THE MAKING OF MODERN BRITISH POLITICS

1867–1945

THE MAKING OF MODERN BRITISH POLITICS

1867–1945

Third Edition

Martin Pugh

The right of Martin Pugh to be identified as author of this work has been asserted in accordance with the Copyright, Designs and Patents Act 1988.

First published 2002

2 4 6 8 10 9 7 5 3 1

Blackwell Publishers Ltd
108 Cowley Road
Oxford OX4 1JF
UK

Blackwell Publishers Inc.
350 Main Street
Malden, Massachusetts 02148
USA

British Library Cataloguing in Publication Data

A CIP catalogue record for this book is available from the British Library.

Library of Congress Cataloging-in-Publication Data has been applied for.

ISBN   0631225900 (pbk)

Typeset in 10 on 12 pt Plantin
by Graphicraft Limited, Hong Kong
Printed in Great Britain by Antony Rowe, Chippenham, Wilts

This book is printed on acid-free paper

Contents

Tables

Illustrations

Preface

In revising *The Making of Modern British Politics* for a third edition I have
made one strategic decision – to extend the book by writing a new chapter
on the politics of the Second World War. In addition to meeting the needs
of students, I hope that this will bring the book to a more satisfying
conclusion in that it follows through the changes that began during the
last 40 years of the nineteenth century. I have also felt the need to revise
several of the existing chapters in the light of research and discussion
amongst historians, notably chapter 7, dealing with Edwardian electoral
politics, which continues to arouse interest, chapter 10 (which replaces old
chapter 11) dealing with the high politics of 1918–31, and chapter 12
(which replaces old chapter 13), which now takes much fuller account of
the Popular Front, fascism and the evolution of the Labour Party into a
national rather than a sectional party. I have felt for some time that
Labour represents the biggest puzzle for political historians, and although
I do not claim to have resolved it here, I think we are, after a century of
the party's history, at last getting closer to a credible overall explanation
for what is, by international standards, an unusual phenomenon. I have
also taken the opportunity to rewrite the three chapters on the First World
War by turning them into two, one dealing with the high politics and
including the 1918 election, and the other focusing on the impact of war
on ideas and attitudes. Needless to say, the guide to further reading has
been revised and updated for all chapters.

Martin Pugh, Slaley, April 2001

PART ONE

1867–1900

CHAPTER ONE

Party and Participation 1867–1900

We have only to imagine, if we can, a Pitt or a Castlereagh stumping the provinces, and taking into his confidence, not merely a handful of electors, but any crowd he could collect in any part of this island.

The Times, 26 December 1879, on the first Midlothian campaign

Between the 1860s and the turn of the century, British politics, in the constituency, party and parliamentary spheres, took on recognizably modern characteristics. Although the transition necessarily proved a lengthy and patchy process, the 1880s stand out as the key decade of change. Indeed the general election of 1880 may, with some justification, be regarded as the first modern election. It was a *general* election in that five-sixths of the constituencies were actually contested, and in that it produced a national campaign as distinct from the sporadic, localized contests typical of mid-Victorian elections. Voters were offered an unusually clear-cut choice, largely through the initiative of the *de facto* leader of the opposition, W. E. Gladstone, who promised to reverse the imperial and foreign policy of Disraeli if he was returned with a majority. In contemporary eyes the novelty of the Midlothian campaign, that 'ten days' waterspout dealing with all human affairs', as *The Times* put it, consisted in a prospective prime minister taking voters so seriously as to deliver to them lengthy speeches on weighty subjects more properly addressed to the Houses of Parliament. The year 1880 brought to a climax that polarization of loyalties between the two party leaders which, since Gladstone's championing of franchise reform in 1866, had begun to transcend the local and personal patterns of allegiance; and which imprinted upon British politics for decades thereafter two stereotyped party positions in both foreign and domestic affairs.

Moreover, the 1880 election physically resembled a modern one. Hitherto the leaders had usually avoided speaking in other men's constituencies after nominations lest they be seen to interfere in a community's private affair; now they found ever more excuses to permit the electorate the novelty of oratory from outside. Gladstone pioneered the nearest approach to a whistle-stop tour as he journeyed up to Edinburgh, descending from his train at Grantham, York and Newcastle to deliver short harangues, somewhat to the annoyance of the ordinary passengers, thence proceeding to an intensive programme of two daily speeches for a fortnight on his second campaign in Midlothian. Though many of the thousands who attended his progress around the constituency could not hear his speeches, Gladstone's every word at West Calder or Dalkeith was caught up by eager journalists to be reprinted in the dense black columns of the provincial and national press, to be bandied about by the more obscure participants up and down the country. 'This duty of making political speeches', Lord Salisbury complained to Queen Victoria in 1887, 'is an aggravation of the labours of your Majesty's servants which we owe entirely to Mr Gladstone.' One should not allow Salisbury's weary cynicism to obscure his own successful adaptation to a variety of political practices, including regular speech-making, of which he disapproved. It would be rash to conclude that the mass of voters felt moved to return Gladstone to power in 1880 because they shared the same concern with the affairs of Afghanistan and the Balkans. The impact of the controversy that had begun in 1876 over the Bulgarian atrocities and culminated in the Midlothian campaigns fell more forcefully upon the partisan activists and local backers of Liberalism, that vital intermediate group whose voluntary efforts and high morale were increasingly indispensable in harnessing the voters at large; but these party workers comprised a characteristic and central element in the political transition of late Victorian Britain.

Voting and Non-voting

Victorians did not claim that their system was democratic, a term that smacked of continental abstraction and implied an excess of equality characteristic of American society; rather, it produced effective government, it guaranteed 'liberty', and it was representative. What it represented directly was those considered fit by reason of their independence, their material stake in society, their education and political knowledge to exercise the parliamentary franchise with beneficial effects upon political life. Men wholly absorbed in the daily struggle for existence were unlikely to develop the capacity for political judgement, still less the opportunity to exercise it freely. Conscious of the defects of even the existing electorate, radicals of the 1860s accepted that drastic and ill-considered extensions of the franchise would only open further opportunities for corruption; the business of a reformer was to find a form of words in law which in practice would define those who were beyond corrupting pressures. Moreover, the late Victorian conception of corruption extended beyond the traditional individual type to the more formal, institutional forms practised in the United States in which politicians offered groups of voters specific pledges of material gain in return for support. Political integrity required that a man who depended upon the state for his maintenance should be ineligible to vote for the government; hence in Britain men in receipt of relief from the poor law guardians remained disqualified until 1918.

In fact an election was not primarily about the individual's rights, but about the representation of his *community*, from which it followed that the interests of non-electors could be represented quite adequately by the leaders of their community. Thus a landowner spoke for his labourers politically as an extension of his other duties towards them; similarly the interests of the largest single group of non-voters, women, were upheld by their fathers and husbands. In a family, as in any other community, there was no special merit in every individual member voting in person, for 'mere numbers' provided no guarantee of efficiency or morality. Women were generally perceived by male politicians to be deficient in the intellectual and temperamental qualities appropriate for politics, to lack the independence, inclination and even the energy, which was devoted instead to the vital task of childbirth.[1] 'Woman', in short, was equated with 'married woman', despite the fact that nearly a quarter of adult females were actually spinsters or widows in the 1860s, many of whom paid local rates and managed property; even wives were permitted, under the Married Women's Property Acts 1870, 1874 and 1882, to retain their property instead of surrendering it to their husbands on marriage. Faced with the fact that some women were 'fit', even on men's terms, for the franchise, politicians allowed female participation, in discreet numbers, in municipal elections, on school boards and on boards of guardians. However, despite the growing similarity between local and national government in the late nineteenth century, most politicians stuck to the view that the great parliamentary issues of Empire, war and national security ought not to be exposed to the vacillating and emotional judgements of women. Moreover, once a majority of men had obtained enfranchisement after 1884, the impetus behind Victorian reform waned noticeably; the remaining male non-voters stood pat upon their superior status as *men*, and eschewed making common cause with women.

The male non-voter himself was by no means uninvolved in the political process. Particularly in smaller boroughs, elections were characterized by popular participation, if only in the form of processions, rioting and

THE POLITICAL EGG-DANCE.
Mr. Disraeli's dexterous management of the Reform Bill in
Committee enabled him to defeat several amendments moved by
the Opposition. – 1867.
Punch, 29 June 1867

intimidation. This attendant disorder obliged the authorities to extend the
poll over two to three weeks (as in modern India) in order to allow the
police to transfer scarce resources from one group of constituencies to
another; not until 1918 did they feel confident enough to risk one-day
polling. However, popular involvement also took on a political tone. Since

the days of the Chartists non-electors had made a practice in some towns of gathering at the hustings when nominations were due, proceeding thence to elect, on a show of hands, an 'MP' as an alternative to the formal poll. Also, disfranchised radical working men in such towns as Rochdale, Stockport, Warrington, Stoke and Morpeth took to boycotting the shops and pubs of their political opponents, thereby playing a more independent role than some enfranchised workers who were more subject to employers' pressure at elections.[2] In addition, the disfranchised invariably shared with the electors themselves a vicarious sense of participation in elections by aligning themselves with one candidate or party; millions of people wore ribbons and rosettes in party colours, or sported primroses on Disraeli's birthday. For a generation not yet in thrall to the personalities of football, films or popular music, political leaders and their contests provided a great entertainment or spectacle, a cause to belong to, and a link with, the lives of the great.

Although the debate over franchise was conducted on the high ground of principle, the translation of 'fitness' into law proved to be severely limited by sheer ignorance of the numbers involved, by the exigencies of parliamentary management, and by assumptions about the help or hindrance newly enfranchised groups would lend to the legislating party. Disraeli's inability to patch together a temporary majority in the Commons in 1867 except by offering concessions to radical Liberal backbenchers produced a dramatic increase in the borough electorate, extending the suffrage to householders and to occupiers and lodgers paying an annual rent of £10, while leaving the county electorate but slightly modified. This lopsided, typically English pattern proved indefensible, and led to the rationalization of 1884 when the new borough franchises were extended by Gladstone to counties. The numerical effect of these changes provided the underlying dynamic to late Victorian political evolution (see table 1.1).

Under this system the proportion of adult males entitled to vote fluctuated usually between 63 and 66 per cent; the more imminent a general election the greater incentive for the parties to ensure that their supporters were on the register. However, the figures overstate the true proportion since half a million men were registered more than once; therefore, no more than six

TABLE 1.1 *Parliamentary electors in the United Kingdom 1866–1911*

1866	1,364,000
1869	2,445,000
1883	3,152,000
1885	5,708,000
1911	7,904,000

TABLE 1.2   *Parliamentary franchises 1885–1918*

		Proportion of the 1911 electorate (%)
Household	franchise for inhabitant occupiers, whether owners or tenants, of a separate dwelling house	
Occupation	franchise for those who occupied as owners or tenants, any land or tenement of £10 annual value	84.3
Lodger	franchise for those who rented rooms valued unfurnished at £10 p.a.	4.6
Property	franchise for 40s freeholders and other freeholders, copyholders and leaseholders (almost wholly confined to counties)	8.4
Service	franchise for inhabitant occupiers of a separate dwelling house through their employment or office, not as owner or tenant	1.8
University	franchise for graduates	0.6
Freemen's	franchise for freemen by birth or apprenticeship in boroughs where the qualification had existed before 1832	0.3

Source: Parl. Papers 1911, LXII, pp. 679–700.

out of every ten men, at most, were parliamentary voters before 1914. Industrial towns, where enfranchisement had traditionally been much lower than that in medieval boroughs and counties, experienced particularly dramatic rises: in Blackburn 1,800 voters became 9,700 in 1868; Newcastle's 6,600 voters had increased to 21,400 by 1872. However, considerable unevenness persisted until 1914 in that residential towns (Oxford 75 per cent) and counties (Cornwall 80 per cent) enjoyed substantially higher enfranchisement than industrial boroughs (Oldham 63 per cent), the extremes being characteristic of large conurbations (Glasgow 52 per cent, Bethnal Green 42 per cent). This pattern was in fact a built-in consequence of the system adopted in 1884. For although the third Reform Act rationalized the existing pattern it nonetheless bequeathed a complex structure of seven distinct types of qualification (see table 1.2).

Those who were expressly excluded by the electoral law fell into three groups; first, women who had been eliminated since the 1832 Act which adopted 'male persons' for the first time; secondly, such categories of men as lunatics, aliens, criminals, peers, receivers of poor relief, those guilty of corrupt practices in elections, and some officials involved in elections; thirdly, men such as sons living in their parents' home and servants residing with their employers who were effectively excluded as they could not claim to be householders. In this way some 1.5 million men (by 1914) found themselves excluded. However, this still left a much greater number – 3.75 million by 1914[3] – who failed to make good their claim (usually as householders or lodgers) simply because of the complicated process of registration. To introduce his name on to the register a potential householder or lodger had to demonstrate continuous residence for 12 months at a given address from July of one year to June of the next. On this basis his name could be entered on the preliminary list in April or May, and if it survived the scrutiny in September–October, would appear on the new parliamentary register in December, which became operative in January of the next year – an 18-month cycle. If the voter moved outside his borough or county constituency, or if his move involved a change of qualification, say from householder to lodger, he had not maintained continuity of residence for 12 months and forfeited his place. Since in working-class boroughs in the large conurbations up to 30 per cent of the population commonly moved each year, massive disfranchisement was inevitable.

The system was also less than democratic in allowing the opportunity to vote many times. Joseph Chamberlain apparently possessed six qualifications, though this was by no means a record; given the leisurely spread of polling, some men claimed to cast as many as ten votes. Overall the plural voters amounted to over half a million or 7 per cent of the total,[4] concentrated in commercial seats, in London and in county seats adjacent to or surrounding parliamentary boroughs. Supporters of plural voting argued that it properly reflected the stake a man had in each particular community. However, if every piece of property a man possessed fell within a single parliamentary borough or in a single division of a county he could vote but once; plural voting was possible only if his property was spread over different constituencies. Moreover, under the anachronistic convention that a borough was part of a county, freeholders in parliamentary boroughs exercised this vote in a neighbouring county seat with which they often had no interest or connection.

The final dimension of inequality lay in the marked variation in constituency size, despite the effect the 1885 redistribution had in correcting the historic over-representation of the South and South-West. By adopting a basic population unit of 50,000 to justify new seats it proved possible to grant 39 additional metropolitan representatives, 15 to Lancashire and 13 to Yorkshire. Some 36 constituencies whose population was above 15,000 but below 50,000 lost one of their two members, while 72 boroughs under 15,000 were simply merged into surrounding counties. However, this still left many small boroughs returning their own members, for example Windsor, Durham, St Andrews and Salisbury, all with around 3,000 actual electors. At the other extreme the largest electorate by 1910 was the Romford division of Essex (61,000). An imbalance, moreover, remained marked between certain areas of the British Isles, notably Ireland, whose 103 members represented an average electorate of 6,700 by contrast with the English average of 13,000. Ireland's exaggerated representation at Westminster had profound effects upon British politics before the First World War. In abandoning the traditional two-member constituencies for the more geographically restricted single-member seats in 1885 the legislators hoped to preserve the community basis of politics. However, the effect in the mature industrial society of late Victorian Britain was a system of constituencies frequently characterized by one dominant class; this was the reality behind what seemed to MPs rather artificial entities – North-East Norfolk, North-West Manchester – that were deficient in the prestige previously attaching to the representation of a county or major borough. This was symptomatic of the changing orientation of politics from the local to the national level, and from community to class.

Electoral Practice and Malpractice

Victorian elections were expected as a matter of course to be punctuated by excessive drinking, mob action ranging from exuberance to intimidation, an exchange of cash and a judicious application of the 'screw'. However, 'influence' covered a multitude of practices and forms, many of which were regarded as perfectly natural and proper. By tradition county politics was the preserve of landed gentlemen who both provided candidates and effectively determined the outcome through the loyalty they commanded among farmers and smallholders. The exercise of such influence could be effortless and inconspicuous, not necessarily coercive or unwelcome to the lower levels of rural society. So long as party politics remained a remote and intangible concept the typical county elector would act within the ambit of his local community; it was the county or community that his MP represented rather than either individuals or a party. Moreover, as the person who remitted rent in bad years, provided work in inclement weather, and contributed financially and socially to the life of the village or estate, the squire could legitimately expect political support; the relationship between squire and local electorate rested upon a mutual sense of duty and responsibility. Insofar as voters anticipated a flow of benefits from an election it was these regular, tangible ones rather than legislative programmes at Westminster. Studies of politics in counties such as Lincolnshire from the 1830s to the 1880s suggest that 'politics' comprised certain agricultural matters, notably the malt tax and the tariff, which tended to unite farmers and landowners, thus offering few openings for genuine party alternatives.[5]

However, this is to describe an ideal situation of rural stability characteristic of the capital-intensive and profitable agriculture of the mid-nineteeth century; it could not survive unscathed the contractions and changes in ownership brought on by falling agricultural profitability after 1875.[6] As unprofitable estates were disposed of and the gentry rented out a number of country houses to families without local, traditional connections, influence inevitably waned or, at least, required to be more deliberately exercised than before. While a landowner who was resident or played a full part in the life of the community might legitimately command loyalty, one who attempted to exercise it as an absentee or negligent owner encountered opposition and resentment.[7] This had always been the case; influence had never been easy to extend to a second candidate connected merely by party, not by ties of family or county.[8]

Nor was a coercive element entirely absent, though it had always been more prevalent in Wales and Ireland than in the English counties, at least in the obvious form of eviction of tenants after elections. As late as 1894, however, Northamptonshire farmers took reprisals against agricultural labourers who had shown the temerity to stand successfully for election in the new parish councils.[9] On the whole influence was most effective when no active steps were necessary to exercise it; in the 1860s it was still regarded as bad form, as well as being futile, to canvass a landowner's tenants without first seeking his permission. Significantly the formal canvass seems to have become more normal from 1885, and was widely associated with undue pressure; Joseph Arch (founder of the Agricultural Labourers Union and Liberal MP for N.W. Norfolk) carried his inbred fear of the canvass to the extent of refusing to adopt it when himself a candidate, describing it as a 'mean subterfuge. Its object is to get at a man's vote in an indirect way.'[10]

It is often asserted that the apparently slight impact of the secret ballot, introduced by Gladstone in 1872, is an indication of the general absence of undue pressure. This is by no means consistent with the actions of many politicians themselves. In order to arrest their declining control in rural areas Conservative landlords often stationed an estate manager or agent outside the polling station to take down the names of those who voted;[11] and since ballot boxes were separately counted it was known how many votes each village had cast for the other side.[12] It was thus not difficult to undermine the rural elector's confidence that the ballot really was secret as the radicals claimed. Naturally voters who were habitually deferential towards their social superiors did not suddenly change their practice in the absence of strong political pressures to do so. Ireland provided a dramatic exception following the introduction of the secret ballot in the form of 57 Home Rulers elected in 1874. In Wales 1874 brought gains for the Liberals, despite a national tide against them, but this was no more than a continuation of a well-established trend. In both these countries the basis of political revolt lay in the fact that landlord and rural voter were frequently not of the same community; a well-developed alternative community of a cultural-religious type generated an early break with political practice. In Scotland large landowners were often Liberal, albeit Whiggish, in allegiance and therefore pulled in the same direction as their tenants wished to go. In England the ballot made little impact under the restricted franchise before 1884; but it was a different matter under the reformed electorate and the subsequent widespread politicization of the counties. It is unlikely that Liberal gains in hitherto Conservative counties in 1885 would have been so extensive had the poll remained open, or that the rebellious Crofter candidates would have prised Highland seats from Whig control.

Influence in the boroughs had for long been more obviously corrupt and coercive. Small boroughs often saw an election as the best means of attracting money to the town. Indeed, an immediate objection to the Ballot Act was that it facilitated the taking of bribes from *both* sides by electors. Contemporary alarm over excessive levels of expenditure during the elections of 1868, 1874 and 1880 stimulated the Gladstone government to enact a Corrupt and Illegal Practices Prevention Act in 1883 which set maximum expenditure limits according to the size of the electorate, imposed upon a single designated agent the responsibility for making a complete return of his candidate's expenses, and made it the duty of the Director of Public Prosecutions to initiate cases where corruption had occurred. Although this appears to have been relatively effective in setting limits to spending during campaigns, it would be optimistic to think that it radically altered attitudes. Neither a politician guilty of corrupt practices nor a voter who took bribes was ostracized for what were regarded as minor peccadilloes. In ancient parliamentary boroughs bribery amounted to a tradition rather than a venal sin; as late as 1911, for example, when Worcester was investigated by a Royal Commission, no less than 500 electors emerged guilty; by this period bribery had settled at an unspectacular level of 2s 6d, or 5s,[13] plus a few drinks per vote, and the Worcesters had ceased to be typical. Such practices dwindled essentially because they ceased to be efficacious; in substantial boroughs with 10,000–20,000 voters large-scale bribery was hardly worth the cost and was too blatantly obvious.

However, politicians circumvented the Act of 1883 to a considerable extent by spending money outside the election campaign period and by allowing others to spend it on their behalf, or in their interest. For the public still regarded it as a proper function of the MP to assist the borough, notably as an employer, and as a regular investor in community projects, charities and sporting clubs. MPs frequently distributed coal and blankets in winter, showered sweets upon the children, and saw that tea parties and 'knife-and-fork' suppers were thrown on suitable occasions. In addition the member's postbag would be full of begging letters from individual constituents seeking money or jobs. On top of this came the costs of being in Parliament. After 1885 expenditure of £800 to £1,000 was typical for a campaign; the candidates paid the often exaggerated costs of the returning officer; and the member commonly provided a salary of £100 to £300 per annum for his agent, plus additional sums for registration work each year. Thus the fact that by the First World War petitions alleging electoral malpractice had shrunk to a handful cannot obscure a certain continuity in the relation between a politician and his constituents.

Victorian reformers who hoped that judicious expansion of the electorate would foster a mature and informed debate on political issues in place of corruption and influence invariably lived to be disillusioned. Historians have rightly grown sceptical about any quick emergence of a 'politics of opinion' based upon the thinking individual voter after 1867. Indeed, good evidence has emerged to suggest that the pattern in new industrial boroughs often repeated in certain respects that of county or medieval borough seats. Some employers, for example, appear to have mobilized the votes of their workers as effectively as any rural squire, and many a self-made manufacturer was known to give his men breakfast on polling day before marching them off to cast their votes for himself or his candidate. A number of medium-sized towns made it a practice to return the largest employer of labour – J. J. Colman the mustard manufacturer at Norwich, Joseph Pease the Quaker ironmaster at Darlington, or Charles Mark Palmer, whose shipyards supported the economy of Jarrow; similarly, industrialized county seats such as Northwich (Cheshire) returned the local chemical magnate Sir John Brunner, and the Mansfield division of Nottinghamshire elected the coal owner Arthur Markham. Detailed study of Blackburn and Bury has demonstrated a distinct pattern in which working-class voters who resided near and worked in a factory owned by an active Liberal or Conservative reflected overwhelmingly his allegiance.[14] In such circumstances the result of an election could be as predictable from the relative strength of Liberal and Conservative employers as in a county from the number of the landlords' retainers. This is explicable, especially in 1868, if one envisages the 1867 Act as enfranchising urban villages in which the factory served as the rural estate; here the pressures for unity around one's place of work against rival, external forces could be stronger than the individual's political opinion. Though dismissal of the politically rebellious introduced an occasional coercive element it was apparently the exception;

coercion was more likely to be applied by a voter's own workmates than by his employer.[15]

Lest this should be seen as the universal pattern of urban politics in the late nineteenth century certain qualifications may be entered. Employer influence was characteristic of medium-sized towns where the range of employment was limited to one or two trades, and where the owners still resided near their workers in the 1880s. Where there existed a more varied economy and no dominant employers, a more rapid emergence of political opinion was a natural consequence.[16] Also the greater likelihood of residential separation of owner from worker in the larger conurbations, and even in the smaller Lancashire and Yorkshire towns by the 1890s, undermined the paternal relationships of the 1860s. Nor was the voter–employer relationship merely a passive, non-political one on the worker's part. In the constant shifting of house and job a workman of, say, Liberal views could deliberately seek a connection with a radical mill-owner. Just as a rural magnate who changed his politics did not expect the tenantry to switch allegiance automatically, so the employer had to recognize the existence of loyalties that were political or party as distinct from personal. Finally, the exercise of influence was naturally marked in the election following immediately upon the 1867 Reform Act, when large numbers or working men voted for the first time but under the old conditions of open voting. By the 1880s even entrenched MPs were vulnerable to political issues; Brunner lost his seat in 1886; Palmer found himself almost unseated by a socialist in 1900. Moreover, any owner had to be known as a good employer or face a battery of criticism and innuendo during a campaign. As a result of personal and political considerations, by the turn of the century entrepreneurs with political ambitions were migrating away from the seats of their business: Richard Holt of Liverpool found a constituency at Hexham in Northumberland; Walter Runciman of Tyneside sat for Dewsbury; Alfred Mond of Cheshire represented Swansea. Such movements reflected the fact that it was no longer enough to be a local employer; allegiance to a political party furnished the safest guide to a constituency's representation.

The Rise of the Party Activist

One of the most striking features of mid-Victorian elections is that barely half the constituencies actually experienced a contest; and where seats were contested a third or more of voters normally split their two votes across party lines – an indication that Whig and Tory were not sharp political divisions but amorphous and overlapping groupings. Since two members had to be returned, Whigs and Tories frequently agreed to nominate a single candidate each with a view to avoiding the trouble and

TABLE 1.3   *Uncontested seats at general elections 1857–1910*

1857	333	1880	109	1900	243
1859	383	1885	43	1906	114
1865	302	1886	225	1910 (Jan.)	75
1868	212	1892	63	1910 (Dec.)	163
1874	188	1895	189		

expense of a contest. Thus an election was often the result of a split *within* one side, between radicals and Whigs or individual rivals, rather than between parties. Such cosy arrangements were, of course, anathema to the dedicated party activists of the late Victorian era whose objective in manning the constituency organization on a permanent basis was to ensure a fight at every election. After 1885 single-member constituencies[17] eliminated traditional Whig–Tory collusion, and the advance of formal party organization, stimulated by franchise extensions, may be measured from the decline in unopposed returns (see table 1.3). As the table shows, 1885 marked the nearest approach to the mid-twentieth-century practice in which virtually every constituency is contested; around thirty of the unopposed returns occurred in staunchly Nationalist areas of Ireland which the Unionists found it futile to fight. Even so, the large totals for 1886, 1895 and 1900, when the Liberal organizations were either split or starved of resources, indicate how incomplete the evolution remained.

Hitherto parliamentary election campaigns had rested in the hands of small groups of landowners, professional men or employers who used solicitors to organize the poll and the registration. However, an alternative approach based upon the assumption of a regular party conflict evolved particularly in those towns whose government had been re-formed under the 1835 Municipal Corporations Act;[18] the municipally inspired prototype did not generally displace the improvisations at parliamentary level until politicians had to face the challenges and problems raised by the new franchises, the redistribution, and the restrictions upon expenditure in the 1880s, which generated a permanent, institutional framework eventually covering the whole country.

Three major manifestations of organized party activity may be identified. First the professional party agent began to displace the solicitor for whom electoral work was just a sideline. This was no more than a natural consequence of the complexity of the franchise and registration process after 1885. The agent's responsibility was to ensure that his party's supporters appeared on the preliminary list of voters in May, to put in further claims and defend them before the revising barristers in the autumn, and particularly to lodge objections against the names of known opponents. Such work could make all the difference to the lodgers' vote since they had to make a fresh application every year; if they or householders shifted house the party agents pursued them in an annual charade. Some found that lodging objections paid higher dividends than making claims. In Newcastle the Conservatives objected to 9,500 names between 1888 and 1891 and in nearby Gateshead, where the population rose by 16 per cent between 1885 and 1891, the electorate dropped by 301![19] In 1908 the Leeds Liberals secured a net advantage from registration of 257 (98 claims, 159 objections) over their opponents; in Keighley the Conservative agent claimed net gains ranging from 69 in 1892 to 238 in 1897.[20] In dozens of seats a turnover of these proportions was enough to determine the result of an election, and the party that neglected registration work for a year or two suffered badly. Where both agents were alert and thorough they habitually met privately before the revising courts got to work for a mutual withdrawal of objections; there is thus no little substance in the view that the parties, as much as the law, determined the franchise before 1918. Agents had also to keep abreast of legal cases which modified the interpretation of the Act; for example the 'latchkey' decision of 1907 by which 'lodgers' who held a front-door key to the building could qualify as 'householders' produced a sudden influx of new voters. Sensible of their role in winning elections the party agents asserted their status by establishing professional associations, the Liberals in 1882 and the Conservatives in 1891; they adopted examinations for full membership, endeavoured to impose minimum salary levels upon the parties, set up benevolent funds, and published semi-secret journals to brief members on the latest tricks of the trade.

A second characteristic of the post-1867 system was the local party-sponsored club. Especially in Lancashire and Yorkshire, working men's clubs were a long-standing feature, but politicians felt so apprehensive of losing touch with the urban electors of 1867 that they threw considerable resources into extending the network. A typical neighbourhood club was a modest affair of two or three rooms, one for lectures, one for reading, drinking, billiards or smoking; even a strongly radical town like Keighley boasted 13 such Conservative clubs in 1907. A popular extension of club activity during the summer involved mass picnics and excursions by train to the country home of the MP, candidate or other party dignitary; in September 1900, we learn, 600 North Salford Liberals picnicked at Matlock Bath in Derbyshire by day and enjoyed a Venetian fête on the river by night.[21] On a more regular basis, urban party associations developed their own brass bands and football clubs which the MP was expected to subsidize. In such ways the parties helped to fill the role nowadays occupied by a vast and varied entertainments industry. Their motives in moving deliberately beyond strictly political activity were to inculcate the values of the parliamentary system among the new voters, to impart political education at least to the activist elite, and to foster an habitual loyalty on the part of those who were uninterested in or ignorant of politics. In addition the parties frequently sponsored benefit societies, friendly societies, sick and burial societies, and even building societies; according to one Liverpool Tory in 1879: 'working men in the north country always wanted to see some return for their money, and would therefore more willingly join a benefit club than an association for a purely abstract object'.[22] The success of the clubs and the Primrose League shows how misleading, in the British context, is the assumption that traditional parliamentary parties were simply parties of 'individual representation' that failed to involve their supporters except intermittently at election times; the evidence suggests that the Conservatives, rather than any of the extraparliamentary socialist or labour bodies, approximated to a party of 'social integration' in that they permeated the daily lives of their members.

Finally, party growth manifested itself in the emergence of formal constituency associations based upon individual membership running into hundreds or thousands, divided between branches for each ward or polling district. This provided the centre for volunteer activists whose time and efforts now provided free much of the canvassing, transport and propaganda work previously paid for on an *ad hoc* basis. Representative constituency bodies were pioneered by radical Liberals – it was dubbed the 'caucus' system – who gave it central institutional form in the National Liberal Federation (NLF) of 1877. Rank-and-file Conservatives encountered greater opposition from landed and parliamentary patrons who sensed a threat to their own control, and eschewed the Liberals' pretensions to policy-making and selection of candidates; nonetheless, after a slow start in 1867 the National Union of Conservative and Constitutional Associations (NUCCA) attained official approval and spawned affiliated associations across the country during the mid-1880s. By this stage few candidates stood without the benefit of an agent, a permanent association, or the backing of a network of social organizations which gave them links with the mass of voters no longer attainable simply through the personal connections of leading families. By building up habitual party loyalty the politicians themselves helped to replace older forms of community and group influence with institutional, political ones.

Party, Parliament and the 'Independent Member'

By 1900 observers of British politics had begun to draw certain conclusions, often pessimistic ones, from the experience of the reformed system since 1867. Graham Wallas, in his *Human Nature in Politics* (1908), highlighted the irrationality of a mass electorate in contrast to the liberal ideal. Also in 1908 the American academic A. L. Lowell, in *The Government of England*, dwelt upon the centralization of power in the Cabinet and the corresponding decline in the authority and independence of the House of Commons. The roots of this change had already been identified in M. Ostrogorski's *Democracy and the Organisation of Political Parties* (1902), which drew attention to what he saw as the debilitating effects of caucus politics upon Parliament. Seen in perspective Ostrogorski's pessimism seems exaggerated, even misplaced, since, despite the pretensions of Victorian party organizations in the 1870s, by 1900 both Liberal and Conservative parliamentary leaders had harnessed their extra-parliamentary forces to serve their ends; they appealed directly to the voters over the heads of their critics for the 'mandate' as the fashionable term had it; their command of patronage and policy was rarely challenged successfully even in the Labour Party, whose roots and strength lay, as yet, outside the House of Commons. Very few politicians used the party organization as their high-road to power; even Joseph Chamberlain and Lord Randolph Churchill merely toyed with it before reverting to playing the game by the existing rules.

However, this should not obscure the very real changes that took place in the career and functions of the backbench politician in the late nineteenth century. Until this time membership of the House of Commons was still widely regarded less as a career than as a part-time activity undertaken along with other unpaid duties towards the community. This was held to be no small advantage in deterring carpetbaggers and in attracting to public service representatives of independent means. 'Once pay a member for his votes collectively,' declared Sir William Harcourt, 'and he will very soon make a market for his individual votes.'[23] Yet both tighter party discipline and the growing demands made by governments upon MPs undermined the conventional conception of the MP in our period. By tradition membership of the Commons impinged lightly upon the MP's time. Government business occupied only a fraction of the time of the House; attendance was frequently fitful and whipping slack, even unnecessary, for a ministry rested upon administrative rather than political support. Each August Parliament rose for the shooting season, members displaying a marked reluctance to return until the following February.

However, under Gladstone and his successors the parliamentary year grew longer. Governments appropriated sittings hitherto reserved for backbench legislation; and severe pressure upon government business caused by regular Irish Nationalist obstructionism prompted Gladstone in 1882 to pioneer the procedure for closure of debate by simple majority vote, a practice ritually condemned but nonetheless adopted by all governments anxious to squeeze legislation through. With the burgeoning scope of official activity came both lengthier and more complex legislation and financial proposals. Both the Public Accounts Committee of 1861 and the Estimates Committee of 1912 represented attempts to maintain the principle of Commons' scrutiny and control of finance without absorbing excessive amounts of time on the floor of the House. In practice Commons debates on Supply evolved into a largely ritual aspect of Parliament's work; in 1896 A. J. Balfour simply fixed the number of Supply days after which all remaining votes were taken by closure; they ceased to be opportunities for criticism of expenditure in detail and became instead occasions for general discussions initiated by the opposition. Thus governments grew to dominate the timetable and members to depend upon the party whip to keep them in touch with business from hour to hour. As attack by the opposition became normal practice so the whips displayed increasing intolerance of non-attendance or revolt. Life gradually ceased to be congenial for what Lord Salisbury described as 'the old judicial type of Member who sat rather loose to his party'.

Whereas the governments of the 1850s regularly suffered 10 to 15 defeats each year, by the 1900s their successors experienced only one per session on average. We may measure the growth of disciplined party behaviour by the number of Commons divisions in which 90 per cent of a party's representatives went into the same lobby (see table 1.4). Two features are particularly striking. First, the Conservatives in office and in opposition displayed tighter discipline or cohesion than the Liberals. This is quite at odds with contemporary criticism of the caucus for supposedly subjecting the politicians to its dictates; in practice the NLF invariably lent encouragement to MPs in rebellion against the leadership. Secondly, the lax discipline prevailing up to the 1860s tightened up after 1868, but

TABLE 1.4   *'Party votes' in the House of Commons 1850–1903*

	No. of divisions	Conservatives (%)	Liberals (%)
1850	321	45	37
1860	257	31	25
1871	256	61	55
1881	199	71	66
1883	253	65	52
1890	261	87	64
1894	237	92	84
1899	357	91	76
1903	260	83	88

Source: H. Berrington, 'Partisanship and Dissidence in the Nineteenth Century House of Commons', *Parliamentary Affairs*, 21 (1967–8), p. 342.

weakened somewhat during the early 1880s when the party leaders were inclined to seek co-operation from their opponents against their own rebellious supporters. However, the great divide on Home Rule in 1886 drove both sides towards greater cohesion than ever before, reaching a peak under the management of Salisbury and Balfour. A fundamental alteration had taken place since mid-century when government and opposition had been more fluid and relaxed, and neither side represented rigid parties. After 1886 governments ceased to be able to rely upon support from oppositions which now criticized everything but without prospect of defeating anything. All now turned upon maintaining the allegiance of one's own party majority; the older traditions of cross-bench voting by a large proportion of members gradually died out. Thus when Edwardians looked back nostalgically to a golden age of the 'Independent Member' they had in mind what we would think of as a House of 'moderates' whose fluctuating votes reflected the blurred and ambiguous lines of party demarcation.

Such developments seemed to many contemporaries to undermine the status of the MP while encroaching upon his time and freedom. Life in the Commons began to lose its attractions for young gentlemen. This is not to say that landed families did not continue to play a prominent role in both parties; simply that they had to make more deliberate efforts than before and acquiesce in the restrictions of parliamentary life. But the social composition of the Commons underwent a steady modification during the late Victorian era. It has been found that between 1868 and 1910 land-owners fell from 46 to 26 per cent as a proportion of Conservative members and from 26 to 7 per cent among Liberals;[24] in the same period those whose livelihood lay in industry and trade rose from 31 to 53 per cent of Conservatives and from 50 to 66 per cent of Liberals; while those from legal and professional occupations grew from 9 to 12 per cent among Conservatives and from 17 to 23 per cent among Liberals. The dominance of lawyers in particular at cabinet level was a noticeable feature of the Liberal governments of 1906–14 which included very few industrialists. This march of the middle classes, which some Edwardians professed to abhor as an invasion by 'wirepullers', professional politicians and men on the make, reminds us how very protracted was the process of penetration initiated by the famous 'middle-class' victories of 1832 and 1846.

In fact by 1900 many a rising bourgeois had discovered a short cut, if not to power, at least to prestige, by obtaining a knighthood, baronetcy or peerage, often after (though not necessarily because of) generous contributions to party funds, aid to ailing party newspapers and services at elections. The rate of creation of peerages during the 1880s and 1890s was twice that of the 1830–60 period. Moreover the proportion of industrial and professional middle-class men among the newly ennobled reached 43 per cent during 1897–1911 by comparison with 14 per cent during

1867–81.[25] Certain types of recruit, notably brewers and newspaper proprietors, attracted criticism for their prominence; Guinnesses were elevated in 1880 and 1891, and a Bass and an Allsopp both in 1886; Lord Glenesk arose from the *Morning Post* in 1899, Lord Burnham from the *Daily Telegraph* in 1903, and Lord Northcliffe from the *Daily Mail* in 1905. Yet the solid centre of British industry was well represented by Lords Armstrong (armaments) in 1887, Inverclyde (shipping) in 1897, Joicey and Allendale (mining) in 1906, and Mount Stephen (railways) in 1891, to take only a few examples. Though both parties, especially the Liberals, were under more pressure to raise central funds from wealthy men by the 1880s, financial contributions were not the sole factor. After 1886 Gladstone had to fortify the depleted Liberal ranks in the Lords. Conversely Salisbury, whose 1885–6 ministry was a turning point in rapid creations, felt obliged to dispense honours as an alternative to posts now thinly spread between Conservatives and Liberal Unionists.

In the quest for office the new men competed under the old rules in that until 1911, when MPs were awarded a £400 salary, the backbencher had to live off a fortune amassed before his entry into politics; by 1900 of course many a second-generation industrialist could use his father's business to launch him into politics in his youth. But party loyalty now demanded that aspiring members should first tackle one or two hopeless or marginal constituencies before being nominated for a safe seat for life. For the politician's essential lifeline lay through his party rather than in his roots in his locality. As Augustine Birrell remarked to Asquith and Haldane one day as they gazed out across the Firth of Forth to the country beyond: 'What a grateful thought that there is not an acre in this vast and varied landscape that is not represented at Westminster by a London barrister!'[26]

CHAPTER TWO

The Evolution of the Gladstonian Liberal Party 1867–1895

A Liberal reform is never simply a social means to a social end, but a struggle of good against evil.

Sidney Webb, *Nineteenth Century*, September 1901

'Like the Kingdom of Heaven,' Sir William Harcourt could say as late as 1891, 'the Liberal Party is a house of many mansions.' Indeed, before the 1870s the 'Liberal Party' was so amorphous and diverse, both politically and organizationally, as to be quite unlike a twentieth-century party. Mid-Victorian parties were primarily loose parliamentary parties, and such cohesion as the Liberals possessed derived initially from their role as the normal governing party of the period, and subsequently from Gladstone's dominating effect from 1866 until his retirement in 1894. Yet although diversity and dispute attended the party during these years, historians simplify too much if they overlook the steady and emphatic evolution of Liberalism towards a cohesive modern party framework and approach. The 1850s had seen the emergence of the parliamentary party under Palmerston; the 1860s brought new links between Liberals in the country and politicians like Bright and even Gladstone. In the 1870s formal party organization began to characterize the constituencies; and during the 1880s came the climax of political radicalization and a purging of the ranks which left popular Liberalism closer to parliamentary Liberalism than ever before. Gladstone's last government, 1892–4, saw the nearest approach to a programmatic party government and a drastic departure from the Palmerstonian era.

The origins of the parliamentary party may be traced back to 1850 when the death of Sir Robert Peel released his free-trade followers to find permanent homes. Aberdeen's Coalition of 1852–5 provided a vital step in the transition by permitting the absorption of the Peelites into the

Whig–Liberal governing group. Although this ministry came to grief in the Crimean War it provided the formula that was repeated with greater success by Palmerston in 1855–8 and 1859–65. On this latter ministry, which is usually thought of as the first Liberal one, Palmerston stamped his leadership effectively enough to ensure that the Whig–Liberal–Peelite combination would be more than a mere stopgap. Its breadth of support and its range of leading administrators made it the natural ruling party of the time.

However, Palmerston's party was essentially a parliamentary one quite unrepresentative of many of the people who regarded themselves as Liberals in the country. Half of its members were landowners or gentlemen with private incomes; indeed, despite the famous victories over reform in 1832 and the Corn Laws in 1846, government remained largely in the hands of the traditional landed men. Yet if the middle classes had not acquired power they showed an increasing interest in penetrating the world of politics; and what made the Liberals more of a national party than their rivals was that they embraced much more of commercial and industrial Britain. They also incorporated many of the most active politicians who devoted themselves to causes, to public speaking in the country, and to building links with the press and pressure groups. In contrast, politics for most politicians remained a part-time affair rather than a profession, and a local rather than a national or party matter. The other 'professionals' were the frontbenchers, often Whig peers like Granville, Kimberley, Spencer and Ripon, who, immersed in the great departments of state, addressed their energies more to administration than to a party audience outside Parliament; they resembled civil servants as much as modern politicians. In 1880 Gladstone still packed five earls, a duke and a marquess into his Cabinet of only 12 members. Later in the century many Whig peers abandoned politics, or at least Liberal politics; but those like Ripon and Spencer who chose to adapt continued to play a major role even on the Liberal side. However, their hold on cabinets was relaxed in favour of men who were typically party politicians such as Joseph Chamberlain, Sir Charles Dilke and John Morley. As the 1880 Cabinet shows, Gladstone had no prior intention of promoting these men, convinced as he was of the virtues of government by disinterested gentlemen. Yet the talents of Chamberlain, Dilke, Morley, W. W. Forster, Sir William Harcourt, John Bright, Henry Fawcett and H. H. Asquith won them posts under Gladstone notwithstanding their radical views; in fact after 1886 a Liberal cabinet could hardly be formed without such men.

Liberalism, Reform and Religion

One of the consequences of the detailed study made by historians of policy-making and internal party debates has been to create an exaggerated impression of division and disunity in Victorian Liberalism. To some extent the quantity of high politics source material makes this unavoidable. But it sometimes leads to the assumption that nothing held Liberals together except power and opportunism; asked to explain what it meant to be a Liberal in late Victorian times, the student is often perplexed for an answer.

Nonetheless, the common basis of Liberalism is tolerably clear. Above all the party was dedicated to the cause of free trade, which many Liberals saw not merely as the key to economic prosperity but as a great moral good. In addition Liberals advocated a range of constitutional, legal and religious reforms which reflected their desire to restrict excessive privilege, to open up opportunities and to improve civil liberties for the individual. One expression of this was parliamentary reform which, after the row over the 1866 Reform Bill had subsided, became a characteristic Liberal theme. This, however, was qualified by the developing split over women's suffrage. Similarly, on the religious front some Liberals wished to travel further down the road than others; while the disestablishment of the Church in Ireland commanded general assent in 1868, most stopped short of disestablishing the Church of England. Again, Liberals usually disliked autocratic and clerical regimes abroad, hence their support for self-determination among Greeks, Italians and Germans; but few were as yet ready to extend this principle to Irishmen and Indians. On this basis, however, it is clear that by the 1860s Liberalism represented something coherent and distinct from Conservatism. Indeed, it was largely because of his stand on these questions that Gladstone himself eventually became a Liberal after his early career as a Tory politician.

Recently historians have begun to go rather further than this in emphasizing the significance of ideology in Victorian politics. This has taken the form of reasserting the centrality of religious and moral issues for Whigs, Liberals, radicals and Conservatives alike. It is certainly striking to note how much time and energy late Victorian governments devoted to questions with troublesome religious complications. After 1868 Gladstone was embroiled in arguments with Nonconformists over elementary schools and disestablishment, and his government suffered defeat over the Irish Universities Bill. The 1880s brought the Church Burials Act, repeated attempts by the atheist Charles Bradlaugh to take his seat in Parliament, the Deceased Wife's Sister's Bill and the Welsh Sunday Closing Act. The 1890s saw debates over clergy discipline in the Church of England, Church tithes, Welsh disestablishment, rate aid for Church schools and the Marriages Act of 1898. The Conservatives were equally troubled – notably by the controversy about ritualism in the Church – and the downfall of Balfour's government was partly the result of the religious implications of the 1902 Education Act.

A number of circumstances help to account for the preoccupation with religion in this period. Since the religious census of 1851 Victorians were afraid that large sections of society had escaped the influence of the Church. Thus Anglicans had been investing heavily in the construction of new urban churches, in Sunday Schools and, after the 1870 Education Act, in new elementary schools. Competition within the Christian world was growing fiercer both because of the challenge posed by Nonconformists and because of the general advance of Roman Catholicism. Gladstone spoke for many when he expressed concern about the resurgence of papal authority in Europe – on the assumption that the citizen could not be loyal both to the pope and to his queen and government. Yet there were many prominent conversions to Catholicism, including Lord Ripon (Liberal) and Henry Matthews (Conservative). Moreover, the steady growth of High Church practices provoked a running controversy over 'ritualism' from the 1870s to the end of the century. And the continuing influx of Catholics from Ireland fuelled Protestant extremism in several parts of the country.

There was a close connection between the role of religion and the peculiar centrality of Gladstone during this period. For he both benefited from and contributed to the prevailing mood. Though suspect to many as a High Churchman and a zealot, he undoubtedly articulated religious and moral questions in a way that neither Disraeli nor, significantly, Joseph Chamberlain could do. He had to pay a price for his position, for example, in steadily accepting the grievances of Nonconformists as political objectives. But equally Gladstone's followers surrendered themselves to his unique status as spokesman for the 'Nonconformist Conscience'; no one could rival his capacity to articulate a sense of morality in politics and lift men's sights above vulgar materialism. The classic example of Gladstone's approach in action was provided by his famous campaign over the Bulgarian atrocities in the late 1870s. While many Whigs and Tories regarded his efforts with suspicion, his crusade aroused notable enthusiasm among both Nonconformists and High Churchmen.

The Building Blocks of Liberalism

Important as Gladstone was, the Liberal Party had a life of its own, and was evolving steadily by the third quarter of the nineteenth century.

Until the 1870s few MPs had to deal with organized parties in their constituencies. But whatever the Liberal forces lacked, as yet, in formal organization they made up for in vociferousness. Most had been drawn into political activity for a specific objective or cause, often through a pressure group such as the United Kingdom Alliance (temperance), the National Education League (free, undenominational, state education), or the Liberation Society[1] (Church disestablishment); the outstanding common element here was Victorian Nonconformity engaged in a prolonged campaign to eliminate other grievances such as the payment of church rates, denial of burial rights in churchyards and exclusion from the ancient universities. Other causes, represented by the Ballot Society, the Reform Union and the Peace Society, were fragments of the anti-Corn Law movement of the 1840s. Still others catered more specifically to radical working men organized in radical clubs, the 'new Model' unions and in the Reform League which harked back to Chartism. In addition there were the campaigns for moral improvement, including not only temperance but the abolition of the Contagious Diseases Acts (which permitted the army to license prostitutes in certain garrison towns), the trade in child prostitution and capital punishment. The foot soldiers in this phalanx of pressure groups ranged from self-made manufacturers and merchants through the lower middle class of shopkeepers, teachers and journalists to craftsmen and miners. Whereas the parliamentarians were typically landed, Anglican and Whig, provincial Liberals were more commonly urban–industrial, Nonconformist and radical.

Disparate as these elements appear, they did in fact provide the fabric of local Liberalism; and although much of their energy was devoted to fighting Whigs rather than Tories, during the 1860s and 1870s they were harnessed to parliamentary Liberalism so effectively that by the 1890s it had come to reflect their views fairly well. Articulate in its incoherence, pressure-group Liberalism was much more cohesive than it appears at first sight. For its forces were concentrated socially and geographically in the towns of midland and northern England, Scotland and Wales. Membership of the groups overlapped so much that there was a natural attraction in the idea of an institutional umbrella such as the Liberal Party. This was especially true for middle-class Nonconformists, whose desire to become integrated into national political life and throw off the stigma attaching to them led them to the parliamentary Liberal Party, which, for all its imperfections, provided the best quick route to power. It is no exaggeration to say that Nonconformity was the factor that turned many Victorians into active politicians, for those who neglected to exercise their political influence were, in the words of the Congregationalist minister R. W. Dale, 'guilty of treachery both to God and man'. Only 64 Nonconformists were elected to the Parliament of 1868, but their numbers rose steadily to 95 by 1886, 177 by 1892 and 210 in 1906.

Unity also arose from a common perception of the means and purpose of radical politics. While some objectives could be realized at municipal level or by pressure applied through bodies like the Trades Union Congress (TUC), all were hindered by the essential unresponsiveness of Parliament. By the 1860s it seemed plain that the key to further advance lay, as Cobden and Bright had perceived years before, through extensive reform of the franchise and the ballot. Political reconstruction invested Liberal politics with an elevating and unifying theme; its business was the removal of privilege and artificial restriction and the opening up of political opportunity to the talents of every man. Herein lay the basis for common action through the identification of common enemies by middle- and working-class radicals which had been pioneered in such places as Birmingham and Rochdale. Radicals discerned a model and a moral reinforcement in the politics of the United States.[2] Working people were encouraged by reports from emigrants who dilated upon the greater opportunities there, the social equality and the absence of a dominant landed elite. Similarly, for middle-class radicals a system that was democratic in being open to energy and talent at the grass roots represented their ideal. America played an important role in drawing together not just popular radicals of Bright's stamp, but also many of the intellectuals and academics of the 1860s. James Bryce, Henry Fawcett and John Stuart Mill were all drawn towards Liberal politics at this time, partly through their sympathy for the North in the American Civil War;[3] this gave them not only contact with urban radicals, but also a sympathetic appreciation for working men who appeared to take a moral view of politics by their advocacy of the Northern cause. Indeed, along with Oliver Cromwell and the Italian nationalists Mazzini and Garibaldi, Abraham Lincoln remained for years a hero to British radicals; and 'John Brown' and other American tunes served as rallying songs for reformers right through to Edwardian times.

This need for leadership and unity was also appeased to some extent by the provincial press, which in its Victorian heyday was highly political and disproportionately Liberal in sentiment. Papers like the *Leeds Mercury*, *Manchester Guardian* or *Newcastle Chronicle* provided a focus for radical activity, and by extensive reproduction of major speeches built a vicarious bridge between the people and leading politicians. The keystone of this arch was undoubtedly Gladstone. For until his emergence as a popular figure in the 1860s Liberalism continued to run on two parallel lines; the movement in the constituencies looked to parliamentarians like Bright, who was only a backbencher, remote from the seats of power. Thus when Gladstone began to speak on franchise reform and to visit industrial centres like Tyneside (which led to his abandonment of his university seat in favour of a popular constituency in 1865), he found a huge reservoir of 'virtuous passion' waiting to be tapped. As Chancellor of the Exchequer and destined Liberal leader Gladstone was the first major figure to take the trouble to come to the people; the experience proved immensely flattering for both sides.

It is a distinctive feature of British politics that by the 1860s most politically active working men seem to have been content to operate under the umbrella of Liberalism. They found their champions in such men as Gladstone, Abraham Lincoln and Charles Bradlaugh, the radical member for Northampton; and many of their ideas were derived from intellectuals such as Henry Fawcett or John Stuart Mill, or Henry George, the American land reformer, whose book *Progress and Poverty* had sold 400,000 copies by the time of his triumphant tour of Britain in 1882. Though Chartism had dwindled after 1848, there was a good deal of continuity of ideas and individuals who rallied to John Bright, and were eventually led into the pale of the constitution by Gladstone when he championed the cheap press and parliamentary reform in the 1850s and 1860s. The culmination came in 1874 when the first working men – Thomas Burt (Morpeth) and Alexander McDonald (Stafford) – were elected MPs. Known as 'Lib–Labs', these members took the Liberal whip and fervently espoused Gladstonian causes. Lib–Lab candidates were usually miners' union officials who stood in constituencies where their members were so concentrated as to enable them to bargain with the local Liberal Associations for the nomination. Burt and McDonald were joined by other miners, notably William Abraham (Rhondda), Charles Fenwick (Northumberland Wansbeck), John Wilson (Mid-Durham) and Ben Pickard (Yorkshire Normanton). But the other Liberal working men should not be overlooked, for example, Joseph Arch, the agricultural labourers' leader (N. W. Norfolk), and in London George Howell, a former bricklayer (N. E. Bethnal Green), Randall Cremer, a carpenter (Shoreditch) and James Rowlands, a watch-case maker (East Finsbury). Clearly the Liberalism of this era enjoyed a powerful democratic reputation; it represented 'the people', at least in the sense of the artisans and small shopkeepers who derived a gratifying sense of self-respect from their participation in Gladstonian politics. The link was consolidated by the popular radical press, particularly the *Daily News*, and by the mass circulation working-class Sunday papers, *Lloyds Weekly News*, *Reynolds Newspaper* and the *News of the World*.

Yet historians have sometimes found it surprising that a traditional party could mobilize working-class support on a frugal diet of constitutional reform, retrenchment and moral causes. However, the relationship evidently also had a material rationale. The obvious element was free trade, which provided cheap food; working men looked for the further lifting of duties levied on essential items of consumption. Social reform as yet generated no significant demand. This was partly because existing social policies represented an unwelcome interference in working-class life, and because the benefits were not seen to be justified by the costs in terms of local rates and national taxation. Approximately 70 per cent of government expenditure was devoted to the army, navy and the national debt; then there was the police, civil service, and civil list to be paid for. Since much of the revenue required derived from taxes on consumption paid by relatively poor people it followed that the Gladstonian cry of retrenchment commanded much popularity. This also helps to explain the loyalty of working-class leaders to Gladstone over foreign and imperial questions. His preference as Prime Minister after 1868 for settling disputes with other powers by negotiation rather than by war, his efforts to withdraw troops from colonies such as New Zealand, and his reluctance to be dragged into fresh imperial expansion all made eminent sense. In fact in 1869 and 1870 Gladstone's government met expectations by reducing expenditure and lowering taxation. The only flaw was that it proved difficult to sustain this strategy. Moreover, the rise in money wages in the early 1870s carried growing numbers of working men over the annual income threshold of £100 which made them liable for income tax. In this context Gladstone's promise in 1874 to abolish the income tax was wholly consistent with the popular appeal of Victorian Liberalism.

However, Gladstone retained his control of the popular and parliamentary strands of Liberalism more by inspiration than by skilful management, and showed an alarming penchant as leader for withdrawing altogether in times of difficulty. Eschewing the vulgar arts of party management, he tried to hold to the higher ground of national interest. No doubt this reluctance to become involved was a useful tactic for keeping him above the sectional interests, and indeed reflected his own distaste for pressure-group politics, which he thought would lead to mediocrity among politicians and the corruption of class legislation. This was a characteristic view for a man of his generation; yet Gladstone also levelled criticisms of self-interest at the 'upper ten thousand', and cultivated the lower classes because he discerned in them a capacity for moral and responsible behaviour that would improve political life. He therefore engaged in a dual enterprise of trying to govern through the best representatives of the traditional ruling class, while involving the lower classes in morally improving issues rather than pandering to their material welfare. The collapse of Whiggery and the aggrandizement of the caucus had defeated these aims well before his retirement, but his struggles decisively influenced the development of Liberal politics. Although Gladstone's reputation for radicalism was exaggerated, he made the Liberal party a vehicle for a certain kind of reform during 1866–74 and gave the radicals their best means of determining government policy; yet his evident alienation from many specific items in the radical programme commended him to the Whigs as a bulwark against drastic change until the 1880s. So long as both sides accepted his leadership and manoeuvred for his support, Gladstone could play a pivotal and unifying role in the evolution of the party.

The Programme versus the Single Issue

Although Gladstone's followers were often captivated by the novelty of participation in national politics they also expected their support to be translated into precise reforms; yet their expectations were bound to be dashed because neither Gladstone nor the MPs as a whole approved of demands for church disestablishment or temperance reform. Instead of allowing his priorities to be influenced by the rank and file, Gladstone intended rather to use their 'virtuous passion' to strengthen his case in Parliament for the changes he did believe necessary. This strategy hinged upon his ability to create a single transcending issue which both Parliament and the constituency activists would accept as the priority. In this process the Reform Bill promoted by him and Lord John Russell in 1866 formed a vital step. For when the Bill perished as a result of Whig opposition Gladstone declined to carry on in office as, on past precedent, he might have been expected to do. His resignation meant that although the Whigs had won a limited victory over that particular Bill, they were going to lose the wider battle for control of future Liberal policy; the incoming minority Conservative administration would sooner or later be driven to an election that Gladstone intended to fight on the franchise question, thereby purging the rebels and producing a majority pledged to reform.

Since in the event Disraeli managed to pass a bill of his own by making concessions to radical backbenchers, Gladstone promptly found another overriding cause – disestablishment of the Church in Ireland and Irish land reform. On this basis he won a majority in 1868 which enabled him to impose both Irish reforms and several other measures during 1868–73. In this period of reform the authority of the gentry was curtailed by Forster's elected school boards and by the secret ballot; upper-class privilege was limited by reforms in the civil service and the army; and the status of the Church and the rights of property were encroached upon in Ireland. This was all of a piece with franchise reform itself as far as the radicals were concerned, in that it attacked the sources of privilege and inefficiency which many had been criticizing since the Crimean War and even earlier. By 1874 the Palmerstonian mould had been decisively broken.

However, while the attack upon privilege furnished a fine theme, the omissions and shortcomings in detail strained the loyalty of Gladstone's supporters sufficiently to produce his defeat over the Irish Universities Bill in 1873. Many radicals believed that Irish disestablishment should lead rapidly to Welsh and Scottish; temperance men were highly iritated by the Licensing Act which regulated public houses and thus made drinking more acceptable not less; trade unions gained legal standing but their right to picket was left in doubt; and Nonconformists felt outraged at the use of ratepayers' money for subsidizing Anglican schools through the new school board system. The 1870 Education Bill best demonstrates the divisive tendencies in the party, for 132 Liberal members voted against it, while 133 abstained; it passed only with Conservative support. These examples show Gladstone's difficulties in trying to govern in the general interest on the strength of sectional interests, many of whom he believed to be propagating unpopular 'fads'; these he pronounced 'unripe' and urged their proponents to convert a majority in the country before expecting the government to risk adopting them. Unfortunately for Gladstone he could not easily command the country without the active assistance of the pressure-group radicals. Temperance fanatics and militant Nonconformists were the quintessential volunteer workers whose withdrawal could cripple the party locally; and the Liberal defeat in 1874 was widely ascribed to the recalcitrance of disappointed groups like the National Education League (NEL). No doubt the NEL deliberately fostered the impression that without them victory was impossible, and they overlooked the loss of support from those who considered that Gladstone had been far too sweeping. Eventually the 1874 defeat sobered many of the 'faddists'; they applied themselves to filling the gap left by conservative defections because the Liberal Party was still their best route to power.

However, the erosion of upper- and middle-class support was a more permanent phenomenon because they did have a political alternative. In 1874 many urban seats returned Conservatives, while in the counties – another portent – Whigs often withheld money and influence from Liberal candidates. The fact is that although in retrospect Victorian Liberalism may seem basically the party of free trade, individualism and self-help, by the 1880s contemporaries were more aware of the growing emphasis on state intervention and compulsion at the expense of individual rights. Temperance and education were two major spheres in which radicals had rapidly concluded that the inadequacy of individual effort could be remedied only by state compulsion. And during Gladstone's second ministry the 1880 Employers Liability Act and the 1881 Irish Land Act, which introduced tribunals empowered to revise rents, were seen as an even graver threat to private property than his earlier measures. Consequently the 1880s saw the resignation of men like the Duke of Argyll from the Cabinet and the creation of the Liberty and Property Defence League. By 1885, with Joseph Chamberlain in full flood against those 'who toil not, neither do they spin', many a traditional Liberal was inclined to take seriously the warning of the jurist A. V. Dicey that if one gave up individual freedom 'you can find no resting place until you reach the abyss of Socialism'.

In fact Gladstone's tactics in 1874 had been to offer abolition of the income tax. But after his defeat he retired for two years before re-emerging in September 1876, 'pamphlet in hand', to assume the leadership of the

'WOODMAN, SPARE THAT TREE!'
LORD BEACONSFIELD sings. –

{'*Woodman, spare that tree!* | THE *Asian Mysterie,*
{ *I love it, every bough;* | *That it has lived till now!*'
Punch, 26 May 1877

provincial crusade against Disraeli's pro-Turkish policy in the Balkans. This campaign was a classic illustration of his capacity for drawing the radicals from their narrow concerns by an appeal to moral righteousness. He began by condemning the Prime Minister for condoning the massacres of Bulgarian Christians merely because he thought it in Britain's interest to back up the Ottoman Empire; and by the time of the two Midlothian campaigns of 1879 and 1880 he had widened the attack to one on 'Beaconsfieldism', that is, the use of military power for imperial aggrandizement as in South Africa and Afghanistan. In fact the policy of their governments was much closer than the rhetoric suggested. Disraeli had been drawn unwillingly into the conflicts with the Boers and the Afghans by British representatives on the ground, Sir Bartle Frere (high commissioner) and Lord Lytton (viceroy), respectively. Gladstone was to encounter the same problems, especially in Egypt and the Sudan.

Nevertheless, as an expedient for polarizing politics and recapturing the leadership of radicalism the campaign against 'Beaconsfieldism' proved a triumph; but it was no solution to the problem that led to 1874. Others had begun to consider how to overcome the incoherence endemic in Liberalism. In particular Joseph Chamberlain, Mayor of Birmingham 1873–6, diagnosed the problem in terms of the dispersion of radicalism over innumerable causes. To be successful radicals had to concentrate on a single question as Cobden and Bright had done over the Corn Laws; the trouble was that their success had led to the disintegration of the forces that had brought it about, and ever since 1846 Bright had vainly sought a similar rallying point. Initially Chamberlain himself believed that either disestablishment or education would serve to concentrate radicalism and tighten its grip on the party, but 1874 had shown him the inadequacy of such causes when it came to rousing the electorate. Making a virtue of necessity, therefore, he abandoned the single-issue strategy in favour of programme politics. His main vehicle for this, the NLF was established in 1877 from the ruins of the NEL with the object of radicalizing both the policy and the organization of the Liberal Party. It would represent the active, democratic constituency Liberals in the country who would select candidates who reflected their views. The annual assembly of the NLF would become a kind of Liberal Parliament in the country, especially when the party was out of office; and being representative of the party's supporters it could legitimately prepare a programme of measures and indicate the priorities to the leaders. In this way it was hoped to harness radicalism's scattered forces to the governmental machine.

The basis of the NLF's claims to represent Liberalism lay in local parties whose membership was open to all supporters. The Birmingham Liberal Association, two-thirds of whose membership was reckoned to be working class, provided a model for others to emulate. Although middle- and working-class co-operation had long been a feature of Birmingham politics, similar systems had been pioneered in Oldham and Rochdale which inspired popular organization in places like Newcastle in the 1870s.[4] Every Liberal in the city was entitled to attend his local ward meetings which elected representatives to a 'Liberal 600', and this in turn chose an executive committee. At its inauguration in 1877 the NLF drew representatives from 95 such organizations.

Initially Gladstone's dislike of the pretensions of the caucus and programme politics was obscured; for when the NLF timed its inaugural meeting in May 1877 to catch the wave of excitement over the Bulgarian issue the Liberal leader graced the occasion with a speech at the Bingley Hall, Birmingham. Each believed they had caught the other. By hitching Gladstone's prestige to the NLF Chamberlain calculated that he was bound to strengthen radicalism at the expense of the Whigs, who were undoubtedly embarrassed by the Bulgarian campaign. Ultimately this proved a shrewd assessment. But in the short run the NLF found itself swept along in Gladstone's crusade in which its own objectives were obscured. By maintaining his grip on radical affections, especially in imperial and foreign affairs, Gladstone succeeded for some years in checking the programmatic form of politics desired by Chamberlain. The year 1877 thus began the process of driving the two men apart.

As a result the Liberals swept home in the 1880 general election on a wave of moral righteousness with a negative mandate to undo Disraeli's policy, but little else. The victory seemed unrelated to the issues of radical politics, and as the new administration staggered on without achievement the whole Midlothian strategy began to appear as a ruse designed to sidetrack radicalism. In fact Gladstone's difficulties during 1800–5 were partly due to the engrossing problems of South Africa, Afghanistan and Egypt; to the coercive measures for Ireland and the consequent obstructionism of the Nationalist MPs; and to time-consuming controversy over the entry into the Commons of the atheist MP, Charles Bradlaugh, who had refused to take the oath. However, the Prime Minister had no priorities for legislation, and important reforms of land and local government were frustrated. Consequently the faddists grew voluble again, and their clamour was stilled only by the introduction of a major measure, the 1884 Franchise Bill, which was passed before the government broke up over its defeat on the budget in June 1885.

In fact the two leading radical ministers, Dilke and Chamberlain, had already resigned in May, the latter to concentrate on a ferocious campaign against the landed upper class which was designed to win the newly enfranchised county voters for radicalism at the 1885 elections. In interpreting Chamberlain's proposals (dubbed the 'Unauthorised Programme'), one has to disentangle the ideological element from the tactical objective. His list included free elementary education, elective county government, land reforms, graduated taxation, death duties, disestablishment, devolution-all-round, manhood suffrage and payment of MPs. In part this grew out of Chamberlain's municipal experience in Birmingham where the council had shown its middle-class ratepayers the virtues of public enterprise in the provision of such services as gas, water, sewerage and lighting. This willingness to extend the collective element in economic and social matters marked Chamberlain out as what was often called a 'constructive radical'; conversely, eminent 'radicals' like John Morley shrank from 'construction' on both economic and political grounds, the more so as it was increasingly coupled with the demand for graduated taxation.

In other respects, however, Chamberlain's approach was less radical. The idea of local government reform or devolution was really to allow divisive matters such as temperance or education to be settled outside

Parliament. Nor did he wish to offend the middle-class belief in private enterprise, witness his cautious approach to housing.[5] For him the chief issue was land, because it served to concentrate the attack upon the upper classes and to pre-empt any separate working-class onslaught on property in general. In the long run, he believed, middle-class radicals had to mobilize the new mass electorate before someone else did.

The tactical significance of the Unauthorised Programme is less obvious. On the face of it Chamberlain's object was to gain such a preponderance of radical MPs in the new Parliament that it would be impossible for Gladstone to repeat the experience of 1880–5. Historians have therefore tried to calculate the number of his supporters. One study suggests a growth from 80 in 1874 to 120 in 1880 and 160 after the 1885 election when 333 Liberals were returned altogether.[6] Another writer suggests 180, using as the criterion for radicalism an MP's support for even one point in the programme;[7] but this contrasts sharply with the chief whip's estimate of only 101 'Chamberlainites'. Retrospective assessments exaggerate Chamberlain's strength because they define radicalism in domestic terms and forget that the foreign–imperial dimension was equally important. Most radicals had inherited their creed from Cobden and Bright: trade not rule was the virtue of Empire: Britain should abstain from entanglements abroad and avoid expenditure and armaments. The irony is that on these matters the two leading radicals, Dilke and Chamberlain, were out of step with most radical opinion; they resented the failure of Gladstone, as they saw it, to stand up for British interests as much as the Whigs. Another weakness in Chamberlain's appeal was that, though a Unitarian himself, he remained essentially a secular radical, not much motivated by religious or spiritual concerns; the 'Nonconformist Conscience' always remained elusive. Consequently Chamberlain could never prise radicalism away from Gladstone. During the early 1880s he began to recognize this: for many radicals now looked to Morley – a staunch 'Little Englander' – as a more suitable leader than Chamberlain; and the first working-men MPs such as Thomas Burt also followed the Gladstonian line on foreign affairs. Thus 'Chamberlainites' should not be equated with 'radicals'. There was little prospect of a takeover of the party by him in 1885; and herein lies the explanation for his otherwise extraordinary abandonment of the Liberal Party in the company of Lord Hartington and the Whigs in 1886.

1886: The Radicalization of the Party

The fall of Gladstone's government over the 1885 budget was followed by a minority Conservative administration and a general election in which the Liberal lead of 86 over the Tories was matched by the election of 86 Irish

Nationalists. The deadlock was resolved by the launching of the 'Hawarden Kite' in December 1885 when Gladstone's son, Herbert, released the news of his father's conversion to Irish Home Rule. Thereupon Liberals and Nationalists combined to eject Salisbury from office; Gladstone introduced a Home Rule Bill which failed, owing to the opposition of 93 Liberal MPs who withdrew under Hartington and Chamberlain to stand as Liberal Unionists at the ensuing general election of 1886.

This crisis reflected much more than a simple division of opinion over the principle of Home Rule. It was easy for men like Sir William Harcourt, who disliked the Bill intensely, to remain loyal to Gladstone. In so doing he had opted for one strategy; Chamberlain in withdrawing had opted for another. Having absorbed the lesson of 1880 he had no intention of allowing the Grand Old Man to lead the party off on another crusade, and thus forget the real business of radical politics. Since the 1885 election had confirmed that he could not dominate the party Chamberlain had sought a short cut by co-operating with Hartington and the Whig elements to topple Gladstone. The basis for a Hartington–Chamberlain government consisted in their common dislike of Gladstone's supine and unpatriotic foreign policy; within such a government Chamberlain believed that Hartington, lacking Gladstone's influence with the radicals, would be obliged to allow him to determine the pace of domestic reform. This prospect of an alternative Liberal ministry posed a dilemma for Gladstone from which he escaped successfully by seizing the initiative over Home Rule. The joint withdrawal of Hartington and Chamberlain was a logical consequence in that it reflected their common failure to ditch Gladstone, and Chamberlain's inability to win control of the radical forces.

The ultimate significance of this turning point in politics is as much misunderstood as its origins. Superficially the Home Rule crisis appears merely a divisive, weakening factor that deprived the party of its radical strength. The reality was different. It clarified Liberal politics by introducing a simple test of orthodoxy, and completed the process initiated unwittingly by Gladstone in 1866 when he refused to abandon franchise reform. The purging of the Whig elements had been proceeding apace during 1880–5 when the Dukes of Argyll and Bedford and the Marquess of Landsdowne, to name only the most illustrious, had left the party. Of the 73 Liberal Unionist MPs who survived the 1886 election only 20 were radical supporters of Chamberlain; by 1892 only 11 of the latter remained and several had rejoined the Gladstonians. In short, 1886 virtually completed the radicalization of Liberalism. Although only 191 Gladstonians were returned in 1886 they comprised a much more cohesive party than ever before. For the first time Gladstone appointed radicals such as Tom Ellis and Arnold Morley as party whips, and when next he came to form a government in 1892 he had no option but to draw upon radicals to fill the cabinet posts.

The fact that the majority of radical politicians chose to stay with Gladstone reflected the loyalties of Liberals in the country. Evidence of the attitudes of the three layers of Liberalism suggests that Home Rule sentiment was at its weakest among parliamentarians, stronger among the electors, and as its strongest among the activists. It is easy to extaggerate the electoral unpopularity of Home Rule. Rebellious Liberal Unionists secured election in 73 seats because the Conservatives stood down in their favour, thus presenting them with around two-thirds of the former Conservative vote to add to a quarter to a third of the old Liberal vote. They managed this most easily in areas where the development of party organization had lagged, and where it proved difficult to obtain and finance a new Gladstonian candidate at short notice. In such cases the prestige of the sitting member served to carry sufficient support, particularly in parts of the South-West and western Scotland, where the strategic implications of Home Rule seemed to lend force to the Liberal Unionists' case. On the other hand, in a straight contest between a Gladstonian and a Conservative the loss of Liberal votes was much slighter; in fact many Liberals improved their poll over 1885 and actually regained seats in such places as Huddersfield, Leeds East, Liverpool Exchange, Manchester South-West, Wednesbury and Wolverhampton West.

These victories in the towns constitute further evidence of the strength of Home Rule sentiment where Liberalism was well organized. Indeed one study suggests that only 5–10 per cent of party activists felt sufficiently opposed to Gladstone's policy to leave the party.[8] To them Home Rule appeared an eminently radical issue on which they could sympathize with the Irish for fighting a common enemy. The swiftness with which the caucus fell into line behind Gladstone undoubtedly surprised Chamberlain. Following the introduction of the Home Rule Bill on 10 April 1886 the local organizations selected delegates for an NLF council meeting on 5 May: the 'Newcastle 600', the 'Nottingham 800', the 'Leicester 500' and many others declared emphatically for Gladstone; even at Birmingham the 'Two Thousand' dissented only on details. At the NLF meeting a motion mildly critical of the Bill was thrown out by 575 votes to 25, which led to the resignation of Chamberlain and his Birmingham loyalists Jesse Collings and Powell Williams. Moreover, sitting members who were prevaricating at Burnley, Nottingham West, Buckingham and Hastings found their local caucuses insisting that they endorse official policy; those who remained obdurate, like G. O. Trevelyan and George Goschen, were denied renomination; other prominent figures were ejected by a vote of the local party, notably Hartington at Rossendale and Sir Henry James at Bury. In general the wealthier Liberal supporters were more prone to withdrawal, so that the local parties became noticeably poorer if more cohesive politically. The year 1886 actually helped to reunite Liberal associations formerly in disarray at Bradford, Dewsbury and Newcastle. As many as fifty associations affiliated to the NLF for the first time, thus making its hold more complete than ever. In September 1886 it shifted its headquarters to London, next door to the Liberal Central Association, so that the two bodies could enjoy a common secretary, Francis Schnadhorst, and put an end to the rivalry between them.

The crystallization of the radical forces as a result of Home Rule is particularly noticeable in Scotland, which, though strongly Liberal, had been sharply divided between a Glasgow-based organization of radicals and an Edinburgh-based association of Whigs and moderates. The former vigorously propagated the two central issues of Scottish politics – land reform and disestablishment – and were conciliated by a new Secretaryship of State for Scotland in 1885 and the Crofters Bill of 1886. The radicals had long felt that a reformed county franchise would expose the inability of the Whigs to mobilize public opinion; they therefore established an NLF for Scotland on the English pattern and put up candidates against Whiggish Liberals in 28 of the 72 Scottish constituencies in 1885. Home Rule finally alienated the Scottish Whigs who had been trying to hold on to Gladstone during the 1880s, though the immediate price was the loss of 23 Liberal MPs opposed to Home Rule, 17 of whom secured election in 1886. On the other hand, the disestablishment radicals and land reformers who had grown impatient with Gladstone saw the futility of leaving and rallied to the Irish cause; Gladstone was now thrown into their arms.

Similarly the English pressure groups appreciated the tactical advantages of sticking to the Grand Old Man. The loss of so many local patrons plainly left the party more dependent than ever on the network of Nonconformity in the provinces. Even before 1886 the faddists had steadily reconciled themselves to long-term work within the party. The NEL had actually disbanded after 1874 to channel its energies through the NLF and into school board elections, thereby becoming an integral part of Liberal electoral machinery. Similarly the Liberation Society dropped its coercive tactics after 1874 in the hope that loyalty would bring its reward, which it did in the shape of a Welsh Disestablishment Bill in 1894. The more closely these groups associated themselves with the Liberals the more their opponents backed the Conservatives; then the faddists could plausibly argue that Liberal candidates could not poll the full potential radical vote unless they aroused the enthusiasm of their own adherents. On balance, the changing relationship between the party and the pressure groups between the 1860s and 1890s was to the advantage of the former. After the franchise extensions and introduction of the secret ballot it was much more difficult for the proponents of any cause to claim credibly that the abstention of their supporters had brought about the defeat of a candidate. By the 1890s, therefore, 'faddism' was for the most part neatly marshalled in the annual programmes of the NLF.

One major element of weakness hampered the post-1886 Liberal Party: the absence of an effective radical leader in the front rank of parliamentarians who could succeed Gladstone whose age and intellectual rigidity increasingly limited his usefulness. It was indeed an irony that Chamberlain should have left the party at the very moment when it became the embodiment of programmatic radicalism. Initially he expected his severance from the party to be temporary, which is why the Liberal Unionists tried to avoid voting with the Conservatives in the Commons; this was intended to facilitate their return to Liberalism when Gladstone retired. In fact he stayed on, and the overtures for reunion in 1887 were easily rebuffed by those like Morley who disliked Chamberlain's brand of politics. While the Grand Old Man remained leader until 1894 Chamberlain gradually learnt to work with Salisbury, whose government he joined in 1895. Gladstone and Morley were content to await the gradual return of the lesser figures embarrassed by association with Salisbury. The drift would have been faster but for Chamberlain's ability to secure certain reforms during 1887–92, particularly those for land and education.

Some writers still regard Home Rule simply as the 'most potent divisive force' in Liberalism after 1886;[9] this is a natural conclusion to be drawn from the correspondence of a few leading politicians, who disagreed on the details of Home Rule as on the details of every policy. However, this is scarcely applicable to the party as a whole which, as we have seen, rallied round the principle of Home Rule. By 1888 the Conservative coercion policy in Ireland had given Gladstone a useful angle on the Irish Question because it allowed him to avoid discussing details and concentrate his fire on a simple moral issue. Resistance to government oppression dramatized the Irish Question for English audiences; 'Justice to Ireland does not arouse enthusiasm', observed the cynical Labouchere, 'unless it be wrapped up in what they regard as justice to themselves.'[10] English working men were therefore urged to see the threat to their own rights of combination, and organization inherent in the suppression of similar bodies in Ireland.

In time, however, Home Rule assumed a less prominent role in Liberal politics. The destruction of Parnell's career in 1891 as a result of a divorce scandal sapped the will of many British home-rulers; and the inevitable rejection of the second Home Rule Bill by the peers in 1893, followed by Gladstone's retirement in 1894, turned the issue into a cul-de-sac for ambitious Liberals instead of the highway to office that it had been for Morley in the 1880s. Since the party had to have a post-Home Rule policy, programme politics enjoyed a heyday encouraged by Harcourt and the faddists. The culmination of this process occurred at the NLF's New-castle conference in 1891 which endorsed the full range of reforms: taxa-tion of land values, ground rents and royalties, death duties, free elementary education, Welsh and Scottish disestablishment, a 'direct popular veto' on the liquor traffic, parish councils, home-rule-all-round, the 'free breakfast table', and reform of the franchise and the House of Lords.

This had been the staple radical diet for some years. What made the 'Newcastle Programme' significant was its apparent endorsement by Gladstone only a year before his victory in an election fought on its provisions. In fact Gladstone paid only cursory attention to the items on the list at Newcastle, ignoring those he disliked and concentrating on Ireland. Regardless of his real attitude, the programme's importance became evident when his Home Rule Bill suffered rejection at the hands of the peers. Their action posed a dilemma for the Cabinet. If Home Rule was so vital then they must resign and ask the country to overrule the House of Lords. But Gladstone's colleagues declined to take this course. In 1892 they had compelled him to embody much of the party programme in the Queen's Speech, and it seemed to them that after six years out of office they must press ahead with the reforms on which they had recently won election. The ministers, in short, now thought along the same lines as the NLF. Hence 1894 brought Harcourt's famous 'Death Duties' budget and the establishment of parish and district councils, as well as unsuccessful attempts at legislation for employers' liability and Welsh disestablishment.

It would, therefore, be beside the point to say that the Cabinet never allowed the NLF to dictate its policy, for the two had moved so close together that as a rule aggressive tactics were not necessary. The 1892–5 Liberal Government represented an important stage in the party's evolution insofar as it showed the absorption of programmatic radicalism both in principle and in detail. Where the rank and file chose to adopt aggressive tactics, as on Welsh disestablishment, it was not because of disagreements on the merits of the issue but because the leaders felt that the peers' hostility made it a futile cause; they nonetheless went ahead with a bill. Undoubtedly the party still had major unresolved problems, notably a solution to the House of Lords question, the emergence of independent working-class politics, and the resurgence of imperial sentiment. Yet it had substantially resolved the problems of the 1860s; and in the process it had abandoned the passive, parliamentary form of politics and shaken free from the upper-class control that had inhibited both its role as assailant of privilege and its evolution as a modern political party.

Gladstone's role in all this is ambiguous. As we have seen, his brand of Liberalism was a viable, not an anachronistic, one, especially in the 1860s and 1870s. However, it is also clear that by the 1890s many of the changes in the party had come about in spite of Gladstone, not because of him.

Moreover, the conditions of politics were now changing in several ways. First, Home Rule inevitably waned as it became clear that the electors would not give the Liberals a mandate on this question alone. Second, by the mid-1880s religious issues had reached their peak. Many of the Nonconformists' grievances had now been settled. Although the bulk of Liberal candidates were now committed to disestablishment, the force behind the issue was fading; this is clear from the loss of members and funds by the Liberation Society in the late 1880s and 1890s, especially in England. Third, it emerged that the Gladstonian formula based on retrenchment and low taxation was not viable in the long run. Far from being abolished, income tax rose under Liberal governments. In fact Chamberlain's emphasis on land taxation and a graduated income tax offered a more realistic way forward. But Gladstone proved reluctant to recognize this, as his resignation over higher government spending in 1894 underlines. Liberalism's new agenda was beginning to be born.

CHAPTER THREE

The Conservative Revival 1874–1900

It is significant that . . . the reformed constituency of Westminster should have preferred the unknown Conservative who sold books [W. H. Smith] to the famous Liberal – JOHN STUART MILL – who wrote them.

The Times, 7 October 1891

At the death of Disraeli in 1881 the Conservative Party stood in some apprehension about its future. Since the repeal of the Corn Laws in 1846 it had not won a majority at a general election except for 1874, and, in view of the drastic reforms made and anticipated, no one could feel confident that the pattern had been decisively broken. Before 1846 the Conservatives had established themselves as a national party representing agriculture while also promoting the economic innovation desired by urban, industrial England. But for the defection of the Peelites in 1846 they might have gone on to perform the role subsequently filled by Victorian Liberalism. Instead they lingered for 30 years a sectional rump, suspect in the eyes of the electorate for their inexperience of office, the prominence of the distrusted Disraeli, and the protectionist tendencies of the country gentlemen. As late as 1874 Queen Victoria noted with evident relief that Disraeli's new ministers included only one duke and were 'not at all retrograde'!

Yet the Conservative reputation for wildness and instability was somewhat exaggerated. Their dilemma really lay in the absence of any distinctive policy with which to win the electorate. There was little that a mid-Victorian Conservative government might do with respect to Empire, economy, property or monarchy that one under Lord Palmerston could not do better.[1] Not until the forces of popular radicalism gained the ascendancy in the Liberal Party, and Palmerston's chauvinistic conservatism gave way to Gladstone's moralistic reformism, did the Conservatives begin to appear a better vehicle for the aspirations of 'respectable' England once again. Disraeli was lucky, if rather late in life, in the events of the 1860s; but he knew how to exploit his opportunities. He saw how to divide and rule the House of Commons in 1866–7 by taking up franchise reform; and how to appropriate Palmerston's mantle by seizing upon the radical 'conspiracy' to dismember the Empire, and by pursuing the Crimean War policy in 1875–8.

Yet Disraeli's contribution to the Conservatives' restoration as a governing party and as a majority in the country has been much exaggerated. When Derby and Disraeli expanded the electorate by enfranchising many working-class householders and lodgers in 1867 they were not making a bold appeal for new Conservative voters. Had they wished to do that it would have been natural to extend the new franchises to the *counties*, where the party was strongly entrenched; but this would almost certainly have provoked a Tory revolt and thus torpedoed the Bill. What Disraeli was really attempting in 1867 – largely by judicious manipulation of the constituency boundaries – was a limited experiment in making the existing Conservative support count for more. Nor is there much evidence that the newly enfranchised voters, outside Lancashire, gave the party additional support in 1868. Even the Conservatives' great victory in 1874 was won on the basis of a smaller share of the popular vote (1.09 million to 1.28 million) than the Liberals; clearly the maldistribution of seats gave Conservatives a major advantage. In the long run the most important aspect of the new electorate was its *indirect* effect in accelerating the radicalization occurring within Liberalism, thereby allowing the Conservatives under Lord Salisbury to inherit the naturally conservative forces in the country. In the long run the party grew less in a 'Disraelian' mould than a 'Peelite' one. Disraeli's own pilgrimage from impecunious notoriety to the peerage left intact his fondness for pre-industrial society united by the deference of the labourer and the duty of the landowner. He could not easily accommodate an urban middle class or an organized proletariat and, like Gladstone, he regretted the explosion of wealth in the hands of men who did not recognize it as a duty 'to endow the Church, to feed the poor, to guard the land, and to execute justice for nothing'. For him government was best conducted by disinterested gentlemen through local communities, not central bureaucracies. This reluctance to come to terms with industrialization restricted the scope for an active policy for the working classes because this implied bureaucracy and taxation; instead Conservatism returned to an accommodation with middle-class industrial wealth. The return of the latter-day Peelites, though not at all what Disraeli envisaged, nevertheless gave the party its increasing strength and much of its organization and policy in the late nineteenth century.

The Impact of Middle-class Conservatism

In 1865 the Conservatives' strength lay in England where 221 of their 294 MPs held seats, particularly in counties and small boroughs. Their representation even in counties was threatened by urban expansion. Yet their perilously narrow electoral base was to be modified in three ways. First, the Liberal hold on Scotland strengthened slightly, and on Wales greatly, while in Ireland the Home Rulers mopped up 80 per cent of the seats after 1874. In this way the Conservative position as the English party was considerably accentuated. Second, the Liberals extended their base in the counties following the 1884 franchise reforms. Thus, whereas in 1868 Conservatives had won 115 out of 154 English county seats, in 1885 they held only 105 out of 239; counties had become a key element in an overall Liberal majority.

Conservatives were saved only by their growing support in large boroughs and suburban seats, which reached a climax in 1900 when they took 177 English boroughs as against 162 English counties. There were indications of this trend in Lancashire after 1852 and in London after 1859; and in 1868, despite its overall defeat, the party gained 34 seats in boroughs whose population exceeded 20,000. Loss of formerly radical constituencies like Middlesex and Westminster was a warning to the Liberals that urbanization had created middle-class residential communities whose aspirations were not those of radical artisans.

However, the large towns remained under-represented in the Commons, and, since they returned two members from undivided constituencies, the improved Conservative poll frequently left the party a larger minority but still unrepresented. If Conservatives were to realize their strength, tactics required a drastic redistribution based upon equal constituencies and a single-member system. This is why one finds such radical notions being urged by Salisbury and Sir Michael Hicks-Beach in 1884–5; they seized their opportunity when Gladstone, hoping to close a somewhat barren term of office with a radical triumph, introduced a bill to extend the household suffrage to the counties. This the peers could plausibly reject unless a redistribution scheme were attached. In the ensuing compact between the party leaders the Conservative desire for equal single-member seats coincided with the objectives of the Chamberlainites who hoped to eliminate Whigs in small boroughs. Thus, boroughs with a population under 15,000 lost their separate representation, while those with under 50,000 lost one of their two members. This drastically reduced the representation of the South-West to the advantage of London and Lancashire, both of which proved to be Conservative for 20 years. All counties and all but 23 boroughs were divided into single-member seats along boundaries that were designed to reflect 'the pursuits of the people'.

TABLE 3.1   *Conservative MPs in London 1859–1900*

Pre-1867 (total 18)		Post-1867 (total 22)		Post-1885 (total 59)	
1859	0	1868	3	1885	35
1865	0	1874	10	1886	47
		1880	8	1892	36
				1895	51
				1900	51

This scheme helped the Conservatives, first, by increasing the scope for plural voting in the divided constituencies at a time when the propertied classes were coming adrift from Liberalism. Second, the Conservatives believed that by keeping agricultural areas separate from mining or urban areas they could maintain the territorial influence of the landowners. Third, in conurbations the same principle involved creating separate working-class, commercial, and residential middle-class seats. This would at least save the Conservative minority from being swamped. Liberals like Leonard Courtney and Sir John Lubbock argued in vain that minority representation would best be secured by a proportional system. At the time few politicians perceived that in a mature industrial society characterized by residential separation the effect of trying to preserve homogeneous communities would be to promote class-based voting. The consequences were obvious in formerly radical cities like Leeds where Conservatives subsequently won two of the five seats, and Sheffield where they took three of five. London, however, provided quite the most striking example of Conservative gains (see table 3.1). Redistribution could not, of course, have had this effect without shifts of allegiance, but it facilitated the translation of urban votes into new members. Indeed his work in 1884–5 alone entitles Salisbury to be considered a major architect of his party's revival; in combination with the Home Rule crisis of 1886 the redistribution of 1885 made these years the decisive turning point for Conservatism.

The broader base of Conservatism gradually modified the party's social composition in Parliament; an analysis of the MPs according to the date of their election to the Commons brings out the extent and timing of the change (see table 3.2). Only among MPs elected in 1885–6 who had previously sat in Parliament was the landed element the predominant one; in each new set of recruits after 1885 a substantial majority were drawn from the industrial and professional middle classes, a reflection of the fact that suburban seats, which were likely to adopt bourgeois candidates, had become safer for Conservatives than many counties.

TABLE 3.2   *Social origins of Conservative MPs 1885–1900*

Parliamentary group		Landed classes	% from		
			Industry and commerce	Professional and public service	Other
1885–6	Old	54.8	28.7	15.2	1.4
1885	New	34.1	34.2	26.5	5.1
1886	New	36.7	27.5	29.2	6.7
1892	New	41.9	32.0	19.6	6.0
1895	New	36.0	28.0	24.9	10.9
1900	New	28.7	42.5	18.1	10.6

Source: J. P. Cornford, 'Parliamentary Origins of the Hotel Cecil', in R. Robson (ed.), *Ideas and Institutions of Victorian Britain* (1967), p. 310.

TABLE 3.3   *Social origins of Conservative MPs 1885–1900* (%)

	1885	*1886*	*1892*	*1895*	*1900*
Landed classes	45.8	43.3	46.2	41.2	38.5
Industry and commerce	31.1	29.5	28.1	28.3	32.0
Professional and public service	19.9	23.2	20.7	23.2	21.3
Others	2.9	4.0	4.7	7.3	8.6

Source: J. P. Cornford, 'Parliamentary Origins of the Hotel Cecil', in R. Robson (ed.), *Ideas and Institutions of Victorian Britain* (1967), p. 310.

On the other hand an examination of the entire parliamentary party after each election brings out the continuity (see table 3.3). Clearly the composition of the party changed rather gradually. For whereas the sons of the upper classes normally entered the Commons before the age of 30, the businessman had first to establish his financial independence by building up his company, so that a seat in Parliament crowned his career in his fifties. Professional men, especially barristers, could enter earlier, but were apt to treat politics as an aid to their legal careers rather than as the prime objective. Both groups were more likely to take on marginal or hopeless constituencies, and to die or retire after short periods as MPs. The squires elected before 1885 enjoyed particularly long terms as MPs, but began to drop out in substantial numbers only after 1900.

Consequently the ultimate reward of cabinet office, being the due of men who had established their reputation in the House, fell disproportionately to the landed gentlemen. A businessman could be caught between the need to attend his business and to devote time to a minor role as parliamentary private secretary or junior whip, which was a necessary step on the ladder of office. It is not surprising that both Disraeli and Salisbury drew criticism for neglecting the claims of middle-class supporters, though the latter quickly learnt to make lavish use of honours to compensate for shortage of jobs. Despite the competition a number of bourgeois recruits obtained major office under Disraeli and Salisbury as a result of the dearth of administrative talent and debating skills to combat the Liberal heavy artillery. The 1874 ministry saw Richard Cross as Home Secretary, Gathorne–Hardy at the War Office, Sclater-Booth at the Local Government Board, and W. H. Smith, whose elevation to the Admiralty in 1877 caused a flutter at the palace and W. S. Gilbert's satirical creation 'Sir Joseph Porter' in *HMS Pinafore*. Salisbury appointed C. T. Richie to three ministries, George Goschen to the Exchequer, and relied heavily on Smith as Leader of the Commons from 1886 until his death in 1891. Smith and Cross, derided by Lord Randolph Churchill as 'Marshall and Snelgrove', reached the top through personal ability rather than as representatives of urban middle-class Toryism, though business expertise was, perhaps, a factor in Goschen's appointment as Chancellor in 1887. Yet it took more than a few pioneers to kill Lord Randolph's snobbery or the ingrained condescension of the traditional leaders. Witness Arthur Balfour's advice to Salisbury on the choice of a new Postmaster-General in 1891 in which he commended W. L. Jackson (MP for Leeds North), who

> has great tact and judgement – middle class tact and judgement I admit, but good of their kind . . . he is that *rara avis*, a successful manufacturer who is fit for something besides manufacturing. A cabinet of Jacksons would [be] rather a serious order, no doubt: but one or even two would be a considerable addition to any cabinet.[2]

What is clear is that middle-class ministers were chosen, apart from the special cases like Chamberlain, on the strength of administrative competence and forensic talent. The epitome of urban Conservatism and the National Union, Sir John Gorst, conspicuously failed to make the Cabinet; however, Gorst, who largely ruled himself out by rebelliousness over labour questions, was never dangerous enough to command a place at the top. Indeed the only politician who can in any sense be said to have used the National Union to advance himself to the Cabinet, Churchill, was an aristocrat without a real following.

Organizing the Democracy

As the Conservative leaders contemplated the growth of urban political organization on the Liberal side they realized that they would have to match it eventually; yet it was Salisbury rather than Disraeli who actually came to terms with this distasteful necessity.

Since the 1830s the party had made do with a rudimentary organizational structure emanating from the Carlton Club whence amateur officials attempted to stimulate registration work in the constituencies. However, continued electoral failure and the establishment of the Liberal Registration Association in 1861 were so worrying that by 1867 Disraeli was ready to respond to John Gorst's passionate demand that the party should deliberately consolidate its traditional links with the people. One expression of these links already existed in working men's Conservative clubs, and the first modest gathering of these – the NUCCA – in 1867 received Disraeli's blessing. Whether through dismay at the election defeat of 1868 or through being apprehensive of the popular body, he also created in 1870 a separate Conservative Central Office which was designed to stimulate new associations, maintain contact with them and compile lists of candidates. Since these functions duplicated those of the NUCCA the dual system inevitably produced friction. Initially, however, both bodies made progress in the declining years of Gladstone's administration; and by 1872 Central Office and the National Union were closely linked through a common headquarters and Gorst's position as both principal agent and honorary secretary of the National Union.

The objects of the National Union were modestly conceived. As Gorst had reminded the approving delegates in 1867, it was 'not a meeting for the discussion of Conservative principles on which we are all agreed, it is only a meeting to consider by what particular organization we may make these Conservative principles effective among the masses'.[3] Initially the task of extending Conservative associations through the country proved congenial; and by 1877 some 791 bodies had affiliated, though many of these were clubs and registration societies, not constituency associations. The victory of 1874, when 65 of the 74 Conservative gains in England and Wales occurred under the auspices of active Conservative associations, encouraged the National Union to ignore the indifference and hostility exhibited by much of the party, which preferred to rely upon traditional *ad hoc* committees of solicitors and gentlemen to organize elections. Particularly in the rural areas local dignitaries disliked anything that smacked of the caucus. They were also deeply suspicious of the voluminous body of literature eulogizing Disraelian reforms generated by the National Union in the 1870s; the Conservative case, they believed, should never be based upon programmes of exceptional legislation for the working class.

Gladstone's surprise victory in 1880 emboldened the National Union delegates to offer the party advice on the shortcomings of its attitude towards organization. They demanded more attention to speeches in the country by parliamentary leaders, and greater expenditure on new Conservative clubs which considerably facilitated registration work; and they condemned the habit of leaving organization in the hands of amateur 'gentlemen who practically knew nothing of election matters and undertook the management merely as a professional duty in their capacity of lawyers'.[4] In addition they pointed out that the 1883 Act on expenses and illegal practices would curtail the practice of paying for canvassing and conveyancing to the poll, and leave the party greatly handicapped against the radicals.[5] The expectation of an extended county franchise at this time was one of the considerations that impelled Lord Randolph Churchill to champion the party organization.

He was not the only one who was alive to the dangers posed by the rapidly changing rules of the electoral battle. Gorst, aware that the associations often existed only on paper and lapsed between elections, tried to encourage them to contest the municipal elections regularly and to find extra money for the building of clubs. But although the National Union took pains to dissociate itself from the NLF and to abjure pronouncements on policy, its conferences eventually became the scene of lively debates, and not simply on organization. After 1885 the rank and file showed enthusiasm for various issues that the parliamentary leaders studiously avoided – alien immigration, women's suffrage, state subsidies for house purchase, and an imperial tariff policy; indeed the successful battle for protectionism waged in annual conferences during the 1880s and 1890s prepared the way for the Chamberlainite takeover after 1903.

Despite these undercurrents the National Union never directly confronted the leadership except in the early 1880s, and then not over policy but over organization and the role of urban middle-class Conservatism. By 1880 Gorst, frustrated by Disraeli's neglect of the machine and by personal chagrin at not being offered a major post, sought a leader for his cause. Through his membership of the 'Fourth Party' (a self-appointed group of four MPs who tormented the Gladstone government), he found one in Churchill; it is significant that it took someone of Churchill's rank to spearhead the campaign. After securing election to the Council of the National Union in 1882 he proceeded to attack the practice of co-opting on to the Council 12 members nominated by Central Office which had little interest in improving organization in the country. He railed against the Central Committee, which Disraeli had established, and was dependent on the leader for funds and personnel, for effectively reducing the National Union to an impotent, advisory role. Churchill demanded that control of organization and funds be removed from the irresponsible body to the elected Council. Culminating in a meeting with Salisbury in 1884,

Churchill's campaign produced a face-saving compromise. The Central Committee was abolished, the Council freed of co-opted members and a little more money granted to the national Union. None of these details, however, materially improved the power or status of the National Union.

Beneath the rhetoric Lord Randolph Churchill had never shared Gorst's objectives, and certainly not his hostility towards the traditional leaders of the party from whose ranks he came.[6] In 1882 he declined an invitation to contest Manchester, preferring to remain safely in the family borough of Woodstock until its abolition in 1885. He made a single foray on behalf of urban Conservatism by fighting a Birmingham seat against John Bright, but thereafter reverted to a safe seat at Paddington. Churchill had no intention of putting his career at risk for the cause of middle-class Conservatism, which is why, once he felt he had done enough to win a place in the next government, he dropped the National Union. It would be flattering both Churchill and the National Union to suppose that he endeavoured to use it as a power base from which to secure the party leadership – he was too young, too inexperienced in office and too lacking in support in Parliament. Salisbury pandered to Churchill's pretensions because he appreciated that his campaign was not directed against himself but against Northcote, and because he recognized that Churchill's platform oratory was an asset to the party. There was consequently no objection to elevating him to cabinet rank in 1885 provided that nothing of substance had to be conceded to the National Union. Churchill was safe because he was no Chamberlain.

Thus, after 1884 the National Union settled down to its functions of branch-building, propaganda and speech-making; and from 1885 all Conservative associations were automatically affiliated to it. A signal indication of the leadership's control over the organization was Salisbury's ability to ensure the withdrawal of Conservative candidates in all but a handful of the 93 seats held by Liberal Unionist MPs in 1886. Local constituency interest was simply overruled by parliamentary strategy. The party in the country was tended by 'Captain' R. W. E. Middleton, the principal agent from 1885 and honorary secretary of the National Union from 1886, who co-ordinated his work smoothly with Salisbury and the chief whip. Where Gorst had been prickly and ambitious Middleton was loyal, tactful and ready to accept the subservient role of the organization. This was congenial to Salisbury who enjoyed consulting him both over election statistics, of which he became a keen student, and over the awarding of honours in the party, which he was determined not to neglect. Much of Middleton's work consisted in creating a network of professional agents that covered half the constituencies by 1900 with an intermediate layer of officials in each region. They provided headquarters with electoral intelligence, and reports about public reactions to legislation, particularly Liberal legislation that might be safely rejected by the Lords. In retrospect, the electoral successes of the Middleton era seemed to prove the advantages of a professional corps of organizers over the larger but more troublesome structure of associations represented by the National Union.

Tradition and Change

In the past much of the writing about Conservative history has approached the subject by considering how liberal or progressive the party was; hence the prominence traditionally accorded to men like Peel and Disraeli who are seen as great reformers who helped to modernize the Tory Party. Yet concentration on such exceptional figures may well produce a distorted idea of Conservative history. The 'reactionary' Lord Salisbury, for example, enjoyed a more successful career than Disraeli, and, as we have already seen, was rather more alive to the needs of a modern electoral system. Salisbury serves to remind us that historically the purpose of most Conservatives involved resisting change and limiting it when it proved to be unavoidable. On the face of it, Disraeli's impressive record of social reform after 1874 appears to contradict this view. But its significance seems to be very limited. Not only did Disraeli himself display little interest in the subject, he had opposed social reforms in the past – 'those Gallic imitations' – through a dislike of central bureaucracy. Most of his reforms emerged from civil service attempts to extend or improve legislation passed by previous Liberal governments.

A more consistent interest of Disraeli's, both in and out of office, was to cut national taxation, relieve the burden of local rates and generally to restrict government. For example, the Artisans Dwellings Act was simply permissive legislation allowing the demolition of slums but not requiring replacements; in practice those few local authorities that did wish to build homes for the working class found themselves prevented from doing so because Conservative governments refused to allow them to raise the necessary loans.

This negative approach to taxation and social policy was arguably more popular than the interventionist one; and it was certainly more typical of late Victorian Conservatism. From the 1870s onwards the party relied little on novel policies and instead resorted increasingly to *traditional* causes. Essentially this involved defending the Church establishment, religious education, private property, the Empire, the monarchy, and the union with Ireland against the depredations of radicalism. The surprise in all this was not that Conservatives adopted such a strategy but that it seemed to be successful even under a larger electorate. Thus, late Victorian Conservatism presents an interesting paradox. On the one hand there is a strong impression from the improved electoral fortunes that the party adapted more successfully than its opponents to the conditions of a mass electorate. On the other hand this seems inconsistent with the leaders' patent distaste for popular organization, and their determination to keep the National Union strictly within bounds; indeed, although constituency associations became the norm after 1885, the organizations were often a mere formality, as small and remote as ever. The need to match the radicals in practical political skills was only partly met by the Conservatives' superior finances and the creation of full-time constituency agents. For they could by no means dispense with the efforts of a large corps of volunteer workers. In this respect the deficiencies of the formal party structure in the National Union and the constituency bodies were more than compensated for by the Primrose League, a key political institution in this period which has been remarkably neglected by the historians of the Conservative Party.

Founded in November 1883, the 'Primrose Tory League', as it was originally known, claimed to promote 'Tory principles – viz. the maintenance of religion, of the estates of the realm, and of the Imperial Ascendancy of Great Britain'; by adopting both the primrose – supposedly Disraeli's favourite flower – and such slogans as 'True Union of the Classes', its leaders sought to emphasize the Disraelian source of their inspiration. The League offered one class of membership at a guinea a year for 'Knights' and 'Dames', and another for associate members whose much lower dues went to their local branches; these branches were actually known as 'Habitations', the honorary president as the 'Grand Master', the ruling body as the 'Grand Council', the executive head as the 'Chancellor', official notices as 'Precepts', and subscriptions as 'Tribute'. All this delightfully anachronistic escapism made the Primrose League as appealing as a Masonic lodge or a collegiate university, and it reminds us that the members created a political role that was as enjoyable as it was useful. By 1886 membership had reached 237,000, by 1891 it exceeded 1 million, and by 1910, 2 million. These figures are exaggerated because the League invariably added new members to the total while making no deductions for losses. However, the pattern of its growth broadly reflected Conservative fortunes. Membership more than doubled in 1886–7 under the stimulus of the Home Rule crisis, slackened in the early 1890s as Salisbury's government ran out of steam, quickened dramatically before and during the Boer War, and stagnated thereafter until 1910. By that year some 2,645 Habitations existed in the British Isles. Far from being a purely rural phenomenon, the League entrenched itself in industrial Britain too, and claimed that ninetenths of the members were working class.

Why was the Primrose League such an asset to the Conservative Party? Fundamentally because it provided a practical application of class and rank as a unifying force in society. Part of the difficulty with a body like the National Union was that Conservatives had felt uncomfortable with an organization designed for working men or the urban middle class. 'I have never been myself at all favourable', Disraeli once said, 'to a system which would induce Conservatives who are working men to form societies confined merely to their class.'[7] Whereas the National Union suffered embarrassment at the lack of participation by working men, the League adopted a frankly hierarchical structure that not only mirrored the gradations of society but dramatized them; by accepting class as a virtue, not as a matter for apology, the League comfortably embraced the Conservative view of social unity.

In the same way the League enjoyed an advantage over the National Union in that though it was a popular body it never appeared a threat to the leadership. Its relationship with the party remained spiritually close but organizationally loose. By confining its politics to fairly general principles like the Empire which would endure beyond the passing excitements of legislation, the League avoided either taking sides on divisive issues or presenting programmes to the parliamentary leaders. This is why Salisbury and Balfour were quite content to accept roles as 'Grand Master' and to present annual addresses. This arrangement gave them a friendly alliance with a large body of like-minded people who, by remaining separate, could not make unreasonable demands upon them.

As an electoral machine the League served the party in several crucial ways. It deluged the constituencies with its own and Central Office propaganda. The Warden of a Habitation was frequently entrusted with responsibility for preparing annually lists of voters and canvassing those on the register; its dense network of local contacts, especially in rural areas, enabled the League to mobilize the Conservative vote efficiently at elections. However, it was the League's regular round of activities *between* rather than during elections that gave Conservatives the edge over their Liberal rivals, whose activity and vote was apt to fluctuate much more according to the ebb and flow of national political issues. By avoiding a formal 'Conservative' title the League also made it easier for non-Conservatives to participate in their events. Indeed they offered a great deal more than mere politics: Habitations readily accepted the warning that meetings should not be 'so distinctly elevating as to be pronounced dull'. They offered cheap dances, their own brass bands, and evening entertainments involving singing, conjurors, ventriloquists, jugglers, waxworks, marionettes and pierrots. Such programmes, available in each locality, formed an irresistible attraction, especially in country areas, where they might be the only form of regular social event. In this way the League often integrated itself into the fabric of a community more effectively than political parties could do. Frivolous League activities provoked much hilarity and contempt from

Liberals and socialists, who were not convinced that politics was meant to be enjoyable. However, they saw that the teas, fêtes and visits to country houses served a real function by providing a coveted opportunity for the lower ranks to mingle briefly with the great. Nor was the mixture purely social, for a fête or evening entertainment usually included its political address. A political message was delivered less directly though doubtless more effectively by techniques that were a novelty in themselves, such as magic lanterns and *tableaux vivants* which displayed a series of images of imperial splendour such as the Queen enthroned as Empress of India, Gordon at Khartoum, Nelson on the *Victory*, Lords Roberts or Kitchener in Afghanistan or South Africa. This blend of patriotic history with recent controversial incidents was more shrewdly aimed than many more cerebral pieces of propaganda.

Another merit of the Primrose League lay in its capacity for involving women in the political process. From 1883 women had been admitted as members, and sometimes formed their own Habitations. Middle- and upper-class ladies threw themselves enthusiastically into arranging League functions, canvassing, contacting the outvoters, conveying electors to the polls in private carriages, raising funds and generally keeping the grass roots of Conservatism vigorous. By the 1890s the sight of the Primrose Dame speeding through villages on her 'safety' bicycle or descending *en masse*, as the 'Primrose Cycling Corps', at by-elections, became a painfully familiar sight to radicals. Here again, it suited the men of the party that women should involve themselves so constructively but without pressing for power or for their enfranchisement. Nonetheless both Salisbury and Balfour followed Disraeli's example in indicating personal sympathy for votes for wealthy women. This early association between women activists and the Conservative Party doubtless laid the foundations for the party's organizational superiority in the twentieth century. More immediately the Primrose League generated the voluntary labour so necessary under the reformed electoral system of the 1880s and challenged the radicals' political skills effectively. By extending the Conservative influence beyond small groups of partisans the League succeeded where politicians invariably failed in keeping the cause healthy between elections, which goes some way to explaining the stability of the Conservative vote between the 1880s and 1914 by comparison with the more volatile Liberal performance.

Salisbury and Liberal Unionism

The third Marquis of Salisbury, who led no less than four governments between 1885 and 1902 from the lonely eminence of Hatfield and the House of Lords, was a most unlikely leader in a democratic age of which he thoroughly disapproved. This period of dominance has long been neglected by historians; even by Conservatives his accomplishments have been ignored in favour of the more superficially attractive figure of Disraeli. This is not altogether surprising: Disraeli does have a contemporary appeal where Salisbury seems inflexibly old-fashioned; Disraeli's name is easily linked with a creed and with a watershed in history, whereas Salisbury seems to have left no permanent tradition; most of all, Salisbury basically despised his party, accepting it merely as the best available vehicle for his objectives; with his austerely intellectual approach he detested any pandering to the sentimental nostrums of Conservatism.

His opportunity to become leader arose after Disraeli's death in 1881 which inaugurated an unhappy experience in dual leadership by Sir Stafford Northcote in the Commons and Salisbury in the Lords. The outcome of this period – Salisbury's premiership in 1885 – was not expected in 1881. For Salisbury's record suggested the dangerously ideological backwoodsman; Northcote was safer, and was for some time the queen's first choice. This failed to materialize because as Leader of the Opposition Northcote, by his conciliatory and lacklustre performance, threw away his main advantage over Salisbury, that he could directly confront Gladstone in the Commons. This was repeatedly emphasized by the lively attacks made by the 'Fourth Party' comprising Churchill, Gorst, Arthur Balfour and Sir Henry Drummond Wolff. It is now clear that one object of Churchill's activity in the Fourth Party, as in the National Union, was to facilitate Salisbury's attainment of the leadership in place of Northcote.[8] For his part Salisbury appreciated that Churchill's popular oratory obscured his traditional Conservatism, and welcomed a compromise that weakened Northcote's supporters in the National Union. The effect of the protracted controversy was to focus attention upon Salisbury as the one who could handle the popular body, and to edge Northcote off stage as an irrelevancy.

However, if the rumpus served to elevate Salisbury, it also drew attention to his political rigidity. Unlike most politicians he thought seriously about the long-term development of society. A quintessential conservative, Salisbury believed that the defects in man's condition were to a large extent congenital and consequently not susceptible to new ways of ordering society. Since what could be achieved through politics was quite limited it was desirable to restrain the state from trenching too far upon the private sphere, as most reforms threatened to do. In government one should concentrate on administration rather than mere 'politics'. Like several other late Victorians with experience of India (Secretary of State 1874–8), Salisbury absorbed a firm belief in the superiority of strong, just, arbitrary government by a highly qualified elite, as opposed to systems in which authority hinged upon representation and efficiency was hampered by political parties and assemblies.

Herein lay the menace of contemporary British society. In 1867 Salisbury had resigned from the Conservative government in disgust at franchise reform, and spent much of his nervous energy composing withering attacks upon Disraeli for his unprincipled opportunism and betrayal of Conservative principles – much as Disraeli had once berated Peel. The slide towards a democratic franchise seemed to him destructive of a stable and unified society. For once the Commons had, in the name of the people, aggrandized all power at the expense of the other elements in the mixed constitution (the monarchy and aristocracy), government would fall into the hands of men without property and lose its impartiality. Britain could easily slide into an American type of corruption in which politicians gained office by offering specific rewards to distinct groups or classes, thereby helping their society towards eventual disintegration.

Although these sentiments were never far from the surface they reflect the younger Salisbury, a man who had not yet acquired the mellow confidence that political success and a happy marriage gradually gave him. In practical terms, much as he preferred the 1832 system, he accepted that he could never hope to reverse the drift away from it.

Salisbury's apprehensions had materially abated by the time he became Prime Minister. He grew to appreciate Disraeli's desire to make Conservatism the British national party rather than the organ of a sectional interest. He realized, too, that the defence of 'liberty' could be accomplished within the framework of democracy; even the United States took on a more attractive appearance, for its federalism, its Senate and its judiciary imposed admirable curbs on the power of central government. The problem was how to extend the role of local against central government in Britain without simply handing over power to the radicals, as had happened with the school boards. The best substitute for an American arrangement of checks and balances lay in reliance on the House of Lords and the Conservative Party.

Therefore Salisbury set himself to master some of the arts of party leadership, gratefully relying on his chief whip and principal agent. Yet he resented the obligation to immerse himself in the trivia of political life: 'Why should I spend my evenings being trampled upon by the Conservative Party?' He retreated to Hatfield as often as possible and kept social contact to a minimum. Fortunately his chief whip, Aretas Akers-Douglas, a congenial country gentleman from Kent, helped to save him from the consequences of his own aloofness, and managed efficiently an increasingly loyal parliamentary party. Though Salisbury could never attain popularity, his followers were in a sense grateful, for, as one historian has put it: 'A nobleman from a Tory family with illustrious forebears, Salisbury came from the class among which Conservatives wanted but rarely managed to find a leader.'[9]

NAILED TO THE MAST!
Punch, 16 March 1889

His practical strategy was determined by the knowledge that his party had won a general election only in 1874 followed by what appeared to be traditional Liberal victories in 1880 and 1885. This, he believed, was simply because the party alignment still reflected the divisions of 1832 and 1846 – now irrelevant. Since the Liberal reforms had been absorbed into the system the Whigs ought logically to join the Conservatives in defending the *status quo.* Eventually Salisbury's major achievement was to facilitate the post-1886 realignment without forfeiting his own control. For him the detachment of the Whigs would ensure either a Conservative government, or, still better, a radical government with such a small majority that it lacked the authority to force through drastic changes; in such circumstances the House of Lords would step in as the guardian of the national will against sectional interests entrenched in the House of Commons.

The critical point in the unfolding of this strategy came after December 1885 when Gladstone's commitment to Irish Home Rule became public knowledge, and began to alienate a substantial section of Liberals under Lord Hartington's leadership. However, Salisbury had to move skilfully, for Hartington had ambitions of his own. He seemed acceptable to a sufficiently wide range of opinion in both Liberal and Conservative camps to form his own government, which would have been tantamount to a restoration of the Palmerstonian alliance in the centre. Since this made him a threat to both Salisbury and Gladstone they endeavoured to prevent any coalescence in the centre. Gladstone forced the issue by preparing a Home Rule Bill, speedily dissolving Parliament after its defeat and elevating Home Rule as the test of Liberalism. For his part Salisbury contributed a strident anti-Home Rule speech in May 1886 in which he derided the Irish as comparable with the Hottentots in their unfitness for self-rule, and advised them to emigrate to Manitoba to alleviate their hardship. This inflammatory speech was calculated to polarize the debate between himself and Gladstone so as to drive Hartington to one side or the other, thereby losing the centre ground.

What was to be the relationship between the 93 Liberal Unionists, of whom 78 survived the general election, and the Conservatives? It was no part of Salisbury's intention in 1886 to absorb them immediately. Co-operation in the constituencies had served its purpose by reducing the Gladstonians to 191 while leaving 316 Conservatives. In view of the dangerous concatenation of Joseph Chamberlain and Lord Randolph Churchill he refused to bring the Liberal Unionists into his government; their joint energies harnessed to programmes of reform would certainly disrupt the Cabinet or take it out of his own hands. When in 1886 Churchill rashly offered his resignation as Chancellor of the Exchequer in protest at the Cabinet's refusal to accept economies, the Prime Minister made a tentative offer to Hartington because he felt confident it would be declined; thereupon the vacancy was filled by recruiting another ex-Liberal, Goschen, leaving the party relationship unchanged. Similarly the Liberal Unionists declined to throw in their lot fully with the Conservatives. Susceptible to their Liberal critics in the country who had rebelled solely over Home Rule in many cases, they seized every chance to distance themselves from the new government by refusing to vote for it except over Ireland or when it stood in danger of actual defeat, which was rare.

However, the Gladstonian revival prior to 1892 convinced Salisbury that it was unwise to take Liberal Unionism for granted. He therefore determined to incorporate them into his next government by offering four cabinet posts. His belief that Chamberlain would accept the limitations of a Conservative cabinet was vindicated when the ex-radical asked only for a committee of investigation on old-age pensions, and, for himself, the Colonial Office. In the long run this led to new problems, but for the time being it served to draw the two together and harness Chamberlain to a cause that was dear to the Conservative Party. Technically Salisbury, with 341 members in 1895, could have dispensed with a coalition. Yet he found some advantage in diluting his embarrassingly large majority with Liberal Unionist elements. For one thing he had discovered that the Nonconformists brought in by Chamberlain were not necessarily subversive radicals; and even radicals contributed to the checks and balances within the coalition. In practice major measures like the 1896 Education Bill succumbed entirely to Conservative attack; and the 1897 Bill for Workmen's Compensation only reached the statute book emasculated by the peers. While this process created friction on particular matters, Salisbury could at least rejoice that it served the higher purpose of setting limits on central government.

The State and Social Reform

Though Salisbury's approach to domestic affairs sprang from a cynical distrust of government, it was softened by fear of adopting an entirely negative policy and by a modicum of compassion towards the poor. Fortunately elections could be won without stooping to 'class legislation' at the expense of the propertied section, for, as Churchill's meteoric rise had demonstrated, the working classes would respond to quite traditional Tory appeals in defence of Church, Empire and monarchy. However, this strategy succeeded best only when the opposition co-operated by concentrating on such questions as Home Rule. When in office after 1886, Conservatives felt obliged to adopt a constructive attitude on domestic matters, if only to disprove the Gladstonian argument that all progress was blocked by the refusal to concede Ireland's demands. This accounts for the quantity of minor legislation, designed to be economical and undisturbing, enacted under Salisbury's premierships.

This policy should not be interpreted, as it sometimes is, as a resurrection of a Conservative tradition for strong paternalist government, unhampered by liberal individualism, which developed into a pragmatic collectivist ideology.[10] The origins of such a view lie in the historic Tory preference for strong government which had been characteristic of the revolutionary and Napoleonic War period and which did reassert itself in exceptional circumstances such as the First World War; but this is not to be confused with or causally linked with collectivism. Conservatives of the 1880s inherited the prevailing Victorian preference for curtailing government in favour of local autonomy and economy, where this was seen to be effective. The basis of Salisbury's *laissez-faire* convictions was more political than economic; they sprang from his veneration of private property and hostility to interfering government rather than from the business liberalism that inspired many of his colleagues. Though he did not shrink from a little judicious state assistance for the poor, he believed that little could be accomplished by this means without causing financial and social damage; on the whole, therefore, he prescribed self-help as a general rule, but without the optimism that an early Victorian Liberal might have displayed. Conservatives also accepted the inevitability of free trade, though their candidates in agricultural constituencies still pandered to protectionism;[11] but as free-traders they lacked the intense moral conviction with which many Liberals invested the issue. Salisbury, like many Conservatives, seems to have been undogmatic about free trade, accepting in principle by the 1890s the idea of retaliation against other countries.

There was, of course, a tradition of Tory radicalism from the early Victorian period when some politicians had attempted to defend the workers against the effects of a rampant capitalism; typically this took the form of support for limiting the working day to ten hours and opposing the new poor law. However, by the 1880s these traditions had begun to wither from neglect. Conservatives were increasingly to be found among those who defended the principles of 1834, while the critics of the poor law were radicals and Fabians who looked to the county councils and central government to shoulder its responsibilities. Similarly the demand for an eight-hour day often met a stony response in the 1880s from the middle-class employers who were now joining the Conservatives. In fact by 1892 the official party view condemned the eight-hour day for raising prices and lowering efficiency, as well as for interfering with the worker's freedom to determine his own conditions of work;[12] in short, the party was preaching the arguments of classical economics more readily than its opponents. Nor was Disraeli's recognition of the right to picket in 1871 followed up by his successors, who were more impressed by unions and militancy; indeed the Salisbury–Balfour era culminated with the Conservatives putting themselves at odds with labour by refusing to reverse the Taff Vale judgement of 1901 (see p. 116). The working man now seemed too assertive and powerful to fit the Disraelian conception.

By the 1880s the remnants of Disraelian Tories, Lord John Manners and Lord Cranbrook, were old and uninfluential. The real reformers were C. T. Ritchie (at the Local Government Board, the Board of Trade and the Home Office successively); A. J. Balfour, at least on education and Ireland; and Chamberlain from outside. Yet Chamberlain's influence proved less formative than that of men like George Goschen who, in becoming Chancellor in 1886, intended to help 'purge them of the cant of Tory Democracy', and irritated even Salisbury in his defence of the rights of property and hostility to social reform. Goschen's career demonstrates the crystallization of the naturally conservative forces around Salisbury and the abandonment of Disraelianism; he epitomized the middle-class recruits who had not quit Liberalism in order to pay higher taxes or suffer more legal regulation under the Conservatives.

Yet there was much more consistency in the negative approach than is often recognized. Ever since 1846 Disraeli had been keen to compensate landowners for the loss of protectionism; the favoured method involved relieving their tax burdens by grants-in-aid from the Exchequer to local authorities. Thus after 1874 Disraeli doubled grants to local authorities, transferred the costs of prisons to the Exchequer, and raised the limit for income-tax liability from £100 to £150. This proved to be the real legacy of Disraeli. Between 1887 and 1892 the Conservatives doubled central support for local authorities from £4 million to £8 million and lowered the income tax rate to $6\frac{1}{2}d$ in the pound. Later in the 1890s they found an extra £1.5 million to relieve rates on agricultural land, several times reduced rates for voluntary schools, and even attempted to relieve Anglican parsons of rates. Two aspects of this policy are significant. First, it enabled the Conservatives to claim the Gladstonian ground as the party of retrenchment, which Liberal governments could no longer do with credibility. Harcourt's achievements in 1892–5, for example, were to raise income tax to $7\frac{3}{4}d$ and add some £9 million to taxation. Second, by the 1890s Tory finance had become a blatant exercise in providing doles for the party's wealthy landed supporters, which urban Conservatives resented as much as Liberals. Any Disraelian claim to represent all classes began to look implausible.

Land reform epitomized the Conservatives' dilemma, for radical propaganda among agricultural labourers threatened electoral disaster, while legislation for Scottish Crofters and Ireland provided precedents. Hence the passage of an Allotments Act in 1887 (extended in 1890), which empowered local authorities to purchase land for letting at economic rents, and the 1892 Smallholdings Act. Salisbury resisted these measures on the grounds that compulsory purchase was tantamount to confiscation, and that infringement of the rights of property owners would be economically counter-productive; yet his colleagues forced him to give way.[13] Some anticipated that the legislation would be relatively ineffective in view of the reluctance of landowner-dominated county councils, especially in the south, to make use of their powers.

Indeed the establishment of county councils in 1889 and the peers' amendments of the Liberals' Parish Councils Bill in 1893 proved an effective check on social reform. Though loath to disturb the existing management of county affairs through the Courts of Quarter Sessions by JPs appointed by the Lords Lieutenant, Salisbury knew that reform was a radical priority from which the 1880–5 government had narrowly been deflected;[14] further radical attempts had to be forestalled. Many Conservatives resisted direct elections for county councils because they would be expensive and, by introducing a political element, would exclude the best men – an argument typical of Salisbury. However, Ritchie, backed by Chamberlain, who saw this as a test of his influence with the Conservatives, managed to scotch the idea of indirect election. Yet the county franchise was restricted to occupiers, and a quarter of the membership of the councils was reserved for co-opted aldermen; in addition special restrictions on expenditure were imposed, and the poor law administration was withheld from them for fear that the radicals might gain control.

Fear of popular involvement also inspired educational reform in this period. Salisbury himself largely lacked sympathy with the idea of education for the masses, which would deprive employers of child labour; but he failed to stop the extension of free elementary education in 1891 by Balfour and his ally Chamberlain for whom it was a long-standing objective. The problem lay in the school boards, always seen as subversive bodies, which had taken to widening the range of subjects taught and had established secondary schools in many places. Apart from the cost to ratepayers it was thought to be destructive of social harmony to educate people beyond their station in life. The 1896 Education Bill, which proposed to remove control to county councils, proved abortive due to opposition within the Cabinet. Thereafter other ways were found of undermining the school boards. In 1899 the Board of Education instigated a case against the London School Board for spending money from the rates on science and art schools; the resulting 'Cockerton Judgement' made higher-grade education illegal. Balfour's famous Act of 1902 finally ended the school boards by placing responsibility for education with committees of the county councils.

In contrast, housing did engage Salisbury's interest to the extent that he personally initiated the 1885 Royal Commission on Housing. Nonetheless his government refused to allow any infringement of the urban landlords' and landowners' rights over their property; they resisted any state involvement in housebuilding, though permitting the London County Council to act; and they adhered to permissive legislation in the bleak hope that market pressures would disperse the population away from overcrowded urban centres.[15]

In Ireland dire necessity pushed the Conservatives well beyond what was thought safe for England. After 1881, when a shocked Salisbury found that the landowners did not want him to save them from Gladstone's Land Act, the rights of property were effectively thrown overboard. A combination of rents lowered by tribunals, agricultural depression and rural violence gradually destroyed the landowners' resolve to the extent that by 1900 they were ready to sell their land, given attractive terms. During the 1880s the Conservatives had begun to appreciate the idea of creating peasant proprietors (at least in Ireland) in the conviction that to turn tenants into small owners was tantamount to converting agitators into supporters of stable government, and thereby undermining 'Home Rule'. Beginning with the £5 million allocated for land purchase in Ashbourne's Act of 1885 and continuing with similar measures in 1888 and 1891, this policy culminated in Wyndham's Land Act of 1903 under which a quarter of a million Irishmen bought farms before 1914. As Salisbury observed dolefully in 1887, 'It is the price we have to pay for the Union, and it is a heavy one.'[16] It is significant that those Conservatives most closely associated with this policy, Horace Plunkett, Lord Dunraven and George Wyndham, suffered a permanent check to their careers.

Ireland also afforded more scope for experiments in social interventionism than England. As Chief Secretary, Balfour applied state funds to pay wages for relief work in the most distressed counties and for the construction of light railways. His Congested Districts Bill of 1890 created boards in the west of Ireland (where the people were too poor to take advantage of land-purchase schemes) with resources to acquire land, amalgamate uneconomic holdings, distribute seed potatoes and assist tenants to migrate from congested districts or to emigrate. The nearest approach to a similar policy in England came in 1905 in the form of Walter Long's Unemployed Workmen's Act, which involved using rate finance for relief work schemes in London. However, Balfour, now Prime Minister, retreated from the radical implications of the measure by limiting it to a three-year experiment only, and by appointing a Royal Commission on the Poor Law to avoid the necessity for further action.

This reluctance to deal boldly or constructively with social problems brought the Salisbury–Balfour era to an unimaginative end. Throughout these years Conservatives had been caught in the dilemma of financing social policies under a free enterprise system. Although this is sometimes seen as a Liberal problem it afflicted the Conservatives more, partly because they found themselves more frequently in office, but also because, in the absence of the political reform espoused by the Liberals, they felt an obligation to pass safe social legislation. Paradoxically Chamberlain's influence was probably greater during 1886–92, when he remained outside the government and felt anxious about justifying his co-operation by means of the measures for county councils, education and allotments. Later he sought influence through a vigorous imperial policy and a formidably long list of social reforms which he presented to Salisbury in a memorandum of 1894: compensation for industrial injuries, amendment of the Artisans

Dwellings Act, loans to working men for house purchase, an eight-hour day for miners, reduction of alien immigration, old-age pensions, labour exchanges, arbitration courts to settle industrial disputes, earlier closing for shops, and cheaper train travel for workmen. In fact his colleagues were amenable to action on several of these items, notably immigration and workmen's compensation. But by now Chamberlain had reconciled himself to playing a limited role. Although pensions did receive official sanction in the *Campaign Guide* for 1895, there was agreement only on a contributory scheme that would have omitted those most in need. The Cabinet drifted into the South African War and lost its opportunity to outflank the Liberals. Its whole approach to social questions was crippled by its addiction to retrenchment and inhibited by apprehension about the pressure of organized labour and the social investigations of the 1890s. Innovation was to be adopted only where it would forestall a more radical change. In this way Conservative thinking stagnated until the explosive reappraisal triggered by Chamberlain's disastrous tariff campaign of 1903.

CHAPTER FOUR

The Social Roots of Political Change in Late Victorian Britain

> When you stand in the voting booth with your card and your pencil in your hand, think of this: I am going to vote either for robbing God or against it.
>
> Warwickshire clergyman, quoted in *The Nonconformist*, 3 December 1885

Up to 1841 British general elections remained essentially parochial in character: that is, the shifts of opinion from one constituency to another fluctuated over a wide range that reflected the multitude of local factors at work. Thereafter the range narrowed as more general influences common to the whole country made an impression. However, historians have characterized this as a regional rather than a national pattern, which reached its height around 1868–85.[1] Using Dr Pelling's calculations[2] of the Conservative and Unionist share of the poll we may distinguish the broad party loyalties of the regions as they appeared in 1885 (see table 4.1). To

TABLE 4.1 *Conservative and Unionist % vote 1885*

Strongly Conservative		*Intermediate*		*Anti-Conservative*	
S-E England	54.5	East Anglia	49.2	Northern	
Wessex	51.5	Bristol region	48.7	England	41.7
Lancastria	51.4	Yorks region	45.8	Peak–Don	41.5
London County		West Midlands	45.5	Wales	39.6
Council area	51.0	Central England	44.7	Scotland	36.3
		Devon and			
		Cornwall	44.3		
		East Midlands	43.7		

a considerable extent these regional loyalties already reflected the uneven distribution of social classes in each area. But classes had by no means come to behave in a uniform fashion across the country. Working men in London and Lancashire were much less inclined to Liberalism than working men in north-east England or Wales; the middle classes of Scotland and Yorkshire were far more likely to vote Liberal than those of south-east England.

Trends and Issues

In terms of party fortunes the period from 1865 to 1900 falls into two phases with the watershed in 1885–6: the first saw a continuation of the mid-Victorian Liberal dominance interrupted only in 1874; and the second, from 1886, saw it replaced by Conservative predominance, with the partial exception of 1892 (see table 4.2).

Broadly two kinds of changes are at work here; there are certain underlying movements in the allegiance of social, religious and cultural groups, in the entry of new groups of voters, and modifications of the constituency boundaries; and there are also short-term factors to be considered – the impact of particular issues and controversies, the timing and tactics of each election, and switches by the leading personalities. We have already noted one important long-term trend, namely the shift of middle-class and propertied interests towards Conservatism from the 1860s, culminating in the schism of 1886. However, long-term group loyalties never entirely account for fluctuating election results, for every group has its soft, wavering fringes that respond to the ebb and flow of events and personalities. It would be too much to claim that the great Victorian issues, however passionately debated by the politicians, actually influenced more than a

TABLE 4.2   *General election results 1865–1900 (seats won)*

	1865	1868	1874	1880	1885	1886	1892	1895	1900
Conservative	294	274	356	238	250	316	268	341	334
Liberal Unionist						78	47	70	68
Liberal	364	384	245	353	334	191	273	177	184
Irish Nationalist			51	61	86	85	81	82	82
Labour						(ILP) 1		(LRC) 2	

fraction of the electorate directly; party loyalty tends to be an impervious thing. But a small turnover of votes always produced drastic effects; as Lord Salisbury observed, a mere 2,000 strategically placed votes made 1880 a Liberal victory instead of a Conservative one. In addition, although economic questions had not yet become the staple of election debates, it does seem that party fortunes were vulnerable to sudden economic fluctuations; the downfall of Disraeli in 1880 and of Rosebery in 1895 was sealed by a slump immediately preceding each election, while Salisbury was saved from heavy losses in 1900, in part by the sudden buoyancy in the economy.

In 1868 Gladstone rallied radical sentiment with his bold programme of Irish reform; but the election, despite the extended electorate, essentially confirmed the traditional Liberal majority, marred only by a distinct ebbing of middle-class Palmerstonians. Coming after a plethora of innovations, 1874 exacerbated this trend. Essentially a reaction by those whose interests seemed to have been threatened by Gladstone's reforms, this election saw both a suspension of Whig support for Liberalism in the counties, and a subsidence of radical-Nonconformist enthusiasm owing to dissatisfaction with recent legislation. In the long run the regular school board elections necessitated by Forster's Act probably consolidated the Nonconformist habit of voting Liberal, while also strengthening Conservatism among Anglicans and Catholics; for Conservative defence of independent religious schools was one means of neutralizing the Liberal appeal to the Irish. After 1875 the prevailing sense of economic depression, though exaggerated, shook Conservative loyalties, especially among farmers suffering bad harvests and high grain imports; and social distress doubtless told more forcefully with the lower classes than the scarcely perceptible benefits of Disraelian social legislation. Although ostensibly the election turned upon the Midlothian onslaught on 'Beaconsfieldism', the outcome reflected this issue only indirectly in that the anti-imperial campaign restored radical morale and thereby helped the Liberals to poll their full strength again.

The election of 1885 appears more complicated. That it was less of a victory for the Liberals than 1880 was due primarily to Parnell's decision to withhold the Irish vote in England, to the unpopularity of Gladstone's imperial policies culminating in the death of General Gordon at Khartoum in 1885, and to renewed alarm among the urban middle classes at the radical tone of Chamberlain's 'Unauthorised Programme'. Yet Conservative urban consolidation was balanced by Liberal gains in the counties now under a new franchise. The question of Church disestablishment attained considerable prominence in England in 1885. For many years Nonconformists had been strenuously engaged, through the Liberal Party, in removing the obstacles to their participation in national life, so much so that religious assignation had become central to party loyalty; wherever the 'free churches' were thickly distributed (as in Wales, Scotland, the North-East, Yorkshire, Cornwall and the midland and East Anglian towns), Liberalism was very strong. But the party still commanded much Anglican support too; the MPs were still mostly Anglicans and led by a prominent Anglican. However, this proved to be a waning asset in this period. Gladstone steadily eliminated Nonconformist grievances such as church rates in 1868; he disestablished the Church in Ireland in 1870, passed the University Tests Act in 1871, and the Church Burials Act in 1880. The next obvious step was disestablishment for Wales and Scotland, and the Liberation Society hoped to exploit the new county franchise to generate sufficient pressure to oblige Gladstone to take action. Since Chamberlain gave prominence to disestablishment, the Conservatives raised the cry of 'the Church in danger' in 1885, hoping to win over middle-class Anglicans from Liberalism. Even Nonconformists, once their keenest grievances were rectified, showed some tendency to side with Conservatism as the embodiment of the status quo to which they now belonged. In fact the political behaviour of the free churches did increasingly reflect the social class of their members; furthest down the social scale – and highest in political radicalism – were the Primitive Methodists, followed by Baptists, Congregationalists and, finally, Wesleyan Methodists. The latter were longer in existence, more comfortably middle class, nearer to Anglicanism, less antagonistic to the established Church, and more receptive to a national political outlook. Hence Wesleyans displayed some reluctance to join radical campaigns by comparison with other Nonconformists; and by the 1890s many of them preferred Rosebery's brand of Liberal Imperialism to Gladstonianism, and provided recruits for the Conservatives.

The Home Rule crisis of 1886 proved to be a watershed because it crystallized the attitudes of many Liberal followers already wavering for other reasons, and enabled them to take a coherent position as Liberal Unionists. Yet the impact of Ireland varied greatly from region to region. Western Scotland was considerably stirred because of the proximity of both Ireland and the Irish, while eastern Scotland remained relatively unmoved; north-east England and Yorkshire stayed largely Gladstonian while Lancashire moved even further to Unionism; in East Anglia the question seemed remote, yet in the South-West Home Rule seemed strategically relevant, and the St Ives division of Cornwall manifested the most marked shift to Unionism. Today it seems remarkable that for years afterwards the Irish Question provided a staple item in constituency campaigns; both parties clearly thought it worth keeping the issue alive. When taking the high ground of principle the Gladstonians urged the virtues of self-determination, and the Conservatives the threat to imperial unity and security. However, on the low ground of self-interest it was articulated differently. Conservatives repeatedly urged English working men to remember that a Dublin Parliament would destroy business confidence and thereby cause an even greater influx of destitute immigrants into English cities. The Gladstonians countered by warning that the bloody suppression of Irishmen's rights implied a threat to those of English workers too, and by arguing that an independent Ireland would in fact retain the population presently compelled to seek its livelihood abroad. While the Liberals plainly forfeited working-class support, notably in the North-West, they enjoyed the compensation of a solid and organized Irish vote which gave them the edge in many urban constituencies right up to 1914.

By 1892 the Gladstonians had managed to effect a limited recovery from the débâcle of 1886, but one based more upon county seats, a sign that they had revitalized the issues of 1885 but could not restore their full 1880 strength. Three years later, after expectations had been dashed by the inability of both Gladstone and Rosebery to deliver the innovations promised, the party went down to a heavy defeat. Essentially a negative reaction, the election saw Liberal abstentions and Conservative victory by default. The year 1895 also brought into general prominence the local veto on alcoholic sales (or 'Local Option'), partly because it was taken up by Sir William Harcourt as he cast around rather desperately for fresh issues. Although temperance reform had acquired some political salience as long ago as 1871 as a result of Bruce's Licensing Bill, there had not been as sudden or complete an alienation of the drinking classes to the Conservatives as contemporaries often alleged. For years Gladstone fended off demands for the Local Veto in the belief that free trade and competition would eventually reduce the harmful effects of alcoholic consumption; also a number of brewers and publicans remained in the Liberal camp despite its connection with temperance; and in any case temperance became an election issue only where a candidate adopted a belligerent attitude on the subject. Although it was undoubtedly advantageous to the Conservatives in working-class seats to be able to defend a man's right to his beer, the party's association with the drink interest could not be too vociferously asserted. For one thing the improving working man was often a keen abstainer; for another, the party actually incorporated much middle-class temperance sentiment in the shape of organizations like the Church of England Temperance Society. Moreover, 1886 had brought many Liberal Unionists to their side who would merely be driven back to the Gladstonians if they were antagonized over licensing or education. Despite these qualifications, however, it is true that many a Liberal candidate risked alienating his staunchest backers if he remained lukewarm about temperance.

Between 1895 and 1899 the Liberals again appeared to claw back much of their support; but the by-election trend in their favour was suddenly interrupted shortly after the outbreak of the Boer War. There can be little doubt that the preservation of the 1895 Conservative majority was due to the shrewd timing of the 1900 general election fought in an atmosphere of embattled patriotism and an economy stimulated by the demand for war production. The government lost only ten English and four Welsh seats while gaining five in Scotland. In fact, in terms of votes there was a swing in their favour everywhere except in Wales, where foreign adventures seemed less relevant, and traditional issues, which favoured the Liberals, reasserted themselves. To a lesser extent the same was true of the remoter parts of England; Conservatives benefited most in the big towns, especially London, which was always quick to grow excited over international crises.

Rural Radicalism

The introduction of the secret ballot in 1872 produced little immediate impact upon English county politics; 1885, when the electorate was trebled, proved to be the turning point in that it led to an attempt to politicize areas hitherto somewhat insular and remote from national politics. Whether the traditional, conservative and Conservative pattern of rural politics could resist the new depended upon certain underlying social characteristics, notably the type of settlement pattern and the prevailing religious affiliation. For radical politics flourished only where it could establish roots in an alternative community to that epitomized by the joint authority of the squirearchy and the Church. The links between politics and religious figures – Anglican, Nonconformist and Catholic – were often active and blatant; one Lincolnshire vicar piously informed Lord Salisbury in 1885:

> I am canvassing the labourers here in Mr Stanhope's interest, and find that a Liberal canvasser has been endeavouring to gain votes with the false assertion that the Conservatives are the enemy of the agricultural labourers, and wish to give the country a dear loaf. . . . As it is part of my duty to protect my parishioners from false doctrines of all kinds and from the father of lies and his progeny, I shall be glad to receive your reply on Saturday so that I may be able to state the truth publicly on Sunday.[3]

Political management by parson and squire attained maximum effectiveness in the 'closed' villages typical of the southern and midland counties and great estates in which all who lived depended upon the landowner for their cottage and employment. However, over the years the surplus population drifted to the 'open' villages which, in consequence, often grew into small towns. Here housing and sanitation were sometimes inferior and more expensive, while employment was irregular. Yet the residents, freer from the influence of their social superiors, tended to deviate in social and religious behaviour, often becoming islands of radicalism.[4] Nonconformists had frequently worsted the Church of England in the struggle for the allegiance of such communities; and the prevalence of their chapels in the small towns and villages of Wales, East Anglia and the South-West underpinned radicalism there. Nonconformity thrived also in areas of more scattered settlement based upon small farms and holdings remote from villages; this was typical of much of the heath and fenlands in eastern counties such as Norfolk, Cambridgeshire and Lincolnshire, of Cornwall and parts of Devon, and in the vast upland chain of Pennine country stretching from Derbyshire north to Yorkshire, Durham and Northumberland.

The significance of settlement and religion is very evident in a highly agricultural and traditionally Conservative county such as Norfolk, where less than half the agricultural population resided in closed villages and where the chapels were vigorous. Enfranchised in 1884, the labourers promptly delivered four of Norfolk's six county seats to the Liberals in 1885. Realization that the county electorate was not so amenable as previously led the Conservative chief agent to advise Salisbury in both 1892 and 1895 that the election should ideally coincide with harvest time, when the labourers would be distracted and less politically involved.[5]

From the 1870s rural radicalism was being integrated with national politics at several levels. It enjoyed national leadership from Gladstone, through whom Liberalism spoke for the small man again the Establishment, and from Chamberlain's three-acres-and-a-cow approach. Radical newspapers like the *Daily News* also took a keen interest, for example by assisting the new agricultural trade unions in the 1870s by writing up the story of their strikes and encouraging urban radicals to provide funds urgently needed to sustain their action. Urban workers such as dockers often thought it worthwhile subsidizing land reform propaganda on the grounds that this would eventually retain the population on the land and thus mitigate the overcrowding and wage-cutting caused by migration to the towns. Similarly, during the 1880s, all kinds of essentially external organizations propagandized the counties, often through mobile vans bearing lecturers, leaflets and lantern shows; the Land Restoration League's Red Van, the Land Nationalisation Society Van, the Sunrise Radical Van, the Beaconsfield Van, the Church Association Van, and the Home Rule Van were some of the entertainments from both parties at this time.

However, neither pressure groups nor national leaders could make lasting inroads against the underlying Conservatism without a network of subcontractors able to link the party cause with the lives of the people. Without missionaries from small towns or chapels it was often difficult to find speakers and chairmen for village meetings, and a small shopkeeper or merchant, Nonconformist minister or even a travelling lecturer would fill this role. When parish councils were established in 1894, many labourers did come forward as candidates, though it was felt safer for an independent entrepreneur to take the risk of offending his superiors. One valuable source of stump orators was the agricultural labourers' trade unions which sprang up especially in Warwickshire, Oxfordshire, Norfolk and Suffolk during the 1870s. Regular union activity proved very difficult to sustain, for even in the strongest counties only a third of the men became members; farmers could therefore draw upon plentiful supplies of labour unless strikes were well co-ordinated and coincided with harvest time. Consequently, after initial successes the membership of the National Agricultural Labourers Union fell from a peak of 86,000 in 1874 to 10,000 by 1886. However, the experience increased the assertiveness of the labourers, and failure drove their leaders towards political solutions of which the first fruit was the county franchise of 1884. Like the Union's founder, Joseph Arch MP, the labourers' leaders greatly strengthened radical Liberalism in this period.

While great national issues like Home Rule remained somewhat remote, the rural radicals worked the villages with a mixture of demands for political rights (county franchise, county and parish councils, disestablishment, the burials question) and material improvements; the latter included eliminating duties on basic food items (the 'Free Breakfast Table'), provision of allotments and smallholdings, poor law reform, and the local veto on licensed premises. The vicar frequently appeared as an obstacle due to his prominent role in vestry meetings which controlled charitable endowments and lands that were regarded as a potential source of new allotments.[6]

Despite the radical upsurge of 1885 the Conservatives managed to retain the bulk of their territory, especially in the Home Counties and Wessex, though it could no longer be taken for granted. Whereas their strength had its roots in agriculture, radicalism had to be sustained by penetration from outside; and the continual migration, or even emigration, of the most active and discontented village radicals steadily enfeebled their cause. It was assumed that the reservoir of rural radicalism could be tapped only when the labourer was made more independent of his employer by possessing sufficient land to feed his family; yet this required more drastic local government reform than was provided either by county councils – still often under landowners' control – or parish councils, which were starved of resources. Conservative strength lay among landowners and farmers; Gladstone made some efforts to win over the latter by repealing the malt tax, by compensation to tenants for improvements, and by the 1880 Ground Game Act. However, this was overtaken by the more radical proposals of the mid-1880s, pitched primarily at labourers. Finally, as we have seen, the Conservatives produced a constructive response to the challenge in the shape of the Primrose League which gave a new lease of life to landed politics.

Working-class Politics and Socialists

As the world's most advanced industrial society, Britain appeared to contemporaries to be certain to generate a mass working-class movement. In
1852 Marx had optimistically forecast that the introduction of universal
suffrage in England would be 'a far more socialistic measure than anything
which has been honoured with that name on the Contiment. Its inevitable
result, here, is the supremacy of the working class.'[7] Of course neither
1867 nor 1884 ushered in universal suffrage, but the reforms did make
working-class voters numerically dominant in at least 89 constituencies with
95 MPs;[8] had they been at all cohesive they could rapidly have emerged as
a substantial and discrete force, like the Irish. Yet such expectations were
regularly dashed. Not only was there no significant movement in Britain,
even the emergence of an effective and independent political party for the
working class proved to be a protracted affair. Why was this so?

One line of explanation grows from a recognition that in the past historians have exaggerated the impact of the industrial revolution on British
society. Even in the late nineteenth century industry was organized on a
surprisingly small scale, with the average workshop comprising only 29 men.
Also, many workers found themselves in service occupations and highly
dependent on the patronage of employers. By the 1890s trade union
membership stood at only 1.5 million, though the figure rose towards
2 million, in a labour force of over 13 million. This was not such a large
basis for an organized proletarian movement. Further, there is evidence that
many British workers, though dissatisfied with their lot, were not basically
alienated and entertained quite positive attitudes towards the political and
social system. Some at least experienced the benefits of economic expansion in terms of free trade and rising real wages. Although the political
system was weighted in favour of property and the legal system often
biased against the working man, neither were impervious to change. Since
1858, when property qualifications for MPs had been abolished, it had
been possible for a working man to stand for Parliament, though not until
1894 was the same true of poor law boards. In 1867 and 1884 several
million working men won a parliamentary vote and from 1874 a handful
sat as MPs. Those who were ratepayers also played a direct part in the
fast-growing number of elective local authorities. Certain practical obstacles still hindered their participation. For example, polling stations were
sparse and polling hours rather inconvenient (8 a.m. to 8 p.m. after 1884),
so that most men were at work when the booths opened in the morning
and had to hurry in to vote in the last half-hour at night. Most municipal
authorities held meetings during working hours, which made membership
a serious burden. Even after the reforms of 1883, parliamentary elections

were still expensive to fight, and MPs received no salary until 1911. This made it all but impossible for the working man unless he was subsidized by his union or could support himself by journalism and lecturing, as Keir Hardie and Philip Snowden did.

However, the system at least remained open to pressure and reform on the part of those working men who were literate, politically aware and not worn down by poverty. Though the trade unionist was by no means typical of Victorian working men, he was sufficiently well entrenched in the traditional skilled crafts, in expanding industries like iron and steel and shipbuilding, and in textiles and coal, to constitute a significant pressure group. However, this section has sometimes been regarded as a 'labour aristocracy' by which it is implied that the men were complacent and passive, and deficient in a sense of class-consciousness. Such men often placed a high priority on self-help strategies, such as providing friendly-society benefits for their members, of which the middle classes approved. They also sought recognition by the employers with a view to establishing regular collective bargaining and arbitration rather than having frequent recourse to strikes. Some working men shared social, religious and political attitudes with employers; and the skilled artisan could still hope to emulate them by becoming a small entrepreneur himself. Yet these workers were also proud, independent and capable of asserting themselves in both industrial and political contexts. By 1868 they had established the TUC as a pressure group monitoring and influencing industrial legislation and promoting its members' political interests through the Parliamentary Committee. By the 1870s the legal status of the unions had been much improved by the action of both political parties. Moreover, traditional ideas about the damaging effects of trade unionism had been effectively challenged by Liberal intellectuals like Henry Fawcett and John Stuart Mill, who argued that the free market would not operate satisfactorily without the active participation of combinations of working men; the free pursuit of higher wages was a wholly legitimate objective.

On the other hand the working class contained a tremendous range of experience and attitudes which inevitably limited and complicated its overall political impact. Between the skilled minority and the unskilled, unorganized majority, between those enjoying a regular wage and those condemned to casual labour, a major gulf still existed. The relative comfort of, say, a blastfurnaceman earning £2 to £3 a week marked him out from the casual labourer in London's East End or a Wiltshire farm worker on 14s. Those involved in irregular or seasonal employment in the low-paid or 'sweated' trades, or those who depended on employers' patronage or charity, were the least likely to generate independent political institutions or aspirations. Even among railway workers, for example, contemporaries noticed a distinction between 'the goods side and drivers and firemen not brought into touch with the public [who] are Radicals, [and] passenger guards and porters who are also underpaid but with funds augmented by tips and the patronage of the rich [who] are Conservatives.'[9]

By the 1880s, however, change was under way. Realization that British industry was losing its former dominance and an awareness of extensive urban poverty shook prevailing attitudes. In this decade socialism enjoyed a revival, though many of its early advocates were middle-class men and women. It often proved a frustrating task for the late Victorian socialist to wean the politically aware working man away from his Gladstonian brand of politics; self-help and free trade appeared to make more immediate sense than a new and vaguely understood philosophy. For some the route led via their existing religious principles towards an ethical version of socialism rather than to an economic creed. Nor was it yet obvious to many workers that state social policies were desirable. Especially from the perspective of poorer families, schemes of reform and improvement invariably appeared intrusive and humiliating because of the interference, inspection or taxation they involved. Government so often manifested itself in unwelcome forms, such as the poor law or the post-1870 educational innovations. The latter led to loss of children's earnings, payment of fees at least until 1891, inspectors trying to enforce compulsory attendance, and, after 1907, medical inspection. Beneficial measures such as vaccination against contagious diseases aroused much resentment; the stern individualist Thomas Burt declared he 'did not intend to have my children treated as if they were cattle'.[10]

Nonetheless, these negative attitudes should not be exaggerated. In time state intervention came to be seen as necessary and desirable, but it was not yet a practical basis for a major political movement, even in the working class. The last 20 years of the nineteenth century saw a series of experiments among labour and socialist organizations before a new, viable strategy emerged. Most of the labour leaders regarded the really impoverished slum populations as too passive and dependent to respond to their relatively sophisticated appeal. As Ramsay MacDonald put it in 1911: 'It is the skilled artisan, the trade unionist, the member of the friendly society, the young workman who reads and thinks who are the recruits to the army of socialism.'[11] Yet for many years socialist parties met with little success. The Social Democratic Federation (SDF), founded in 1883, represented the nearest approach to a Marxist socialist party. By the late 1890s the SDF claimed only 10,000 members though its true membership has been put at 2,600; it was always crippled by its inability to win more than a derisory vote at parliamentary elections, although it scored some successes in municipal contests. Like most organizations that took their socialism seriously the SDF attracted articulate middle-class people, but men like H. M. Hyndman, H. H. Champion and William Morris tended to reduce the Federation to disputatious fragments, all energetically defining their ideological position in numerous journals rather than converting the working class. It has been calculated that no less than 800 Labour and socialist newspapers were published between 1890 and 1910, most of them with tiny circulations and very short lives. Even Keir Hardie's *Labour Leader* struggled against perennial losses. The only viable socialist paper, Robert Blatchford's *Clarion*, outsold all the rest of the socialist press put together with a circulation of 40,000. Blatchford's formula, not unlike that of other successful working-class papers, was a lively, readable blend of socialist radicalism combined with a vigorous, patriotic nationalism. It was Blatchford more than any of the politicians who articulated 'socialism' for the rank and file in pre-1914 Britain.

A far more realistic and pragmatic approach than that of the SDF was adopted by the Independent Labour Party (ILP) founded in Bradford in 1893. Though socialist, the ILP displayed a certain flexibility absent from the SDF; for it espoused a shrewd mixture of radical Liberal causes and current trade union demands. Also its members reflected much more closely the working class of provincial England, and its leaders, especially Keir Hardie, spoke a socialism of a moralistic, humanitarian, revivalist kind. For some years the ILP-ers put their main emphasis on the local rather than the national sphere, working through municipal bodies, and also through trades councils, which were often the most successful means of co-ordinating the efforts of the otherwise disparate elements in the labour and socialist movements. During the 1890s opportunities were seized, for example, in boards of guardians such as the one at Poplar in London to which George Lansbury and Will Crooks were elected; they were able to change policy locally by providing outdoor relief to the aged and fit working men temporarily unemployed, and even more importantly, to highlight the problems and thus concentrate the minds of the policy-makers elsewhere. London was also the source of a notable triumph for ILP tactics in 1898 when West Ham Borough returned a majority of Labour members, who proceeded to improve the conditions of council workers by introducing two weeks' annual holiday, a minimum weekly wage of 30s, and a working day of eight hours. Although there was little co-ordination of labour and socialist action around the country, in practice a common platform did exist. This comprised essentially a demand for the municipalization of basic utilities like gas and waterworks where they were still in private hands (this was advocated on grounds of economy – an important consideration to a ratepaying electorate – as much as for fairness and improvement). The second basic proposal was to establish a works department so that the council could be a direct employer of labour; by this means it might both alleviate unemployment locally, and, by inserting a 'fair-wage' clause into its contracts, stimulate improvements in the conditions of men employed privately. Often this was accomplished by means of co-operation with Liberals and Fabians as in the case of the London County Council Progressives, but it certainly gave the labour movement a coherent political programme pitched towards working men. In the long run this experience proved to be immensely important. Local government in Bradford, Glasgow or London provided an invaluable apprenticeship in elections and office-holding that was eventually built upon at the parliamentary level; indeed, it left Labour's mainstream in the twentieth century with a pronounced municipal flavour, and probably compounded the neglect of ideology.

Yet despite this progress the ILP found it all but impossible to break into national politics. Though Keir Hardie was briefly the MP for West Ham (1892–5), the ILP's membership fluctuated around 6,000 to 9,000 by the end of the decade; financially starved and without access to trade union strength, the party remained a somewhat ramshackle and diffuse organization which, after the early successes, seemed to stagnate in the face of the trend to Conservatism during 1895–1900. However, the ILP leaders had grasped the fact that the key to effective independent labour politics lay in tapping the funds and organization of the trade unions; and the events of the later 1890s and early 1900s enabled them to translate their strategy into practice in the form of the Labour Representation Committee (LRC). The emergence of the LRC at the turn of the century has sometimes been explained in terms of an outflanking of the traditional craft unions by the more socialist and radical leaders of the 'new unions'. Undoubtedly several groups, like the Gas Workers and General Labourers Union, succeeded in extending industrial organization to many semi-skilled and unskilled men hitherto outside the movement. Moreover, the successful strikes of 1888–90 threw up many new trades councils, and leaders such as Will Thorne and Ben Tillett, who were ardent exponents of independent labour representation and critics of the TUC. With their advocacy of the eight-hour day they took the initiative in the TUC away from Henry Broadhurst, the Parliamentary Secretary and champion of Lib–Lab strategy. By the 1890s the Lib–Lab MPs were not, apparently, achieving much except respectability for themselves. Broadhurst himself served as an under-secretary in Gladstone's last government, but neither this nor his work on industrial legislation impressed the younger working-class activists with political ambitions who did not enjoy similar advantages. Lib–Labbery worked well enough for the miners, but this no longer seemed sufficient.

Nonetheless, too much should not be made of the new unions. They remained comparatively weak and soon lost much of their membership; by 1900, in fact, only 100,000 of the one million affiliated to the TUC were members of the new unions. Thus the emergence of what was to become the Labour Party in 1906 could hardly have occurred at that time but for the willingness of the well-established unions who still dominated the movement to indulge in an experiment. They had been much influenced by the experience of economic stagnation during the 1890s which exposed hitherto well-placed skilled men such as shipwrights, ironfounders, steel smelters and blastfurnacemen to 10 per cent unemployment rates. Further, the employers now displayed a tendency to take advantage of higher unemployment by combining for concerted action to curb union activity, as in the case of the Shipping Federation and the six-month lock-out of engineering workers in 1897. On top of this the legal status apparently achieved in 1875 now appeared to have been undermined by a number of legal decisions, notably the *Lyons* v. *Wilkins* case in 1896 and 1899 which infringed the right to picket. All this seemed to point to the need for unions to be represented in Parliament on a similar scale to employers; industrial weakness, in short, stimulated a characteristic turn towards political remedies. It was in this spirit that in 1899 the TUC approved by 546,000 votes to 434,000 a resolution of the Amalgamated Society of Railway Servants to establish a new and independent political organization. As a result 129 delegates representing unions and socialist societies met in February 1900 to set up the LRC. Its leading supporters at this stage included printers, boot and shoe operatives, gasworkers and dockers, and those like the railway workers who were trying to win recognition from their employers. Their purpose may best be defined as 'Labourism', that is, to achieve a greater degree of direct working-class representation than was possible within the scope of existing Lib–Lab arrangements. The chief authors of the strategy, Hardie and MacDonald of the ILP, recognized the futility of attempting to commit the LRC to any distinctive left-wing ideology lest they play into the hands of the many unionists who were anxious to 'bury the attempt in good-humoured tolerance'. Hardie contrived to obscure the inconsistency between a wholly independent party, which the LRC nominally was, and the relationship with Liberalism, which the bulk of the unions still desired. Thus the new organization was not in 1900 expected by most participants to differ dramatically from earlier experiments in labour representation. The LRC had to begin life as a loose federal organization with an executive of twelve, comprising seven trade unionists, two from the ILP, two from the SDF and one Fabian, and with an unpaid secretary in Ramsay MacDonald. The unions continued to hold on to their money and declined any ideological innovation. It was a modest start for a party that was to form a government only 24 years later.

Women, Politics and Labour

During the last 30 years of the century women impinged increasingly upon public affairs in Britain. They extended their range of employment in the expanding service sectors, notably as teachers, clerks, typists, Post Office employees and shop assistants; they also established a formal role both in the political parties and in local government. This process began to introduce a fresh element into conventional divisions along lines of social class and party ideology.

Although marriage and motherhood were seen as the inevitable lot of women, a high proportion of Victorian females remained single or became widows quite early in life. Working-class girls usually found themselves driven by necessity to paid employment at some stage in their lives. But most trade unionists regarded women workers as a threat because of their willingness to accept low wages. Working men used their growing foothold in Parliament to extend 'protective legislation' which was designed to exclude women from certain occupations. This conflict made women aware of the need for state intervention to impose minimum wages on the low-paid trades, as well as of the wider need for the vote. There are some grounds for thinking that women generally had a different view of politics, partly because of the different experience in employment. Obviously they were much less likely to be members of trade unions than men; around 20,000 joined in the early 1870s, though there were 166,000 by 1906. This reflected the temporary nature of their work and also the type of occupations they held. They were strongly concentrated in domestic service and similar jobs, where unions hardly existed and where they came into close contact with the middle class. There is some evidence that their attitudes and aspirations diverged as a result of this. Women clearly played a major role in giving their families 'respectable' status; they were more skilled at handling money; and were widely believed to be more interested in religion, temperance and other moral questions.

Gradually all this began to impinge upon the world of politics. In the 1880s new organizations like the Women's Co-operative Guild appeared which aspired to turn the concerns of ordinary housewives into political issues for the first time. The Women's Trade Union League provided a ladder by which young women like Margaret Bondfield began the long ascent to the cabinet. The political parties in the shape of the Primrose League, the Women's Liberal Federation and the Independent Labour Party made extensive use of women volunteers from the 1880s onwards. Some women, both middle-class and working-class, also gained a local government vote as ratepayers in 1869, and subsequently many were elected, especially to the school boards and as poor law guardians. Apart from the direct implications for women's public role, this experience in municipal affairs had a broader significance. For in the late nineteenth century local government served as an important experimental field for novel social policies. Elected women played a major role in this, partly because as women they noticed and understood things which men neglected. Such innovations as school meals, modestly attempted in this period, were to become the subject of national policies during the Edwardian period.

Working-class Conservatism, Empire and Patriotism

Even today studies of voting behaviour suggest that around one-third of working-class voters consistently support the Conservatives. In the mid-nineteenth century, when voters were offered two parties drawn from broadly similar social backgrounds and eschewing a class appeal, there could be no neat general relationship between class and party allegiance. But investigation has always been difficult because working-class Conservatism largely lacked organization, and therefore a record, and also because of the somewhat equivocal attitude of the party itself. While recognizing the division of society into ranks as natural and desirable, Conservatives feared the potential for class conflict in an industrial society; their leaders were thus anxious to avoid being drawn into a competition for votes by appeasement of material demands. As a result Conservatives approached the matter in two distinct ways. One involved appealing to working men as working men by cataloguing the beneficial measures enacted by Conservative administrations since Disraeli's time, and reminding them of how badly the Liberals fell down on their promises. This approach was typical of the National Union, which printed huge quantities of literature on the theme. The alternative was that usually adopted by the leaders and the Primrose League, which amounted to an appeal to working men as patriotic Britons, as soldiers of the queen, as English workers and as Protestants. To Salisbury the drawbacks of the former approach were only too obvious. National Union conferences were regularly troubled with complaints by working-class delegates that 'the time had come when the Conservative Party should have its Burts and its Broadhursts'.[12] Yet James Mawdsley of the cotton spinners enjoyed a lonely eminence as one leading Conservative trade unionist: he ran in harness with Winston Churchill in the double-member constituency of Oldham in 1899. But in the absence of payment of members, which the party thoroughly disliked, this experiment was unlikely to be repeated.

Two kinds of explanation are usually advanced to account for working-class Conservatism. The first is in terms of deference. This implies a willingness by the voter to be governed by his social superiors who are equipped to rule by birth and training, and a tendency to identify with the traditional values and institutions of his society, which invariably seem closely associated with the Conservative Party. This may well suggest the pattern for rural Conservatism; and is also consistent with the tendency noticed by some writers on local politics for Conservatives to do particularly well in both the wealthiest and the poorest wards.[13] There are signs of this in parliamentary elections too, notably in the East End of London, and in strong Conservative seats such as Bristol West, which combined the wealthy with the dependent poor. The other explanation sees the Conservative working man as a pragmatic or secular voter whose choice implies some assessment that his self-interest is best served by supporting the Conservative Party. In the nineteenth-century context the deferential and the pragmatic element was combined in the concept of Tory paternalism in the sense of government by hereditary leaders fully alive to their obligations, material and moral, towards the lower orders of society.

Although deferential attitudes were widespread in the nineteenth century they did not automatically make for Conservative voting. For until the 1860s the natural ruling elite in Britain – the Palmerstonian Whig–Liberal combination – was more closely identified with the symbols of national pride than the sectional and peripheral Conservative Party. However, there is a strong prima facie case for thinking that this changed during the Disraeli–Salisbury era as the Conservatives began to reap the benefit of association with patriotism and Empire. By his firmness over the Congress of Berlin, the Suez Canal, Afghanistan and South Africa Disraeli contrived to sharpen his disagreement with Gladstone, who could plausibly, if inaccurately, be accused of planning the dismemberment of the Empire and of showing weakness towards the United States and Russia when British interests were threatened. Thereafter Conservatives ceaselessly propagated their claim to be the party of national interests, and cast aspersions on their opponents' patriotism; they catalogued the radicals' failures in the 1880s – defeat by the Boers at Majuba Hill, abandonment of Kandahar, death of General Gordon – and pinned the label 'pro-Boer' indiscriminately on their rivals during 1899–1902. One conference speaker summed it up in 1905: 'in all those places where the enemies of England foregather, the advent of a Radical government would be hailed with undisguised rejoicing'.[14]

Some historians have gone to considerable lengths to exonerate the working classes from any sympathy with 'imperialism', arguing that this was characteristic of the lower middle and middle classes. However, this is tenable only if imperialism is fairly tightly defined, and if selective groups of working men are examined. The argument, for example, that the greater imperialism of the lower middle classes was manifested in their greater readiness to fight in the Boer War[15] is surely vitiated by the fact that, as in 1914, a huge proportion of working-class volunteers were rejected on grounds of physical unfitness to which others were less subject. There is more plausibility in the contention that working men regarded, or at least articulated, their patriotism in a different way, namely that they perceived a connection between vigorous imperial policies and material well-being. Such links obviously underpinned the popular Conservatism of centres

THE BOER AT BAY
A comment on Joseph Chamberlain's prominence in the
South African war.
Punch, or The London Charivari, 5 July 1899

like Woolwich, Newcastle and Sheffield, where jobs depended on the
fortunes of munitions manufacturers, and also in the dockyard towns of
Plymouth, Chatham, Portsmouth and Southampton. However, Empire
was hardly without its material advantages for the other classes; and it
would be rash to assume that the range of attitudes from patriotism to
chauvinism was especially concentrated in any level of Victorian society.

In recent years the debate over the popularity of imperialism has been
modified by the examination of a wider range of evidence. As a result it
has become increasingly clear that ideas associated with Empire were very
generally diffused by cultural rather than merely political mechanisms. For
example, the growing body of children's literature typified by the *Boy's
Own Paper,* the teaching of patriotic history and geography, the popular
music-hall songs, the Empire Exhibitions and the fiction, biographies and
press accounts of British achievements in exotic parts of the world all
familiarized the Victorian public with the idea of Empire. Moreover, the

rapid growth of commercial advertising helped remind people of the close connection between many items of their diet and British colonial possessions. Many working-class families enjoyed personal links with the colonies to which they had dispatched their sons, and with the Royal Navy in which sons and brothers enlisted. Their feelings were heightened by the growing fear of other European powers and the threat of invasion which was so characteristic of the 1871–1914 period. Empire was clearly far from being a remote or abstract notion in late Victorian times.

However, it is still difficult to assess *how* important popular imperialism was in political terms. Much imperial sentiment seems superficial and thus liable to fluctuate sharply, as the evaporation of enthusiasm in the latter stages of the Boer War suggests. A good deal also depends on how and how far vaguely patriotic sentiment was focused in formal political ways. The great imperial crises and the general elections provided good opportunities, and organizations like the Primrose League maintained a steady stream of imperial propaganda for the Conservative Party.

Dislike of foreigners and defence of British interests formed complementary sides of a currency extensively coined by Conservative propagandists in the late nineteenth century at constituency level; they furnished the unifying theme behind the Irish Question, the aliens issue and the tariff. For example, it was argued that Home Rule would bring 'thousands of ruined and desperate Irishmen over to England to compete in our markets';[16] and much play was made with the common interests of the Irish Party, British Liberals and Britain's enemies. The pattern that had evolved in the Irish case was extended to the attack upon the immigration of aliens, usually described as 'pauper Jews' in the propaganda, who were similarly represented as undercutting wages, overcrowding accommodation and imposing a heavy burden upon the poor-law authorities and ratepayers. The free trade in people was also blamed for conditions in the sweated industries; rather than advocating the imposition of minimum standards by law that would annoy small employers, Conservatives thrust the responsibility upon the influx of Poles and Russians.[17] That this struck a ready response even in radical working men is evident in Joseph Arch's disgust that Britain lost men through emigration every year while taking in immigrants who were 'the scum of their own countries, three of whom cannot do the work of one honest Englishman'.[18] When finally Balfour passed an Aliens Act in 1905 Conservatives continued to attack the new Home Secretary for not implementing it, and reopening the door to 'the diseased and pauper aliens who are so dear to the Radical party'.[19]

Similar themes are evident in the tariff reform propaganda; material interests were articulated in the same emotive terms, namely the need to stand up for Britain by retaliating against the import of inferior foreign goods produced by cheap labour, which, owing to the spinelessness of the free traders, were depriving British workers of jobs. Protectionism characterized Conservatism locally well before Chamberlain's campaign was launched in 1903; in places like Sheffield, where employment seemed threatened by imported German cutlery, it became an integral part of the party's appeal and helped Conservatives to win three or four of the five seats throughout 1885–1914.

While these essentially nationalist themes provided the staple attack, more constructive elements were also included. Conservatives were keen to throw back at Gladstone the radical plea that Ireland blocked the way to reform by pointing to the combination of 'firm' government from Dublin with measures of improvement at home. Only a few of these produced tangible benefits, such as the elimination of elementary school fees in 1891, and the Truck Act of 1897 which placed limits on the much resented practice of paying workers in kind rather than in cash. On the whole, however, the Conservative Party stood to gain more by abstaining from too much costly improvement and allowing its rivals to provoke hostility to interference and regulation, particularly in the fields of temperance and education. Even apparently constructive measures like the 1875 Artisans Dwellings Act assisted the Conservatives indirectly; for where energetic municipalities like Liberal-run Birmingham availed themselves of the powers in the Act for slum clearance, they fuelled working-class resentment against themselves.[20] Thus, for late Victorian Conservatives the key to their appeal lay in capitalizing upon the unchanging and unifying issues like Empire and the foreigner, while leaving the radicals to suffer the consequences of dashed expectations and disturbing innovation.

Three major conurbations became notable bastions of working-class Conservatism in this period. In Liverpool and west Lancashire generally the party's predominance was inextricably bound up with the working-class Protestant backlash against Irish immigrants as Catholics, aliens and rivals for employment and homes. As early as 1868 Gladstone's burgeoning interest in Ireland contributed to his ejection from a Lancashire seat. As a result the Conservatives enjoyed a popular and organized base in the working class; by the 1890s the Liverpool Workingmen's Conservative Association claimed 6,000 members, and under Archibald Salvidge they held seven or eight of the city's nine constituencies after 1885, the only regular exception being the Scotland division, where the Irish comprised a majority. Nor was this sectarian pattern seriously shaken until 1945. Glasgow and western Scotland, also a point of arrival for Irish immigrants, displayed similar tendencies, though with the difference that more here were Protestants from Ulster; even before 1886 the Glasgow Conservatives had successfully brought the Orange Lodges under the party's umbrella where, in combination with the Liberal Unionists, they made a formidable force.

Another region conspicuous for its popular Conservatism was Birmingham and the west Midlands. This was not simply the result of the detachment of Chamberlain and the Liberal Unionists from the Liberals in 1886, for by 1885 Birmingham Conservatives had steadily raised their vote to 42 per cent. The party often ran working men and small tradesmen as municipal candidates and gained strength, particularly in the poorer wards antagonized by the rule of the Chamberlainite machine.[21] Tariff reform won popularity among the west Midland metal trades, many of which were organized as small workshops where a close master-and-man relationship was more typical than large-scale production and unionization. After the amalgamation of Conservative and Liberal Unionist forces in 1886 Chamberlainite candidates were virtually unchallenged in every Birmingham constituency until 1929; and the west Midlands as a whole remained relatively resistant, even to the Liberal revival of 1906. What is distinctive is the assertive, even populist character of Conservatism in both Birmingham and Lancashire.

By comparison the rural areas were more passive and deferential, as was the East End of London. In fact a formidable catalogue of poor East End constituencies elected Conservatives in the late nineteenth century: N.E. Bethnal Green, Walworth, Rotherhithe, Bow and Bromley, Mile End, Limehouse, Stepney, St George's (Tower Hamlets) and Deptford, to take the best examples. Conservative strength here was, however, at least partly a reflection of Liberal and socialist weakness. London was notably irreligious, it was not strong on temperance, its workers were comparatively non-unionized; its population was quickly excited by the great imperial war-and-peace issues; and alien immigration from eastern Europe assumed considerable proportions from the 1880s. The poverty of East End workers was the result of the casual and seasonal nature of their employment, and of the abnormal role of the service industries which fostered an abject dependence upon middle-class patronage. Also, much of the population were catered to by a wide range of charitable enterprises. All of this was apt to undermine any spirit of independence and self-help, and to leave the working population comparatively indifferent to politics. The small size of the East End electorate facilitated the survival of the older pattern of politics in which constituencies looked to candidates as providers of employment or as distributors of largesse. This made for a working-class Conservatism of a more passive and less consciously political nature than elsewhere, lacking a strong organizational base, and able to win by default. Thus in London, even more than in other regions, popular Conservatism turned out to be very vulnerable in the Edwardian period when the Liberals posed a vigorous challenge with free trade and social reform, which raised the level of participation and swamped the limited Conservative vote.

The Lower Middle Class

In Britain it has been easy to overlook those who fall between the 'working class' and the 'middle class', possibly because they seem to have played a less dramatic role than elsewhere in Europe, or because of an assumption that such groups tend to diminish. No doubt the lower middle class is far from being a cohesive section of society, but for our purposes its members are defined by the very ambiguity of their situation, frequently working class by origin yet precariously clinging to the bottom ranks of the middle classes by occupation and attitudes. They were a key element in Victorian political evolution, and a rapidly expanding, not a declining, group from the 1860s. In occupational terms the lower middle class falls into two categories: first, the essentially pre-industrial group of small entrepreneurs, particularly shopkeepers, many of whom were hardly to be distinguished from the elite of craftsmen such as tailors and printers; second, the administrative, technical and professional occupations whose numbers were greatly augmented in a mature industrial society, notably clerks, civil servants, elementary school teachers, journalists, travelling salesmen, insurance and friendly society collectors, and policemen.

The political significance of what Victorians often called the 'shopocracy' is readily apparent. For not only did its members enjoy the time and independence for local political activity, they also comprised a large proportion of the pre-1867 electorate; even in industrial towns the shopocracy often formed 30–50 per cent of the total, with craftsmen making another 25 per cent.[22] In their ambitions and frustrations lay the seeds of formal political organization in boroughs. Municipal reform in 1835 presented an opportunity to challenge the exclusive control exercised by superior classes of merchants, landowners and lawyers. The basis of the controversy over parliamentary reform in 1866 lay in the Whig belief that, in view of the radicalism displayed by the urban shopocracy, the franchise had been extended as far as was safe, whereas Gladstone's proposal to lower the qualification from £10 to a £7 rental value was tantamount to a complete enfranchisement of small shopkeepers and craftsmen. Contemporary assumptions that they leant to radical Liberalism have been corroborated by evidence from surviving poll books for the mid-Victorian period which suggests that both shopkeepers and artisans supported the Liberals against the Conservatives by up to two to one, a markedly higher proportion than that of those immediately above or below them. During the 1870s local caucuses and the NLF opened up further avenues of participation for them and for journalists and teachers, who were quick to appreciate the moral fervour and individualist tone of Gladstonian Liberalism.

Although franchise reform in 1867 and 1884 rendered the traditional lower middle class less numerically significant, non-manual jobs increased from 2 million to 4 million in Britain between 1881 and 1914. In particular the number of clerks shot up from 100,000 in the 1860s to nearly 700,000 by the First World War; together with commercial travellers, teachers, and central and local civil servants they numbered approximately 920,000. Moreover, since they increasingly resided in distinct suburbs somewhat apart from working-class or solidly middle-class communities, they often became a major element in the single-member constituencies. Conscious of having risen just above the working class and existing frugally on yearly incomes in the £75–£150 range, Victorian clerks were distinguished more by a belief in respectability and social mobility than by higher living standards. Frequently teetotallers, active Nonconformists, and imbued with notions of self-improvement through individual industriousness and thrift, the new lower middle class was often as predisposed to Liberalism as the shopocracy. This is easily overlooked in the assumption that the urban clerk was typical of the sections detached from Liberalism in this period. There is, of course, a strong case for the view that their identification with their social superiors manifested itself in patriotic Conservatism and demonstrative loyalty to king and Empire on the part of those who volunteered to fight in the South African War. No doubt military service in such circumstances added zest and adventure to the lives of ambitious men confined to tedious jobs without prospects, just as it raised their status and self-regard. However, it remains unproven whether the lower middle class were especially prone to imperialism; and if the *Daily Mail* catered to the imperialists among them, the *Daily News* was read by their pacifists and Little Englanders.

Alternatively, lower-middle-class politics may have been determined by the pressures arising from a frustrating and ambiguous social position. Commercial salesmen were particularly vulnerable to economic fluctuations during 1875 and 1896. The supply of clerks and administrators, now beginning to be swollen by female recruits, was so plentiful as to make for stagnant wages and poor promotion prospects. Small shopkeepers, too, felt the competition of co-operatives and the rapidly spreading chain stores. These economic pressures coincided with an apparent loss of political clout as the organized working class claimed a growing share of legislative attention and ensconced their representatives in Parliament. Some occupations – teachers, clerks and railway clerks for example – were driven to form trade unions, though they endeavoured at first to be professional associations rather than militant bodies; otherwise unionization was eschewed as a sign of non-middle-class status.

These pressures on income and employment manifested themselves politically in burgeoning complaints about high taxation and, especially, local rates. The activities of local authorities in urban improvement, education and coping with the pressure of poverty resulted in steep increases in rates by the end of the nineteenth century. However, this bore not upon the owners of land, who were often very wealthy, but upon the occupiers of property, many of whom were householders or shopkeepers of modest means. Many Liberals and socialists saw the solution in terms of effective taxation of land values, but this was necessarily a long-term objective. The Conservative approach seemed more immediately attractive, namely, more grants-in-aid by national government. Lower-middle-class ratepayers were easily mobilized in opposition to schemes of improvement which required expensive loans. This was a recurring theme and it helps to explain the revival of municipal Conservatism in the Edwardian period.

However, the parliamentary loyalty of constituencies characterized by concentrations of lower-middle-class residents, such as Fulham, Hammersmith, Islington, Peckham, N. West Ham and Lewisham in London, and South Edinburgh, South Manchester and North Bristol is not clear. While these seats showed a shift towards Conservatism typical of the late nineteenth century, they also saw a reversion to the Liberals around 1906, as did most areas. In fact the three provincial seats mentioned above were more often Liberal than Conservative during 1885–1914, and South Edinburgh was never won by a Conservative. In London, where Liberalism was markedly weaker, Fulham, Hammersmith and Lewisham had already become Conservative by 1885; and where, as in Lewisham, the lower middle class was mixed with middle-class residents, the Conservative lead seemed unassailable. However, the early Liberalism of the four Islington seats and N. West Ham re-emerged by 1906, and this casts some doubt on the idea that the lower-middle-class electors were fundamentally alienated by the Liberal abandonment of individualism in favour of collectivist reform. If some propensity for radicalism was retained this may have been due to their Nonconformity, or may, alternatively, reflect their changing composition through constant recruitment. Literate, politically conscious young men and women rising into non-manual employment were often exponents of radical Liberalism and indeed of socialism, as figures like Ramsay MacDonald and Herbert Morrison, the son of a Lambeth policeman, indicate; already by the end of the century the Labour movement was drawing upon clerks, journalists and teachers for activists and municipal candidates much as Victorian radicalism had previously done.

PART TWO

1895–1914

CHAPTER FIVE

The Edwardian Crises 1895–1914

There are men who sit still with the fly-blown phylacteries of obsolete policies bound round their foreheads, who do not remember that while they have been mumbling their incantations to themselves, the world has been marching and revolving.

Lord Rosebery, Chesterfield speech, 14 December 1901

The Waning of Radicalism

By the mid-1890s radical Liberalism had lost the drive and purpose it had displayed between 1867 and 1885. No doubt this was partly because so many radical reforms had been accomplished; but it was also because some reforms, notably the franchise, had not produced desirable results. Gladstone's modest victory in 1892 by no means reversed the disaster of 1886; and in 1895 the Liberals won a mere 177 seats against 411 for the combined Conservatives and Liberal Unionists, a performance that was only marginally modified in 1900. It began to seem that the mass electorate, subject as it was to crude appeals to chauvinism and ephemeral emotions, fell well short of the mature, informed body a stable democracy required. As a result many prominent Liberals felt disinclined to transform the 1884 franchise into one-man-one-vote, not least because this would now mean opening the pandora's box of women's suffrage. Both older Liberals like Gladstone and younger ones like H. H. Asquith often perceived women as the epitome of a mass electorate – politically ignorant, emotional, vacillating. They took refuge in the argument that since women were characterized by Anglicanism and were likely to be enfranchised on a property basis they would inevitably lean to the Conservatives. Yet they felt embarrassed in this illiberal attitude by the pleas of the National Union of Women's

Suffrage Societies, a rather Liberal and moderate organization, and by the Women's Liberal Federation, which steadily and successfully worked to convert the MPs to suffragism. It was fortunate for the anti-suffragists that the Conservatives also remained too divided to formulate a policy, and were, as a group, even more resolutely hostile to women's suffrage. Thus by the end of the century the great Victorian reform crusade was in danger of petering out amid the manoeuvres to block the women's claim.

Disillusionment became evident, too, in the new regard for the American system of government on the part of such 'radicals' as James Bryce. Once the model for popular radicalism, America now served to demonstrate the viability of stable, conservative democracy, characterized by devolution of power, legislative inertia at the centre, and a strong second chamber.[1] It was no accident that, despite their difficulties with the House of Lords, the Liberals were so slow to produce a scheme for reforming the powers and composition of the upper chamber. In the 1860s the anti-Liberal majority there had been 60–70; this widened steadily even before the withdrawals of 1886, so that in the 1893 vote on the second Home Rule Bill the Gladstonians found themselves outnumbered by 419 to 41. Much of the work of the 1892–5 administration was crippled by the peers, more so than in the past. Yet the obvious response, an appeal to the country, required a more popular cry than was provided by any of the rejected measures. Indeed, an unreformed House of Lords constituted a useful insurance for voters who felt it safe to vote Liberal as long as Home Rule remained an impossibility. Thus despite much rhetoric from Rosebery, 1895 came and went without either a new issue or a determined plan to reform the chamber. Not until 1908 did the leadership think seriously about reform, and not until the budget of 1909 did the party risk linking a major social question with the constitutional issue. Meanwhile it seemed safer to accept the status quo than to challenge it; yet the consequence was to undermine the credibility of any Liberal social policies in the eyes of the electorate.

The electoral setbacks and inhibitions of post-1886 Liberalism have led some historians to argue that it was congenitally incapable of sustaining the role of a reforming party in a mass electorate. The grounds for such a view rest, first, on the party's inability to organize its following as effectively as its rivals, and secondly, on the individualism and rationalism that inhibited the Liberals from making the demagogic appeal required by an unsophisticated electorate.[2] This case appears convincing if based on the aloof, temperamental, parliamentary figures of Liberal Imperialism or on timid, faltering radicals like John Morley. However, it does tend to overlook the tough partisans such as Harcourt or Labouchere, the adept, manipulating whips such as Herbert Gladstone, J. A. Pease or the Master of Elibank, as well as the more obscure organizers like J. Renwick Seager of the Liberal Registration Department. The legendary organizer Francis Schnadhorst remained secretary to the Liberal Central Association until 1893 though evidently well past his peak; and the activities of the Society of Certificated and Associated Liberal Agents indicate no less professional an attitude towards organization than that of their opponents.[3] The difference between the two parties lay not in attitude so much as in resources. By the 1890s far less money fuelled the Liberal machine, but this by no means indicated a revulsion from this aspect of politics. Similarly the party of Lloyd George and 'Limehouse' can hardly be suspected of eschewing a demagogic approach; what is true, however, is that in the period between the defection of Chamberlain and the emergence of Lloyd George the Liberals badly missed their former monopoly in popular platform oratory. The restoration of Liberal supremacy in all the coarser arts of politics by 1903–6 should warn us against portraying them as a special kind of party too encumbered by scruples to succeed. Their manifest weaknesses during the last 20 years of the century should not be mistaken for a congenital distaste or inacapacity for modern politics.

The attrition of Liberal strength may be discerned in the late Victorian press where the earlier predominance slipped somewhat. Many Liberal proprietors and editors no doubt liked to see their brand of political journalism as morally uplifting for the people while the Tories pandered merely to their baser emotions; radical papers were sometimes handicapped by proprietorial distaste for gambling and racing results, which were a mainstay of the cheap evening press.[4] But the basic problem lay in the fact that it became increasingly difficult to sell strongly partisan newspapers of any variety by 1900 (see table 5.1). Moreover, the capacity of newer national newspapers to reduce their costs and draw a bigger circulation inevitably reduced the significance of the sober provincial press which had been disproportionately Liberal in sympathy; no major Liberal equivalent of the *Daily Mail* emerged. With its restricted audience and declining profitability the provincial radical paper stood in growing need of subsidies for survival; but at a time when commercial wealth was drifting further towards

TABLE 5.1 *Political loyalties of English daily newspapers 1868–1910*

	1868	1886	1900	1910
Liberal	26	66	71	57
Conservative	9	40	40	35
Independent	1	19	35	14
Neutral	8	13	25	15

Source: A. J. Lee, *The Origins of the Popular Press 1855–1914* (1976), p. 287.

Conservatism this naturally meant a thinning out of the Liberal press in relation to its rivals. Yet although by the Edwardian period the Liberal advantage had been narrowed by comparison with the 1860s it had not been destroyed by any means.

In another respect the transition from the 1860s to the 1890s involved a more drastic curtailment of the Liberal lead over the Conservatives. When the Liberal Unionists withdrew in 1886 they took with them not only wealthy and influential Whigs in the counties, but, more importantly, middle-class men in the industrial areas who gave Conservatism in the north and Scotland vital infusions of business and Nonconformist, especially Wesleyan, strength.[5] With far fewer subscribers, constituency Liberal associations often had to neglect the costly annual work of maintaining the electoral register, and even to abandon contests; no less than 163 Unionists were returned unopposed in 1900, for example. Although local Liberal poverty was partly redressed after 1900 by infusions from central funds under Herbert Gladstone, the Edwardian party undoubtedly depended heavily for its finance on a small pool of really wealthy, progressive industrialists – Sir William Lever, Sir John Brunner, George Cadbury and Joseph Rowntree in particular.

A further consequence of the withdrawals was to leave the remaining subscribers in the constituencies with a greater influence over candidatures. The caucus system had never been as representative as its proponents had claimed; after 1886 it became increasingly a vehicle for the 'faddist' radicalism of the NLF, which blocked the aspirations of working men to parliamentary representation. Usually a local caucus felt obliged to seek a candidate able to make annual contributions and pay his own election expenses; not only would a working man require support from the association, he would also be unable to administer the material assistance either to individual constituents or to the economy of the town itself which was expected of a middle-class politician. Hence it was often felt by working-class as much as by middle-class Liberals that a working man could not carry a radical constituency. The problem is well illustrated by Newcastle Liberalism. John Morley seemed an admirable candidate for this two-member seat in 1885; but as a journalist he had little money to devote to the association, which consequently succumbed to the temptation to adopt as his partner a wealthy but nondescript local businessman in preference to a working man like Arthur Henderson, who would have widened the party's electoral appeal. Morley's defiant opposition to the eight-hour day compounded the alienation of organized workers, thereby precipitating the loss of one of the Newcastle seats in 1892 and both in 1895.[6]

By contrast, the concentration of miners in certain counties and the availability of financial support from the miners' federations facilitated the effective adoption of trade unionists by Liberal associations, especially from 1884, when miners benefited from the extension of the county franchise. In this way such seats could be economically secured for Liberalism; for the Lib–Lab members were much appreciated by Gladstone as sound radicals quite independent of the Chamberlainite caucus. However, though the Lib–Lab experiment was a novel and significant asset, by the 1890s it seemed incapable of extension beyond a handful of constituencies dominated by the miners. Paradoxically the weakness of the strategy lay in the ease with which the miners' leaders were absorbed into the party establishment. Elderly men for the most part, who had sat at the feet of Bright and Gladstone, the Lib–Labs breathed life into traditional Liberal individualism; indeed, the aversion of men like Burt for state intervention (outside the mines) made them more orthodox than many of the younger middle-class Liberals of the 1890s. Thus, although they symbolized the common interest of working men and radicalism, and contributed positively to labour legislation, the Lib–Labs failed to make a significant programmatic or intellectual contribution to Liberalism; lacking a distinctive impact, they were bound to be outflanked eventually by more radical Labour politicians.

These flaws in the infrastructure of radicalism were compounded by the absorption of the leading Liberals with in-fighting and the consequent vacuum in party leadership from 1894 to 1905. The adage that Gladstone became more radical with age has recently gained new support.[7] It is suggested, for example, that he perceived the Irish agitation as an aspect of the wider British working-class movement with which he increasingly sympathized. Certainly he deplored the suppression of workers' discontent in 1886 and 1887; but the Gladstonian defence of trade union liberties was *individualist*, and he could not embrace their economic demands as class representatives. Nor are there more than indirect indications of Gladstone's tentative sympathy for the radical social policies of graduated income tax and old-age pensions. He strongly disapproved of Harcourt's Death Duties budget of 1894 and continued to hold that income tax facilitated extravagance and tended to the social disintegration of the community.

No doubt in the 1860s and early 1870s Gladstone had led Liberalism in a radical direction, but thereafter his energies were devoted more to restraining the forces he had unleashed; his tactics in 1886 obliged him ultimately to compromise with caucus politics to the extent of swallowing such previously unpalatable measures as Welsh disestablishment and land reform. But Gladstone's endorsement of the NLF's Newcastle Programme in 1891 was purely nominal. His reluctance to respond constructively to the social questions of the 1890s marked him as an essentially one-issue statesman who had become a liability to his party; and he found it hard to accept that he had been returned to power in 1892 *in spite of* Home Rule. Now growing deaf and tiring rapidly, Gladstone absented himself increasingly from the Commons and whenever possible avoided meeting his Cabinet, which made his sudden reappearances all the more trying for his colleagues. He took little interest in the development of policy beyond Ireland, and preferred to deal with a few individuals, notably Morley, with whom he felt at ease. But for his negativism and temperamental infirmity Morley might have been groomed as the next leader. Yet, to rest on Morley as Gladstone did was only to advance deeper into the cul-de-sac of mid-Victorian radicalism, not to face the industrial society of the future.

Gladstone's colleagues took his somewhat pitiful retirement over increased expenditure and naval rebuilding in 1894 with relief mingled with apprehension; for they failed entirely to compensate for the inspiration he had long provided for Liberalism. 'Neither Harcourtian iconoclastic crusades nor Roseberian grand panjandrum secretiveness will do any good,'[8] as one Liberal put it. Now the party counted the cost of losing its two outstanding radical statesmen: Sir Charles Dilke, ruined by a divorce scandal in 1885, and Joseph Chamberlain, soon to become Lord Salisbury's Colonial Secretary. No one adequately filled the vacuum. Rosebery, in many ways an attractive successor, rapidly proved congenitally unsuited to be Prime Minister and party leader; impaled upon a small, fractious Commons majority he did no more than inveigh ineffectually against the House of Lords in which he was himself incarcerated. In 1896 Rosebery threw up the leadership to spend the next decade exacerbating party divisions without making a determined attempt to regain his title. During 1896–8 Harcourt and Lord Kimberley shared the leadership in the two Houses; upon the former's retirement in 1899 Sir Henry Campbell-Bannerman attempted to consolidate a party rent by imperial controversies until he was rescued around 1904 by the discovery that he could win a general election. As a leader Harcourt was too narrow and negative, and too unpopular with his colleagues; Campbell-Bannerman and Herbert Gladstone were worthy but uninspiring; Morley and Bryce too detached, irresolute and pessimistic. Among the imperialists, apart from Rosebery, there was only Asquith, cold, remote and absorbed with his legal career; Grey, too dilettante; and Haldane, too much the intellectual and intriguer.

Liberal Imperialism

Absence of constructive leadership greatly exacerbated the discontent of young middle-class Liberals. For Herbert Samuel, Charles Trevelyan, Willoughby Dickinson and others of their generation the 1890s brought a heightened consciousness of the poverty and inhumanity of urban life. As sensitive young men growing to adulthood amid the dismal investigations of Charles Booth and Seebohm Rowntree, they felt a certain guilt in the contrast between their own inherited wealth and privilege and the condition of the majority. Imbued with a Victorian sense of duty and public service, many of this generation served a form of apprenticeship in social work connected with Toynbee Hall in the East End, or served on municipal councils, school boards and boards of guardians before entering the Commons. They admitted, too, the moral charge of socialism against the existing order of society even if they rejected its analysis and solutions. Moreover, they identified the danger of a mass electorate generating insatiable pressure for penal taxation and the confiscation of wealth, which threatened to reduce politics to a struggle between a party of property and a party of labour. Such a prospect was not to be avoided by Morley's dogmatic resistance or by faddism, but through the adoption of a constructive social policy. This explains why Rosebery was acclaimed and for years regarded as the white hope of younger Liberals; as the first chairman of the London County Council he seemed in tune with progressive politics and urban England.

Indeed Rosebery provided the link that bound up men like Trevelyan, Samuel and Runciman with 'Liberal Imperialism'. The label is a confusing one since the strength of Liberal Imperialism was by no means simply a reflection of imperialist sentiment; though it incorporated a right-wing element, it also included those who, rebelling against faddism, sought a positive social policy. This incoherence renders measurement of the number of Liberal Imperialists difficult. Analysis based strictly upon imperial issues indicates that in the parliamentary Liberal Party the Imperialists comprised one-eighth in 1892, rising to over a third by 1905.[9] This trend reflects the death, retirement and defeat of elderly Gladstonians and their replacement by younger men less committed to party traditions.

The Liberalism of free trade, self-help and non-interference did not drive them to open conflict, though it seemed an inadequate programme. However, the Gladstonian approach to foreign and imperial questions had always been contested, and it was this that crystallized the revolt. Strictly, Liberal Imperialism was a coherent force only at the top, where it comprised essentially Rosebery, Asquith, Grey, Haldane, Sir Henry Fowler and R. Munro-Ferguson. They criticized Gladstone for his obsession with Home Rule, which was undesirable in itself and had led him to pander to NLF programmes. 'Mr G.', said Haldane, 'thoroughly demoralised the Liberal Party by the policy of sop-throwing in the two years before 1892.'[10] As a result, they believed, the party had alienated moderate middle-class support and forfeited its claim as the national party; it had degenerated into a rabble of protesters and faddists unlikely to inspire the confidence of the country as a whole.

Shaking off Home Rule and the Irish Party thus seemed essential; for even if the policy was right it remained inexpedient because it could not be forced through the Lords, and presented the Tories with a useful cry.

To some extent, however, this split could be obscured by merging the Irish issue into a home-rule-all-round approach and a wider policy of imperial federation for the Empire. They regarded further British expansion as an inevitable consequence of the competition of the great powers, though they do not seem to have argued the economic case for this. The Liberal Imperialists shared with Chamberlain and many Conservatives a concern for drawing together the white colonies under an Imperial Parliament at Westminster so as to facilitate a closer defence policy. In the context of imperial federation the devolution of authority to Ireland would be less disturbing, while general devolution would enable Westminster to disperse many of the radical fads to the regions for settlement.

In foreign affairs the Liberal Imperialists desired continuity of policy between the parties. Although their disagreements with the Gladstonians began to manifest themselves during Rosebery's tenure of the Foreign Office in 1892–4, the split reached a climax only in 1899–1902 as a result of the Liberal Imperialists' support for Sir Alfred Milner in his negotiations with President Kruger; they adopted the somewhat naive view that the conflict was about defending the rights of British settlers in the Transvaal, from which it followed that the South African War was just. However, the 'pro-Boers' were so voluble that it seemed they would stamp their view upon the party in an election. To check this an Imperial Liberal Council was set up in April 1900 under Robert Perks MP, from which the frontbenchers stayed aloof lest they be charged with creating a faction. The Council claimed the allegiance of 109 MPs and 142 candidates, a considerable exaggeration. Most MPs adopted the compromise position that while the war had been forced on Britain, the government had been inept in diplomacy and negligent in its military planning. Until 1901 Asquith attempted to keep on the periphery of Liberal Imperialism so as to ease Campbell-Bannerman's task of holding the party together. He was dismayed, therefore, by the latter's celebrated speech in June of that year in which he condemned as 'methods of barbarism' Kitchener's use of concentration camps in South Africa. This seemed ominously to echo Midlothian and was interpreted as an abandonment of the middle ground by Campbell-Bannerman. When in September a Liberal Unionist candidate at the N.E. Lanark by-election was denied the party leader's support and that of other Gladstonians who preferred the ILP contender, they began to fear being squeezed out of the party. Their immediate response was to set up the Liberal Imperial League under Grey. However, only Rosebery could mobilize their strength in the country, and he now took another of his fitful initiatives in a speech at Chesterfield in December, which contained a striking appeal for Liberals to adopt a 'clean slate' and free themselves of the 'fly-blown phylacteries' in domestic as much as foreign politics. Campbell-Bannerman responded to this clear challenge simply by inviting

Rosebery to define his relationship to the Liberal Party. By establishing a new Liberal League in February 1902 Rosebery virtually admitted that he was outside the fold.

Although divisions seemed to be crystallizing as the South African War approached its end, Liberal Imperialism was in fact about to be submerged in the tide of Gladstonian revivalism. Asquith, Grey and Haldane did achieve high office in 1905, but the group had lost its coherence well before then. Rosebery finally parted company with his colleagues on account of their radical financial policies; but even before 1906 he had shown himself to be a handicap because of his steadfast failure to sustain his initiatives. At heart he had no desire to regain the Liberal leadership, preferring instead to lead a coalition; and for a time it was conceivable that the disintegrating Salisbury government and squabbling opposition would present him with the opportunity. However, the Liberal Imperialists failed to exploit the situation; always inept in the basic political arts, they neither organized themselves in the Commons nor built up a grass-roots organization; remote and elitist, they absorbed themselves with policy and office more than with in-fighting. Tactically the Liberal Imperialists sought the middle ground when the war was driving opinions to extremes; and their acquiescence in the policy of Milner and Kitchener proved genuinely offensive to Liberals who were not 'pro-Boers'. Nor did they compensate by launching a bold social policy; instead they conveyed only a distaste for programmes in general and Liberal fads in particular. Eventually they were wrecked by the ramifications of the war, particularly Balfour's 1902 Education Act which most Liberals attacked, and the revival of the free-trade issue to which all rallied. Asquith in particular reworked his passage to Liberal affections by pursuing Chamberlain around the country. He appreciated that by 1902 the party was thoroughly tired of factionalism and anxious to unite on the causes presented by the Tories. Unity and revivalism swiftly made Liberal Imperialism irrelevant as a discrete force.

'National Efficiency' and Tariff Reform

The Liberal Imperialists were by no means alone in their attitude towards party politics, imperial and social questions. In a sense they simply represented a Liberal expression of the wider movement for 'National Efficiency' around the turn of the century which embraced Fabian socialists like Sidney and Beatrice Webb, as well as collectivist Conservatives like Milner, Chamberlain and even Balfour. Though they sprang from every political tradition the enthusiasts for National Efficiency shared certain qualities and convictions. Fundamentally they were reacting to the perceived decline of industry and agriculture during the previous 20 years,

A 'MISTAKEN ROAD.'
(*A Scene from the Patriot-Pilgrim's Progress.*)
An early comment on Chamberlain's move to protectionism.
A Penny Popular Monthly, November–December 1897

and the corresponding enfeeblement of Britain as a world power, a process that appeared to culminate in the disasters of the South African War and subsequent revelations about the degeneracy of the British urban population in the Report of the Inter-Departmental Committee on Physical Deterioration in 1904. Apprehension about British decadence stimulated a variety of remedies, including the improvement of secondary education, particularly technical and scientific, to enable Britain to compete with Germany. On the military side the critics fastened upon the crippling role of the Treasury, the lamentable amateurism of army officers and the inadequate training of their men; military training for civilians was commended for both its physical and moral advantages. Also typical of National Efficiency advocates was the bold application of state power in the field of social welfare, for Bismarckian rather than humanitarian reasons: a healthy population was a more efficient workforce and more stable politically.

The other unifying theme lay in the identification of the nineteenth-century system of parliamentary government as the underlying cause of Britain's decline. Critics argued that popular democracy had warped parliamentary politics by rendering it vulnerable to sectional pressures. Governments were run increasingly by amateurs adept at party warfare but incompetent in administration and the development of policy. They were obliged to indulge in sham conflicts on irrelevant issues that turned Parliament into an entertainment for a few partisans. 'Party is an evil,' declared Rosebery, 'its operation blights efficiency.' One striking consequence of this was held to be that too much authority had been acquired by the Treasury, whose narrow retrenchment philosophy killed both military innovation and social reconstruction; it also tended to eliminate the contribution of the expert and businessman to administration. This debilitating process was evident, too, at local level, where specialists such as doctors and engineers were losing out to the generalist and bureaucrat. In addition local government was hopelessly fragmented among 133 county, county borough, district and parish councils, 643 poor law boards, and 2,500 school boards. In short, there were too many elected authorities with insufficient powers and expertise for coherent, efficient administration. Balfour's Education Act and the Webbs' proposals for poor law reform in the famous Minority Report of 1909 were very much in accordance with National Efficiency thinking. Ideally it was hoped to bypass the lackadaisical, garrulous 20-member Cabinet by cabinet committees fortified with specialists and the practical wisdom of businessmen as a means of curbing party and Treasury influence. The cult of the expert found typical expression in the Committee of Imperial Defence established by Balfour in 1902 as a vehicle for the evolution of defence policy unimpeded by parliamentary interference.

Despite such notable initiatives along National Efficiency lines Balfour could not as Prime Minister (1902–5) avoid reaping the political whirlwind of the South African War. While attempting to sort out the problems bequeathed by his uncle he was overtaken by the tariff reform wave set off by Joseph Chamberlain in May 1903. His tariff reform campaign was designed in the short run to restore the initiative to a government faltering between the need to reduce high wartime taxation and to raise revenue for social reform. But it sprang from a long-term concern for national decline. During the 1880s and 1890s the remnants of Conservative agricultural protectionism had begun to receive infusions of support from industry, particularly steel and textile manufacturers subject to foreign competition. Whereas in 1860 only 5.5 per cent by value of British imports had been manufactured items, by 1900 this was 25 per cent.[11] Much impressed by what he took to be the effects of a protected domestic market upon Germany and the United States, Chamberlain argued that these powers were now using their system of mass production to dump goods so cheaply on Britain as to undermine our manufacturing sectors; unless checked the process would denude Britain of industry. Yet for Chamberlain the central virtues of a tariff policy was its contribution to imperial economic unification and its potential for the social regeneration of Britain. The first would be attained through preference for colonial goods in the British market and acceptance by them of our manufactured products; it seemed possible to make a start in 1902 by retaining the temporary levy of 2s a bushel on foreign grain but exempting Empire imports. The second object would be achieved through the increase in employment once the home market had been secured, but also through the application of the new source of revenue from tariffs to social welfare schemes. This desire for a constructive social policy reflected Chamberlain's long-standing belief that politicians must come to terms with the working class; yet while very many Conservatives were attracted by the commercial advantages of protectionism, only a minority of imperialist–collectivists like L. S. Amery appreciated his wider vision and strategy.

However, this was the first time that the latent Conservative protectionism had been given a lead from the top, and it is no surprise that the bulk of the party fell into Chamberlain's lap after 1903, although ironically he himself was incapacitated by a stroke in 1906.[12] Before the election Balfour had attempted to hold a middle position between the free-traders – 83 out of the 392 Conservative MPs[13] – and the protectionists on the basis of a retaliation policy, the idea being to force concessions from protectionist states and thus restore genuine freedom of trade. However tactically shrewd, this failed to satisfy the emotional forces unleashed on both sides of the debate; moreover, the two wings of the party soon became so unequal that any compromise proved irrelevant. For in 1906 the free-trade MPs shrank to a handful; a few joined the Liberals, some were denied renomination and others perished in the electoral holocaust; meanwhile the 'Whole Hoggers' came to comprise a majority in the parliamentary party. By 1910 the free-trade elements reluctantly accepted that the overriding threat was now the 'socialism' of Lloyd George; and to defeat it they acquiesced in a tariff policy. However, the rallying of the middle classes between 1906 and 1910 failed to compensate for the unpopularity of protectionism with consumers in the country. Thus after failing in the January 1910 election, the Conservatives made frenzied efforts to reconcile their major constructive policy with the voters' apparent dislike of dear food. By December Balfour had decided on a pledge that no tariffs would be introduced without popular approval in a referendum, a tactic that probably produced a few gains in Lancashire, but left the party out of office and still badly divided. Indeed, Conservative realization that by staking everything on the tariff they had opened up the House of Lords, the Union with Ireland and the Welsh Church to radical attack led many to judge the whole campaign a mistake.

Although Chamberlain had regarded a constructive social policy as integral to his strategy, neither Balfour nor Bonar Law, his successor in 1911, felt inclined or able to develop this. Instead they allowed themselves to be impaled upon a narrowly protectionist case closely linked in the public mind with the peers' revolt against Liberal taxation and welfare proposals. This misjudgement lay at the heart of the Conservative dilemma throughout the Edwardian period.

The Crisis of Conservatism

The origins of the notion that a crisis of dire proportions erupted in Edwardian England lay in events during and after the First World War. An apparent concatenation of more or less violent challenges to authority before 1914 does convey an impression of a violent spasm in which the consensus on which the social and political system rested was disintegrating; it is tempting to see Edwardian governments rescued from this prospect by the outbreak of war, which, however, only interrupted the collapse of the economic, social and political pillars of the Victorian world. In order to substantiate such a thesis it would be necessary to demonstrate, first, that the manifestations of violence were in nature and in effect anti-parliamentary; and second, that they were all symptoms of a common underlying malaise, not just a series of coincidental events. This has never, in fact, been done. Moreover, the thesis has suffered from a prevailing assumption, the under-standable result of hindsight, that the Edwardian crisis was a crisis of Liberalism. Yet, as one writer has wisely observed, it would be quite as appropriate to discuss the period in terms of the crisis of *Conservatism*.[14]

The foundations of the Conservative dilemma were electoral, in the sense that the party proved unable to dislodge from power the Liberal–Labour–Irish alliance; and programmatic, in that the split over tariffs simultaneously restored the unity and morale of the Liberals. It was a misfortune for the Conservatives that their attempt to convert the country to protectionism in 1910 coincided with a distinct economic revival. No doubt this was a 'last innings' for traditional British staples like coal and cotton: shipbuilding would have been in grave trouble but for naval rebuilding programmes; and productivity continued to languish. But the buoyancy of the Edwardian economy undoubtedly took the steam out of protection and, incidentally, robbed it of its appeal to labour.

Much the most ominous aspect of the crisis was Ireland. In particular, the appearance of private armies of Ulstermen and Nationalists and the inability of the government after the so-called Curragh Mutiny of 1914 to use the army to enforce its policy in Ireland presented a severe challenge to an elected administration, especially in view of Conservative connivance with the Ulster rebels. Yet there is a danger of swallowing Unionist propaganda of the time. When the party disposed of Balfour in 1911 after his third election defeat, it chose Bonar Law, a leader whose strength was of a brittle kind. Not only did he lack the patronage of the premiership, he enjoyed a status inferior to at least five colleagues in terms of both governmental experience and social standing.[15] Merely a compromise between Walter Long and Austen Chamberlain, Law had little hold on his party at first except as a vigorous debater on tariffs and Ulster. 'I shall have to show myself very vicious, Mr Asquith, this session: I hope you will understand', he told the Prime Minister privately in 1912.[16] His tough 'new style' was appreciated by the party as a welcome contrast to Balfour's elegant but ineffectual philosophizing. They rallied to him, but only because he was doing what they wanted. Pandering to the extremists had led his predecessor to disaster, and, given his failure to dislodge the Liberals from their Home Rule policy, it was likely to achieve the same for Law. By 1914 he and Sir Edward Carson were anxious chiefly to find a way out of the Irish problem without shattering the confidence of their followers.

Bonar Law's defeat was implicit in the Asquith government's persistence. It could not renege on Home Rule without destroying the hold of the Nationalist Party in Ireland, upon whom it depended for its Commons majority. As Asquith put it, 'An ungovernable Ireland is a much more serious prospect than rioting in four counties.'[17] To some extent both party leaders had to consider the question through English eyes, in that both were playing to win the next general election. The Cabinet believed that by offering Lloyd George's ingenious compromise of a six-year exclusion for Ulster from the Dublin Parliament they had shown themselves reasonable to the English voters, who were antagonized by irresponsible Unionist interference with the army, and who viewed with relief the conclusion of the Irish Question at last. Hence they refrained from prosecuting Law, Carson and Captain James Craig since this would only be to rescue them from their dilemma. This impression is corroborated by the Unionists' own realization by 1913–14 that their attempt to stir the English constituencies over Home Rule was falling flat.[18] The Liberals were not to be caught out on a novel and perplexing policy as in 1886; they had long since lost what support they would ever lose on Home Rule.

Whether Bonar Law would have been rescued by a civil war can only be guessed at. However, one can look for connections between the Ulster controversy and the suffragette agitation or the industrial unrest. Comparison with the Women's Social and Political Union (WSPU; founded in 1903 by Emmeline and Christabel Pankhurst) is illuminating, for while the authorities unhesitatingly used the law against the latter they treated the Ulstermen far more circumspectly. This reflected the inability of the women to mobilize comparable support; by 1914 the Pankhurst militants represented no more than a shrinking rump of the women's movement, increasingly isolated from potential adherents among working women and alienated from middle-class sympathizers.[19] Certainly the Pankhursts' antagonism to Labour and industrial action during 1911–14 runs against the idea of a general or connected revolt. The women's violence amounted to sporadic assaults upon property by a handful of activists designed to win publicity, which obscured the fundamentally conservative nature of the WSPU and the movement generally.

As for the wave of strikes, their basic causes lay in the price rises and stagnation of money wages after 1900. When to this was added the 1906 Trades Disputes Act, which overthrew the Taff Vale judgement, and the increase in employment during 1910–14, it is clear that the major restraints on strike action had been removed. Much has been made of syndicalism as an underlying force at this time. While it is true that certain initiatives towards industrial unions and co-operation between unions, such as the Triple Alliance of coal, railway and transport workers, were consistent with a syndicalist strategy, the actual motives were of much more limited significance. Industrial unionism remained exceptional, and co-ordination of strikes was calculated to minimize the damage to the unions themselves; their objects in bringing pressure to bear was invariably to secure from employers recognition and a regular system of collective bargaining, not to undermine the parliamentary system in favour of industrial democracy. If the authorities had adopted a strategy of unmitigated coercion towards labour unrest and had declined to appease workers' demands, it is possible that the strikes could have developed into revolution. But neither government nor union leaders intended to allow this to happen. Although there were several explosive points, notably the shooting of two miners at Tonypandy in 1910 and the arrest of Jim Larkin during the Dublin transport workers' strike in 1913, these were exceptional. Frequently the unions found allies in ministers like Lloyd George and civil servants like Sir George Askwith of the Board of Trade whose object was to induce employers to engage in collective bargaining. In addition the Trades Disputes Act (1906), the Trade Boards Act (1909) and the Miners Minimum Wage Act (1912) demonstrated how Parliament could be used to further the aims of organized labour. The most striking endorsement of the labour movement's parliamentary strategy came in 1914 when all but three of the 63 unions that balloted on the question of a political fund associated with the Labour Party supported the proposal; this was hardly the action of men alienated from the parliamentary process. The leaders remained keen to take what the system offered in representation and legislation, in terms of employment under the Labour Exchanges scheme, and as approved societies under the 1911 National Insurance Act. This tendency to become integrated into the system rather than to undermine it was typical of the pragmatic approach of British trade unionism, which showed no sign of diminishing before

1914. The handful of syndicalists undoubtedly won a certain prominence in 1911–14 when the average union member was moved by the recent decline in real wages; but they in no sense led or directed the working-class movement, and enjoyed a fleeting eminence only while the special circumstances of 1911–14 lasted.

Thus, with the exception of Ulster the Edwardian agitations cannot be represented as effectively anti-parliamentary in nature; nor did they comprise a single or interconnected phenomenon, apart from a little rhetorical and stylistic imitation of the Ulster Unionists by the WSPU and some unions. Each remained a discrete movement. It is significant that the new light thrown on this period by oral evidence has tended further to undermine the apocalyptic view by showing how little sense of crisis the ordinary, obscure person had.[20] This underlines the point that the concept of catastrophe was essentially an upper-middle-class one, and even then, characteristic of the political 'outs' after 1906. Their exaggerated apprehensions about the arrival of independent working men in the Commons representing their class, and the general assertiveness of labour, were compounded by the demagogy of Lloyd George. Not since Chamberlain had attacked those 'who toil not, neither do they spin' in 1885 had they heard the upper class pilloried from on high. 'They are forcing a revolution and they will get it,' declared Lloyd George at Newcastle in 1909, 'the Lords may decree a revolution, but the people will direct it.'[21] However, it was not a revolution but graduated taxation and a modest redistribution of income that he intended; by preaching against the peerage he sought not to foment class conflict but to harmonize the potentially conflicting working class and middle class, for therein lay electoral salvation. Nor are there sound grounds for the old view that the people were in fact bored and disillusioned by the constitutional conflict of 1910. This is to miss the wider social dimension behind the constitutional argument; it also overlooks the actual evidence for turnout among voters: 86 per cent in January and 81 per cent in December 1910. Such figures have rarely been exceeded before or since; moreover, it is particularly striking that the second election of the year should have produced such a response, for a reduction of 4 per cent was the unavoidable result of the staleness of the register by December. The elections of 1910 can hardly be seen as other than notable indications of popular involvement in the parliamentary process. Though Bonar Law might claim that there were things stronger than parliamentary majorities, the experience of the Edwardian years belies such alien sentiments. Unlike the opposition who stumbled from one problem to the next, the government confronted each obstacle and ultimately imposed their strategy by the strength of representative democracy. They played the parliamentary game with indications of conviction because within the rules it was a game they invariably won.

CHAPTER SIX

Edwardian Progressivism

British Liberalism is not going to repeat the errors of Continental Liberalism.
. . . Let Liberalism proceed with its glorious work of building up the temple
of liberty in this country, but let it also bear in mind that the worshippers at
the shrine have to live.

David Lloyd George, Swansea, 1 October 1908

Origins of the New Liberalism

The history of Victorian Liberalism has often been written as though it is
to be equated with *laissez-faire*. Clearly much of its drive derived from an
industrial middle class bent upon levelling the privileges of the aristocracy
and eliminating restrictions upon individual enterprise. Yet 'economic liberalism' was always distinct from party Liberalism, whose primary achievement was political democracy in Britain. In practice the period from the
1830s to the 1880s was one of continuous experiment with state intervention
in the economic and social affairs of individuals whose actions were re-
strained in the interests of the community; in the process the Victorians laid
the foundations for the huge central bureaucracy of the twentieth century.
Particularly at the municipal level, where Liberalism was often the party of
expenditure and interference not of retrenchment and abstention,[1] the
notion gained ground that certain economic functions, ranging from water
and gas to parks and libraries, were better performed by the community
than by the private entrepreneur.

Moreover, the Liberalism of the Victorians was as subject as most creeds
to reinterpretation by its adherents; and the 1880s and 1890s constitute
an especially important phase of this kind. Reinterpretation for politicians
did not, however, imply any repudiation of essentials. The primary concern

of Liberalism continued to be liberty defined by the law. But confidence in the virtues of the free play of individual energies and talents was qualified by knowledge of the consequences and also by an appreciation that the terms of competition must not be too unequal; where they were, the state might legitimately adjust them, even though infringing the rights of some individuals in the process. In the last 20 years of the century the elements of interventionism waxed steadily stronger, and not only in Liberalism. Why was this so? Undoubtedly the perceived difficulties of the British economy, now facing severe international competition and shrinking profits, eroded the attractions of industrial growth as a panacea for society's ills. Whereas in, say, 1851, it seemed likely that another generation of economic expansion would absorb unemployment and poverty, by the 1880s few could be so confident. Far from being eliminated, poverty, as the investigations of Charles Booth and Seebohm Rowntree suggested,[2] had remained at a depressingly high level. The consequences of advanced industrialism were minutely observed in London, where society seemed to fragment into social classes by residence. Aware of the strains on their society, adherents of Liberalism tended to reaffirm their basic object of maximizing liberty as a means to individual moral improvement; some, like Herbert Spencer, sought to achieve this by advocating a reduced role for the state; others, like T. H. Green, the Oxford philosopher, urged a greater and more positive use of interventionism. What is important historically is that by the 1900s it was those who thought along Green's lines who had come to typify active political Liberalism in Britain.

Thus, by the turn of the century an impressive body of academics and publicists were reinterpreting the Liberalism with which they had grown up. Green himself was no more than a representative, not the most advanced, of new Liberal thinking in the 1880s: while accepting the capitalist system as broadly consistent with social good, he justified state legislation in carefully limited areas to maintain the conditions for individual initiative. D. G. Ritchie, the collectivist radical, took a more emphatic view of the state as a positive agent of improvement. L. T. Hobhouse, the sociologist and journalist, argued that freedom was devoid of meaning to the victim of uncontrolled free enterprise, and urged collective action for mutual advantage. J. A. Hobson, perhaps the best-known propagandist for the 'New Liberalism', urged that the state should maintain a minimum standard of life for all its citizens and operate certain economic functions for the community as a whole. Hobson was most conscious of the link between social and political changes; the idea that 'politics had anything to do with industry or standards of living' was, he noted, somewhat novel. In his view, Victorian politicians had endeavoured to keep social questions out of politics by agitating alternative issues; but by 1900 the broad divide in politics corresponded increasingly with the social divide, with possession and property on the Conservative side.

However, thinkers are not usually politicians, and in Britain especially there is great scepticism about the connection between the realm of ideas and actual historical events. Yet links there were, if only in the shape of the 31 Balliol College men who sat in the Parliament of 1906, four in the Cabinet. Take the apparently unpromising example of H. H. Asquith, whose ministerial career spanned the Gladstonian and the Edwardian phases. Tutored by Green at Oxford, Asquith was a typical politician in being rather uninterested in abstract ideas and not apparently afflicted by a social conscience. Yet he acquired an enduring scepticism about the traditional party platitudes and was unencumbered by ideological inhibitions such as *laissez-faire*; it was he who, as Chancellor of the Exchequer 1906–8, initiated the financial and social radicalism that antagonized traditional Liberals. However, the 'New Liberals' were usually more intellectually curious than Asquith. A typical example is Herbert Samuel, who combined writing on Liberalism, investigation into social conditions and active party politics. Like William Beveridge and R. H. Tawney, he had been at Oxford at a time when young undergraduates were urged to go out and discover why so much poverty existed in British society, and did so. Characteristically the first stop was work in London's East End, often at Toynbee Hall, before moving on to wider political activity. For those who chose to operate through the party system the intellectual basis of their action was twofold. First, it showed the continuity of Liberal thought, a matter of some importance to men like Samuel and Hobhouse, anxious not to repudiate their traditions. Second, it demonstrated the existence of a real alternative, both theoretically and practically, to 'socialism', to which many young middle-class men would otherwise have been driven. As it was they enjoyed a fruitful relationship with the Fabians, particularly Graham Wallas, the Webbs and Ramsay MacDonald. Indeed, much of what in twentieth-century Britain is termed 'socialism' is no more than the 'New Liberalism' of 1900.

The starting point for the 'New Liberals' of this period was a belief that, in the past, liberty, while a proper concern of Liberals, had been too narrowly defined in terms of legal, political and religious liberties; yet it was now apparent that for most men the chief restraint upon their liberty was economic or social in nature. Thus the individual's material welfare should be of equal concern to the state as his moral condition. In this way the New Liberalism came, for many, to imply drastic social reform. In the words of J. M. Robertson MP, 'Laissez-faire is not done with as a principle of rational limitation of state interference, but it is quite done with as a pretext for leaving uncured deadly social evils which admit of curative treatment by state action.'[3]

However, New Liberals looked beyond the symptoms of distress to the underlying distribution of wealth. Did a redistribution of resources threaten the traditional Liberal commitment to private property? The reformers were clear that while the state ought not to infringe what rightly belonged to individuals, what did not rightly belong was a different matter. Wealth was so often the result not of individual enterprise but of community development that society could properly differentiate between earned and unearned income, and tax the latter more heavily for the benefit of the community at large. The death duties introduced by Sir William Harcourt in 1894 were a harbinger of this theme in radical policy which increasingly divided the Liberals from Conservatives. The best target for taxing the 'unearned increment' was, of course, land. For as a result of the expansion of towns and the needs of local authorities, the price of urban land increased spectacularly in the nineteenth century. To radicals, land was a monopoly of the privileged class which they had historically sought to 'free'. To levy a toll upon its increment, therefore, could provide resources for the state while leaving private ownership intact and stopping short of confiscation. In this way land reform provided both a practical expression for popular radicalism and a valuable bridge between Cobdenite traditions and New Liberalism.

New Liberalism also challenged the notion that taxation was inherently or necessarily an evil, and argued that the budget might become a positive instrument of social policy. This view was to be translated into practice by Asquith and Lloyd George as Chancellors in the period 1906–14, though Harcourt had pointed the way. Their policies offended orthodox economic wisdom, which held that the uneven distribution of income in the community was both necessary and beneficial since its concentration in the hands of a few meant it would be channelled into future production; the effect of diverting it to the masses whose expenditure was held to be essentially non-productive would be detrimental to business activity. Now death duties were defended on the grounds that they tapped resources not normally available for investment. However, Liberals, notably J. A. Hobson, began to dispute the conventional financial assumptions fundamentally. Hobson claimed that the uneven distribution of income actually hindered the economy because it deprived the mass of the population of the capacity to consume goods, while diverting the surplus into the hands of those who merely generated more goods for which there was an insufficient market. In short, the real weakness – *underconsumption* by the masses – could be remedied by a reallocation of purchasing power through taxation and social welfare; rising demand would stimulate economic growth. Underconsumptionist arguments enabled the New Liberals to justify their emphasis on social reform as a means of reducing the waste and inefficiency in society, for such expenditure need not be regarded as a cost or burden upon the productive economy. Thus the Edwardian governments were fortified by an assumption that one might helpfully raise the level of expenditure according to the condition of the economy and employment. It is not entirely accidental that in the 1920s Liberals were more inclined than their rivals to espouse Keynesianism.

Yet the New Liberals had to face the political implications of their ideas. Did not a programme of sweeping social reform and graduated taxation amount to a class policy at variance with the party's traditions? Some, like Hobhouse, frankly urged that the improvement in the conditions of the working class was now so overriding a priority that no party that claimed to represent national and not sectional interests could ignore it. Samuel argued that since any expenditure that raised the material condition of the poor was in the interests of the wealthy, the latter should bear their share of the cost. This notion of a fair contribution from those best able to pay became a standard defence much favoured by Lloyd George during the controversy over his 'People's Budget' in 1909–10. By this stage the New Liberal orthodoxy held that the state must accept a wide responsibility for the welfare of the people financed by limited redistributive taxation; it broke with the traditional fondness for retrenchment and individual property rights; and it offended against the Gladstonian belief that taxation should not be a means of marking out different social classes or types of wealth. Even in Gladstone's time these principles had been infringed in special cases such as Irish land reform; and retrenchment had been gradually abandoned out of expediency. However, the New Liberals, fortified both by principle and by necessity, pushed financial and social policy unapologetically into its twentieth-century mould. Thereby they increasingly distinguished the Liberal Party from the Conservatives, who still favoured indirect taxation, objected to graduated taxation on principle, and preferred to restrict government expenditure to basic administrative functions.

Between the 1880s and the First World War the New Liberalism gradually came to occupy the mainstream of Liberal politics. The critical decade was the 1890s, when the 'New Liberal' title began to be applied to various groups and individuals such as the Rainbow Circle, whose members included Samuel, Hobson, Charles Trevelyan, J. M. Robertson and Percy Alden. They developed both a social policy and a political strategy of co-operation between middle- and working-class radicalism, such as that pioneered by the Progressives on the London County Council. By the turn of the century Hobson, Samuel, Robertson, Hobhouse and Charles Masterman, all prolific writers, had generated a coherent revision of their creed and a programmatic refurbishment for the party (see Guide to Further Reading). In 1896 the Rainbow Circle produced its own *Progressive Review*, but it enjoyed much wider support from radical editors such as

C. P. Scott (*Manchester Guardian*), W. H. Massingham (*Daily Chronicle*), J. A. Spender (*Westminster Gazette*), and most importantly, A. G. Gardiner of the *Daily News*, the cheap radical paper widely read by provincial activists which consistently promoted an alliance of Liberal and Labour forces.

Tension inevitably existed between the New Liberals and orthodox stalwarts among backbench MPs, local party chairmen, and municipal politicians who formed the warp and woof of the local party fabric. Impatient with existing organizations like the NLF 'merely reiterating its approval of the Newcastle Programme', New Liberals sought more direct approaches to power. Fortunately for them the electoral defeats of the 1890s and the withdrawal of some wealthy patrons left a vacuum for younger radicals: 1886 had prepared the ground; and by the 1900s those employers and other wealthy men who remained in the Liberal camp had generally accepted the need to come to terms with Labour.[4] Indeed, among the keenest advocates of old-age pensions, graduated taxation and state intervention were industrial magnates like William Lever and Sir John Brunner (the leading manufacturers of soap and chemicals, respectively), who along with the Cadbury and Rowntree families continued to finance the party up to 1914. Industrialists like James Joicey, the north-east coal owner, found radicalism excessive and quit the party; adherents of strict *laissez-faire* like Richard Holt, the Liverpool shipowner, remained MPs until 1918 but had dwindled in numbers and influence. After 1900 the older generation of social radicals – Sir Charles Dilke, Francis Channing, Sydney Buxton – were joined by younger men in Parliament. In London, where the field was wide open, Charles Masterman, Christopher Addison, T. J. Macnamara and Percy Alden gained seats; here as elsewhere Herbert Gladstone played a vital role as chief whip (1899–1905) in placing radical candidates in winnable seats and often assisting them financially. In the North a similar role was filled by Charles Trevelyan, himself elected in 1899, who helped to place Samuel, Robertson and Runciman in radical industrial constituencies. The steady transformation of the personnel of Liberalism grew into a flood in 1906, for of the 401 Liberals then returned to the Commons, 205 had never sat in the House before.

This change was somewhat obscured by the aftermath of the South African War; none of the Liberal Party's leaders acted as midwife to the New Liberalism as Lloyd George, Asquith and Churchill did after 1906. Indeed, the war divided radicals like Hobson and C. P. Scott, who condemned British policy, from men like Trevelyan and Samuel. After 1902 Liberal rhetoric was diverted towards such tempting targets as education, 'Chinese Slavery' and free trade, and propaganda took the negative line of reversing Toryism. This inevitable attempt to exploit the government's difficulties culminated in the revivalist campaign of 1906. However, this obscures the underlying trend. Examination of the 1906 campaign material shows the general commitment of candidates to old-age pensions, graduated taxation, poor law and land reform, which was soon reflected in backbench impatience for legislation after the election. The governments of Campbell-Bannerman and Asquith turned out to be more radical than the campaign rhetoric had suggested. Retrenchment had been a useful stick with which to beat the Conservatives but it was rapidly abandoned by the incoming administration. Asquith's 1907 budget proved to be a key point in the overthrow of financial orthodoxy. He asserted the principle of income differentiation by retaining the rate of tax on earned income at 9d while raising that on unearned to 1s in the pound; he made compulsory personal declarations of every class of one's income; he forced the Treasury to accept the idea of a super-tax, and insisted that social reform obliged governments to plan for rising expenditure several years ahead. The widespread support for his non-contributory pensions scheme and the measures for the feeding and medical inspection of schoolchildren is some indication of changed attitudes in Britain; the individual was no longer seen as wholly responsible for his family's welfare; nor, significantly, was there any question of disfranchising the recipients of the new benefits as the recipients of poor relief were. In short, the strength of the Liberals' position was that although they were reformers they were not dangerously in advance of opinion in the country. Similarly, Lloyd George's 1911 National Insurance Act reflected Victorian self-help traditions in incorporating the contributory principle and by involving existing friendly societies and insurance companies in the scheme. His celebrated budget of 1909 embodied elements of redistribution in the shape of the £10 income tax allowance for children under 16, the super-tax on incomes above £5,000, the additional 2d on unearned income, the extra rates for death duties and the modest levies on land values; although the purchase tax increases on tobacco and spirits did bear upon poorer families. Of the £17 million deficit that Lloyd George intended to make up by these means £8 million arose from pensions, only £3 million for Dreadnought building, and the rest from a fall in revenue as a result of reductions in trade. The emerging strategy for dealing with an economy subject to serious unemployment involved three items: the Labour Exchanges of 1909; the attempt to replace the income workers lost through ill health, unemployment or old age; and third, the Development Commission. In the 1909 budget the Chancellor set aside £200,000, with a promise of any surplus accruing to the Exchequer, for use by the Commission on experimental farming, forestry, rural transport and land reclamation. This reflected the thinking of radical industrialists in favour of state investment in those sectors of the economy that private enterprise failed to finance. Because fairly full employment returned in 1910 little use was made of the Development Commission, but it signified governmental

MEASURE FOR MEASURE.

FIRST TOPER (*discussing Mr. Asquith's Licensing Bill*).
'*DOES HE WANT TO STOP OUR BEER?*
SECOND TOPER. *NOT LIKELY. IF HE DO, 'OW'S 'E GOIN'*
TO GET THE MONEY FOR OUR OLD AGE PENSIONS?'
Punch, or the London Charivari, 12 February 1908

intention to regulate expenditure as and when the state of the labour market made it desirable.

By the time of the campaigns on the 'People's Budget' in 1909–10 Lloyd George had reduced the New Liberalism to a tangible, popular form. He based his case squarely on a free-enterprise economy under free trade. In this system, he contended, Liberalism represented the interests of those who created wealth, that is, employers and workers, who were in conflict with a parasitic landowning class and their political agents. He often delighted to point to the wealth of the Liberal candidates on whose platforms he spoke, noting how much extra they would pay in taxation. What distinguished such men from their opponents, he claimed, was their willingness to shoulder a fair share of the cost of national defence and social reform, thereby proving the sincerity of their concern for the people's welfare, and also demonstrating that the Liberal Party was not bent upon the confiscation of wealth. Thus Liberalism served the vital function of unifying the social classes who worked for a living by seeing fair play between them in the national interest. The Liberal Party was the most efficacious vehicle for the working classes because it harnessed to their cause large sections of the middle class who would be frightened into reaction by a party based solely on labour. Here lay the political and intellectual rationale for the New Liberalism.

The Politics of the Pact 1903–1914

Though never an outstanding politician either as orator or administrator, Herbert Gladstone became a pivotal figure, particularly in the decade after he became chief whip in 1899. As heir to his father's 'Little England' views he greatly appreciated the rapprochement of Labour and Liberal forces as a result of the South African crisis. To Gladstone it was axiomatic that nothing of significance divided Liberals like himself from the mainstream working-class politicians: all parties, he believed, tended to develop a left, centre and right: the emergence of organized labour was thus essentially a natural expression of radical Liberalism, whose inclusion under the Liberal Party's umbrella was both logical and necessary if progressive Liberalism was to be strengthened against the imperialist right now so much in evidence. To this end the Campbell-Bannerman–Morley–Gladstone leadership had declined to support an official Liberal candidate of imperialist views at the Mid-Lanark by-election of 1901 in favour of Bob Smillie, the ILP nominee. When another seat fell vacant at Dewsbury in 1902 they attempted, unsuccessfully, to secure the nomination of a working man, Sam Woods. In calling in the workers to redress the balance of middle-class Liberalism the party leaders clearly risked alienating their own local activists; however, without a large measure of common sentiment between Liberal and Labour forces in the country Gladstone's initiative in 1903 in seeking terms with Ramsay MacDonald, Secretary of the Labour Representation Committee, would not have been practicable at all. This appeared to be the lesson of three by-elections at this time. When the safe Liberal seat at Clitheroe fell vacant in 1902 it was filled unopposed by David Shackleton, a trade unionist of essentially Liberal convictions standing for the LRC, because of the approval of local Liberals. Similarly Liberals abstained at Woolwich, where they were weak, on behalf of Will Crooks (LRC), who gained the seat from the Conservatives. But it was the Barnard Castle by-election in 1903 following the death of Sir Joseph Pease that caused the greatest stir, for in a three-cornered contest the seat went to Arthur Henderson (LRC) by 47 votes. Although a Liberal defeat, the election's significance lay in demonstrating the vitality of Liberal–Labour sentiment among working-class voters. For Henderson won because he enjoyed the tacit support of the Liberal leaders; because as Pease's former agent he was well known locally as a *Liberal*; and because the local Liberal association blundered by nominating a tariff reformer at a time when free-trade sentiment had been sharply aroused. Henderson, sound on free trade, was thus the best Liberal available. For Gladstone this underlined the dividends to be won by Liberal–LRC co-operation. For the elections did not indicate that the LRC was about to sweep the country in its own right. The Labour leaders appreciated this, though socialist activists often did not; at Norwich in 1904, for example, an ILP candidate obtained only 13 per cent while the Liberals gained the seat. This rubbed in the point that if socialists were unlikely to succeed as socialists, Labour candidates of Liberal views would flourish.

For MacDonald this was by no means an unwelcome reading of events. His own inclinations and record as a candidate led him to seek accommodation with the Liberals, but to do so from a position of strength. However, in 1900 the newly launched LRC had been too weak. Only 376,000 union members had been affiliated (at only 10s per thousand) by 1901, although delegates representing 546,000 had voted for the creation of the LRC, and TUC membership was over three times this figure. However, the notorious Taff Vale judgement of 1901 which made the Society of Railway Servants, and therefore any union, liable for the financial losses arising from strikes, transformed the situation by stimulating union leaders to extend their political influence. By 1903, 861,000 had been affiliated, the fees had been raised, and a fund established to pay a £200 salary to MPs elected under LRC auspices, thereby enabling the National Executive Committee to exert a degree of control for the first time.

As a result of these developments MacDonald found himself able to impose his strategy upon a labour movement now anxious to obtain rapid representation in Parliament, while at the same time he had something to offer Gladstone – not only votes, but the LRC's financial resources. This latter was important, for hitherto a labour alliance had always appeared a financial liability to the Liberals. Thus by 1903 MacDonald and Gladstone had identified a common interest in victory over a crumbling Conservative government and the danger of jeopardizing it by splitting the Progressive vote. Later, when under attack from his own party, MacDonald tried to minimize his role in the pact by arguing that no formal bargain had been struck. But this was only because neither could guarantee to withdraw candidates in specific constituencies and both feared that a public announcement would provoke criticism. Gladstone's private papers show that the pact was very deliberate; MacDonald made great exertions to kill Labour candidatures in Liberal seats not covered by the pact,[5] and, though he could not control the socialist societies he often emasculated their efforts by denying them the LRC ticket. For Gladstone it was relatively easy to secure a clear run for the LRC in derelict seats in Liverpool, Lancashire or Birmingham, and not difficult to share candidatures in double-member constituencies such as Preston, Bolton, Leicester, Derby and Newcastle, particularly as this was frequently marginal or Conservative territory. As a result 31 of the 50 LRC candidates in 1906 were unopposed by Liberals.

In retrospect the pact appeared an unnecessary mistake for the Liberals in that 24 of the 29 LRC MPs won by virtue of Liberal withdrawals, while the Liberals' own 401-seat landslide would not have been materially smaller in the absence of co-operation. However, in 1903 this had not been obvious. Labour had saved Gladstone a lot of money and tied the Conservatives down in all constituencies. Moreover, since the Labour members were for the most part 'sober, earnest Liberals', they reinforced the progressive drift of Liberal politics admirably. The significance of this strategy is underlined by the availability of an alternative during 1903–5. For Chamberlain's tariff campaign and the consequent hounding of free-trade Conservatives from their constituencies after 1903 presented the Liberals with a golden opportunity to reverse the losses of 1886 by clawing back the centre-right. They largely succeeded in doing this among the electorate, at least temporarily, as their victories in southern and middle-class seats show. Yet how much of the personnel and programme of the rebel Conservatives should be absorbed? Those Conservatives who expected free trade and retrenchment to provide an adequate bridge between them and the Liberal Party were mistaken, as Trevelyan reminded Winston Churchill:

> The Liberal Party is not a free trade party. It is only satisfied with Free Trade as an economic base to work from. . . . The whole raison d'être of present day Liberalism is constructive reform. . . . What I want to know is how much common ground can you find with reforming Liberals on economic and social questions? . . . the reform forces in the party are vastly stronger than ten years ago and I am certain will never check themselves for the sake of a few Tory votes.[6]

As a result Liberal–Conservative co-operation in 1906 was limited to a few exceptional cases; 12 MPs crossed the floor before the election, including Churchill and J. E. B. Seeley, who won election in Manchester and Liverpool, respectively; others, like Arthur Elliott (Durham City) and Richard Cavendish (North Lonsdale), enjoyed a free run from the Liberals. But the pact with Labour pre-empted any general arrangement; Lancashire, the centre of free-trade Conservatism, was already the scene of the most widespread application of the Gladstonian strategy.

Faced with the bleak prospect of an overwhelmingly radical House of Commons the tactics of the 157-strong Conservative opposition were initially rewarding. By employing their majority in the Lords to reject or emasculate legislation of concern to Liberal pressure groups, especially on education, licensing and land, they shrewdly maximized discontent within the government's ranks. For while traditional radicals became exasperated at the failure of their huge majority to overawe the peers during 1906–8, the social radicals resented the time wasted on bills that were clearly doomed. This feeling was exacerbated by unmistakable evidence that the peers were studiously accepting measures like the Trades Disputes Bill and the feeding of schoolchildren for fear of antagonizing the workers. So long as the government ploughed the issues that left the country as a whole unmoved it deprived itself of the option of a successful dissolution and exposed itself to attack from backbenchers and Labour for neglecting social questions; the loss of two by-elections to Labour at Jarrow and Colne Valley in 1907 appeared to underline the point. Thus so long as the Conservatives applied their destructive tactics judiciously they could oblige the Cabinet to soldier on while indirectly encouraging Labour to loosen its ties; by redividing the radical forces the opposition could reasonably expect to return to power at an election around 1911–12.

Unhappily for the Conservatives they had not thought out their tactics quite so rationally, nor did they apply them so precisely. So much emotion, fear and pride underlay their politics that they failed to resist the provocation offered by Lloyd George in 1909. There are now no real grounds for thinking that the Chancellor deliberately prepared his budget with a view to its rejection by the peers. His object was rather to use the budget as a Trojan Horse that would gain legislative entry for such items as land and licensing reform, rebuffed in ordinary bills.[7] Yet when he perceived in the rising antagonism of the Tory Party the possibility of a first-class constitutional–social controversy he grasped it quickly. His budget also raised two matters of longer-term significance. The first was not the land taxes themselves but the consequent provision to undertake a valuation of all the land in the country, a necessary preparation for an effective radical policy for the land. To avert this more distant threat many peers felt obliged to reject the immediate proposals, modest as they were. Secondly, the increase in revenue demonstrated that social reforms could be paid for without abandoning free trade, and thereby knocked away a central prop of the tariff reform argument. Hence the particular prominence of protectionist Conservatives in the move to reject the budget. However, no one could be sure how far the Liberals would capitalize politically on the financial breakthrough, nor how soon. For the present their proposals were not self-evidently revolutionary in character; extra taxation could be justified by the need to pay for pensions, which the opposition dared not oppose because they were too popular, and the Dreadnought programme for which they had loudly clamoured. In throwing out the budget, therefore, the Tories placed themselves in a dilemma exacerbated by the weight of constitutional precedent that heavily favoured the government. Had they stuck to their original tactics and left the budget alone, the Liberals would have borne the unpopularity for higher taxes, which fell upon all sections to some extent, without any immediate compensation. Instead, by assailing the innovations with great passion they invested them with a revolutionary significance, thereby burnishing brightly the progressive credentials of the government in the eyes of labour – the key to continued power. They enabled the Liberals to claim, with some plausibility, that their opponents were a lot of rich men trying to evade their taxes, and were intending to renege on old-age pensions now that they realized the cost, a point which, significantly, Conservative candidates tried to refute at length during the 1910 general elections.

The opposition did derive some immediate gain from the constitutional crisis in that they obliged the Liberals to go to the country twice during 1910 and, in the process, removed the overall Liberal majority of 1906. However, the circumstances of the elections so greatly reinforced the 1903 pact as to keep the Conservatives more firmly out of office. Many a northern town that had not seen the landed aristocrat of radical demonology for years was now treated to the spectacle of elderly peers gracing the platforms of Conservative candidates; even Lord Curzon let slip the typically arrogant aphorism that 'all civilisations are the work of aristocracies', a remark that was endlessly repeated by gleeful radicals. The effect of all this on Labour was of crucial importance. It could not but welcome the government's initiatives as a step in the right direction; if the peers condemned the budget as red socialism MacDonald had no desire to dispute it. The Labour leaders' only doubts, justifiable ones, were whether the Cabinet would shirk the ultimate task of curbing the powers of the Lords permanently. Driven both by sentiment and by tactical necessity, therefore, Labour threw its efforts more strongly behind the Liberals, even to the extent of reducing its candidates from 78 to 56 between the January and December elections. Thus the triumph of Lloyd George's tactics in 1910 was a dual one; he dictated the terms of the debate by forcing the Conservatives into wild negativism and leading Labour into loyal acquiescence.

The Chancellor's achievement was not simply a short-term rhetorical coup, however. The New Liberalism had not begun with the budget of 1909, nor did it end with it; for the Cabinet could not cease to deliver social reform for fear of disappointing expectations aroused in the country. This undoubtedly made for certain difficulties in the short run. For example, the 1911 National Insurance Act seemed to threaten so many vested interests[8] that the opposition exploited their fears effectively in the by-elections of 1911–12. By 1913, however, when the insurance benefits began to be paid out, the credit redounded to Lloyd George. Indeed, for all their vehemence in public some Conservative leaders had seen from the start that national insurance would only consolidate the Liberals' reputation, and by 1913 the most they could do was to promise to improve, not to repeal it. In order to counter the negative siege mentality that fell over the Conservative Party in the reaction from protectionism, prominent Conservatives like F. E. Smith established the Unionist Social Reform Committee in 1912. Yet it proved difficult to shift the party from its obsession with Ireland in these years. Perhaps there was truth in Bonar Law's characteristic comment that if the country wanted social reform it would not vote the Conservatives back into office. This prospect was enhanced because every stand the Conservatives took tended to compound their alienation from the bulk of the working-class vote which was what kept the Liberals in power. It is easily forgotten that even the Ulster question, on which the Labour Party remained as consistently nationalist as the government, helped to reinforce the electoral pact when it showed signs of breaking down. Hence the futility of a Conservative strategy that united their opponents instead of dividing them.

Despite this it is sometimes assumed that the New Liberalism was bound to destroy the Liberal Party by alienating the middle classes, or alternatively, that fear of a middle-class reaction would bring reform to a halt, thereby losing the working-class vote. The electoral evidence bearing on this will be considered in chapter 7. Here it must be noted that the idea of a termination of social radicalism in terms of policy and programme around 1911 is largely theoretical; it is scarcely borne out by the empirical evidence. The budget of 1914 projected a record national expenditure of over £200 million; Lloyd George continued pushing out from the bridge-heads already established. Income tax relief for children was doubled; he introduced a graduated tax rising to 1s 4d in the pound on earned income over £2,500; super-tax now became payable at £3,000 instead of £5,000, and at steeper rates rising to a maximum of 2s 8d; and the scales for death duties were also increased to a maximum of 20 per cent on estates over £1 million. Also in 1914 a further instalment of radical social measures were introduced, including government grants for local maternity and child welfare clinics, £4 million in loans for local authority house-building, compulsory school meals, and proposals for minimum wages in agriculture.

These unmistakable signs of the government's intention to stick to its new course are all the more impressive in view of the criticism it continued to provoke in some quarters. Throughout 1906–14 there was evidence of middle-class protest against higher taxes and especially rates, which helps to explain Conservative municipal successes on the basis of ratepayers' revolts. Some industrialists also articulated their misgivings at the trend in policy; Alfred Pease, for example, explained his refusal to appear on a Liberal platform in Cleveland by his dislike of the 'disposition to multiply laws and restrictions. . . . The idea that the State can take from one class and give to other classes and take the place of individual enterprise is a very corrupting one.'[9] There was also a discernible feeling that too much legislation bestowed special advantages on labour. In 1908, for example, there had been pressure from colliery owners and shipowners, reflected in Cabinet by Runciman, against minimum wages for miners as tantamount to 'truckling for miners' votes'.[10] However, the Liberal Party had already parted company with the Yorkshire coal owners without, it transpired, impairing its grip on the Yorkshire constituencies. So long as sums of £5,000 and £10,000 at a time were donated by Lever and Rowntree the party did not need to fear the loss of the remaining Gladstonian businessmen.

However, the criticism made it all the more important not to neglect issues of traditional concern to Liberals: hence the time devoted to Welsh disestablishment, Home Rule and the franchise in 1911–14, in a shrewd attempt to balance the novel and the traditional elements in the programme. By 1912 the Cabinet was also well aware of the desirability of relieving the burdens of the lower ranks of the middle classes, especially by sparing local rates from some of the cost of education, roads and the poor law.[11] This was one of the considerations that drove radicals and Lloyd George 'back to the land' in the last years of peace.

The Land Campaign, launched in October 1913, has often been misunderstood as an anachronism. Yet seen in all its ramifications it amounted to a drastic extension of social radicalism. Lloyd George capitalized on the widespread agreement that the previous 30 years had seen a disastrous weakening of British agriculture with serious social, economic and strategic consequences. His Rural Land Enquiry showed, as did official statistics, that 60 per cent of agricultural labourers earned only 18s or less per week, and that despite a reduction in the labour force housing conditions remained appalling since few landowners were now willing to invest in new cottages. Not only was it difficult for the opposition to deny the underlying case for action, but in addition land was an ideal means of arousing the enthusiasm of Liberals of all shades. In any case, research into the distribution of wealth in Britain has undermined the old assumption that after the industrial revolution the chief source of great wealth was industrial in character; as late as 1900 the large fortunes in Britain were still to a remarkable degree concentrated in land, urban landholdings, and commerce.[12] In taking land as a target, therefore, the radicals were by no means mistaken. Finally, they expected to derive a considerable short-term electoral advantage in the shape of extra votes from labourers and farmers in many rural seats in the West and North narrowly held by Conservatives. This potential was underlined by the by-election successes scored in 1912 and 1913 by candidates who concentrated on land reform to the exclusion of all else (E. G. Hemmerde at N.W. Norfolk and R. L. Outhwaite in the urban scat of Hanley).

While Lloyd George publicized the campaign, much of the detailed preparation was undertaken by Runciman at the Board of Agriculture. Realizing that labourers tolerated low wages through fear of losing their cottages, Runciman planned for the construction of 90,000 houses by the state, each with up to one acre of ground to give the labourer a measure of independence. This was to be undertaken by a new Ministry of Lands and Forests which would also enjoy compulsory purchase powers to acquire undercultivated and waste land, thereby bypassing the county councils which had proved useless for the purpose. It was to appoint commissioners to fix the price of land and wages boards to fix fair minimum wages in each locality; farmers faced with higher wages would be able to appeal to tribunals for revision of their rent.[13] The government had already adopted such methods to regulate wages in the sweated industries under the Trade Boards Act and for the miners; the extension of the idea of establishing a 'minimum standard' restored the initiative in social policy to Lloyd George. Invited to join his Land Campaign, MacDonald and Keir Hardie admitted privately that land was the economic bedrock of reform, but feared losing the initiative to the Liberals.[14]

By the end of 1913 an equally important urban dimension had emerged partly due to the vociferousness of land taxers in Parliament, who wanted Lloyd George to offer precise policies for the towns. They urged in particular a national tax on land values so as to enable the government to relieve local rates; and also the rating of site values by municipalities instead of the levying of rates on the value of buildings and improvements. Lloyd George was evidently keen to respond to the pressure for relief of small property-owning ratepayers and small businessmen. He could claim with some justification that state-financed social policies had the effect of reducing the pressure of the poor on local rates; from 1911, for example, paupers were made eligible for old-age pensions. During the winter of 1913 he committed himself to a measure of site value-rating and promised the Town Tenants League compensation for small businesses faced with exorbitant demands by landlords for renewal of their leases. However, radical policies could not be implemented quickly – land valuation would not be completed until 1916. By 1914, therefore, Lloyd George had agreed to offer additional rate support from national taxation.

In short, the Liberals embodied in the Land Campaign moves to shore up their exposed middle-class flank and simultaneously strengthen their standing with a number of working men. The expediency of this strategy is borne out by the Conservative reaction to it. After 1910 Austen Chamberlain had warned his colleagues that unless they could offer alternative policies on land they would not win back the urban support they had lost. The Tory party chairman, Arthur Steel-Maitland and the chief whip, Lord Edmund Talbot, believed it wise to avoid provoking controversy and thereby giving Lloyd George more credit over land reform. Indeed, Leslie Scott MP, of the Unionist Social Reform Committee, offered Conservative co-operation over his legislation if only he would not 'Limehouse' the landlords again.[15] But with the opposition at a disadvantage the Chancellor pressed on with the campaign, and there are few grounds for thinking that the New Liberalism had been checked on the eve of war in 1914.

Edwardian Labourism

With hindsight the evolution of the Labour Party is easily depicted in terms of a deterioration in ideological purity as the socialist inspiration of Keir Hardie gave way to the pragmatic leadership of Ramsay MacDonald. However, studies of both men and of the Labour movement generally have entirely revised such a picture. MacDonald was remarkably consistent in his views and objectives, while Hardie differed from him in style and temperament rather than in ideology or programme. The careers of both were characterized by a history of radical Liberalism and a practical grasp of electoral collaboration combined with persistent advocacy, vehement in Hardie's case, of independent political action by working men. As with most Edwardian Labour politicians the mainspring of their action lay in the social condition of working people, but the form taken by it was moulded by the ideas and institutions prevalent in the 1880s, notably the chapel, the trade union and the municipal council. A survey of the reading of the 29 Labour and 24 Lib–Lab MPs elected in 1906 revealed that hardly any had drawn their ideas from explicitly socialist sources; only two mentioned any knowledge of Marx, and only two had read the *Fabian Essays* of 1889. Much more widely read were Henry George (author of *Progress and Poverty*, 1879, a bible for land reformers), John Stuart Mill and John Ruskin, along with the Bible, Dickens, Scott, Bunyan and Tennyson. Keir Hardie, while by no means unaware of Marxism, made no serious study of it; he found attractive the notion of the historic struggle of the working class and the prospective degeneration of capitalism prior to a co-operative, classless society; but he had no patience with the idea of a revolutionary overthrow of capitalism or of the growing immiseration of the workers. For him the object of political action in the British context was to take advantage of the available means for improving the lot of working people. This meant enacting social reform; adopting allies outside the Labour movement; and (what was most distinctive) increasing the direct representation of the working class by working men – in short, 'Labourism'.

The economic ideas of Edwardian Labour were an amalgam of three main strands. First, they shared many of the Victorian assumptions about the economy, particularly the necessity for wage levels to be regulated according to the price commanded by the products of labour in the market. They shared enthusiastically the Liberal loyalty to free trade. This is a striking indication of the basic orientation of the movement, for while cheap bread had obvious attractions, free trade had not been an obviously desirable policy to the Chartists; nor would it have been a natural policy for a party seriously contemplating socialism. Indeed the Edwardian tariff reformers and right-wing apostles of National Efficiency were a good deal closer to advocating an economy operating on socialist lines than most Labour politicians. In addition the Labour Party espoused the radicals' predilection for graduated taxation and using the unearned increment of land to finance social reform. Henry George's *Progress and Poverty* seems to have stimulated Hardie as much as it did the young Lloyd George. 'Land Nationalization' was also used loosely as shorthand for compulsory purchase powers for local authorities; in 1892 Hardie referred to 'nationalizing the land by taxing land values' much as a radical Liberal would have done. Finally, Labour politicians adopted a range of trade union demands for employers' liability and workmen's compensation for accidents, a shorter working day to spread the available employment, amendment of the Truck Act, and recognition of unions by employers. There was nothing here that looked out of place in the manifestos of Liberals in the 1890s.

Before the First World War the Labour Party never accepted state ownership and operation of industry as a general principle, and even limited forms of control like tariffs were automatically ruled out. Neither MacDonald nor Hardie had more than the haziest notion of the administrative implications of nationalization, or of the bureaucracy necessary for a comprehensive system of welfare services. Indeed the only grounds that some writers have found for justifying the description of Hardie as a 'socialist' is his advocacy of the nationalization of coal mines. Yet the significance of this was quite limited. He believed simply that state control would facilitate the achievement of union objectives, the eight-hour day and minimum wages, which he had found from experience in the Ayrshire coalfield difficult to win. In short, coal nationalization was not part of an analysis of how industry should be run, but a special case. Consequently while the Edwardian Labour Party undoubtedly had coherent ideas about economic affairs they were hardly *distinctive*; and any description of Labour as socialist must be modified by the fact that its 'socialism' had little basis in economics. At this time it meant essentially humanitarianism and fraternity, a generous-spirited belief in co-operative action for and by the disadvantaged which owed its inspiration to Christianity as much as to politics. The same tendency led Labour towards a pacific, anti-imperial, Gladstonian approach to international affairs. The South African War threw Labour and the radicals together in common outrage; hence J. Bruce Glasier of the ILP could say of John Morley, of all people, that he 'stood for much that [was] essential to a socialist state and international peace'.[16] In denouncing Kitchener's 'methods of barbarism' in 1901 Campbell-Bannerman rekindled the torch of Gladstonianism, and this was taken up in 1914 by MacDonald, who stood thereafter as the heir to a common tradition.

While Hardie was not a systematic thinker, MacDonald gave Labour a more coherent, historical framework, and, perhaps confusingly, he employed the language of socialism. Not only did he have no time for the class struggle; he never conceived of Labour as merely a working-class party. Not for nothing had he been secretary to a Liberal MP and an active member of the Rainbow Circle in the 1890s (as well as a member of the SDF in 1885, the Fabian Society from 1886, and the ILP from 1894). For him all that was wrong with the Liberal Party was that it had served its historic function and might obstruct the coming of the New Liberalism and socialism. Initially the ILP and later the LRC were seen by him as successors to the Liberal Party which would eventually take the form of a more effective alliance of middle-class and working-class radicalism. If there was a difference between him and Hobson or Hobhouse it was that he was trying to recruit the middle class and they the working class. Though MacDonald spoke of socialism it was not for him a policy but a vision that would evolve gradually rather than spring from the ruins of the present system. Society's progress in that direction was perceptible in small steps; when Balfour's government adopted the Unemployed Workmen's Bill in 1905, for example, this was worth having because it drove politicians closer to admitting an obligation to provide work or maintenance for every worker, and thus made Labour's own Right To Work Bill seem much less utopian after 1906. Despite his talk of socialism, MacDonald's own economic observations largely involved condemning the dead weight of landownership and rent upon industry rather than an economic critique of capitalism. However, it has rightly been urged that the virtue of presenting socialism as an evolutionary growth from existing society lay in giving Labour its own objective which, if vague, did not frighten those who had to be won over; MacDonald's strength was a capacity to convey to radicals a reassuring sense of continuity and parliamentarianism and to Labour a comforting belief in ultimate, inevitable triumph.

Although MacDonald's approach clearly owed a great deal to his early Fabianism, it is significant that the Labour Party never availed itself of the full Fabian programme before 1914. As a forcing house for investigation and ideas the Fabians inspired the respect of both Liberal and Labour politicians, but their claims to direct influence have been regarded as exaggerated by historians. The Fabian Society and the Labour Party were kept apart partly by the sheer elitism of the former, anxious not to waste time trying to build a new party based on what it saw as intellectually destitute trade unions. As a result, from the late 1880s much of the Fabian effort had been diverted into municipal affairs, especially in London under the umbrella of the Progressives. The Fabian approach showed little of the humanity of the typical working-class politician but more of the hardheadedness of the National Efficiency school. Fabians believed that labour exchanges would facilitate the identification of shirkers; they criticized health insurance because it was wasteful to subsidize the sick; they welcomed the 1902 Education Act, which was generally condemned by Labour leaders; most of them supported the South African War and lacked sympathy with Home Rule and even with women's suffrage. They thus remained for long a middle-class pressure group largely isolated from the sentimental radicalism inherent in the working-class movement. However, this relationship began to change during the last two years of peace. Faced with the refusal of Lloyd George and Churchill to be guided by Fabian remedies as laid down in the Minority Report of the Royal Commission on the Poor Law, and impressed also with the potential strength of the labour movement as demonstrated in the strikes of this period, Sidney and Beatrice Webb recognized that Labour could serve both as a vehicle and as a power base; the fruits of this were garnered during the war and afterwards.

Thus, what seems indisputable and central in the emergence of Labour as a separate party is not a novel ideology so much as a struggle by politically conscious working men to achieve direct representation in Parliament. Consequently the MPs followed a course barely distinguishable from the Lib–Labs in the Commons before 1914 in that they threw their weight behind the Liberal causes and made a distinctive contribution only on strictly trade union issues. Hardie, despite the vehemence with which he sometimes attacked the Liberals, departed from the Lib–Lab approach only in seeking more seats for working men and in declining to take the Liberal whip. For most of the LRC MPs returned in 1906 the pact was perfectly consistent with long-held attitudes; they regarded the LRC as no more than a continuation of earlier efforts to elect working men with a view to defending their interests in parliament; few expected or wanted to transform the LRC's role as a separate pressure group into that of a governing party.

However, events conspired to eliminate the distinction between the Lib–Lab and the LRC contingents to the advantage of the latter. In the early 1900s the leading working-class politicians, John Burns, Ben Pickard, Thomas Burt, Richard Bell and Charles Fenwick, were Lib–Lab in sympathy but all elderly figures who had reached or passed their peak. Burns, the impassioned strike leader and SDF militant of the 1880s, had graduated by way of Progressivism on the London County Council and a parliamentary seat at Battersea from 1892 to an honoured position in the Liberal Party and cabinet rank in 1905. It is significant that when invited by Hardie to lead the LRC in 1903 Burns found it unattractive. Indeed before 1906 only two of the LRC MPs, Hardie and Crooks, stuck strictly to the independent line; Henderson, Bell and Shackleton became more or less identified with Liberalism. In 1903 there had thus been some danger that Lib–Lab forces would persuade the LRC conference to allow the affiliation of bodies like the National Democratic League, which would have stifled the independence of the LRC and kept it as a Liberal pressure group. However, attempts of this kind only provoked support for the ILP proposal for an extra levy on the unions to finance new candidatures. Yet in 1906 the Lib–Labs still numbered 24 in the Commons; but Burns, the symbol of the Liberal/working class alliance, spent his declining years complacently enthroned as President of the Local Government Board, an object of attack by Hardie for his reluctance to initiate remedial measures for unemployment. Meanwhile changes in leadership and militancy led the Miners Federation to seek affiliation to the Labour Party in 1908, a step that virtually ended Lib–Labbery as a separate body. Insofar as the miners were incorporated into the Labour Party they tended to undermine still further its political coherence and minimize its distinctiveness from Liberalism.

Although specific aims and policies had been avoided in 1900 at the foundation of the LRC, nonetheless the typical Labour candidate of the 1900s offered the electorate a battery of proposals including the eight-hour day, reversal of the Taff Vale decision, employers' liability, old-age pensions, poor law reform, the feeding of necessitous schoolchildren, taxation of land values, free trade, Home Rule, nationalization of mine royalties, mines and railways, payment of MPs, curtailment of the powers of the House of Lords, and universal suffrage. There was little in this that was not acceptable to the New Liberals, or to Gladstonians for that matter. Nor was this merely a tactic to win Liberal votes. The annual conference in 1906, for example, apart from reaffirming many of the items already listed, pledged itself to the Local Veto, condemned the Education Act of 1902, and welcomed the entente with France provided it was not used against Germany. It is only fair to note that at least one delegate protested at 'tinkering with the out-worn pledges of the Liberal Party'. Occasionally, as in 1908, a resolution calling for the socialization of industry slipped through without debate, apparently because it was not taken seriously enough to warrant the time, and served to encourage the socialists.

In the Commons. MacDonald demonstrated a clear idea of the appropriate tactics. 'Governments are not afraid of socialist speeches,' he observed, 'they are very much afraid of successful criticism in detail.'[17] This approach enabled Shackleton and MacDonald to play a useful role, especially during 1906–8. The government proved quick to adopt Labour bills on trades disputes and the feeding of schoolchildren, and compromised on the Workmen's Compensation Bill. For Campbell-Bannerman, Labour thus helped the government in the direction in which it was already going. But it is not the case that the pensions scheme was the result of by-election losses to Labour in 1907, for their introduction had been carefully planned well beforehand by Asquith. What is true is that when Labour members voted for motions critical of the Cabinet on such matters as pensions they usually did so in company with larger numbers of Liberal backbenchers, all impatient to drive the Cabinet in the same direction. Unemployment provided the best issue on which Labour could distance itself from the Liberals by means of its Right to Work Bill and Hardie's dramatic interventions at Burns's expense. However, by 1908 the initiative was passing to the Liberals; after 1909 there were only occasional revolts by a handful of Labour members over the Insurance Bill and women's suffrage. Once the Liberals had lost their overall majority in 1910 Labour became nearly as reliable in the division lobbies as the Liberals: moreover, after the 1909 Osborne Judgement (which checked the rights of trade unions to use their funds for political purposes) Labour felt the need of cabinet help in changing the law. Eventually this concession was granted in 1913, and in 1911 Labour obtained payment of members.

However, co-operation between the parliamentary party and the government naturally provoked fierce criticism in the movement, notably from Victor Grayson, who had been elected as an Independent Socialist in 1907 and declined the Labour whip; there flourished a mutual antagonism between Grayson and the other Labour MPs who felt relieved at his defeat in 1910. A more persistent critic, the dockers' leader Ben Tillett, waged campaigns to make the parliamentary party responsive to conference, and published a famous pamphlet *Is the Parliamentary Party a Failure?* in 1908. Yet the leadership of MacDonald, Hardie, Snowden and Henderson – 'softly feline in their purrings to Ministers', as Tillett put it – always carried the conference with them; from 1909 when he became chairman of the parliamentary party, MacDonald went a long way to establishing himself as leader in a traditional sense, and to confirming the right of MPs to make party policy.

The Workers and State Welfare

The evidence of so much common ground between Edwardian Liberals and Labour has led to the abandonment of the old assumption that a working-class party was bound to outflank its rival. However, some questions have rightly been raised about the new orthodoxy, especially from the perspective of working-class reactions to policy innovations. For example, even if social reforms were welcome it is likely that workers placed a *higher* priority on such issues as wage rates and unemployment. Are we justified in assuming that reforms were generally poular in view of the suspicion with which they were often regarded in the Victorian period? Clearly this is a large subject still under analysis, but several general comments can be made. First, reactions do seem to have varied according to the type of reform; the unmistakable enthusiasm for pensions did not extend to the medical inspection of schoolchildren, or to the Children Act, which allowed children to be taken into care. Second, some innovations which were initially greeted with scepticism won acceptance in time. Unemployment insurance is a case in point. Another example is the labour exchange scheme. Workers were reassured that they were under no obligation to accept jobs at below union rates of pay or jobs that involved strike-breaking, and by 1914 three times as many men were being placed in employment as in 1909. Third, the importance placed upon government intervention almost certainly varied within the working class. Lower-paid men, for example, were more likely to value health insurance because they often had no adequate existing scheme of self-help. Similarly unskilled men, and of course many women workers, had a greater interest in state intervention to fix minimum wages since they lacked the bargaining power to defend themselves; in chain making, for example, the effect of the government's Trade Boards Act was to raise wages by approximately 50 per cent by 1913. It seems clear from the Land Campaign that Lloyd George was alive to the implications of all this.

CHAPTER SEVEN

The Electoral Struggle 1906–1914

Nothing has hampered our movement in the country more than this false idea of independence, that only Labour or Socialist votes should be given to Labour or Socialist candidates. It is humbug.

Ramsay MacDonald, *Labour and Electoral Reform* (1914)

The traditional view of Edwardian politics reflected the assumption that an industrial and urbanized society such as Britain inevitably develops a class-based pattern of politics. Influenced partly by continental perspectives and by political science, many historians accepted that a middle-class parliamentary party such as the Victorian Liberals could not ultimately accommodate a working-class electorate or adapt to the expansion of state interventionism in social and economic affairs. Hence the emergence of a political system polarized between two large parties, one representing property and the other representing labour, which appeared to have been reached by the 1950s, when the Conservatives and Labour won an overwhelming share of the vote. However, during the 1970s historians became sceptical about this approach. Studies of Liberal social and financial ideas suggested, as we have already seen, a capacity for adaptation to change between the 1890s and 1914. Detailed examination of the Labour Party revealed the limited nature of its support, thereby casting doubt on assumptions that by 1914 it was displacing the Liberals. Of course, several counter-arguments to this revisionist view soon appeared, as we shall see. It is important to stress that the debate depends partly on how one interprets the evidence provided by parliamentary elections; but it also involves evaluating the importance of one type of evidence against other sources.

The revisionist approach to Edwardian politics draws on the concept of 'Progressivism' and involves several related propositions about political change in this period. It argues that during the quarter-century before 1914 a synthesis of Liberalism and socialism gained credence on the left, and that the emergence of a generation of professional politicians helped accelerate the movement of the Liberal Party away from its localized Victorian roots into a national, reformist movement. These changes restored the intellectual vitality and the popular appeal of Liberalism, and the appearance of the Labour Party was less a means of outflanking the Liberals than a reinforcement to its Progressivism. From this it was argued that the 1906 Liberal landslide was not simply a traditionalist revival based on free trade and Nonconformity, but part of the long-term shift towards more novel ideas and a general widening of the agenda of British politics away from constitutional questions to social and economic issues. A shift was taking place away from the community and religious basis of voting which had characterized the nineteenth century towards the class-based pattern of the twentieth century; this change occurred substantially *before* the First World War rather than after it, as had usually been assumed. Thus the party divide already reflected fundamental social cleavages. Of course, it could not be disputed that the extent of the Liberal victory in 1906 reflected extra support from voters influenced by tariff reform, education and other traditional radical issues. However, by 1910 their importance had diminished, as was demonstrated when the Liberals lost middle-class and county constituencies in the south of the country. Yet the withdrawal of some middle-class support still left the Liberals in power because of their retention of the working-class vote, especially in areas such as Lancashire and London where the Conservatives had formerly been strong. Indeed, in 1910 the Liberals were still gaining working-class seats not won in 1906. Thus, the 'Progressive' interpretation amounts to more than a claim that the Liberals survived the Edwardian elections; it suggests that they were adapting to the basic trend in modern politics on the basis of an economic appeal to the working class. The wider implication of this was that there was nothing inevitable in the rise of Labour as a governing party.

The Containment of Labour

If the general election of 1906 had stood in isolation as the last Liberal victory before the war it might be regarded as a freak; it would remain difficult to explain why a party capable of winning 400 seats was in fatal decline, but the suspicion would still be there. However, the two elections of 1910, though less spectacular, corroborated the view that 1906 was part of a long-term change. Comparison with 1892, the only late Victorian Liberal victory, shows that by 1910 the Liberal–Labour forces had a higher share of the vote and won more working-class seats.

TABLE 7.1   *General elections 1892–1910*

	Conservative		Liberal		Labour		Irish Nationalist	
	% vote	Seats	% vote	Seats	% vote	Seats	% vote	Seats
1892	47.0	314	45.1	272	0.3	3	7.0	81
1895	49.1	411	45.7	177	1.0	0	4.0	82
1900	51.5	402	44.6	184	1.8	2	2.5	82
1906	43.6	157	49.0	401	5.9	29	0.6	83
Jan. 1910	46.9	273	43.2	275	7.7	40	1.0	82
Dec. 1910	46.3	272	43.8	272	7.2	42	2.5	84

But what was the relative position of Labour and the Liberals in this period? Although the evidence is restricted by their electoral pact, it is sufficient to indicate relative strength and a trend. Twenty-four of the twenty-nine Labour victories in 1906 were achieved in the absence of Liberal opposition under the pact; but the party's standing appeared to enjoy a significant boost in 1907, when it gained seats in by-elections at Jarrow and Colne Valley at Liberal expense. However, 1908 seemed to mark a turning point in that the introduction of old-age pensions, followed by Lloyd George's 1909 budget, restored the initiative to the government. Thereafter Labour experienced losses down to 1914. In January 1910 the party had eight losses and three gains, for example. This left Labour with 40 members, simply because the affiliation of the Miners' Federation to the party in 1909 meant that technically the Lib-Lab M.P.s took the Labour whip; this gave Labour 45 before the election and 40 after. Naturally, the controversy with the House of Lords over the budget aroused the common feelings of Liberal and Labour voters and made the politicians anxious to avoid splitting the Progressive vote in 1910. Many leading Labour figures, including MacDonald, Hardie and J. H. Thomas, were elected in two-member constituencies in co-operation with Liberals and on the strength of some Liberal votes. As a result they kept the pact going despite an expansion of local organization; Labour ran 51 candidates in 1906, 78 in January 1910, and fell back to 56 in December.

Significantly, amongst the voters the electoral co-operation appeared to work even more effectively in 1910 than in 1906, as is impressively demonstrated by the cohesion of the vote in two-member seats. If either Labour or Liberal supporters had been unhappy with the pact they could have shown this by simply casting a single vote, but a negligible number did so (see table 7.2). The vast majority split their votes, that is, they used them

A WAITING GAME.

LABOUR PARTY (*to* CAPITALIST). 'THAT'S ALL RIGHT,
GUV'NOR. I WON'T LET HIM BITE YOU.
(*Aside, to dog.*) WAIT TILL YOU'VE GROWN A BIT,
MY BEAUTY, AND YOU'LL GET A BIGGER MOUTHFUL!'
Punch, or the London Charivari, 29 January 1908

for a Liberal *and* a Labour candidate. Thus, within the confines of the
pact Labour did well; but outside it the party enjoyed little success. In the
35 three-cornered contests in the two elections of 1910, its candidates
came third in 29 cases, second in 6 and first in none. Attempts to break

TABLE 7.2   *Leicester: general election voting December 1910*

Result	Crawshay-Williams (Lib.)	13,238 elected
	MacDonald (Lab.)	12,998 elected
	Wilshere (Con.)	7,547
'Plumpers' (cast *one* vote)	Crawshay-Williams	728
	MacDonald	547
	Wilshere	7,245
'Splits' (cast *two* votes)	Crawshay-Williams/MacDonald	12,316
	Crawshay-Williams/Wilshere	194
	MacDonald/Wilshere	108

TABLE 7.3   *Gateshead parliamentary elections 1906 and 1910*

1906		January 1910		December 1910	
Labour	9,651	Liberal	6,800	Liberal	8,763
Conservative	5,126	Conservative	6,323	Conservative	5,608
		Labour	3,572		
	4,525		477		3,155

out of the pact against Liberals met with failure except in two cases (West Fife and Gower) where the Conservatives withdrew in Labour's favour. In addition, the Liberals displayed a capacity to recover seats lost in by-elections (Jarrow and Colne Valley), and even some such as Gateshead that had been conceded to Labour in 1906 (see table 7.3). Clearly, the independent Labour vote was, as yet, too small to elect many M.P.s without the addition of Liberal support.

On the other hand, the 1910 elections were fought in fairly special circumstances. Whether Labour's advance resumed during the last few years before the war is less obvious, and historians have scrutinized the by-elections of 1911–14 for evidence, some seeing a decline and some an improvement in Labour's performance. Mid-term by-elections offered excellent opportunities for the Opposition to make gains at the government's expense, but it was the Conservatives rather than Labour who took advantage. Vacancies in industrial constituencies coincided with severe industrial unrest, which might have helped Labour, while the Liberals encountered unpopularity over their National Insurance Act in 1912. After its pact with the National Union of Women's Suffrage Societies in 1912 Labour also benefited from an influx of voluntary election workers in the by-elections. In spite of this, however, Labour came bottom of the poll in each of the fourteen industrial seats it contested, polling 10–20 per cent in six and

TABLE 7.4   *Labour's share of the poll in Huddersfield 1906 and 1910 (%)*

1906	1906 by-election	January 1910	December 1910
35.2	33.8	31.6	29.0

20–30 per cent in eight. The Liberals retained almost all their seats, though several of the marginal ones were lost to the Conservatives. Even in seats dominated by mining, fewer than half of the coal miners supported Labour.[1] The best results were in places such as Holmfirth, a Yorkshire mining seat, where the Labour poll rose from 14.9 per cent in January 1910 to 28.2 per cent in June 1912, but this fell short of the performances in 1907. The worst results occurred in the four seats defended by Labour, all of which were lost, one (Bow and Bromley) in a straight fight with the Conservatives and the others in three-cornered contests where Labour came last in the poll (Hanley, Chesterfield, and N. E. Derbyshire). Taking the Edwardian years as a whole, one can say that Labour gained ground sharply in the early 1900s, reached a peak around 1906–7, and fell back slightly thereafter. This is best illustrated in the, admittedly few, constituencies where a succession of contests indicate a trend (see table 7.4). On this showing, there seem to be few grounds for seeing Labour as poised to displace the Liberals by 1914.

The Franchise Factor

Nonetheless, impressive as the evidence of parliamentary elections seems, it may be flawed. After all, approximately four out of every ten men were still excluded from the electoral register, and it was not until the reforms of 1918 that 95 per cent of adult males voted in Britain. Some historians have discerned in this structural change the key explanation for Labour's ability to overhaul the Liberals after 1918 and correspondingly the reason for their inability to do so before 1914. The implication is obviously that a large reservoir of working-class support existed that could not be tapped by Labour without a drastic reform of the voting qualifications.

This is such a compelling way of explaining the major fluctuations in party fortunes that it requires careful examination – especially as it suffers from fundamental defects. The interpretation rests on two assumptions: first, that the pre-war non-voters were disproportionately working class, and second, that the working-class non-voters differed from the working-class voters in ways that made them more disposed to support Labour. However, both assumptions are implausible.

The electoral register of 1911, which was less accurate than usual, excluded some 42 per cent of adult men, comprising 12 per cent who failed to meet one of the qualifications and no less than 30 per cent whose names failed to appear because of the complications of the registration process and the residence requirement for householder and lodger voters.[2] Thus, most of the non-voters were not under *permanent* legal disqualification, but reappeared on the register from time to time as their circumstances changed or as the parties improved their efforts at registration. Similarly, those on the register could easily drop out following, say, a change of address which interrupted their residence qualification. In short, the composition of the electorate fluctuated, and the differences between voters and non-voters are easily exaggerated.

The next question is: what sort of people were able to vote? Certain categories of people are known to have been disqualified, notably those who received poor relief, those renting rooms of below £10 annual value, those who moved frequently, perhaps because of inability to pay rent, and interrupted the 12-month residence requirement, those who lived with their parents and could not be 'householders', servants residing with their employers and soldiers living in barracks. However, these causes of disqualification were not essentially connected with social class but more with age, housing tenure and marital status. Most men qualified as household voters, a status they usually achieved by marrying and setting up a separate household, typically around the age of thirty. Conversely, single men in their twenties were more likely to live with their parents or to be in lodgings and thus not to qualify for the householder franchise. This affected *middle-class* men, who were more likely to marry late, just as much as working-class men. It has been estimated that of the 4 million disfranchised men, 2.5 million were unmarried, including 450,000 middle-class bachelors.[3] In short, the system discriminated against younger and unmarried men in *all* social classes, and if there was a bias in the electorate it is unlikely to have been large enough to constitute a significant handicap to the Labour Party.

This still leaves the question of the political leanings of the disenfranchised working men. Those who worked as servants and as soldiers, for example, were assumed by politicians to be pro-Conservative either out of deference or personal interest. Certainly they were isolated from the kinds of influences that fostered Labour voting. Similarly it is doubtful whether the poorest families, who were so vulnerable to patronage, charity or the poor law, were likely to develop pro-Labour views in this period. The Irish, a community whose level of enfranchisement was low, were inclined to back the Liberals. Indeed, contemporary Labour politicians seem to have recognized the difficulties they faced in many urban constituencies. As Ramsay MacDonald put it: 'In places like the Potteries [of Staffordshire] where poverty and degradation is of the blackest kind, the Labour Party is bound to be weak.'[4] By contrast, Labour found it easier to establish its organizations in areas where working-class communities were more stable, skilled, literate, unionized and politically aware. In these circumstances the limited extent of the electorate may not have been a drawback at all. This impression is corroborated by the attitude taken by the non-Conservative parties towards franchise reform. Although Edwardian Labour supported full adult suffrage in principle, it never regarded this as a priority or as the key to immediate success. The party appreciated that at this early stage in its development it could not effectively appeal to the whole of the working class; indeed, even in the 1920s and 1930s this proved beyond the party's power. In 1911 the Liberal whips sought advice from their regional federations as to the likely effect of one-man-one-vote by means of simplified registration and a shorter residential qualification. On the whole the local organizers believed this would give them a significant advantage, especially if combined with the abolition of plural voting, but some exceptions were made for some of the Yorkshire constituencies where it was felt that *younger* voters might give Labour an advantage.[5] Generational differences may well have been the most promising aspect of electoral reform from Labour's point of view. For example, it seems on the face of it unlikely that the 45 per cent of miners who lacked the vote would have held different opinions from the very pro-Liberal 55 per cent who were enfranchised, unless one recognizes that among the minority were some young men who may have been less committed to Liberalism than their fathers and more inclined to socialism.[6] This apart, the franchise factor cannot be considered a valid explanation for Labour's electoral weakness before 1914.

However, there is another dimension to the franchise question: the *local government* franchise. It can be argued that the evidence of municipal elections undermines the Progressive thesis in several ways. Most obviously, the losses suffered by the Liberals in pre-war local government could be taken as symptomatic of an underlying decline at the grass roots, in spite of the party's success in national government. Moreover, Labour advances in municipal elections threatened to drive the Liberals into local alliances with Conservatives, thereby undermining their parliamentary strategy and preparing the ground for the widespread Conservative–Liberal collaboration in local government between the wars. However, the evidence requires much more study than it has so far received. Both before and after 1906 the government of the day lost seats to the Opposition in local elections, which suggests we are looking at ephemeral protests and indications of improving morale amongst the Conservatives rather than evidence of a fundamental Liberal decline.

Also, the municipal electorate differed from the parliamentary one; it was *less* democratic in that it excluded many more working men, but it

TABLE 7.5   *Labour's municipal record 1907–1913*

	Candidates: 'Labour & Socialist'	SDF/BSP	Elected	Net loss/gain
1907	274	66	86	10
1908	313	84	109	−33
1909	422	133	122	23
1910	281	49	113	33
1911	312[a]	32	157	78
1912	463[b]	95	161	42
1913	442	52	196	85

Notes: [a] +23 undefined   [b] +38 undefined.
Source: Labour Party Archives.

also included women who were ratepayers. Consequently, the concerns of small property owners, shopkeepers and the lower middle class, upon whom local rates pressed hardest, loomed large in local elections. In contrast to the parliamentary voters, most of whom paid no income tax, municipal voters often regarded financial retrenchment as a great virtue, which obliged all the parties to take economy very seriously. As a result all three parties behaved differently at local level.

Above all, Labour's progress in local government was surprisingly limited (see table 7.5). Though the number of candidates elected did increase, they represented a tiny fraction of the opportunities in Edwardian local government. On the other hand, as the table indicates, municipal elections offered scope for socialists to drive a wedge between Labour and Liberalism and thereby go some way to challenging the parliamentary strategy. How successful this was remains uncertain. The nomination of anti-Liberal candidates often had the effect of alienating local trades councils and dividing the Labour organization. When, as in 1908, Labour lost seats this was ascribed to the effect of socialists in antagonising moderate Labour voters and to collaboration between Liberals and Conservatives.[7] Whereas in places such as Bradford Liberal–Labour clashes were traditional, in towns such as Bolton the two parties managed to co-operate in both parliamentary and municipal elections. This makes generalization very difficult.

Regional Political Culture

For a long time discussion about the rise of Labour and the decline of Liberalism revolved around the timing of the shift towards class-based politics; but during the 1990s many historians became increasingly doubtful about the importance accorded to social class as a key determinant of party loyalty. As research turned to the inter-war period it became obvious that even after working men had won the vote, Labour continued to be very slow to win majority support and that working-class communities behaved very differently in different parts of the country. Conservative support amongst the working class remained so extensive and persistent that the importance accorded to class appeared to be an exaggeration or even a misrepresentation. Hence historians became very critical of sociological explanations for voting behaviour, especially before 1914, which appeared to make the connection between class and voting too mechanical and the participants in the process too passive. In fairness, it should be recognized that political scientists themselves felt obliged to qualify the centrality they had formerly given to class in the face of an apparent breakdown of class loyalties during the 1980s and 1990s. As a result, in recent years historians have focused on the process by which political parties built up their support in specific communities, in effect returning to local and regional studies. A regional approach is especially helpful in evaluating the strength of the 'Progressive' strategy before 1914, and in explaining the long-term evolution of the Labour Party in Britain.

Some critics of the 'Progressive' thesis always argued that it reflected developments in only limited parts of the country. Lancashire was an obvious example, partly because of the role of exponents of the New Liberalism such as C. P. Scott and enlightened Liberal entrepreneurs such as William Lever and John Brunner, as well as Winston Churchill from 1904 to 1908. Also, the traditional Liberal weakness in Lancashire facilitated electoral co-operation with Labour which produced no fewer than 13 Labour M.P.s in the region and delivered 47 of the 62 seats to the alliance in 1906. London can be seen in similar terms, for it already enjoyed a tradition of Liberal–Labour co-operation through the Progressives on the London County Council, and had a concentration of New Liberal writers and politicians including Charles Masterman, Sydney Buxton, Christopher Addison, Willoughby Dickinson and T. J. Macnamara. In London, too, the pact reversed the previous Tory dominance by returning 49 Liberals out of 58 in 1906, though there were only two Labour members.

At the other end of the spectrum stood Scotland, where Labour's organization remained more independent and hostile to the Liberals. In fact in 1906 the Scottish Liberals regarded all but two of the eleven Labour candidates as socialists and the pact never really operated there.[8] Interestingly, Labour did win seats at Glasgow Blackfriars and West Fife, but there are indications that the party drew support from the Conservative and Unionist side as much as from the Liberals, and that in the absence of a Labour candidate the party's supporters were less willing to vote Liberal.

The withdrawal of Unionist candidates at West Fife, N. W. Lanark and Leith seemed to benefit Labour. Yorkshire is another region where, because the Liberals had retained their strength even through the late Victorian period, there was more resistance to a pact with Labour. As in Scotland, the ILP had branches and often fought the Liberals, especially in West Riding towns such as Bradford and Leeds. However, the pact did operate and gave Labour representation at Halifax and East Leeds. Moreover, Yorkshire's traditional Liberalism was changing and the region boasted some of the leading exponents of New Liberalism – Charles Trevelyan, Herbert Samuel and Walter Runciman. In Wales, despite the presence of Lloyd George, politics still revolved around traditional Nonconformist issues, which minimized the need for a change of personnel or policy among the Liberals. During the last few years of peacetime there were increasing tensions in the South Wales coalfield between Liberal owners and socialists, and here, most of all, the pact may be said to have been breaking down.

But this was not typical. In north-east England, for example, where Lib–Lab traditions also remained strong, Labour enjoyed co-operation from the Liberals in Sunderland, Newcastle and Darlington. Significantly, when three-cornered contests arose in mining seats such as Houghton-le-Spring and N. W. Durham in 1913–14, the Liberals retained their lead. But despite the presence of some elderly trade unionists of Liberal loyalties (Thomas Burt, Charles Fenwick and John Wilson) and local Liberal employers (Palmer, Joicey & Furness), the personnel of Liberalism was changing by 1914 as the older men retired. This underlines the point that some regions had advanced further towards the 'Progressive' pattern than others according to the strength of traditional Liberalism; but almost all seemed to be moving in the same direction as the older men were replaced by New Liberals, often from outside the region. The most striking industrial region was the Midlands, where the coalfields of Derbyshire, Nottinghamshire, Leicestershire and Warwickshire were notable for their profitability and relatively good industrial relations; this made for political collaboration between owners and workers and continued Liberal strength. The region attracted advanced radicals such as Leo Money, R. L. Outhwaite and Edward Hemmerde, as well as progressive business Liberals such as Arthur Markham and Josiah Wedgwood. Labour seemed particularly weak here, losing several seats in by-elections between 1911 and 1914 when it stepped outside the pact. All the indications are that the working-class electorate was content with the progressive brand of politics.

A regional perspective also reminds us that research on the Labour Party has been unduly concentrated on the Liberal and Socialist traditions of the movement as epitomised by pioneering figures such as Keir Hardie. The point is encapsulated by the 1900 election in which Hardie spent most of his time as a candidate at Preston which, with its working-class Tory tradition he failed to win; but he was elected in Merthyr, where the prevailing Nonconformist–Radicalism suited his outlook far better. For all his attributes, Keir Hardie was cut off from a good deal of working-class life and opinion – a dilemma which goes a long way to accounting for the slowness of Labour's advance as a national party. Some important areas of the country were dominated by a Tory working-class political culture, notably Birmingham and the West Midlands, much of Lancashire, the East End of London, parts of Clydeside and the naval towns. In some of these – such as Birmingham, where both the Liberal and socialist traditions were too weak – Labour made no significant progress before 1914 because the well-entrenched and populist Conservative machine mobilised both middle- and working-class support. On the other hand, Labour *could* adapt to this political culture. Many of the successful Edwardian Labour leaders, including J. H. Thomas, J. R. Clynes and Will Thorne, actually held Tory views – pro-monarchy, pro-empire, hostile towards foreigners and immigrants, and militant Protestant; they also reflected the social life of the working class better than Keir Hardie in championing the working man's enjoyment of beer, the music hall, gambling, boxing, horse racing, and scurrilous newspapers. They articulated a brand of socialism which was not 'improving' or critical of working-class life and which could combine state intervention in the economic sphere with nationalism in external affairs. This was why Blatchford's paper, *The Clarion*, always sold so much better than Hardie's *Labour Leader*.

It is becoming clear that the traffic of ideas and personnel between Labour and Conservatism was greater than has traditionally been recognised. In Lancashire many ILP members came from a Tory background; and after the war many upper-class Conservative men and women were recruited by the party. Before 1914 the best evidence for adaptation to Tory political culture comes from parts of Lancashire, where the Liberal tradition had been comparatively weak. The success of right-wing Labour candidates such as John Hodge and J. R. Clynes in the Tory working-class seats at Manchester Gorton and Manchester North-East in 1906 and 1910 were early signs of a breakthrough which occurred in other areas at intervals up to 1945.

The Unions, MacDonald and the Pact 1911–1914

Despite the evidence of the parliamentary elections there are grounds for regarding Labour as close to a breakthrough by 1914 in that it was beginning to mobilise its potential support from the trade union movement. This may sound surprising since the unions had been among the founders

TABLE 7.6   *Ballots held under the 1913 Trade Union Act on the establishment of a political fund*

Union	For	Against	Turnout (%)
Boilermakers	4,752	4,404	14
Carpenters and Joiners	13,336	11,738	
Amalgamated Society of Engineers	20,586	12,740	25
National Union of Railwaymen	102,270	34,953	
Miners' Federation	261,643	194,800	81
Amalgamated Weavers	98,158	75,893	89
Gasworkers	27,802	4,339	22

of the LRC in 1900. However, many unions had been slow to affiliate and they gave only modest financial backing. Part of the problem was that so many rank-and-file members were Liberals and Conservatives. In 1909 one such worker successfully challenged his union's right to use its funds for political purposes. It was tempting for the government to allow the resulting 'Osborne Judgement', as it was known, to stand.[9] Not until 1913 was this overthrown in favour of a new system, which permitted trade unions to establish a political fund provided their members first approved in a ballot and provided that individuals were allowed to contract out of the political levy. Subsequently, most unions voted to create a fund, though large minorities opposed it. Although there was not sufficient time to collect large sums before the outbreak of war, this system proved to be an enormous long-term advantage for the Labour Party. Total membership of TUC-affiliated unions increased to 2.6 million in 1914, and in practice few members opted out of the political levy, even if they did not support Labour. And whereas previously each union's political contributions had come from general funds and thus been in competition with other calls on expenditure, now substantial sums could be built up for the sole use of the party. Taken in conjunction with the introduction of a £400 salary for all M.P.s in 1911 this left Labour in a much stronger financial position by 1914.

By 1918 the extra resources encouraged Labour to run many additional candidates, but even before this development some local activists had placed the party leaders under pressure to expand. In the by-elections between 1911 and 1914 the pact with the Liberals was so frequently breached that it was an open question whether it could be maintained at the next general election. Obviously the strains of co-operation between the parties were much greater in the constituencies than they were at

TABLE 7.7   *Constituency parties affiliated to the Labour Party 1901–1913*

1901	1902	1903	1904	1905	1906	1907	1908	1909	1910	1911	1912	1913
7	21	49	76	73	73	83	92	155	148	149	146	143[a]

Note: [a] Sometimes given as 158 (i.e. 85 trade councils plus 73 LRCs), because some constituencies are counted twice.

Westminster. On the one hand socialists felt tempted to stimulate their organization by opposing sitting Liberals, while by 1910 the Liberal Party had become reluctant to make any further concessions to Labour. The result was a series of damaging three-cornered by-elections beginning in November 1911 when Labour intervened at Liberal-held Oldham, which fell to the Conservatives. In July 1912 the Liberals retaliated by standing at Hanley, where they gained a seat previously given to Labour, pushing the Labour candidate into a humiliating third place with barely 12 per cent of the poll. The very fact that six Liberal and three Labour seats were lost in this way up to 1914 left both parties in no doubt that to abandon the pact would be to give victory to the Conservatives by splitting the Progressive vote.

For this reason one cannot simply assume that Labour was already on the way to breaking away from its client relationship with the Liberals. These by-election contests proved to be extremely divisive within the party. Labour's National Executive Committee (NEC) spent much effort smothering new candidacies, but it enjoyed limited control, especially over local ILP activists. The NEC regarded many local initiatives as frivolous and unjustified in the absence of any significant constituency organization. Indeed, after expanding up to 1909 the party's local network had stagnated so that it was actually represented in a hardly a quarter of the constituencies (table 7.7). This, like the electoral record, is not really consistent with the idea of an inexorable Labour advance up to 1914.

For Ramsay MacDonald electoral policy posed an acute dilemma in 1913 following the death of the Liberal member with whom he jointly represented the double-member constituency of Leicester. Some of his local supporters insisted that by standing against the Liberals they could prove that Labour members did not depend on Liberal votes to win, but MacDonald flatly rejected what he called 'this false idea of independence'. In his view, so long as the two parties had to co-operate at Westminster they should follow the same course in the constituencies. This exposed him to the charge of condemning Labour to its existing seats and sacrificing any real chance of growth for the foreseeable future. However, MacDonald believed that there was some scope for increasing the number of Labour candidatures in areas dominated by the Conservatives where the Liberals had little to lose. He also accepted that the surviving Lib–Lab working men, whose loyalties were really to Liberalism, were not worth retaining, which implied additional contests in mining seats. Despite this, there is no question that he intended to maintain the electoral pact up to the next general election, if only because to abandon it meant Liberal retaliation and the defeat of many existing Labour M.P.s. By June 1914, according to the party's chief agent, Labour contemplated contesting 37 seats already held, 18 where candidates had been sanctioned by the NEC, 22 where candidates had been chosen locally but not sanctioned, and 40 where a candidate was thought possible but uncertain. Allowing for the fact that four of the Labour-held seats were also included (significantly) in the 'uncertain' category, this represented a maximum of 113. Some historians suggest that this was incompatible with the pact. However, given the NEC's record of suppressing what it saw as propagandist or unrealistic contests which would simply damage the government, it seems certain that many of these would not have materialized. By 1914 the unions were backing Labour candidates in *fewer* constituencies than in 1910 because they had no wish to risk the return of a Tory government.[10] In fact by 1915 the NEC had sanctioned only 65 candidates, which can be taken as a realistic figure because all the parties were working on the assumption that an election would take place that year. This allowed for a slight increase over December 1910, but suggests that they did not yet contemplate breaking away from the pact.

The obvious implication of this line of argument is that, if the Liberals were in no immediate danger of collapse under a Labour advance, the main explanation for their decline lies in the impact of the First World War. Certainly until war broke out the chances of a Conservative victory appeared slight. The government was endeavouring to enhance its own prospects by abolishing plural voting, a move calculated to deliver 30 Conservative seats into their hands. Lloyd George had seized the initiative with his Land Campaign which certainly frightened the Conservatives, who felt they could not afford to oppose proposals for minimum wages and housebuilding. Indeed, though the party remained unsure how to respond to Liberal reform, it was concerned that it could not win back sufficient urban support without adopting a more positive approach.[11] Bonar Law's retreat from 'food taxes' dismayed the tariff reformers and blunted the party's boldest policy. This left the Conservatives placing their hopes on the issue of Ulster and resistance to the Liberals' Home Rule Bill, an increasingly extreme and desperate strategy.

On the other hand, while rejecting traditional assumptions about the inevitability of Liberal decline, one must also recognize the sources of weakness in the party's position on the eve of war. Apart from the need to maintain co-operation with Labour, the Asquith government had committed several policy miscalculations which made it vulnerable on the left. Perhaps the greatest of these lay in the drift of foreign and defence policy under Sir Edward Grey and the former Liberal Imperialists since 1906, which offended many traditional Liberals. What they saw as Grey's obsession with the German threat had led to Britain abetting French imperialism in North Africa, allying with the detested Tsarist regime in Russia, acquiescing in the exploitation of the Congo by King Leopold of Belgium, and committing Britain to military involvement on the Continent of Europe. As one critic put it, this threatened to allow the Labour Party 'the whole honour of voicing the best traditions of Liberal foreign policy'.[12] Asquith's government was also felt to have departed from Liberal traditions over franchise reform, especially as it affected women. Apart from the merits of the claim for women's votes, many Liberals were offended by the forcible feeding of hunger-striking suffragettes in prison and by their repeated rearrest under the 'Cat and Mouse' Act in 1913–14. This had a demoralizing effect on Liberal woman activists, torn between loyalty to their party and sympathy for female enfranchisement; as a result women were leaving the party organization before the war.[13] Meanwhile in 1912 the Labour Party had agreed a pact with the national Union of Women's Suffrage Societies, which attracted female volunteers, including Liberal women, into its by-election campaigns in return for its unqualified backing for female enfranchisement. These two issues are important illustrations of the connection between the Great War and the Edwardian era, for war accelerated the recruitment of Liberals who were discontented about foreign policy or women's suffrage into the Labour Party during the 1920s.

PART THREE

1914–1920s

CHAPTER EIGHT

The Impact of the Great War on British Politics

No one on earth can pretend that we were elected to support this Government.
Richard Denman, MP, to C. P. Trevelyan, 28 May 1915

As if to prove the dictum that in politics the expected rarely happens, H. H. Asquith contrived to take both his Cabinet and the country largely united into war in August 1914. This represented a major political achievement which had enormous repercussions; but how did it come about?

The anti-war tradition was still very lively in the Liberal and Labour ranks in 1914, fuelled by suspicions that Sir Edward Grey had committed Britain to support France and the detested Tsarist regime in Russia in a continental conflict. A Liberal Foreign Affairs Group, led by Arthur Ponsonby, claimed the allegiance of several hundred MPs; but in the crisis of July–August 1914 its support melted away to twenty or so members. The failure of the opponents of war to check their own government can readily be explained. Over the years they had placed their faith in the navy as a cheaper and less aggressive form of defence than the army. Even Haldane's reorganization of the army to create the British Expeditionary Force (BEF) placated critics because of the money it saved, and also because the BEF was believed to be designed for use in the Indian or colonial context, not in mainland Europe. Moreover, Asquith and Grey had always insisted that Britain had given no undertakings of military support to another European power, which was true in the letter rather than in the spirit, for they believed it essential to Britain's interests to save France from another defeat at the hands of Germany; the naval conversations with the French and the plan to convey the BEF swiftly across the Channel had been deliberately designed to frustrate German military plans. When the crisis broke this gave the government the advantage of a precise and carefully prepared strategy.

Events also contrived to make the opponents of war very isolated. By refusing to rush the country into war, Grey convinced his critics of his genuine desire to maintain peace, if possible.[1] Above all the upsurge of patriotism in the country weakened the determination of Liberal and Labour MPs to hold out against the declaration of war. And although half of the 20-strong cabinet were thought to have been more-or-less against British involvement in July, no major leader emerged to challenge government policy. Lloyd George's claim in his memoirs that he had been kept in ignorance of foreign policy was implausible, for although he had often argued for economy in naval spending and for improved relations with Germany, he always accepted the logic of the British commitment to France. He was never likely to repeat the role he had played during the Boer War. In the absence of a lead, other ministers felt reluctant to throw away their careers by a hasty resignation; only Morley and Burns, both exhausted volcanoes by this time, left the Cabinet, but they made little attempt to mobilize support in the country. In any case ministers were genuinely shocked at Germany's action in marching into Belgium, and they believed the German government had deliberately kept its ambassador in London, Lichnowsky, in the dark so that he would be more plausible in presenting his country as non-aggressive.[2] Reluctant members, including Runciman, Simon, Pease and Harcourt, were under the impression that war implied embarking on an essentially naval enterprise in support of the French; had they appreciated how drastically the continental commitment would expand after Lord Kitchener's appeal for volunteers, more would probably have resisted the decision.

There were also major party political considerations. If the Cabinet had failed to agree on entry into the war, Asquith, Grey and Haldane would have resigned, thereby breaking up the government. Asquith made a point of reading to the Cabinet the letter sent by Bonar Law and Lansdowne on 2 August urging prompt support for France and offering 'our unhesitating support to the Government in any means they may consider necessary for that object'.[3] This reminded the critics that the collapse of the Cabinet would lead to a coalition or a Conservative government; war, in short, was not to be avoided by their own resignations. Moreover, since war was expected to cause economic disruption and social distress the Liberals felt reluctant to allow the Conservatives the opportunity to undermine the social reforms they had introduced; if there had to be a war it would be better run on liberal lines. Subsequently the official propaganda machine presented the issue in idealistic terms as 'The War to End War', in the famous phrase of H. G. Wells; and liberal writers including Arnold Bennett, John Galsworthy, John Masefield and Thomas Hardy helped to put Britain's case in terms of defending the rights of small nations against the rule of 'Blood and Iron'.

This combination of political calculation, dismay about German actions, and evidence of popular patriotism led to the swift collapse of the pro-peace meetings planned for early August. Reluctant politicians reconciled themselves to the situation with the thought that they had done their best to keep the peace and that France could not be left in the lurch. This was easier because of the unexpected support from the other elements in the alliance. On 4 August John Redmond, the Irish leader, delighted his allies with a bold speech supporting Grey; proof of Irish loyalty in England's moment of crisis seemed likely to enhance the prospects of Home Rule. The Labour Party also showed its patriotic instincts by voting to back the government, even though this involved ousting Ramsay MacDonald from the chairmanship. Apart from his reservations about the diplomacy that had led to the war, MacDonald understood the deeper implications of the conflict as a decisive event which would enable his party to break free from its client relationship with the Liberals. Although anti-war groups such as the ILP and the newly-formed Union of Democratic Control (UDC) were at first beleaguered minorities, they and their arguments eventually offered a bridge by which disillusioned middle-class radicals would later cross to Labour.

The Disintegration of the Progressive Alliance 1914–1916

On the Conservative side all the manoeuvring for morally acceptable positions was regarded as irrelevant. The Opposition responded to war with a single-minded patriotism unhampered by scruples and fortified by the conviction that they had been correct in their diagnosis of the German threat. However, apart from the 98 Tory MPs who joined the armed forces, it was not clear what Opposition members were to do during the war. Inevitably they became susceptible to the scaremongering in the press, notably the *Daily Mail*, which variously attributed military setbacks to lack of determination in the government and to enemy aliens, spies and sabo-teurs supposedly operating throughout the country and in the civil service. Prince Louis of Battenburg, Richard Haldane and Sir Eyre Crowe, the senior official in the foreign office, were alleged to be among the German sympathizers in high places.

Initially Asquith dealt neatly with these hysterical attacks by appointing as Secretary of State for War Lord Kitchener, whose reputation as a war hero made him difficult to attack with any credibility. Unfortunately, he proved more effective as a poster than as a military strategist, and when the generals began to plead that the insufficiency of high explosive shells was handicapping their offensives, Kitchener became a liability for the government. Officially the Conservative leaders accepted a party truce, though they felt they were being taken advantage of when the government claimed that, on the strength of consultations with Balfour and others, they shared responsibility for war policy.[4] Meanwhile Bonar Law's position became uncomfortable as his backbenchers organised themselves into the Unionist Business Committee and other groups designed to maintain criticism of the Liberals in spite of the truce. Bonar Law could not remain aloof from their attacks without jeopardizing his own leadership. However, he felt reluctant to abandon the truce because the inevitable result would have been a wartime general election by December 1915, when Parliament's term ran out. Though he would probably have won, he and his party shrank from running the country in wartime without the full co-operation of the organized working class, which they feared they had alienated during the Edwardian period. The alternative was to join in a coalition, but almost all leading Tories rejected this as calculated to silence their criticism.[5]

It was not until May 1915 that Bonar Law's hand was forced by the crises arising out of Sir John French's complaints about munitions supply and the resignation of Sir John Fisher, the First Sea Lord, in protest at Churchill's campaign in the Dardanelles. He was greatly relieved when Asquith seized the initiative by inviting him to join a coalition. However, as Bonar Law failed to settle policy issues or to secure a fair share of the major ministerial posts before agreeing to join, the new arrangement was resented by his colleagues and never regarded as more than a stopgap solution.

In the short term the Coalition at least postponed the election and kept Asquith in office until December 1916. But in the longer run it involved a fatal step towards the disintegration of the Liberal Party by exposing the prime minister to charges of abandoning liberal principles. The notorious Official Secrets Act of 1911 had been a foretaste of the illiberal measures ushered in by the war, including the Defence of the Realm Act, strict censorship, the Aliens Restriction Act, the National Register Act and the tariffs in McKenna's 1915 budget. Liberals felt less willing to accept such policies under a coalition government. Asquith's failure to consult the party about joining with the Tories rankled: 'The more I contemplate this Coalition,' observed one Liberal, 'the more I revel in the new sense of freedom it gives us all. No one on earth can pretend that we were elected to support this Government.'[6]

Consequently, from May 1915 much of the Liberal rank and file became detached from its leadership, and meanwhile, the pre-war alliance began to break down. One of the immediate consequences of entering the war had been the suspension of controversial legislation including the Irish Home Rule Bill. Relations began to deteriorate when Redmond declined to join the Cabinet in 1915 while the Unionist, Sir Edward Carson, became Attorney-General. Yet things only became irretrievable for the nationalists in 1916 when their own policy of loyalty to the government was fatally undermined by the Easter Rebellion. The authorities allowed the army to put down the rebellion with calculated brutality, as though administering a lesson to a colonial people, and compounded the effect by executing Roger Casement for his role in the affair. Consequently a revolt that had begun with little support quickly gained retrospective sanctity, with the result that by 1917 the country had rejected the Nationalist politicians in favour of the Sinn Fein and in the process destroyed one part of the Liberal alliance. Asquith bore the blame for failing to persuade the Conservatives to accept the settlement hastily negotiated by Lloyd George after the rebellion.

Asquith also undermined his position by his handling of conscription. Under the Coalition the generals, who demanded more men than were being produced through the voluntary system, gained support from the new Conservative ministers. In October 1915 Asquith tried to maintain voluntaryism by introducing the Derby scheme, but when this failed he agreed to conscript single men in January 1916 and married men in June. This kept the government together but led many Liberals to conclude that he was no longer serving his purpose as a guarantee against authoritarian measures. Meanwhile the more right-wing Liberals looked increasingly to Lloyd George for an energetic approach to the war. Much of the subsequent confusion in wartime and post-war politics arose from the way in which right-wing politicians attached themselves to Lloyd George, leaving Asquith as the leader of the Left – a role the prime minister was ill-equipped to play.

Lloyd George and the Conservatives 1916–1918

For the Conservatives the Coalition achieved what all their efforts before 1914 had failed to achieve – the break-up of the Progressive alliance. It also strengthened their position in that their withdrawal would have forced an immediate general election once the life of Parliament ran out in December 1915. Asquith's skill in managing his colleagues enabled him to live with the situation until the end of 1916 but the lack of military and naval victories steadily undermined his authority. Appreciating Lloyd George's ability to focus on a specific problem, Asquith placed him at the new Ministry of Munitions. However, Lloyd George, knowing he could not afford to fail, insisted on removing the obstacles to higher production of munitions, one of which was the voluntary recruiting system which deprived industry of thousands of skilled workers.[7] Though not hitherto an

DELIVERING THE GOODS.
Lloyd George emerges as the leading 'war' minister.
Punch, or the London Charivari, 21 April 1915

advocate on conscription, he now adopted it and threw his weight behind the Conservatives, who were pressing for it. Asquith's next move was to make Lloyd George Secretary of State for War, following Kitchener's death. However, as some of the powers had already been stripped from this office, and the politicians feared too much controversy with the generals over military strategy, Lloyd George soon became frustrated in his new position. As a result he became attracted by schemes designed to reorganize the war effort particularly by re-forming the cabinet and bypassing civil servants and generals. This brought him into co-operation with Bonar Law and Sir Max Aitken, his *éminence grise* and an arch-schemer. Just as in 1915, Bonar Law felt vulnerable to the criticism of his own backbenchers for failing to influence government policy sufficiently. Along with Carson, the two men hatched a proposal to improve the efficiency of the war machine; they sought to replace the large, talkative Cabinet with a three-man War Cabinet which could meet daily to make quick decisions unhindered by departmental responsibilities.

Though neither Lloyd George nor Bonar Law intended to drive Asquith from the premiership, they were presenting him with a humiliating ultimatum. After complicated negotiations Asquith overplayed his hand by turning them down, which led to resignations by both Lloyd George and the Conservative ministers. The king invited Law to form a new ministry, which he refused. Lloyd George was then given the chance, but he had to demonstrate that he could command majority support in the Commons. Though the Conservatives had not wished to make him prime minister, they shrank from restoring Asquith and felt tempted to serve in any new administration. It soon emerged that Lloyd George could form a viable government when a canvass by Christopher Addison revealed that 49 Liberals were firmly committed to him and many more would acquiesce in his premiership. After an eloquent appeal by Lloyd George the Labour members voted to back him by 18 to 11, a decision later confirmed by the party's NEC. In this way Asquith, who had so recently appeared to be indispensable, lost his grip on power.

Although most of the responsibility for the Liberal split was subsequently placed on Lloyd George's shoulders, it was Asquith who first split the party by refusing to serve under the new premier in 1916. Henceforth the Liberals suffered from having two leaders, one as prime minister and one as Leader of the Opposition, along with two whips in the House. Though initially seen as a temporary division the spilt hardened as members got into the habit of voting for or against the new Coalition. On the whole Asquith shrank from opposing the government, except in the 'Maurice Debate' in May 1918. At a black period in the war General Frederick Maurice alleged that Lloyd George had lied to the Commons over his role in reducing British troop numbers on the Western Front. In the subsequent division 98 Liberals voted against Lloyd George and 71 for, thereby formalizing what was now a well-established situation. Although some progressive Liberals such as Christopher Addison and Edwin Montagu stayed with Lloyd George, many regarded him as a traitor to Liberal principles. For many of his colleagues the Coalition was to be a stage on the road to

Conservatism. Conversely many left-wing Liberals, especially those who disapproved of the war and conscription, felt little loyalty to either leader. Some were to retire from politics in 1918, while others, like Charles Trevelyan and Arthur Ponsonby, fell out with their local parties and drifted towards Labour. In the country Liberal activists lost their sense of purpose and direction in contrast with their rivals; for Conservatives patriotic war work seemed integral to the party's cause, while for Labour the opportunity to defend working-class interests under wartime pressures helped to maintain unity and cohesion. National policies of reconstruction accentuated this situation. For example, the housing reform of 1919 encouraged local Labour activists to throw their energies into plans for building council houses for rent after the war; in this way they occupied the leading role in social reform previously played by the Liberals, who drifted towards the right of politics. In such ways the war proved crucial in reshaping the party political configuration.

Meanwhile the new relationship between Lloyd George and the Conservatives developed so that it endured until 1922, and unofficially for longer than that. Recognizing Bonar Law as the chief prop to his government, he elevated him as Chancellor of the Exchequer and Leader of the House; Law, after all, had the essential task of managing the Tory backbenchers who provided the bulk of the government's majority. Lloyd George also took care to include in the War Cabinet two influential right-wing Tories, Lords Curzon and Milner. This, combined with his commitment to winning the war by the 'knock-out blow', reassured the Conservatives that growing pressure for a negotiated peace with Germany would be resisted. Whatever their doubts about Lloyd George, most Conservatives determined to maintain him in power for fear of Asquith's return. The worse things got, the more essential Lloyd George became. From 1917 industrial unrest began to rise sharply as workers sought to raise wages to keep pace with prices. Discontent over living standards was believed to be making workers susceptible to pacifist propaganda by the ILP and the UDC. With Russia disintegrating under the impact of two revolutions and with the French and Italian armies experiencing widespread mutinies, Lloyd George's combination of determination and inspiring oratory seemed crucial to the maintenance of a united and efficient war effort.

Conversely, Lloyd George used his position to drag reluctant Tories into unexpectedly sweeping reforms of the electorate. In January 1917 a Speaker's Conference, set up under Asquith, reported to him with agreed proposals which included the enfranchisement of men at the age of 21 and votes for women aged 30 who possessed a local government qualification or whose husbands were local government voters. Many Conservatives now believed that the patriotism shown by ordinary people during the war made this a less risky move than it would have been, but others had to be pacified with concessions. A special vote was given to 19-year-old men for war service, while conscientious objectors were disfranchised for five years; men in the forces received a vote by post or by proxy. There was also a vague undertaking to reform the House of Lords with a view to restoring its lost powers, though this was not fulfilled.

Even so, many politicians felt alarmed about a new electorate of 21 million, including 8.4 million women, and a working-class majority for the first time.[8] Fear of the spread of revolutionary doctrines from Russia led many Conservatives to anticipate that the demobilized soldiers, returning to face unemployment, might create a left-wing landslide comparable to that of 1906, or even worse. This goes some way to explain the readiness of Conservatives to extend their alliance with Lloyd George into peacetime. His popularity with the people offered the safest means for effecting a transition to peace; in effect he was to be their bulwark against the rise of Labour, which seemed increasingly inevitable. This was the foundation which kept the Coalition in being until 1922.

Despite the entry of the United States into the war and improvements in food and shipping supplies, it was widely expected that the war would last until 1919 before the Allies won a clear victory. But as Parliament was several years beyond its proper term, Lloyd George felt tempted to put his Coalition on a stronger footing by appealing for a mandate to finish the war. However, the complicated arrangements designed to allow soldiers to vote delayed the election until the autumn of 1918. Nor was it easy for the prime minister to decide on what basis to go to the country. Though seen as an indispensable war leader, he had no real party of his own. He needed as many Liberals as possible in order to bargain effectively with the Conservatives, and to this end he held out proposals for reforms in housing and education, land reform, free trade, Home Rule, a fair peace settlement and a league of nations. There was an element of deception in all this, for his agreement with the Conservatives included protectionism and House of Lords reform but ignored Home Rule. However, by July 1918 his whip, F. E. Guest, had embarked upon negotiations with Sir George Younger for the Conservatives to allocate constituencies so as to ensure the two sides would not oppose one another in the election.[9] Arrangements were not quite complete when military events suddenly closed in. On 11 November the Armistice was signed, and three days later the Labour Party withdrew from the Coalition. Lloyd George knew that he had to fight an election while his prestige as 'The Man Who Won the War' was at its height, and before the Conservatives woke up to the fact that they did not really need him. Consequently he and Bonar Law issued a letter of support – dubbed 'The Coupon' by Asquith – to 374 Conservatives, 159 Liberals and 18 Labour or National Democratic Party candidates for an election designed to effect the transition from war to peace.

Labour's Change of Course

Superficially Labour's divisions over the war mirrored those of the Liberals; a minority criticized pre-war diplomacy and worked to end the conflict by a negotiated peace, but the majority rallied to the patriotic cause, some reluctantly but many with enthusiasm. However, these divisions were far less damaging to Labour than they were to the Liberals, and by 1918 the party had managed to rally round a new programme and a new constitution. Part of the explanation lay in the fact that the Labour movement was less fundamentally affected by parliamentary splits, and international affairs remained a slightly remote concern for many members. Also, both sides acted with restraint. Arthur Henderson, who replaced MacDonald, made no attempt to purge the opponents of war, and MacDonald and Snowden propagated their views through the UDC and the ILP rather than through the Labour Party – an illustration of the advantages of having a loose federal structure.

In May 1915 Labour improved its standing by joining Asquith's Coalition, with Henderson serving as President of the Board of Education, though his chief function was to mediate between government and the trade unions and promote working-class co-operation. More surprisingly, Labour joined the more right-wing Coalition under Lloyd George because, on balance, working-class interests seemed better served by working within government. This reflected rank-and-file opinion, not just that of the MPs. At the party conference at Bristol in 1916, delegates representing 73 unions, 39 trade councils and 41 local Labour parties approved by 1.5 million to 0.6 million votes resolutions pledging support for the war effort and backing Labour participation in the Coalition; the next conference endorsed membership of Lloyd George's government by six to one. Nevertheless, Labour had to perform a precarious balancing act. On the one hand the role of Henderson and the other ministers boosted the party's status and confidence; yet at the same time they could not risk compromising Labour's role as guardian of working-class interests. That this was possible owed much to the activities of the War Emergency: Workers' National Committee (WNC) which contrived to maintain links with the party's grass roots and also to use Labour's influence with the authorities. Though originally conceived as a peace committee in August 1914, the WNC quickly accepted Britain's participation as an inescapable fact over which little influence could now be exerted. Disengagement from war was sometimes deliberate; socialists such as G. D. H. Cole, for example, were anxious to avoid discrediting their cause by any association with the anti-war campaigns. The WNC therefore constituted itself as a body representative of the working class devoted to defending its immediate interests by intervening with the authorities over price rises, housing, rent controls, benefits and pensions for servicemen and their families. It grew to some forty members under Jim Middleton, the assistant secretary to the Labour Party, and included a wide spectrum from patriotic union leaders (Will Thorne, Havelock Wilson), right-wing MPs (James O'Grady, C. W. Bowerman), near-jingoes (Ben Tillett, John Hodge), middle-of-the-roaders (Arthur Henderson, Fred Bramley, J. A. Seddon, Sidney Webb), moderate critics of the war (Bob Smillie) and ILP leaders (MacDonald, W. C. Anderson, Fred Jowett, H. Dubery). The WNC concentrated on winning concessions without becoming drawn too far into the official machine; Henderson, for example, resigned from the committee on becoming a minister and Smillie refused to become the Food Controller.

Even more importantly, the work of the WNC at national level was complemented locally by the trades councils. War generated all kinds of local bodies such as committees on food control and profiteering, on which representation by trades councils and Labour municipal groups was required. They attempted to resist pressure for retrenchment, to maintain the value of council employees' wages and relieve the suffering of the families of servicemen. War also stimulated Labour interest in the housing issue, one of the neglected topics of the pre-war period. As Minister for Reconstruction Addison endeavoured to persuade local authorities to prepare plans for housebuilding, which Labour councillors were especially keen to do.[10] Housing shortages eventually led to the enactment of Addison's bill in 1919, and although it was abandoned in 1921 the policy was taken up by Labour in the form of John Wheatley's Housing Act of 1924; in this way Labour inherited the social reform tradition at the local level, while many Liberals were moving to the right.

Rather surprisingly, Labour's loyalty to the Coalition was not seriously shaken until Henderson's visit to Russia in June 1917, an initiative intended by the government as a means of encouraging the new provisional Russian government under Kerensky to maintain the war effort. However, Henderson, who welcomed the new regime, soon recognized how precarious it was; to persist with the war was to invite overthrow by the Bolsheviks, and he returned convinced that Russia would have to see some hope for a negotiated peace if another revolution were to be forestalled. The episode revealed the extent to which a wider perspective could alter the thinking of a pragmatic, non-ideological figure like Henderson. He began to consider the implications for Britain: when the troops were demobilized and returned home, would they become disillusioned and susceptible to revolutionary and anarchistic doctrines? However, Henderson's colleagues were too obsessed with military victory to sympathize with his view of Russia and he was effectively sacked from the War Cabinet. Although George Barnes took his place, this proved to be a blunder on Lloyd George's part, for it forced Labour into defying the government for the first time. When the

Labour Party conference sanctioned representation at a conference in Stockholm designed to discuss a compromise peace, foreign affairs suddenly began to divide the movement from the government and to promote a rapprochement between the middle-class socialists of the ILP and the patriotic trade unionists.

Thus, by September 1917 Labour had embarked, almost by accident, on a new course. A statement of 'Peace and War Aims', largely written by MacDonald, Webb and Henderson, appeared in October; a new party constitution and a programme entitled 'Labour and the New Social Order' were ratified by a special conference in September 1918; and during 1918 Henderson devoted himself to preparations for a general election. These changes effectively marked Labour's escape from the politics of the pact that had prevailed since 1903. The confidence for this course arose from three sources. In the first place, the parliamentary alliance had ceased to exist, more through Liberal division than through any intention by Labour. With no Liberal government in power the pressures that had dictated Labour's electoral policy had lapsed. Conscious of deteriorating Liberal organization and the detachment of middle-class radicals, Henderson and Macdonald saw the chance to recruit supporters who would make Labour more than a section party.

Another stimulus lay in the expansion of resources. Total union membership had increased from 4.1 to 6.5 million during the war and that of TUC-affiliated unions from 2.6 to 5.2 million; with the machinery set in place in 1913 after the Osborne Judgement, union political funds were at last accumulating. This made it feasible to run more candidates and to extend the organization by establishing a Labour Party in every constituency. As table 8.1 shows, this development occurred quite late in the war. Similarly, the breakthrough in parliamentary candidates came towards the end of the war. During 1917 the NEC stepped up the work of its travelling organizers, who visited 79 districts in that year.[11] After having 117 candidates on its list in 1914 the party added only one additional one in January 1916, followed by two more in January 1917. But in the autumn of 1918, 388 Labour candidates fought the election.

Henderson's initiatives were also accelerated by the knowledge that a comprehensive scheme of electoral reform was proceeding through

TABLE 8.1   *The Labour Party: affiliated constituency organizations 1913–1918*

1913	1914	1915	1916	1917	1918
143	179	177	199	239	389

Parliament during 1917. This seemed likely to assist Labour in several ways: by expanding the working-class vote at a time when the Liberals were in no position to exploit it; by limiting election expenses and thus narrowing Labour's disadvantages; and by revising constituency boundaries which disrupted the other parties' organizations more than Labour's. Also, when Henderson contemplated fielding 500 candidates, he assumed that the alternative vote system (which prevents the election of any member on a minority of the poll) would remain in the bill and thus reduce the danger of splitting the Progressive vote to the advantage of the Conservatives. It was not until February 1918 that the alternative vote was dropped, too late to have a significant impact on the number of candidates. In short, the pact was now dead and for the first time Labour could bid to become a majority party. The potential for this breakthrough had existed for some time, but had remained unrealized; the timing must largely be attributed to the concatenation of favourable events, including the stimulating impact of the war on working-class communities, the Liberal split and electoral reform.

The Coupon Election of 1918

The general election of December 1918, in which no fewer than 21 million people enjoyed the right to vote, proved to be a watershed in twentieth-century politics. Students often overlook the fact that it ushered in a 20-year era of Conservative dominance; it dealt the Liberals a blow from which they never fully recovered; and it gave Labour the chance to emerge as the leading opposition party for the first time.

As with most elections the outcome had been clear well in advance, but the scale of the victory won by Lloyd George and his allies was unexpected; they claimed 526 seats out of 707, which left the government in an extremely strong position, especially as the largest opposition party, Sinn Fein, failed to come to Westminster. It is difficult to interpret the result as anything other than a long-delayed eruption of Germanophobia. Lloyd George himself began the election by speaking about a sane peace settlement and social reconstruction, but he found his audiences excitedly demanding vengeance; one of his ministers, Sir Eric Geddes, notoriously pandered to this emotion: 'we shall squeeze Germany like a lemon; we shall squeeze her until you can hear the pips squeak'. All candidates were put under pressure to prove that they had always been anti-German; in London the *Evening News* sent telegrams demanding: 'For the guidance of your constituency will you kindly state whether if elected you will support the following: 1. Punishment of the Kaiser 2. Full payment for the war by Germany 3. The expulsion from the British Isles of all Enemy Aliens.'

TABLE 8.2   *General Election results 1918*

Coalition	Seats	Vote (%)	Opposition	Seats	Vote (%)
Con.	335 (374[a])	32.6	Lab.	57[b] (388)	22.2
Con.	48 (75)	6.1	Lib.	28[c] (258)	12.1
(Uncouponed)			Sinn Fein	73 (102)	4.5
LG Lib.	133 (159)	13.5	Irish Nat.	7 (60)	2.2
Nat. Dem. Party	10 (18)	1.5	Others	16 (197)	5.3
Total	526		*Total*	181	

Notes: [a] Figures in brackets denote candidates.
[b] Also unofficial Labour victories at Anglesey, North Aberdeen, Kettering and West Ham Silvertown give the total of 61 sometimes quoted.
[c] 37 Liberals were actually elected without the Coupon, but 9 of these took the government whip subsequently.

The timing of the election proved crucial; it took place so soon after the conclusion of hostilities that wartime emotions still ran very high, which was inevitably to the disadvantage of the non-Conservative parties.

However, the swing to the right does not entirely explain the extent of the Conservative victory. The results distorted the poll in that the Coalition won 74 per cent of seats for 54 per cent of the vote, a clear indication that without their pre-war pact the Liberal and Labour Parties were severely disadvantaged by splitting the non-Conservative vote. What seems at first surprising is that the one factor that might have been expected to tell in favour of the Left, the new franchise, apparently failed to help. The government went to some lengths to enable the troops to participate in the election by arranging a postal vote for those in Belgium and France, including a two-week delay in the count to allow their ballots to arrive, and a proxy vote for those who were further afield. In fact, of 3.9 million service voters, 2.7 million were sent ballot papers but only 0.9 million actually voted. Low participation reflected the practical difficulties in voting and an understandable detachment from domestic politics. There are indications that, as in 1945, the troops leaned to the left. Certainly the UDC believed they had the sympathy of discharged servicemen, and many soldiers wrote to pacifist candidates wishing them success. At the count observers noticed that a high proportion of absent votes were cast for Labour and that soldiers had sometimes expressed their resentment by writing 'demobilize first' on the ballots.[12]

Conversely, the evidence, though admittedly impressionistic, suggests that civilian, especially the new women voters, formed the backbone of the

Coalition vote. Isolated from the real war, they often wanted to prove their loyalty to the men who had fought by voting for a tough peace settlement; this was their vicarious blow against Germany. Some candidates formed the impression that women voters strongly favoured the government and voted as they believed their husbands or sons wished.[13] In any case, subsequent studies showed that women invariably gave more support to the Conservatives than men. Their role in 1918 must have been considerable, for apart from constituting almost forty per cent of the total electorate, many women also acted as proxies for male relations.

Inevitably the Coupon arrangement attracted much contemporary comment, particularly from candidates, who ascribed their defeat to its misleading effect on voters. However, this may have been an excuse for many who were heading for defeat anyway. Although 133 of the 159 Lloyd George Liberals who received the Coupon were elected, this was really because it saved them from opposition by their local Conservatives. This is corroborated by the success enjoyed by those Conservatives who stood without the Coupon; 25 of them were Irish Unionists, but on the mainland 23 of 37 uncouponed Conservatives won in such unfavourable places as Barrow, Rotherham, Derby, Salford West, and East Fife, which had been Asquith's seat. It looks as though the Conservatives did equally well with or without the Coupon. Many Liberals occupied an untenable position, being seen as opposed to the Coalition and to outright victory, but also as responsible for the war. Their organization collapsed disastrously in places such as East Bristol, where Sir Charles Hobhouse obtained 7.6 per cent and Glasgow St Rollox, where McKinnon Wood won 8.2 per cent of the vote.

Contrary to received impressions, it is not easy to interpret Labour's performance. Though good enough to enable the party to overtake the Liberals, the 57-seat total was a very modest improvement on the 42 seats won in 1910; moreover, since 33 of these were in mining constituencies there had been no significant breakthrough into fresh territory. No fewer than 51 of the 1918 MPs were nominated by trade unions, including 25 by the Miners' Federation. In this sense Labour's real breakthrough was delayed until 1922.

In 1918 those Labour candidates who showed any sign of criticizing the war effort met an overwhelming rejection from voters, so much so that they often dissociated themselves from MacDonald for fear of damaging their chances. The scale of their defeat came as a shock; at West Leicester MacDonald received only 23.6 per cent in a straight fight, while at Blackburn Snowden won 19.7 per cent in a three-cornered contest. Conversely, Labour candidates such as J. H. Thomas, Will Thorne and Jack Jones who adopted a highly patriotic line were comfortably elected; in the process Labour shifted sharply to the right, at least at the parliamentary level.

However, in the long run the seats won by Labour in 1918 were less significant than the size of the vote – over 22 per cent. This was less a reflection of support from new voters than of the huge increase in Labour candidates from 56 in 1910 to 388. Comparisons between pre- and post-1918 elections are difficult because so many of the boundaries changed. However, historians who have attempted to analyse the Labour performance in relation to changes in the size of the electorate have concluded that the higher the proportion of new voters in a constituency, the *less* well the party did.[14] To some extent this reflected the Conservative bias amongst the female electors. There seems no real grounds for thinking that the reservoir of newly created votes enabled Labour to achieve a breakthrough in 1918. However, in the municipal elections in 1919 and subsequent years the party made sweeping gains. Interestingly, many of the new parliamentary voters were still ineligible to vote in local government; the fact that Labour appears not to have been handicapped by the less democratic character of the municipal franchise or greatly helped by the wider parliamentary one suggests that electoral reform was not by itself the key to success. The important feature of 1918 lay in the demise of the Liberals. The Asquithians put up only 258 candidates for the 707 seats compared to Labour's 388. Both in 1918 and in subsequent elections many Liberal voters were obliged to chose between Labour, the Conservatives or abstention; as Liberal candidatures fluctuated wildly, the habit of voting Liberal was broken and the organization disintegrated at local level. Even in 1918 ex-Liberal activists were found to be helping to run Labour campaigns.[15] Despite subsequent Liberal revivals during the 1920s, the party never quite managed to overtake Labour and to regain its role as the alternative to the Conservatives.

CHAPTER NINE

Patriotism, Ideology and the State in the Great War

As the Labour Party has grown in power, the menace of revolution has dwindled.

J. H. Clynes, *Memoirs 1869–1924* (1937), p. 52

The First World War placed a great strain on the British political and economic system, on the political parties and their ideas. It is tempting to assume that it led to major and lasting changes, for example, in replacing the traditional belief in non-interventionism with state control. However, things were clearly much more complicated than that, partly because many of the changes associated with war proved to be ephemeral and because in some respects war consolidated existing practice rather than undermining it. All three parties responded negatively as well as positively to the pressures generated by the wartime state. For Liberals the experience offered the chance to extend pre-war social policy through the expansion of the state's resources, but on the other hand the authoritarian measures needed to win the war threatened individual liberty. Conservatives welcomed the opportunity provided by war to exclude German imports and extend the empire, but many of them accepted the extension of state control, and especially the higher taxation, on a strictly temporary basis. Fabian socialists derived great encouragement from the pragmatic pattern of state controls built up during the war which seemed to give tangible expression to their ideas; on the other hand, many socialists looked askance at wartime collaboration between the state and industry, which seemed to pose a much more formidable long-term threat to the interests of the workers.

Laissez-faire and Interventionism

Before 1914 the Liberals had already moved some distance from nineteenth-century notions by extending state taxation and intervention in living standards. More surprisingly, Asquith's Cabinet had also considered what steps would be necessary to save the economy from collapse during wartime. Despite Treasury advice to the contrary, they were prepared for intervention in shipping and railways because of the country's dependence on imported food and the danger of disruption to communications. In August 1914 they used their powers under Acts of 1870 and 1888 to impose control over the railways by setting up a Railway Executive Committee including company directors and civil servants, which set a pattern for subsequent extensions of control during the war.

Insofar as wartime economic policy was governed by principle at all it reflected *military* thinking rather than economic ideas. On the original assumption that Britain would fight the war with the navy and a small expeditionary force, a 'Business As Usual' approach would have been feasible. The War Office would simply have relied on its traditional arrangements with the arsenals and some private manufacturers to supply the army with munitions without making great demands on the economy. However, all this was undermined by Kitchener's appeal for troops which created an army of two million by January 1915, in the process making huge demands on the economy and causing shortages of skilled labour in mining, engineering and agriculture. This led to a debate about what size of war Britain could realistically maintain. While the generals demanded ever more men, an alternative strategy was pressed by Maurice Hankey, the Secretary to the War Council, ministers such as McKenna and Runciman, and civil servants such as Sir Hubert Llewellyn Smith of the Board of Trade. In January 1915 they argued that of the 3 million fit men of military age still at home, no more than 1.1 million could be taken by the army without crippling British industry.[1] They believed that Britain's wisest policy lay in using her industrial strength to support her allies, making maximum use of the navy and restricting her offensive role on the Western Front which was so wasteful of manpower.

Domestic pressures also pointed towards a pattern of interventionism. At the outset of war the government stepped in to purchase wheat from the USA and Argentina and sugar from the West Indies, to control Indian wheat, and to secure an agreed scale of maximum retail prices with shopkeepers. Their intention was to interfere with the free market by edging out the middlemen who caused inflation, and by releasing their own supplies on to the market so as to keep prices down.[2] This policy grew bit by bit under all wartime governments until, by 1918, no less than 80 per cent of Britain's food passed through the official machine and was subject to price controls. The migration of workers into areas producing munitions exacerbated housing shortages, pushed rents up and, by 1915, provoked rent strikes. To this the government responded with a Rent Restriction Act, a measure which had long-term consequences for housing tenure. Coal strikes similarly led to state control over the South Wales coalfield in November 1916, which was eventually to the whole industry during 1917. Above all, the insatiable demand for munitions forced the authorities into a series of actions beginning as early as October 1914 when a 'Shells Committee' was imposed upon Kitchener. Under the Defence of the Realm Act the government armed itself with wide powers, including the right to control factories producing munitions, and in May 1915 a fully-fledged Ministry of Munitions was created. Under its auspices the government imposed controls over 250 factories and mines during 1915 and 1916, including the regulation of profits and prices. Lloyd George, who was regarded as the driving force behind much of this interventionism, adopted an unideological approach. On the one hand, he believed nothing should be allowed to stand in the way of higher production, but on the other hand he agreed there were limits to the number of men who could safely be removed from industry; hence his concern to use conscription to bring back skilled workers from the front. The picture of Lloyd George as an arch-interventionist and his Liberal critics as doctrinaire advocates of *laissez-faire* is a caricature. As wartime Chancellor Lloyd George had been no radical; it was McKenna who became responsible for drastic increases in income tax in 1915, who infringed free trade and imposed an Excess Profits Duty at 50 per cent. Much of Lloyd George's policy involved extending earlier innovations; for example, the County Agriculture Committees were incorporated into the 1917 Corn Production Act, which imposed production targets on farmers under the threat of losing their land if they refused to co-operate. Lloyd George also dramatized the key issues by creating many new ministries, departments and committees staffed by experts and outsiders. When his Food Controller, Lord Devonport, proved to be too cautious, he was replaced with Lord Rhondda, who introduced rationing for many staple items of food. None of the wartime governments thought out the principles involved in this system of controls, rather they developed policy in an ad hoc fashion in response to a crisis in each sector of the war effort. As interventionism was essentially a matter of expediency there was little political will to maintain the new structures once the wartime crisis had passed, even in the area of reconstruction to which the government was ostensibly committed.

Labour's Socialist Commitment and the Liberal Inheritance

Up to 1914 socialism had made only a limited impression on the Labour Party, partly because many trade unionists continued to feel suspicious of socialists as middle-class intellectuals keen to tap their funds. Conversely, some Socialists despaired of the lack of ideological coherence in the party's programme and the opportunism of its leadership. While the war by no means destroyed these divisions, it did enable Socialists such as Sidney Webb to participate more fully in the party. This was now promoted by Arthur Henderson who pronounced himself keen to 'enlarge the bounds of the Labour Party and bring in the intellectuals as candidates'.[3] For the Webbs the wartime proliferation of committees representing labour and employers, such as the Whitley Councils, offered an ideal opportunity to experiment with their ideas on state control. The war convinced them that the Labour Party was, after all, a suitable vehicle for the transmission of their version of socialism, and as a result the Fabian approach to nationalization became embedded in the party's long-term policy-making, though its results were not fully apparent until the 1940s. However, socialists such as G. D. H. Cole and R. H. Tawney became alarmed by wartime collectivism which seemed to make capitalism more secure by guaranteeing profits and uniting employers, civil servants and government. This pre-empted genuine socialism in the form of greater control by their workers themselves in industry; and as a result many socialists shared the desire to dismantle controls once peace had been declared.

Despite this, the new party constitution of 1918 appeared to mark a major shift to a distinctive left-wing position, incorporating as it did the famous commitment in Clause IV to 'secure for the producers by hand or by brain the full fruits of their industry, and the most equitable distribution thereof that may be possible upon the basis of the common ownership of the means of production'. However, some historians have questioned the significance of this statement, arguing in the light of the party's inter-war record that it cannot be taken literally. Within the trade unions the war did more to stimulate patriotism than socialism, and their influence was institutionalized in the new constitution. Whereas under the original constitution the representatives of the various affiliated societies had chosen their delegates separately, now they were to be selected by the conference as a whole, effectively allowing the unions to dominate the process. The creation of a local party in every constituency with individual membership and special women's sections appeared to offer greater opportunities for socialists to participate in the organization. Certainly middle-class socialists were more likely to join as individual members, and the sudden expansion of candidacies offered them new scope to rise in the movement. On the other hand, by creating local parties and individual membership the constitution deprived the ILP of its special role in the movement after 1918. Only three of the Labour MPs elected in 1918 were nominated by the ILP, a considerable departure from the pre-1914 situation. Nor did the socialist societies now enjoy their own representation in the national organization, for the NEC comprised 11 union, 5 constituency party and 4 women's representatives, all chosen by conference. It was partly because the unions felt that their power was stronger than ever that they allowed themselves to be persuaded by Henderson to accept the socialist clause in the constitution.

On the other hand, the socialist commitment was by no means devoid of significance, if only as a symbol of Labour's emancipation from the politics of the pact and its determination to distinguish itself from Liberalism. Political movements need a myth or ideal around which to rally, and 'socialism' fulfilled this function for the party faithful by showing where the movement stood in relation to previous developments and by creating a sense of inevitable progress towards a better society. Like Empire for late Victorian Conservatives, 'socialism' was a sufficiently imprecise ideal to be impervious to mere day-to-day events. MacDonald's skill in articulating this idea endowed the inter-war Labour movement with a formidable sense of purpose and optimism in the face of the deteriorating international economy.

The idea of Clause IV as a symbolic rather than a substantial change is corroborated by the party's failure to develop a detailed socialist programme at this stage, and also by the recruitment of former Liberals. Indeed, the entry of men and women from middle- and upper-class backgrounds during the 1920s went a long way to transforming Labour into the *national* party Macdonald had always envisaged, as opposed to a class party. The immediate stimulus leading Liberals such as Charles Trevelyan, Josiah Wedgwood, Arthur Ponsonby, H. B. Lees-Smith and R. L. Outhwaite to join Labour lay in their reaction to the war and disagreement with their local Liberal parties. Others, including Noel Buxton, L. C. Money, Sydney Arnold, Willoughby Dickinson and Percy Alden, were defeated as Liberals in 1918 before switching allegiance. They especially disliked the mandarin diplomacy which had foisted war on Britain and the uses to which victory was being put, notably the extension of imperial control and the exploitation of Germany for the benefit of a few capitalists. The disclosure by the Bolsheviks of the secret treaties of the pre-1914 period demonstrated, in their view, how little British policy had been based on respect for self-determination and how much on cynical manipulation of territory in the interests of power politics. Trevelyan explained his transition to Labour by drawing a comparison with the moral leadership of Cobden and Bright during the Crimean War; like many recruits he saw Labour under MacDonald as continuing this tradition in foreign affairs.

The influence of the ex-Liberals was especially obvious in the way they strengthened the movement's pacifism as the reaction against the war gathered pace in the 1920s. They also served prominently in the first two Labour governments. In 1924 the ex-Liberal ministers included Trevelyan (Education), Haldane (Lord Chancellor), Wedgwood (Duchy of Lancaster), Buxton (Agriculture), Ponsonby (Under-Secretary for Foreign Affairs) and Sir Patrick Hastings (Attorney-General). In 1929 Trevelyan served at Education, Christopher Addison at Agriculture, William Wedgwood Benn at the India Office, Arnold as Paymaster General, William Jowett as Attorney-General, Lees-Smith as Postmaster General, and Ponsonby at the Duchy of Lancaster. The question arises, how far were these ex-Liberals in tune with Labour on social and economic issues; did they inhibit or strengthen the pressure for a more left-wing policy? In some respects, such as Labour's predilection for free trade, they reinforced existing tendencies. Their conviction that Labour now upheld Liberal traditions more effectively than their old party was underlined by Snowden's 1924 budget, which removed the duties introduced in 1915. Believing that wartime protectionism and cartels had curtailed competition and thereby made capitalists more powerful, the Liberals supported further state controls over industry. This is not to say they had become socialists, but the ex-Liberal Sydney Arnold propagated the idea of a levy on capital in the Labour Party. The notion of the 'conscription of wealth' as a means of diverting wartime profits into social reconstruction exercised a wide appeal and was adopted by post-war Labour conferences. However, well before 1924 MacDonald and Henderson had distanced themselves from the levy as an extremist policy. Similarly, a number of the enthusiastic land-taxers joined Labour; but although the party conference backed land nationalization in 1925, there was little chance of Labour governments attempting to enact such policies.

Several of the recruits regarded Labour as the best vehicle for extending the Edwardian social reform policies, notably L. C. Money, Haldane and Percy Alden, whose views combined Liberalism and Fabianism in equal measure. 'All social reformers are bound to gravitate, as I have done, to Labour', wrote Charles Trevelyan.[4] Haldane's enthusiasm for placing the administration in the hands of a trained elite led him to support the nationalization of the coal industry. But perhaps the most central figure in Liberal–Labour politics was Christopher Addison, who had pioneered the policy of state-subsidized council housing under Lloyd George. When he broke with his old party in 1923 Addison identified three areas where Labour enjoyed superior credentials: social reform, free trade and disarmament.[5] He advocated 'Practical Socialism', by which he meant state intervention designed to raise standards wherever private enterprise had proved to be inadequate. Labour adopted Addison's policy of subsidized

council housing, and he effectively designed the party's agricultural programme for a system of agricultural marketing boards that would eliminate
middlemen and offer the producers guaranteed prices. This meant abandoning free trade in favour of import quotas on food, a policy which he
tried, without success, to persuade the 1929–31 Labour government to
adopt.[6] If Addison was strictly a collectivist rather than a socialist, nonetheless his Agricultural Marketing Act demonstrated a better grasp of the
legislative route to socialism than any of his colleagues, apart from Herbert
Morrison. Somewhat in contrast to Addison, William Wedgwood Benn,
who became an interesting late recruit to the party in 1927, seemed to
place the emphasis on economic as distinct from social questions. He
declared that he had for some time questioned 'the theory of private
enterprise and free competition'. As British industry failed to revive during
the 1920s, Wedgwood Benn increasingly saw workers' control as the alternative form of industrial organization, which offered a natural development
from the municipal socialism of the late nineteenth century.[7] However, he
was not typical of the Liberal recruits.

Significantly, neither Trevelyan nor Wedgwood Benn showed much
sense of a dramatic conversion in changing their party affiliation. When
Trevelyan advocated the 'minimum socialist programme' in the 1920s he
included 'the living wage', state-funded public works, especially in housing,
nationalization of the mines and railways, a levy on land values, a capital
levy, and free trade. Insofar as there was an underlying theme here it was
the Hobsonian idea of stimulating the economy by increasing the power of
consumption of the mass of the people. In this sense Labour's advance
from minor to major party status during the 1920s involved change through
continuity rather than a sharp break with earlier practice. This was politically very advantageous; for the Liberals did not decline because their
ideas on free trade, social reform, Home Rule, civil liberties, or colonial
self-determination were suddenly discredited; rather they declined because
Labour increasingly enjoyed a superior claim as champion of these traditional Liberal causes. Transition to Labour involved as much a reaffirmation
of political principles as a repudiation for many of the Liberal recruits.

The Working Class, the State and Patriotism

However, the war did more than promote Labour's inheritance from Liberalism. It greatly accentuated the common ground between Labour and
Conservatism, a relatively neglected theme, but of crucial importance in the
party's eventual emergence as a national majority party. Amid the traumatic
effects of the war it is easy to overlook the fact that by comparison with
the rest of Europe, where empires and royal dynasties were collapsing,

Britain emerged with her political system intact and weathered the revolutionary movement unleashed in Russia with relative ease. This was partly because Britain's liberal democracy worked well in making enough concessions to retain popular loyalty, even under the stress of wartime conditions. But it also reflected the remarkable upsurge of patriotism in the working class. Many of the trade unionist MPs argued that Britain was not to blame for the war, that the aim must be to stop German militarism and that the defeated enemy must be punished for the war. Even socialists were by no means completely aligned with the anti-war pressure groups. Indeed, some argued that socialism was perfectly compatible with nationalism. This led some socialists, for example, to accept military conscription on the grounds that the state had every right to call upon its citizens for service – a view very much in line with Conservative thinking. War also strengthened working-class support for protectionism on the grounds that British producers and workers must be safeguarded against foreign goods produced by low wages and unfair subsidies. More generally, the sense of crisis during the war heightened existing working-class support for the monarchy and the Empire. 'In many respects', wrote J. H. Thomas, one of the most patriotic Labour MPs, 'the workers are more conservative than the Conservatives. No question of Republicanism as a serious proposal ever finds a place in Labour discussions.'[8]

Of course, the two revolutions in Russia in 1917 considerably complicated Labour politics. The March revolution encouraged patriotic Labour because by removing the Tsarist regime it made the war a respectable fight by the democracies against the tyrannies. However, the Bolshevik revolution in the autumn greatly inspired the Left and most opponents of the war. It opened up the prospect of an international revolution and the replacement of 'bourgeois democracy' by workers' soviets and direct action. During the period of industrial militancy from 1918 to 1920 it was not certain whether the Labour movement would succumb to the attractions of direct action. However, the revolution also provoked a reaction among most Labour leaders who condemned Bolshevism as undemocratic and alien, and repudiated the class war in Britain. Apart from maintaining a footing within government, Labour leaders such as J. H. Thomas won praise for their work in keeping vital industries like the railways running throughout the war. This experience created bridges between the working class and the political Establishment, and as a result the Labour movement entered the 1920s broadly content to accept the existing political system. Above all, as Thomas noted, there was confidence that when Labour reached the point of forming a government its advice would be accepted by the king as readily as that of Tory or Liberal ministers.

Leading Conservatives including Lord Milner, Lord Selborne and Sir Arthur Steel-Maitland recognized the patriotism shown by the workers during the war. This led them to accept the sweeping extension of the vote in 1917 and also to recommend extending into peacetime certain forms of wartime interventionism including minimum wages, limits on profits and control of essential industries. War, in short, had accentuated a common Tory–Socialist brand of politics. The elimination of all the more left-wing and anti-war Labour MPs in 1918 made this development even more obvious. But the more important manifestation lay in the entry of upper-class Conservatives into the Labour Party during the 1920s, including Lord Parmoor and his son Stafford Cripps, John Strachey, John Sankey, who chaired the royal commission on the coal industry, Sir Oswald Mosley and his wife, Lady Cynthia, who was the daughter of Lord Curzon, Oliver Baldwin, son of Stanley Baldwin, Hugh Dalton, Hugh Gaitskell, George Strauss, and Lord de la Warr. Even before 1914 several men and women from a Tory family background had joined the party, notably Susan Lawrence, Clement Attlee and Lady Warwick.[9] Two aspects of this were significant. First, these recruits eventually enabled Labour to develop into a national party representing all sections of the community. Second, the former Tories, unlike the ex-Liberals, repudiated the economic thinking of their old party and devoted a good deal of thought to a socialist economic policy; indeed, their complaint about Labour in the 1920s was often that it had failed to take its professed socialism seriously enough, and in the long run they strengthened the party's programme in this respect.

Conservatism, Capitalism and the State 1914–1922

The Conservative Parry entered the war very uncertain about its views on social and economic questions. As we have seen, during several decades before 1914 Conservatives had increasingly adopted the arguments of nineteenth-century economic individualism, though evidence of national decline and electoral failure after 1906 had stimulated a minority within the party to advocate state social reform. This had been overshadowed as the party descended into a bout of in-fighting over tariff reform, an issue which led some Conservatives further towards interventionism but made others even more hostile to the role of the state. By 1914 it was uncertain whether a future Tory government would press ahead with tariffs as the majority of the party clearly wanted, or allow electoral expediency to temper its policy.

The Conservatives' enthusiasm for a vigorous prosecution of the war made the party appear initially as more interventionist than its rivals. However, this interventionism ran to conscription and a willingness to regulate civilian life rather than a to a wider role for the state in social and economic policy. The immediate effect of the war was to stimulate the

THE VICIOUS CIRCLE.
PROFITEER (*to successful striker*). 'YOU GET YOUR BONUS;
I MAKE EXTRA PROFIT AND HE STANDS THE RACKET.'
Punch, or the London Charivari, 11 September 1918

activity of backbenchers in the Unionist Business Committee and the
Unionist War Committee, especially in pressing for a vigorous assertion of
British commercial interests. The suspension of German imports widened
the domestic market and the demise of German overseas trade opened up
fresh opportunities to British enterprise and even to imperial expansion. This

enabled the protectionists to stiffen the party's somewhat equivocal attitude towards tariffs. In 1917, the Balfour of Burleigh Committee endorsed the view that at the end of the war Britain's infant industries, which had filled the gap left by German imports, would require full protection.

These possibilities stirred some sections of industry to exert more pressure on the Conservative Party. In some respects industry's experience of wartime co-operation with the state had proved reassuring, for many firms received large contracts and enjoyed unusually high levels of profit; they were also shielded from the usual competition and to some extent from the pressure of their labour force. These cushioning effects led some industries to seek continued government help in the form of tariffs and subsidies, co-operation with the civil service, and amalgamations designed to control the market. The object was to extend wartime advantages into peacetime while persuading governments to reduce high wartime levels of taxation and abandon controls on prices and profits. Industry's ability to influence governments was weakened because the members of the Federation of British Industry were divided over protection and chary of close association with the political parties. Consequently a new organization, the British Commonwealth Union (BCU), appeared in December 1916, inspired partly by fear of socialism and revolution, and determined to prolong the economic warfare with Germany.[10] The BCU promoted 24 Conservative candidates in 1918 of whom 18 were elected, and subsidized Emmeline and Christabel Pankhurst to speak against strikes in the manufacturing districts. BCU influence was probably wider than the figures suggest, for by 1918 it expressed views held universally in the Conservative Party. The Coalition manifesto included proposals for protection of key industries and anti-dumping legislation, without which Conservatives would not have maintained the government after the war. The government lived up to its promises with the 1921 Safeguarding of Industries Act which imposed a $33\frac{1}{3}$ per cent duty on certain goods, largely imported from Germany.

Beyond this, however, the Conservatives' chief post-war demand was to set industry free from government. In fact by 1922 almost every form of control had been dismantled. Food rationing lingered longest because of the politicians' apprehension about unrest among demobilized men in 1919–20, and the Ministry of Food proved itself by keeping supplies moving during the railway strike of 1919. But in 1920, when world food prices had begun to fall, the government gladly abandoned subsidies and rationing and abolished the ministry itself in 1921. In that year the Ministry of Munitions, the Coal Control Department and the Railway Executive also closed. Sir Eric Geddes, the Transport Minister, prepared a plan to nationalize the railways, but the cabinet dropped it in the face of backbench hostility, and the most he could achieve was an amalgamation of the existing multitude of companies into four groups – a recognition that private ownership was no longer viable. The war also generated some support for public control of coal, and in view of the union's pressure, a commission was established under John Sankey to investigate its future. Recognizing that the economic problems of the industry were unlikely to be resolved through the fragmented and inefficient pattern of private ownership, the majority of the commission's members recommended some form of nationalization; however, the Lloyd George government, reflecting the political backlash against state control, ignored the verdict and proceeded to decontrol coal in 1921.

This failure to derive any lasting advantage from wartime experiments underlines the lack of a real intellectual conversion by most politicians. By contrast, civil servants relished the new and constructive role wear had opened up to them. The pre-war introduction of trade boards and minimum wages was extended during the war to cover agricultural and munitions employees, and by 1921 some 63 trade boards had been established. At this point, however, the policy of minimum wages suffered a decisive check because it conflicted with the Treasury's view that money spent on public services deprived industry of investment, and its belief that the downward movement of wages was essential for a return to full employment.[11] The Treasury still held the whip hand, especially under the orthodox Austen Chamberlain, over the newer, innovatory ministries such as Labour; it even managed to have the Transport Ministry abolished in 1922.

In fact all the wartime innovations proved to be vulnerable to political and institutional pressures. Lloyd George had created the Ministry of Reconstruction under Addison in 1917, which became the Ministry of Health in 1918 with a remit covering housing. However, the prime minister made the mistake of denying the ministry executive powers, thereby obliging it to persuade other departments, notably the notoriously negative Local Government Board, to accept its proposals on housing. The cabinet itself delayed its acceptance of Addison's housing reforms with the result that they were not enacted until 1919, and then ran into the problems caused by post-war inflation. It was unfortunate that the two major post-war reforms in education and housing were the responsibility of Liberals, H. A. L. Fisher and Christopher Addison, which left them exposed to Conservative criticism and obstructionism. Many Conservatives also resented Lloyd George's habit of multiplying the number of departments and insinuating into them assorted 'experts' and businessmen from outside party politics. These included the press barons, Northcliffe, Harmsworth and Beaverbrook. Sir Joseph Maclay, the Shipping Controller, held Parliament in such low esteem that he did not trouble to take a seat in either House. From the perspective of the party politicians the new appointees added to the prime minister's powers of patronage while limiting their own opportunity of office. Consequently peace brought an inevitable reaction against Lloyd

George's practices, and left many Conservatives convinced that extensions of state control were automatically connected with corruption in government. In retreating from interventionism they were also recoiling from the dynamic wartime premiership of Lloyd George.

On the other hand, Conservatives such as Lord Milner appreciated the introduction of experts and businessmen into government; this was, after all, the practical expression of the idea of National Efficiency that had gained popularity around 1900. Milner and his disciples became ensconced in Lloyd George's personal secretariat during the war, where they promoted the cause of imperial expansion and also liberal domestic policies. Milner went further than most of his colleagues in condemning *laissez-faire*, which he blamed for preventing full employment. He regarded the power of the state in a *Bismarckian* sense as a positive good capable of regenerating British society and industry; he even described himself as a National Socialist and was very active in preparing a Tory–Socialist programme through the British Workers' National League. When the cabinet considered the reports issued by the Sankey Committee on the coal industry, Milner was the one Conservative ready to support nationalization, along with George Barnes and G. H. Roberts for Labour and two Liberals, Addison and Edwin Montagu. A number of the younger men who had served as junior officers also believed that the state now had a duty to provide employment and a minimum standard of living for its citizens; among them Harold Macmillan, Anthony Eden and Oswald Mosley were later to play influential roles both inside the party and outside it. Mosley, who was elected in 1918 as a supporter of the Coalition, advocated a strong benevolent state, tariffs and greater development of the Empire. But by 1922 he had lost patience with the caution and negativism of the Conservative Party and moved across to Labour by 1924, as did other prominent Tories. While this weakened interventionism in the party, it also strengthened Stanley Baldwin, who became leader in 1923, in his determination to pursue a progressive domestic policy.

The great stumbling block for Conservatives lay in their wish to reverse the high taxation which had begun in 1909 and had been extended during the war. The major victim of the backlash was Lloyd George's promise to build homes fit for heroes to live in. The government had decided to allow local authorities to determine quotas for housebuilding, buy the land and offer contracts to private builders to construct houses for rent. However, the programme was eventually launched amid the post-war boom when builders were undertaking more profitable work than local authority contracts. As a result the government offered them subsidies which made the programme more expensive than envisaged and a natural target for re-trenchment. The 'Anti-Waste' campaigners regarded housing as the main obstacle to reducing income tax, which stood at 6*s* in the pound by the end of the war. Austen Chamberlain reduced the tax to 4s, which was still high by Edwardian standards, and appointed the Geddes Committee in 1921 to recommend cuts in expenditure. Its report put paid to the housing and education reforms and the vociferous attacks of the Tory backbenchers forced Lloyd George to abandon his progressive social policy by 1922. Not surprisingly, contemporary observers such as J. M. Keynes attributed the reversal of policy to what they saw as the narrow and blinkered businessmen sitting in the post-war Parliament. Most of the 168 Conservative members who entered the Commons for the first time in 1918 were middle-class men; over two-thirds of the parliamentary party were now businessmen (39 per cent) or professionals (31 per cent), while those with traditional backgrounds – the land (15 per cent) and the services (15 per cent) – had become modest minorities.[12] None of the post-war party leaders showed much inclination to challenge the rank-and-file view. Austen Chamberlain, the Chancellor, shared the conviction that the economy would right itself once the burdens imposed by war had been lifted. Bonar Law, who had been Chancellor during the war, sympathized with the idea of a capital levy to reduce the crushing burden of payments on the national debt, but he dropped it when the idea was pronounced suicidal by the party chairman Sir George Younger. Even the most liberal leader, Stanley Baldwin, who had been an advocate of social reform before 1914, bowed to the demand for retrenchment. He, too, accepted the wisdom of a special levy on capital to the extent of imposing one on his personal fortune when he was Financial Secretary to the Treasury in 1919; but as President of the Board of Trade he took his part in decontrolling the coal industry. Thus, as the Conservatives entered the new decade they seemed anxious to return to balanced budgets and low taxation. Apart from strengthening their existing conviction in protectionism the war had engendered in them only a negative reaction against interventionism; it was not until the 1930s that their approach changed under the influence of a younger generation and the economic failures of the 1920s.

PART FOUR

1918–1945

CHAPTER TEN

The Elevation of Labour and the Restoration of Party Politics 1918–1931

The Labour Government's main weakness is vanity; they are all . . . delighted with the good impression they are making on the middle class.

Diary of William Wedgwood Benn, 19 March 1924

The Fragmentation of the Coalition

In view of the critical state of the war in 1916 the formation of Lloyd George's Coalition was not surprising; it was more remarkable that it survived until 1922. For although the prime minister appeared all-powerful as hostilities drew to a close, his power rested upon the illusion that the Conservatives needed him; and to exercise his power he relied upon the Tory leaders, Bonar Law and Austen Chamberlain, to manage the Conservative rank and file for him. Lloyd George himself recognized how unlikely it was that they would accept him indefinitely, so much so that before normal party loyalties reasserted themselves he contemplated launching a new centre or national party. In the post-war years, when traditional loyalties and issues seemed irrelevant, the rearrangement of the party system became a fashionable preoccupation, and Lloyd George could reasonably hope to attract Conservatives such as Austen Chamberlain (himself originally a Liberal Unionist), Milner, Balfour, Birkenhead and Worthington Evans, all of whom disparaged party government and relished coalition. While Lloyd George dispensed patronage he might also retain the opportunists such as Curzon. In the Labour ranks J. H. Thomas and J. R. Clynes were thought likely to join Lloyd George, while his Coalition Liberals provided administrative talent, if little political flair. On the other hand, while such disparate allies could be held together by power and patronage, it was doubtful whether, in the absence of a coherent programme and philosophy, they could become a viable party in the country where they would have required sufficient membership and organization to survive a general election.

Even with power the Liberal side of the Coalition began to disintegrate not long after the 1918 election. Their position had been justified by Lloyd George's reconstruction programme. Yet by 1921 the reforms in housing, education and agriculture had been abandoned or curtailed for the sake of financial retrenchment. Over half the Coalition Liberals voted against the government or abstained over the 1921 Safeguarding of Industries Act which introduced a 33⅓ per cent tariff on certain goods. Even more offensive to Liberals was the recruitment of the 'Black and Tans', an irregular force used to subdue the Sinn Fein in Ireland, a policy actually presided over by a Coalition Liberal minister, Sir Hamar Greenwood. Liberal influence had also been felt over India, where Edwin Montagu issued a pledge of eventual self-government in 1917 and enacted the Montagu–Chelmsford reforms in 1919. However, the Conservatives deplored all this and roared their approval of the so-called 'Amritsar Massacre' of 1919, when British troops shot and killed 400 Indians. The vilification of Montagu drove him to resignation in 1922. This, combined with Addison's resignation as Health Minister the previous year, underlined Lloyd George's inability or unwillingness to defend his Liberal policies. Consequently by 1922 many Coalition Liberals, seeing no future with Lloyd George, began to make overtures to the Asquithian Liberals for reunion, though several, including Winston Churchill and Sir Alfred Mond, moved further towards the Conservatives. The demise of coalitionism had been heralded by signs of electoral vulnerability. Between 1919 and 1922, when the Asquithians made five by-election gains, the Coalition Liberals lost nine seats, seven of them to Labour, an indication that the role of the Coalition as a bulwark against the rise of Labour was played out.

That the Coalition survived four years of peace, despite all this, reflected Conservative appreciation of the prime minister's positive achievements. He had been persuaded to take a strong line against both Sinn Fein and Bolshevik Russia; by 1921 he had bowed to the pressure for financial retrenchment by the Conservatives and the Anti-Waste League. Above all, he had managed to steer a course through the industrial militancy of 1919–20 which culminated in the collapse of the 'Triple Alliance' of miners, railwaymen and transport workers in March 1921. This largely involved making shrewd concessions, notably the setting up of the Sankey Commission on the coal industry which enabled him to avert the pressure for nationalization.

Against this many Conservatives felt that the government had failed to go far enough in giving protection to industry or in supporting agriculture. They were increasingly impatient over the reluctance of Bonar Law and

Lloyd George to honour their promise to reform the composition and powers of House of Lords, which had been a condition of their acceptance of the extension of the franchise in 1917. The core of the opposition to the Coalition lay in some 42 MPs, known as the 'Diehards', who were largely from the landowning and Ulster Unionist elements of the party, as opposed to the businessmen who tended to favour the Coalition. They were also comparatively elderly men representing safe seats who were unlikely to serve in the government; as such they felt little need for the Coalition.[1] The Diehards were especially antagonized by the Indian reforms, the reversal of the coercive policy towards Russia and the concessions which led to the establishment of the Irish Free State in 1920.

However, only 58 MPs voted against the Irish Treaty, and Diehard opposition is by no means an adequate explanation for the overthrow of Lloyd George. Disillusion spread beyond policy and legislation. Many Conservatives had never ceased to dislike Lloyd George on both personal and political grounds, and once the sense of crisis had lifted their resentment over his irregular methods of government resurfaced. They believed that he undermined the Foreign Office and the Treasury through his personal secretariat, and that he exploited incidents such as the Chanak crisis of 1922, when Britain almost went to war with Turkey, to perpetuate a presidential style of government. Though much of the apparatus of wartime had gone, Lloyd George was associated with unsavoury characters including Sir William Sutherland and Maundy Gregory, through whom he lavishly dispensed honours at inflated prices. Though the Conservative Party also benefited from the sale of honours, it chose to foist the guilt upon the prime minister personally when the issue was debated in Parliament in 1921. When Stanley Baldwin condemned the 'morally disintegrating effect of Lloyd George on all whom he had to deal with' he was reflecting a sentiment widely held in the Conservative Party.

In addition Conservatives had to count the cost of coalitionism in terms of their own careers. Since May 1915 the party had been denied a proportionate share of government posts. Even during 1919–22, when the cabinet numbered 21 or 22, only 10 to 12 places were held by Conservatives.[2] Among those deprived of office were senior men such as Lord Selborne and the former party chairman Sir Arthur Steel-Maitland. This was also irksome for the rising junior figures whose promotion was blocked including W. C. Bridgeman, R. A. Sanders, Sir Philip Lloyd-Greame, Edward Wood and L. S. Amery.

The New Strategy 1922

By 1922 these fears and grievances had been crystallized by the realization that the Conservatives no longer *needed* Lloyd George. The original tactical rationale for the alliance consisted in the assumption that the rise of Labour could best be checked by using Lloyd George to attract the ex-Liberals and the new, unattached voters to the national cause. But this assumption broke down when the Liberal Coalitonists' seats started to fall to Labour in by-elections at Spen Valley and Dartford in 1919, Norfolk South, Southwark and Heywood and Radcliffe in 1920, and Leicester East and Pontypridd in 1922. Altogether Labour made 13 gains in these years, including 5 from Conservatives, which suggested that they rather than the Asquithian Liberals (5 gains and 1 loss) were benefiting from the unpopularity of the government. Some Tories concluded from this that they must accustom themselves to Labour as the alternative party of government.

For a time right-wing resentment towards the government was harnessed by independent Conservatives fighting on a retrenchment platform led by Horatio Bottomley, Lord Rothermere and Lord Beaverbrook. By 1920 candidates of the Anti-Waste League were snatching Conservative seats on a policy which most Tories wished to make their own. Lord Salisbury lent respectability to the revolt by forming the People's Union for Economy, which was designed to appeal to both working and middle-class support.[3] The critics argued that if the party continued to tie itself to Lloyd George he would reduce it to the divided and demoralized condition in which he had left the Liberals. Above all the futility of coalitionism in Conservative eyes was demonstrated by the dramatic by-election at Newport in October 1922. There a Conservative, intervening in a seat held by a Coalition Liberal, emerged top of the poll in a three-cornered contest. Newport thus reinforced those who argued that electoral safety now lay in abandoning Lloyd George in favour of a straightforward appeal to voters by an unencumbered Conservative Party; for if seats like Newport could be won they were well within reach of an independent majority. Consequently local Conservative associations began to adopt candidates in Coalition Liberal seats, thereby forcing them to return to the Asquithian fold.

Another key factor in the collapse of the Coalition was Bonar Law's resignation through ill health in March 1921, which meant that 18 months later he was available as an alternative party leader. Meanwhile, his successor, Austen Chamberlain, wholly failed to conciliate disgruntled Conservatives. Aloof and remote, Chamberlain showed no sympathy with the complaints expressed by the junior ministers, perhaps partly because his own background as a Liberal Unionist made him insensitive to party feelings. By stubbornly refusing to acknowledge that the premiership could not remain indefinitely in Lloyd George's hands he fatally alienated his followers and sealed the fate of the government.

Conscious of the danger, the prime minister contemplated snatching an election early in 1922 so as to give himself another five-year term and thus the opportunity to establish a new centre party. However, this backfired by provoking a reaction from Baldwin and Curzon, as well as leading Tories outside the government. The party chairman, Sir George Younger, took the initiative by announcing his refusal to stand as a coalitionist at the next election. Though Lloyd George declared he would not be bullied by a 'second-rate brewer', he was deterred by Younger's move. He thus let slip the chance to abandon his allies on an issue of his own choosing, relying instead on Chamberlain to keep the Coalition running. After consulting his colleagues about the next election Chamberlain agreed to summon a meeting of the parliamentary party at the Carlton Club on 19 October.

Chamberlain offered an election without the Coupon but on the basis of continued co-operation with Lloyd George. He failed to give the party either the chance to fight under an independent programme or an end to Lloyd George's premiership. This played into the hands of Baldwin, who frankly condemned the prime minister as a divisive force, and allowed the moderate majority to contemplate rejecting his advice in the knowledge that Bonar Law was now ready to return to the leadership. Of the 286 MPs present at the Carlton Club only 86 voted to maintain the Coalition and 187 against.[4] The consequences of this vote proved to be immense. Within hours Lloyd George had resigned, and the next day Law was elected as party leader. Having formed a Conservative administration he promptly dissolved Parliament and won a comfortable victory with 344 seats out of 615. By plunging the country into an election which had so recently been resisted by his party Bonar Law caught his opponents unprepared. Lloyd George, forced to adjust to being out of office for the first time since 1905, was unsure whether to attack the Conservatives for rejecting him or to keep open the chance of collaboration with the Chamberlainites who remained aloof from the new government. Though designated a Liberal he was spurned by the official Liberal Party. Suddenly everyone seemed anxious to dissociate themselves from him. By ditching him now that he had become an electoral liability the Conservatives avoided the unpopularity they otherwise risked attracting as members of the government. Speed, in short, was Law's best weapon and he used it to the full.

However, the real significance of the 1922 decision lay in long-term strategy. In effect the Conservatives had adopted a different method for containing Labour. Instead of relying of Lloyd George they hoped to destroy him, along with the Asquithian Liberals, by squeezing their support between themselves and Labour. By focusing the debate on Labour and scaring middle-class voters into seeing it as extreme and Socialist, they intended to win over enough of the former Liberal support to give them a comfortable lead over Labour, despite its advance under the new electorate.

Baldwin and Normality 1923

No one handled the new strategy more deftly than Stanley Baldwin, who had emerged from the relative obscurity of the Board of Trade to become Chancellor of the Exchequer in Law's cabinet in October 1922. The temporary absence of so many leading Tories enabled him to become an unexpected prime minister when Law again retired in May 1923. Baldwin's immediate concern was to exclude Lloyd George from office; his broader policy was to remain calm and realistic about the prospect of a Labour government, to encourage the Conservatives to adopt a conciliatory approach to the working-class and female voters, and to accept changes in the Empire and in relations with Ireland. As such Baldwin was unquestionably a key figure in twentieth-century Conservatism. He was responsible for the next crucial decision that determined the pattern of politics in the 1920s – namely the plunge into another election in November 1923, only a year after the previous one and at a time when his majority was still intact. Ostensibly his motive was to ease the way to introduce tariffs in order to tackle unemployment, which had risen alarmingly since 1921; he was still hampered by Law's earlier pledge not to introduce tariffs without a popular mandate. Since the consequence was to reduce the 344 Conservative members to 258 and to precipitate the first Labour government, the whole exercise appeared to contemporaries an unforced error on Baldwin's part.

Although some historians have accepted at face value Baldwin's own explanation for the decision to call the election, the idea remains implausible. Unemployment was a problem in 1923 but hardly the sort of crisis that would drive a prime minister to take such a grave risk; and no clear evidence has been produced to show that Baldwin was primarily influenced by it at the time. Indeed, his experience at the Treasury had made him lukewarm about tariffs, and his willingness to offer the Chancellorship to the free-trader Reginald McKenna in 1923 suggests that protectionism was less than a priority.[5] But it gave him a plausible excuse for doing what he wished to do for political reasons. He remained obsessed by the need to reunite his party and complete the restoration of normal party politics which had begun under Bonar Law. So long as Chamberlain, Birkenhead and the others refused to join a Conservative government the prospect of a revived coalition could not be ruled out. In any case his own cabinet, which had been derided by Churchill as the 'second eleven', stood in need of the Tory Coalitionists. By announcing his desire for a mandate on tariffs in a speech at Plymouth on 25 October, Baldwin immediately polarized politics. Since the Liberal Party was bound to declare for free trade Lloyd George could not avoid nailing his colours to the same mast if he were to be included in the reunion of the party; but in the process he isolated himself from the Chamberlainites, who backed protectionism. This served Baldwin's purpose by restoring party unity because the Conservative rebels agreed to serve under him in a future administration. The short-term price proved to be heavy, but Baldwin had not appreciated how many seats he would lose; he contemplated reducing rather than losing his majority altogether.

In the event, when the Conservatives lost 107 seats and gained only 18 his gamble was seen to have failed. But although Baldwin suffered criticism for his miscalculation he did not lose the leadership and his underlying strategy survived. As a result he steadied the party in what many regarded as a crisis. One Tory backbencher proposed to lead the Coldstream Guards into the House of Commons to avert the prospect of a Labour government, but the bulk of the party accepted Baldwin's shrewder perception that a minority Labour government would be a safe experiment between two Tory ministries. Such conclusions reflected the parliamentary arithmetic after the election, which left 258 Conservatives facing 191 Labour and 158 Liberal members. In this situation there was no certainty that Labour would even get the chance to govern. For this reason Baldwin declined to resign and remained in office to meet the new Parliament in January 1924 as he was fully entitled to do as leader of the largest party. In this way he forced Asquith to take the deliberate step of joining with Labour to vote the Conservatives out and thus earn some responsibility for putting Ramsay MacDonald into office. Since the effect of the first Labour government was to elevate the party and accelerate the squeeze on the Liberals it served to advance the broader Conservative strategy most effectively.

The 1923 election exposed graphically the lack of unity and leadership on the Liberal side. As early as February 1919 some MPs, responding to the pressure of the rank and file, organized meetings of the 'Wee Frees' and Coalitionists designed to lead to reunion. However, the Asquithians were still too angered by the Coupon election and feared a takeover by the more numerous Lloyd George Liberals to co-operate. When Asquith returned to Parliament in the Paisley by-election in 1920 he failed to give any effective leadership either over reunion or on policy. Instead he allowed the party to launch candidates against the Coalition Liberals, thereby exacerbating the split. Although the Coalitionists had set up their own *Lloyd George Liberal Magazine* and organizations in the constituencies, their political rationale looked increasingly dubious. In 1922 they ran only 150 candidates compared with 320 for the Asquithians. They won 47 out of a Liberal total of 116, and their seats were very vulnerable since only 4 had won against a Conservative. Instead of welcoming them back into the fold, however, Asquith did nothing to check the factionalism of Simon, Runciman, Lord Gladstone and others who wanted revenge and professed to regard Lloyd George as an incubus on the party. Their antagonism was sharpened by the realization that they badly needed subsidies from the fund he had raised.

In the surge of enthusiasm over free trade in 1923 Lloyd George dispensed £160,000 to the party, but thereafter he held on to his money, preferring to wait for his rival's inevitable retirement rather than use it to help an organization that wished to exclude him from influence. After losing his seat in 1924 Asquith clung on as leader until 1926, by which time the Liberals had lost too many Radicals to Labour to make a full recovery.

Despite these failings it is doubtful whether any Liberal leader could have done better in the difficult circumstances following the 1923 election. Having fought the election to defend free trade they could not avoid voting Baldwin out of office, and all the leading Liberals accepted that MacDonald should have his chance to govern, even though this would attract criticism from right-wing Liberal supporters in the country. The Liberals claimed that Labour was following their ideas, but MacDonald's refusal to seek any deal with them made this implausible. If the Liberals had immediately tried to vote the new Labour government out they might have attracted the backing of some Tory members and gained an invitation from the king to form their own government. A united party might have attempted it; but Lloyd George could hardly be expected to relish serving under Asquith again. As a result the opportunity to restore Liberalism as an independent governing force passed.

MacDonaldism and Socialism

How had the Labour Party attained the status of a governing party in so short a space of time? As recently as 1918 it had only 57 MPs, largely regarded as an uninspired set of union leaders who had managed to survive the Coupon Election and failed to conduct themselves like a government-in-waiting. Many of the socialists and critics of the war complained that the MPs offered no serious opposition to the Treaty of Versailles and had nothing to say on the great moral issues of the day. The explosion of industrial militancy in 1919-20 inevitably made the parliamentarians seem a little marginal for a time as it offered the only means of challenging the dominance of the Lloyd George Coalition. As many of the strikes succeeded in winning wage increases they boosted union membership to a peak, and the idea of 'direct action' as an alternative to the plodding parliamentary strategy gained popularity for a time. Direct action took concrete form in the shape of the 'Triple Alliance' of miners, railwaymen and transport workers, and it achieved a famous victory in May 1920 when the dockers refused to load the *Jolly George*, a ship preparing to sail with a cargo of arms for use against the Bolsheviks in Poland. The government's retreat on the issue gave some grounds for thinking that the workers could compel it to abandon its policy of intervention in support of the anti-Bolshevik forces in the civil war in Russia. This, however, proved to be a brief phase. Most Labour and trade union leaders disapproved of direct action and condemned Bolsehvism as anarchism and anti-democratic. 'If you want me to lead the Labour movement as a Bolshevist,' declared Arthur Henderson in 1918, 'I give you notice that I am done with the job.'[6] In April 1921 the Triple Alliance collapsed when the other workers left the miners in the lurch, and thereafter the parliamentary leaders regained the initiative, helped by the knowledge that the Coalition was disintegrating.

In view of the opprobrium later heaped upon him it should be emphasized how much Labour owed to Ramsay MacDonald for its resurgence in the early 1920s. His defeat in 1918 left him free to articulate the party's case in the country and in effect to underline his superiority as a parliamentarian to those who presently occupied the front bench. His advantages as a potential leader were strikingly similar to those of Gladstone for the Liberals in the 1860s, for, despite a tendency amongst socialists to disparage leadership as opposed to ideology, the inter-war Labour Party badly needed a great leader to unify the disparate range of people within the movement. The very ambiguity of MacDonald's thinking enabled the conflicting elements within the movement to look to him as their own best spokesman. His oratorical talents and his principled stand against the war allowed him to articulate a sense of moral righteousness, much as Gladstone had once done. When support for direct action was at its height he avoided condemning it by arguing that the workers' intervention had helped to save the country from another war. In addition to his ability to inspire confidence in ILP Socialists, pacifists and the patriotic trade union leaders, Macdonald was also a key figure in attracting recruits from the other parties, including the idealistic ex-Liberals and some influential figures who abandoned the Conservatives to join Labour, including Lord Parmoor, Stafford Cripps, John Sankey, John Strachey, Oswald and Cynthia Mosley, Oliver Baldwin and Susan Lawrence. These Conservatives especially warmed to his vision of Labour as a *national* party, not a mere class party.

Despite his advantages there was no certainty that MacDonald would become the party's leader. He was narrowly defeated in a Labour seat at Woolwich in February 1921 but then returned at the general election for Aberavon, a safe seat in South Wales. He then defeated J. R. Clynes by just 65 votes to 61 to become the new leader. But although Labour had 142 MPs compared with 116 for the Liberals, there was no certainty in 1922 that the party would retain its new position as the second party. MacDonald, however, had a clear idea of his strategy. Unlike Clynes, he refused to be conciliatory over the occupation of the front bench in the Commons which he refused to share with the Liberals. Like Baldwin, he intended to polarize politics around a Conservative–Labour contest in which the Liberals were marginalized. He was strengthened in this by the prominence of foreign affairs in 1922 and 1923. The problem of German reparations and the French occupation of the Ruhr seemed to vindicate left-wing criticism of Versailles as too punitive towards Germany. MacDonald was a keener student of foreign affairs than either of the Conservative prime ministers and as the reaction against the First World War gained strength he gained in authority.

Nonetheless, as the prospects of a Labour government grew, the party's domestic programme and ideology became increasingly exposed. Much of the debate during the 1920s was cast in terms of capitalism versus socialism; in 1923 the House of Commons even treated itself to a debate on the subject. Yet in fact such a choice was never available. All the governments of the inter-war period thought in terms of orthodox solutions for Britain's economic ills, including a return to the Gold Standard, the restoration of trade and a balanced budget. The chief alternative was not a detailed socialist policy but a reformed, interventionist form of capitalism. The advocates of this alternative approach included members of all three parties, the ILP, pressure groups such as Political and Economic Planning, and individuals such as J. M. Keynes, Lloyd George and Sir Oswald Mosley. They offered a mixture of public works schemes funded by budgetary deficits, devaluation of the pound, cheap money policies and tariff protection, all of which were designed to reduce unemployment by stimulating the domestic demand for British-made goods. By putting the emphasis on the domestic market they effectively abandoned what seemed a futile attempt to manage the world economy.

During the 1920s the major influence on Labour thinking came from the ILP. It moved beyond the debates over whether wartime state control pointed the way towards socialism to focus on the problems of mass unemployment and on techniques for managing a failing capitalist economy. In *The Socialist Programme* in 1923 the ILP revealed the influence of underconsumptionist ideas in the emphasis it placed on raising and stabilizing the demand for the products of industry by a more equal distribution of incomes. This went hand in hand with the strategy which became associated with Keynes. The ILP's programme included state management of banks, a scientific credit policy designed to moderate fluctuations in the economy, the raising of purchasing power as a way of reducing unemployment, and measures of control over key industries.

This was somewhat at variance with the imprecision of official Labour Party thinking at the time. For despite the fresh statements in the 1918 constitution and *Labour and the New Social Order*, the party had not really begun to think through the implications of a commitment to Socialism and economic planning. On the contrary, the parliamentary leaders backed away from the kind of precise proposals advocated by the ILP, and in particular they abandoned the idea for a levy on capital. By reducing the drain of debt payments on government revenue a levy would have gone a long way to enabling Labour to pursue the social policies it favoured.

To some extent this reflected the supremacy of *political* considerations in MacDonald's mind; he wished to minimize fears that a Labour government would be extreme or radical. But as a result Labour arrived in office in January 1924 without a well-defined economic policy, except insofar as it shared with the other governments of the period an optimistic nineteenth-century belief in maximizing trade. The solution to unemployment was expected to be found in restoring the pound to its pre-war value, promoting a high level of world trade and thus recovering Britain's former export markets. Though immensely attractive, this approach proved to be flawed, partly because Britain no longer possessed enough influence over the international economy, which was drifting into protectionism, and because as world trade increased Britain failed to recover her former share of it.

However, when the election of 1923 presented him with the opportunity to form a minority government, even on the basis of just 191 seats, MacDonald showed no hesitation. He appreciated that if he failed to form a ministry, the Liberals would do so, thereby forcing Labour off the Opposition front bench in favour of the Conservatives. Despite the fact that he could have been voted out of office at any moment by the Conservatives alone, MacDonald ignored the apparent logic of the parliamentary arithmetic which pointed to formal co-operation with the Liberals to give him a working majority. Contrary to many textbooks which continue to assume that MacDonald governed with Liberal support, he resolutely avoided any agreement. In part this was a reflection of personal vanity and insecurity; he had no governmental experience and thought his opponents were waiting for him to make a fool of himself. But it was also a deliberate policy designed to kill any client relationship with the Liberals and exclude them from office. MacDonald's minority position in Parliament could even be used to advantage by providing an excuse for the absence of socialist legislation in the face of criticism from the left of the party. Some ILP members argued that the best course would be to invite defeat by offering a full socialist programme on taking office. However, this would merely have played into the hands of Labour's critics and, in view of the king's reluctance to concede a third election so soon, possibly have resulted in a Liberal government. In any case, MacDonald had no socialist programme to introduce in 1924; his aim was simply to operate the machinery of government so as to explode the myth that Labour was unfit to govern and thus consolidate its new standing. He never expected to retain office for more than a short period; indeed the longer he remained in office the greater would be the pressure to tackle fundamental social and economic problems. In this sense he was always seeking a parliamentary defeat, but not too soon; he managed to achieve this with the tacit co-operation of Baldwin.

In pursuit of respectability and competence MacDonald imported into his cabinet a series of former Liberal ministers – Haldane as Lord Chancellor, C. P. Trevelyan at Education, Noel Buxton at Agriculture, and Josiah Wedgwood at the Duchy of Lancaster. More surprisingly, he appointed several Conservatives, including Lord Chelmsford to the Admiralty and Lord Parmoor as Lord President of the Council. Only two posts went to men of undisputed socialist convictions – John Wheatley (Health) and F. W. Jowett (Works). The prime minister faced little criticism over this, perhaps because the party felt awed at the momentous step it was taking and reluctant to rock the boat. MacDonald went out of his way to ensure that his government conformed to expectations, even to the extent of acquiring court dress for his ministers to wear. The ease with which Labour had been entrusted with office also consolidated the strongly monarchist sentiments in the movement. During 1922 and 1923 leading Labour politicians had met the George V and Queen Mary socially, and one of them, J. H. Thomas, had insisted: 'Republicanism [is] no part of the Labour Party's programme. If Labour came to power tomorrow they would find the King prepared to accept their advice as readily as that of the Liberal or Tory parties.'[7] The party's readiness to accept the British constitution as it found it and the prime minister's known disregard for reforms contributed to the overall strategy of establishing Labour as a natural party of government. Philip Snowden, the new chancellor, produced a model Gladstonian budget in which he used a small surplus to reduce duties on food and make a modest grant to public works schemes; though there was no serious attempt to tackle unemployment during the nine months of the government's life, the party remained pleased at the spectacle of a Labour chancellor managing the Treasury in an orthodox fashion. As foreign secretary Macdonald also reassured the country by endeavouring to restore trade with Russia, by reducing German reparations and by improving relations with the French in order to secure their withdrawal from the Ruhr. The one major innova-tion was Wheatley's Housing Act, which reintroduced the council-house building policy of 1919.

The avoidance of anything really controversial made it difficult for the Conservatives to attack the government. Baldwin actually liked MacDonald and approved of the continuity with the previous government's foreign policy. Though he felt obliged to make critical speeches in the country to rally his own followers, for some time he avoided attempts to overthrow Labour in the Commons which could have been achieved comparatively easily. Some defeats on minor matters maintained the illusion that the Opposition was doing its job, but Conservative members were strikingly absent when the government's majority was in danger. In truth it suited Baldwin to keep MacDonald in office until the autumn of 1924, allowing him time to consolidate his own position before the inevitable return to a Tory government. By September the Conservatives felt ready to censure the government over the withdrawal by the Attorney-General of the proposed prosecution of J. R. Campbell, a Communist editor, under the Incitement to Mutiny Act. Meanwhile the Liberals, patience exhausted by MacDonald's refusal to co-operate with them, had put down a motion criticizing the Russian Treaty negotiated by MacDonald. In his diary the prime minister revealed his eagerness to be defeated: 'I am inclined to give the Liberals an election on it if they force it . . . the conditions of office perhaps bribe me to take this chance of ending the present regime.'[8] So determined was he to take the opportunity to be defeated that when the Liberals put a compromise amendment to the Conservative motion seeking a select committee of enquiry he insisted on treating it as a resignation issue. MacDonald's fall was in fact unnecessary, for he knew that Asquith wanted to find a way out of the confrontation. Nonetheless he secured his own defeat by 364 to 198 votes. Of course, there were good reasons for taking this course. After nine months the novelty was wearing off and Labour supporters were growing dissatisfied over unemployment and the cabinet's use of troops in a strike in the docks. He could not go on much longer without doing something substantial to justify holding office. That he was forced out while defending left-wing causes such the Russian Treaty and the Campbell case helped to blunt criticism within the movement. The impression that Labour had been sabotaged by reactionary forces was greatly enhanced by the so-called Zinoviev Letter. This document, which purported to be part of a plot to incite class war in Britain by the President of the Communist International in Moscow, was released on the weekend before polling day for maximum effect. Though the letter was a forgery designed to boost Conservative propaganda, it probably made no more than a marginal impact on the result of the election; its importance lay in diverting attention from the shortcomings of MacDonald's government and convincing Labour that it had been deprived of office by a conspiracy among the capitalists.

Though it appears odd for a prime minister to court an early election, MacDonald knew it was unavoidable and that the Conservatives were bound to recover once the special circumstances of 1923 had disappeared. By-elections at Burnley and West Toxteth, which Labour held, convinced him that the party's support would not collapse. By contrast the Liberal vote looked shaky and the Conservatives could be expected to recover seats lost the previous year. That they would be the major beneficiaries in the short term mattered little to MacDonald, for his main concern was the relative strength of Labour and the Liberals. While Labour's seats dwindled from

191 to 151, the Liberals shrank from 158 to 42. Labour ran 512 candidates and won 33 per cent of the vote while the Liberals fielded only 340 and won 17.6 per cent. In this way the 1924 election served the objectives of both Baldwin and MacDonald by squeezing the Liberals and consolidating Labour's position as the only realistic government-in-waiting. The return to two-party politics was not complete but it had advanced significantly.

The Rise and Fall of the Second Labour Government

The freedom of being back in opposition inevitably led Labour critics of MacDonald to question the wisdom of accepting office without having a parliamentary majority sufficient to enact a radical programme. Despite the pressure, however, the leaders managed to escape being committed to any precise economic strategy in the years up to 1929. In this they were helped partly by the manner of their defeat in 1924 and also by the General Strike of 1926 which deflected criticism on to the enemy. It was while several of the right-wing union leaders had been involved in the 1924 government that the TUC had become committed to the general strike strategy. After returning to the TUC they hoped it would prove unnecessary to implement such a policy. A general strike would have been inconceivable but for the reaction of key leaders like Ernest Bevin of the Transport and General Workers' Union to the fall of the Labour government; they anticipated *general* wage reductions by the employers, who would be backed by the Baldwin government. This diagnosis was sound in that the decision to restore the pound to its pre-war level of $4.87 in 1925 could not be sustained without a significant reduction in the costs, and thus the wages, of British industry. Seen in this perspective the General Strike was not motivated by syndicalism, nor was it primarily an unselfish action to support the miners, but a defensive measure designed to resist a general attack on wages. This explains why 1926 saw both a short general strike and a much longer miners' strike.

In a purely industrial sense the General Strike was not of great significance, though it probably deterred some employers from making the wage cuts they thought necessary. Union membership had been falling for the last five years and militancy had been in decline. Perhaps surprisingly the union leaders, whose conduct of the strike had not been impressive, survived, and, if anything, the episode discredited the advocates of direct action. Similarly MacDonald and the parliamentary leaders, who had given no real support to the strike, benefited from the greater sense of unity it generated. The industrial and political wings of the Labour Movement agreed on the need to win the next election so as to repeal the punitive legislation passed by the Conservatives in 1927 to make general strikes illegal.

THE TREE-SITTER.

PRIME MINISTER (*to himself*). 'I DON'T SAY THIS HAS BEEN
A COMFORTABLE SESSION; BUT SO LONG AS I CAN
COUNT ON A FAIRLY REGULAR SUPPLY OF LIGHT
REFRESHMENT I DON'T SEE WHY I SHOULDN'T
STAY HERE FOR EVER.'

[The latest craze in America is to see how long you can sit on
the branch of a tree. Competitors are supplied with sustenance
by their supporters.]

Punch, or the London Charivari, 30 July 1930

Consequently when the ILP began to propagate its programme in *The Living Wage* MacDonald merely disparaged its authors as extremists – a striking indication of the readiness of the party to accept the authority of its leader. He continued to confine himself to lofty generalizations and avoid a precise economic policy. In fact the most serious challenge to MacDonald came from outside the party, in the shape of Lloyd George, who succeeded in making unemployment the dominant issue by 1929. Since 1926 he had been rebuilding his bridges to radicalism. Old colleagues such as Charles Masterman had been drawn together with the Manchester Radicals, E. D. Simon and Ramsay Muir, as well as an influential group of economists and academics including Walter Layton, Hubert Henderson, J. M. Keynes, William Beveridge and J. A. Hobson, to pool ideas through the Liberal Summer Schools and Lloyd George's Liberal Industrial Enquiry. It was the Enquiry that generated the famous Liberal Yellow Book, *Britain's Industrial Future*, in 1928. This reflected the thinking of Keynes in its proposals to use the Bank of England's control of credit to stimulate trade and to support major schemes of public works by deficit financing. What was unusual, apart from the impressive intellectual underpinning behind the document, was the detailed character of the proposals. It was calculated that every £1 million invested in road building would generate 5,000 man-years of employment. In the first year some 350,000 extra jobs were to be created by such methods. This was the basis of Lloyd George's claim that he could reduce unemployment, which stood at 1.1 million in June 1929, to normal proportions within a year.

Faced with this bold and constructive alternative Labour adopted an ambivalent stance. At the local level many Labour candidates advocated similar policies based on public works schemes. Officially, however, the party accepted the orthodox Treasury view of deficit finance as impracticable. Some socialists chose to dismiss Keynesian methods as palliatives designed to shore up a system in fatal decline, while others, failing to grasp the scale and the rationale, saw them in terms of traditional, local authority works schemes. MacDonald himself disparaged the Liberal campaign as a typical stunt by a man notorious for making unfulfilled promises. The confusion was evident in the party's *Appeal to the Nation*, which boldly promised to deal with unemployment and claimed that Lloyd George had appropriated its own ideas; but the document also contained the lame admission that 'the most important attack upon unemployment is to restore prosperity to the depressed industries'. After 1931 MacDonald bore the brunt of criticism for the failure of Labour's approach to the economic depression. In the late 1920s, however, the party conference repeatedly sided with him against the critics who were attempting to commit the party to a more precise and more radical policy. Yet MacDonald had never concealed the fact that he regarded socialism as the distant conclusion to a gradual transformation of society rather than as something concrete that would emerge in the near future. Insofar as he envisaged achieving the goal at governmental level he believed, not as a Marxist, that it would emerge from the crisis and collapse of the capitalist system, but, as a Fabian, that it would grow from the success of the existing system. Meanwhile, the Labour Party was the best vehicle for guiding society in the right direction.

While MacDonald's approach was sound enough politically, it left him exposed to periods of economic depression. He argued eloquently that the more the world economy deteriorated the more it proved Labour's claim that the system was rotten and would collapse. But Labour's justification for holding office at such times was to protect working people from the effects of unemployment, and in the absence of a short- to medium-term strategy for tackling unemployment this was fatally flawed. The absence of a majority in both 1924 and 1929 offered another alibi for the failure to take any real steps towards socialism, but during the second Labour government's life this wore increasingly thin. To some extent MacDonald's actions were severely circumscribed when he entered office in the summer of 1929 by the magnitude of the economic depression that was sweeping across the world. However, this should not be exaggerated. In November 1929 unemployment stood at 1.3 million – a serious problem, but not a crisis; it reached 1.7 million by April 1930 and 2 million by July 1930. During that period MacDonald failed to get to grips with the problem. He left responsibility in the hands of the highly orthodox chancellor, Philip Snowden, and appointed J. H. Thomas as Lord Privy Seal, with a brief for unemployment but without the executive powers and civil service support necessary to take significant initiatives. By setting up an Economic Advisory Council he merely compounded his original mistake. The prevailing wisdom of the Treasury, as expressed by Snowden, held that public works schemes to reduce unemployment were inherently uneconomic, would take a long time to implement, and would only damage private industry since there were no idle reserves for investment. Although MacDonald had grown privately sceptical about Snowden's faith in balanced budgets and free trade, he failed to challenge the orthodox view. In February 1930 Sir Oswald Mosley, a junior minister under Thomas, drew up a memorandum designed to promote an expansion of purchasing power, place restrictions on imports to help British industry and control banking so as to finance industrial development. However, the Cabinet rejected this, whereupon Mosley resigned and Thomas escaped to the Colonial Office; Vernon Hartshorn, who replaced him, received pathetic letters from the prime minister entreating him to do his job and 'put pressure on industries to put themselves in order'.[9]

Mosley's memorandum was not the only alternative strategy open to Macdonald. Since the election Lloyd George had been anxious to press his proposals for handling the economy upon the new premier. The Liberal leader could offer not just a counter to the negativism of the Treasury, but also the extra votes required to give MacDonald a majority in the Commons. It is clear from MacDonald's papers that he played Lloyd George shrewdly by involving him and his advisers in protracted negotiations, but with little intention of reaching overall agreement.[10] Agreement was reached on a bill for electoral reform which would have introduced the alternative vote system; since this would have boosted Liberal representation it was regarded by many as contrary to Labour's interests, and the bill had been safely emasculated by the House of Lords by the time the government fell.[11] But all this served the purpose of keeping Lloyd George away from negotiations with the Conservatives, which might have brought the government down even sooner. Yet in the process Macdonald missed the opportunities he undoubtedly had to get a grip on the economic problem before the collapse of the international banks in August 1931 forced him into a real crisis at last. Following the Treasury view that the priority was to restore confidence and avoid a devaluation of the pound, Snowden drew up a list of expenditure reductions totalling £78.5 million, including a ten per cent cut in unemployment benefit, so as to balance the budget. But although the cabinet reluctantly approved this by 12 votes to 9, the General Council of the TUC flatly rejected the proposals. This led several of the waverers, notably Arthur Henderson, to retract their acceptance because they feared alienating the industrial wing of the Labour movement. As a result the Cabinet broke up on 23 August. MacDonald resigned but was persuaded by the king to form a new national government; he took with him several leading figures, including Snowden and Thomas, but was repudiated by the bulk of the party. In this way the apparently inexorable advance Labour had made since 1918 suffered a decisive and prolonged check.

CHAPTER ELEVEN

Origins of the Conservative Electoral Hegemony 1918–1931

It is not surprising that the desire to put an end to this plague of annual elections should be uppermost in the minds of many voters.

The Nation, 1924

Although the most striking feature of the 1920s was the sustained surge in popular support for the Labour Party, this should not obscure the Conservative preponderance which so characterized the period. Indeed, during 1918–39 the Conservatives formed or predominated in governments after five of the seven general elections, and were consistently the largest party except during the 1929–31 Parliament. How was this hegemony established and maintained at a time when the terms of the electoral battle had changed drastically, and in ways that might have been expected to present the advantage to a rival party claiming to stand for the working-class majority? How far, if at all, was the political struggle modified as a result of the introduction of a new element of uncertainty in the shape of the female electorate? In this chapter we shall attempt to isolate the chief elements both in Conservative success and in Labour's growth which proceeded apparently unchecked until 1931.

The Impact of the Electoral System

It would be erroneous to assume that the Conservative parliamentary majorities of 1918–39 reflected their transformation into a natural majority in the country. A glance at the voting figures shown in table 11.1 indicates

TABLE 11.1   *Voting figures, 1922–1929*

	Conservative		Liberal		Labour	
	% Vote	Seats	% Vote	Seats	% Vote	Seats
1922	38.2	345	29.1	116	29.5	142
1923	38.1	258	29.6	159	30.5	191
1924	48.3	419	17.6	40	33.0	151
1929	38.2	260	23.4	59	37.1	288

TABLE 11.2   *Unopposed returns 1922–1929*

	Conservative	Liberal	Labour
1922	42	10	4
1923	35	11	3
1924	16	6	9
1929	4	–	–

that the victories of the 1920s were attained on a fairly narrow basis, usually a bare two-fifths of the poll. It can be argued that Conservative strength is in fact underestimated by the figures because of the number of strongly Conservative seats not contested by the other parties and therefore omitted. It is true that Conservatives enjoyed a disproportionate share of unopposed returns, largely in Northern Ireland and south-eastern county divisions. However, the numbers were not large and were diminishing (see table 11.2). In fact the net loss of Conservative votes arising from this source is insufficient to make more than a marginal impression on their share of the poll, even in 1922.[1] In that year only 483 Conservatives stood and a portion of the party's support must have gone to National or ex-Coalition Liberals. But their share is also inflated by the smaller number of candidates fielded by the Liberals whose absence in 1924, for example, from 275 of the 615 constituencies, served to boost the Conservative share. One may generalize by saying that the Conservative–Liberal–Labour share changed from 4–3–3 in the early 1920s to 4–2–4 by the end of the decade.

That such a division generated comfortable Conservative majorities may be ascribed in the first instance to party relationships and the electoral system. Single-member systems invariably produce highly unrepresentative results in which slight shifts in votes lead to exaggerated changes in representation; but the effect is notoriously erratic when three, rather than two, evenly balanced parties are in competition. Whereas before 1914 the Lib–Lab pact had resulted in straight fights in five seats out of six, during the 1920s three-cornered contests became usual. Consequently the division of the Progressive vote between Labour and Liberal gave the Conservatives a major advantage. This was dramatically demonstrated in 1922 when the comfortable Conservative majority of 345 (out of 615) was based on a percentage poll five points *below* that obtained in the disaster of 1906 which had yielded 157 seats (out of 670)! By contrast, the Liberal and Labour parties managed 58.6 per cent in 1922 compared with 54.9 per cent in 1906, yet returned only 258 members instead of 430. In 1922 they divided the vote virtually evenly between themselves, though the seats fell out to Labour's advantage because the greater concentration of its vote in certain industrial counties and conurbations brought its candidates more frequently to the head of the poll. The erratic operation of the electoral system left a major impact on politics during the successive general elections of 1922, 1923 and 1924. Labour came to power with only 191 seats following the 1923 election, when a modest loss of Conservative votes precipitated a net loss of 87 seats, largely to Liberal candidates in constituencies where Labour did not stand. The bizarre logic was reversed the following year in that Labour's increased strength facilitated Baldwin's return to power; for the rise in Labour candidatures from 422 to 512 occurred largely in seats won by Liberals in 1923, thereby producing many of the 107 Conservative gains from Liberals. Labour itself won substantially fewer constituencies in 1924 despite an increased share of the poll.

The long-term effect of the electoral system emerges from a comparison between the 1922 and 1929 elections. Although the Conservative vote was similar in each case they won 85 seats fewer in the latter year. The reason for this lay in a realignment of the non-Conservative vote during the decade. For whereas in 1922 Labour and the Liberals took 29 per cent each, by 1929 they stood at 37 per cent and 23 per cent; despite their party's 'revival' during 1926–9 many erstwhile Liberals regarded Labour as the more probable or desirable winner against the Conservatives. The disproportion in seats – 288 to 59 – was far greater than previously.

Why did the non-Conservative politicians not attempt to deprive the Conservatives of their built-in advantage, either by means of proportional representation using multi-member seats or by using the alternative vote in single-member seats? Before 1914 the Liberal Party, though tempted by the alternative vote, had neglected such innovations so long as the pact held. All parties tended to interpret Edwardian elections as meaning that the bulk of Liberal and Labour voters would use their second preferences to mutual advantage. Therefore when proportional representation (PR) and the alternative vote were debated under the Representation of the People

Bill in 1917–18 most Labour and Liberal MPs favoured the alternative vote, while the Conservatives resisted both schemes. Although the radical parties still retained a majority in the Commons at this time, they lacked leadership on this point, and in deference to Conservative objections Lloyd George induced sufficient coalitionist Liberal and Labour members to reject all varieties of reform. Thus they missed their best opportunity to break out of the traditional system. After 1918, since the Conservatives were unyielding, the Liberal Party hoped to obtain reform from the minority Labour governments. At the Speaker's Conference of 1930 the Liberals proposed PR in urban areas and the alternative vote elsewhere, a formula that seemed likely to maximize their advantage; for they would gain Labour second preferences in rural counties while limiting Labour's clean sweep of industrial regions. Unlike many in his party MacDonald had always disliked PR, but in view of the vulnerability of his government he gave consideration to the alternative vote. Now according to the party's chief agent, if this had been applied in the 313 constituencies whose MP had been elected on a minority vote in 1929 the representation would have been substantially modified: the Liberal total would have risen from 41 to 88, Labour's from 120 to 135–43, and the Conservatives fallen from 152 to 67–82.[2] Yet for MacDonald this would have been a mixed blessing; for the advantages of curtailing the Conservative strength were outweighed by the disadvantages of boosting the Liberals. Moreover, the agent's calculations had to be made on the assumption that each party's first preference votes would remain the same. However, the likelihood was that the new system would have encouraged wavering radicals to vote Liberal instead of backing Labour in order to keep the Conservatives out, and also relaxed the pressure on 'moderates' to vote Conservative rather than Liberal to stop Labour. Already the Liberals under Lloyd George's inspiration were dangerously near to a breakthrough; their 5 million votes in 1929, against 8 million for each of the other parties, threatened a return to three-party politics. MacDonald's whole strategy in the 1920s consisted in using the logic of the first-past-the-post system to drive the Progressive vote into Labour's camp, as the Liberals had used it before 1914. To allow the Liberals a guaranteed parliamentary base of between 100 and 150 members – the inevitable consequence of electoral reform – would have been to destroy the prospect of a majority Labour government which was now within sight. A bigger Liberal representation would have led to coalition which, especially with Lloyd George's participation, foreshadowed a restoration of the Liberals as the senior partner in government. Thus although MacDonald humoured Lloyd George even to the extent of introducing a bill for electoral reform, he relied upon the Conservative peers to delay and destroy it for him; it was a reasonable assumption that his government would not last long enough to have to fight for the measure. The establishment of a National Government in 1931 killed off any prospect of reform, and also undid the Liberal revival of 1929 by shifting the Liberals into a closer relationship with the right, thereby completing the vacating of the left for occupation by Labour. Conservative predominance between the wars was, thus, for Labour a necessary price to be paid in the medium term for maintaining its own elevation as the major alternative at the expense of the Liberals.

The Conservatives and the Constituencies

The second key element in the Conservatives' success is to be found in the reorganization of the constituencies in 1918 and the Conservative response to it. The previous redistribution back in 1885 had left plenty of anomalies such as seats like Kilkenny with 1,700 voters, and the shifts of population since then had only exacerbated the disparities. By 1918 the average English constituency had twice as many electors as the average Irish seat and somewhat more than those in Wales and Scotland. This over-representation told against the Conservatives, though it was to some extent balanced by Conservative command of many small boroughs in England.

It seems obvious that the growth of population since 1885, especially in suburban areas around London, Birmingham, south Lancashire and Glasgow, would inevitably have produced Conservative gains under any redistribution that moved towards equal constituencies. One historian has estimated that if the 1918 redistribution had operated at the previous general election (December 1910) it would have had the effect of adding 3 to Liberal strength, 5 to Labour and 34 to the Conservatives (see table 11.3).[3] However, this calculation of a net Conservative gain of 26 should not be seen simply as the effect of equal constituencies. If one sets aside the 6 net gains in Ireland – for Ireland's representation was exempted from the general provisions in 1918 – one has 20 gains in England, Wales and Scotland; this includes 4 university-seat gains (also exceptions to the population rules), which leaves 16. The key to these in fact lies in the

TABLE 11.3   *Estimated result of December 1910 election under 1918 boundaries*

	Actual result December 1910	*Effect of 1918 boundaries*
Conservative	272	306
Liberal/Labour	314	322
Irish	84	79

overall increase in the Commons to 707 members rather than to any strict application of the principle of equal constituencies. None of the parties had objected in principle to equalization at the Speaker's Conference in 1916; existing borough and county seats were to retain separate representation only if their population reached 50,000, and new ones were to be formed for every 70,000 and for remainders of 50,000. The redivision of residential constituencies, particularly in London, Middlesex, Surrey, Warwickshire and Lancashire, certainly generated additional Conservative, seats. Before 1914, 9 of the 13 largest seats had been Conservative, of which 7 were in London (Croydon, Ealing, Enfield, Harrow, Lewisham, Wandsworth and Wimbledon); Wandsworth, for example, became 4 separate seats in 1918, each returning a Conservative. However, much of this was offset by the disappearance of many small Conservative boroughs like Salisbury, Winchester, Windsor, Taunton, Canterbury, Hereford and Bury St Edmunds, which were merged into the surrounding county constituencies. These modifications had a special significance within the party, for they eroded still further the natural parliamentary base of the landed elements while extending that of the commercial and urban sections, a process discernible by 1900 but greatly speeded up in the twentieth century.

In fact the principle of equal constituencies was circumscribed in ways calculated to assist the Conservatives, such as the increase in university representation from 9 to 15,[4] which the party had expected to lose altogether.[5] In addition, the rules for constituency size were always interpreted flexibly because of the assumption that parliamentary boundaries should coincide with administrative ones. In 1918 the Boundary Commissioners' room for manoeuvre was significantly widened by a Conservative amendment to the instructions to the effect that they should avoid creating constituencies of an inconvenient size or character.[6] This could not save sparsely populated (Liberal) counties like Caithness and Sutherland or Radnor and Brecon from amalgamation; but it did allow a number of English agricultural seats to be given the benefit of the doubt where their population was not too far below the limit laid down in the Act. According to private Conservative estimates at least 17 county seats, which on a strict interpretation should have been abolished, were thus preserved.[7] This was possible only at the cost of inflating the membership of the Commons from 670 to 707, something that the House, though very critical, was prepared to tolerate on the assumption that before very long the Irish element was bound to shrink as a consequence of Home Rule. Thus, so far as England, Scotland and Wales are concerned, the 1918 redistribution gave the Conservatives a modest gain, not so much through the application of equalization as by certain judicious modifications of it.

Ultimately, however, their major gain came from Ireland, where Conservatives had long been anxious for redistribution, in view of the huge

TABLE 11.4   *Seats won by Conservatives in 1900 and 1924* (%)

	London	Southern England	Midlands	Northern England	Scotland	Wales
1900	86.4	79.4	68.2	63.6	51.4	17.6
1924	62.9	90.9	73.6	50.1	50.7	25.7

Nationalist preponderance. In fact in 1918 the total of Irish seats was raised by two to 105 with a slight internal rearrangement. But since the 73 Sinn Fein members elected in 1918 refused to attend Westminster, the Irish element was for all practical purposes removed at this point. After 1922 the separation of the Irish Republic left Northern Ireland with only 12 Westminster MPs, not more than two of whom were ever other than Unionist. Thus, whereas before 1918 the Conservative Party had normally suffered a handicap of around 65 (that is, 84 minus 19) from Ireland, after 1922 they usually enjoyed an advantage of 8–12. Herein lay the real gain; the virtual disappearance of the Irish factor from Westminster in itself made it far more difficult for the non-Conservative forces to obtain a majority than previously.

If one turns to consider the regional distribution of Conservative support in the new constituency system one finds considerable continuity of strengths and weaknesses between the wars. A comparison based on the proportion of Conservative seats held in each region in the 1892–1910 period with that of 1922–35 points to an enduring pattern in which Wales, Scotland and the four northern counties and Yorkshire continued to be the party's weakest areas, and the counties south of the Wash–Severn line the strongest.[8] What modifications there were are best brought out by comparing the elections of 1900 and 1924 when, for England, Wales and Scotland, the party won 67 per cent of the seats on both occasions. If these victories are broken down into six broad regional groups it is clear that southern England, London and the Midlands remained the strongest and Wales, Scotland and the North the weakest (see table 11.4). By 1924 Conservatives had grown even more reliant upon southern and midland England. Their tightening grip on the south reflected, first, some spread of middle-class residential population beyond London (hence a drop in their share within the capital itself), and second, the Conservatives' ability to take up the slack resulting from Liberal decline in East Anglia and the South-West, both areas in which Labour found it difficult to inherit fully the old radical vote.

Inevitably any regional perspective somewhat exaggerates the fundamental north–south divide; on the other hand, if one looks at the spread of

TABLE 11.5   *Distribution of Conservative seats in 1924 (England, Scotland and Wales)*

Total	Middle class 20% or more	Middle class 10–19.9%	Middle class under 10%
409(602)	169(200)	236(356)	4(46)

Source: M. Kinnear, *The British Voter: an Atlas and Survey 1885–1964* (1969) pp. 122–4.

Conservatism socially, the impression is more one of a nationally based party. On the basis of the occupational categories in the census of 1921 it has been found that 200 constituencies had a middle-class element of 20 per cent or above in their occupied male population.[9] Of these 200 the Conservative Party invariably won 130–80 during the 1918–31 period. While this was a valuable base it was by no means the key to their post-war electoral hegemony, for the middle classes had plainly shrunk as a proportion of the electorate. What was therefore vital for the Conservatives during the 1920s was their capacity to supplement their basic 130 with a further minimum 130 in the seats where the middle-class element fell below 20 per cent, thereby making an irreducible minimum of around 260 in the Commons, which rendered it difficult for any other single party to obtain a majority. What is remarkable is that, apart from 1923 and 1929, they usually held another 100 on top of this from the less middle-class areas. A breakdown of the Conservative victory in the 1924 general election illustrated in table 11.5 shows that the party's massive command of the Commons rested upon successes in more than two-thirds of the constituencies where the middle-class element fell between 10 per cent and 19.9 per cent or, to put it another way, where the working class comprised 80–90 per cent.

The corollary of this spread of Conservative seats was dependence upon fully mobilizing their support in each social group by means of an efficient and comprehensive electoral machine. The traditional skill in doctoring the register of voters naturally became redundant under the new simplified system in which the bulk of the work was done by town clerks and clerks to the county councils. Registration gave way to a new emphasis, particularly on increasing the number of volunteer workers; this followed from the curtailing of expenditure and introduction of one-day polling in 1918 which threw most constituencies upon their own organizational resources on polling day. The party activist's role as intermediary between politician and voter became still more important as a result of the increase by two and a half times in the size of the electorate. Many were young voters whose loyalties were less deep or less rigid than those of pre-war voters; one indication of the difficulties this posed is the fall in turnout to 70–6 per cent during the 1920s against the 81–6 per cent in Edwardian elections. There are certainly grounds for thinking that the Conservatives responded more effectively to the challenge presented by this larger, relatively uncommitted electorate than either of their rivals. While the Liberal agents disappeared and Labour made do with union organizers, the Conservatives improved their existing system of training and examinations for agents, some 352 of whom, together with 99 women organizers, received training between 1924 and 1937.[10] Regular attention by professional staff enabled the party to get to grips with the new system of absent voting established in 1918 for those whose occupations kept them away from home; the routine, meticulous work of tracking down such people and ensuring postal votes for loyal supporters probably came more naturally to the clerically minded Conservative organizations than to their Labour rivals.

A new emphasis was also placed upon fund-raising activities and upon raising large numbers of small subscriptions. Indeed, Conservatives from Baldwin down were now heard to criticize the party for relying too much on candidates wealthy enough to relieve constituency associations of any need to finance elections. Rather than widening their choice by adopting impecunious but able candidates, as Baldwin urged, it seems that some constituencies relieved their MPs of bills they normally paid; even this process did not go very far, for only a quarter to a third of local associations appear to have become financially independent by the 1930s.[11]

Labour's Grass Roots 1918–1929

Between the First World War and the 1930s the Labour Party turned itself from the rather loose federal structure it had originally been into a substantial parliamentary party supported by a strong central organization and a comprehensive framework of regional and constituency parties and members. Much of the credit for this achievement must be ascribed to Arthur Henderson who held tight control over head office, the National Executive and its subcommittees until 1924, when he temporarily surrendered the party secretaryship. He was helped by the new national agent, Egerton Wake, who in 1918 appropriately replaced Arthur Peters, a man whose sympathies with Liberalism rendered him a hindrance to the expanding party. Central to Henderson's dominance was his co-operation with the trade unions, whose financial contribution nationally and locally underpinned the whole structure. During the 1920s the union membership affiliated to the party – which was based very approximately on the number who paid the political levy – rose to 3.5 million, though the figure fell sharply to 2 million between 1927 and 1928 as a result of the Baldwin government's Trade Disputes Act which introduced the practice of 'contracting in' for the levy.

At constituency level union branches or trades councils were often instrumental in fighting election campaigns and selecting candidates. On the whole union-sponsored candidates held the safer seats, and even in difficult rural constituencies the key trade union frequently determined the choice. Dependence upon strong union branches explains the patchy but continuous growth of constituency organizations during the 1920s. The number of affiliated constituency parties rose year by year from 397 in 1918 to 626 by 1924, though the latter figure is inflated by some double affiliations. The three general elections in 1922–4 clearly provided a stimulus in that the 140 constituencies lacking a Labour party in 1921 had shrunk to 19 by 1924. Yet there remained a shortfall of up to 100 between affiliated parties and parliamentary contests, which reflects the inability of young organizations to sustain expensive campaigns in the absence of strong union branches. Nevertheless the pattern of continuous expansion which began around 1917 was virtually complete by 1929 when the Labour Party fought on almost as broad a front as the Conservatives. The party's steadily rising share of the national poll is a direct measure of the additional candidates fielded; the average poll per contest, which hovered around the 40 per cent mark, reflects additional candidatures in weak constituencies in 1924 and 1929 which depresses the average figures (see table 11.6).

The dramatic interruption in this pattern of growth in 1931 diverted attention from the flaws in the party's organizational base during the 1920s and it is to these that we must now turn. In the first place it is clear that many constituency parties were little more than nominal, and that the pattern of individual membership projected in 1918 always remained an elusive goal rather than an achievement. Frequently local Labour parties comprised simply the delegates of local union branches plus some socialist societies' representatives. After 1918 in the industrial North-East, Lancashire, Scotland and Wales the old trades councils had frequently adopted

TABLE 11.6   *Labour growth at general elections 1918–1931*

	1918	*1922*	*1923*	*1924*	*1929*	*1931*
% total poll	22.2	29.5	30.5	33.0	37.1	30.6
Candidates	388	411	422	512	571	515
Average % poll per contest	–	40.0	41.0	38.2	39.3	33.0

the title of 'Divisional Labour Party'; consequently at local level the party remained an umbrella organization outside the real centres of power, as it had been before 1914. It is not surprising that the desired mass membership was rarely attained. In 1928, when separate figures became available, individual party membership stood at 215,000; though no doubt a considerable improvement on pre-war strength, this suggests a constituency average of around 350 only. Even this must be qualified by the knowledge that 1928 was a buoyant time for Labour – now anticipating victory over a fading Baldwin administration – and that all parties' official figures tend to exaggerate real membership. Although Conservative figures were not published, local evidence suggests a massive advantage in membership; by 1929 the Glasgow Conservatives, for example, enjoyed an average of 2,000 per constituency. A brighter sign for Labour was the recruitment of women; some working-class towns like Woolwich and Barrow claimed around 1,000 women members by 1924, though these had been unusually well-organized localities before 1914 and remained exceptional in the 1920s; at this time individual membership was often far more female than male in composition. Also among the seats with over 200 women members were mixed industrial and middle-class towns such as York, Colchester, Gloucester and Newport, in each of which Labour either won or ran the Conservatives very close in 1929; they were in fact the crucial battle-ground if the party's total of 288 seats in 1929 was to be turned into an overall majority of 308. In this struggle the disproportionately middle-class Labour women's sections had a vital part to play in taking on the Conservative organization on more equal terms.

It may be thought that individual membership was insignificant in view of the huge affiliated union membership and that the unions somehow endowed Labour with all the apparatus of a mass political party; yet this was by no means the case. For one thing the affiliation to the party of an arbitrary number of union members meant much less, in terms of individual commitment, than taking out direct membership; indeed, recent studies suggest that many of those who pay the political levy are unaware that they are doing so. Also, although total union membership reached a peak of over 8 million in 1920, thereafter until 1934 it steadily declined to almost half that number, so that it was a wasting asset for much of the period. What is most important is that although a trade union-based organization was perfectly adequate for mobilizing voters in overwhelmingly unionized working-class constituencies, this could guarantee only a hard core of MPs; for a party whose path to a majority necessitated winning the more mixed seats this could never be a satisfactory substitute for the efficient machine built up by the Conservatives. Moreover, although the unions were a vital source of funds they remained somewhat inflexible about how the money was deployed. Henderson, who was acutely aware of the need to channel resources through headquarters into needy and marginal areas, never obtained the funds he believed to be necessary. Against the opposition of a number of union leaders he managed to persuade Conference in 1920 to raise the levy from 2d per member to 3d, and this produced £40,000–£50,000 a year. In 1923 he resurrected the fighting fund to assist impecunious constituencies, which had been abolished in 1919. Although some £20,000 was thereby paid out in 1924 this still fell short of Henderson's objective of equalizing the expenditure of the richer and poorer constituencies. Seats fought by the miners, for example, spent on average 50 per cent more on elections in the early 1920s though they could have managed on less than most. Because the trade unions felt reluctant to allow headquarters unlimited powers to redistribute the movement's resources Labour continued to enjoy abundance in its safest seats but failed to make good the deficiencies in areas where it had to make gains. A crucial consequence of this failure to tap resources fully was the poor provision of full-time agents. In 1920 the number stood at 112; it rose to 133 in 1922 and tailed off to 113 by 1924, though it was supplemented by 20–30 agents employed largely by the Miners Federation. By 1929 a maximum of 169 had been recorded, but this fell back to 136 by 1935. Again these agents were concentrated largely in safe seats. Only a total of 300–400 full-time professional agents would have placed the party on an equal footing with its rival.

In many ways, however, the most positive aspect of Labour's advance was in municipal politics, which provided the opportunity to defend working-class living standards even when the party lacked power at Westminster. In the first post-war elections in November 1919 the change of mood since the Coupon Election became clear. Outside London Labour gained 400 seats; and in the London boroughs its candidates were elected for 572 out of 1,362 seats. These gains were not only of a far higher order than pre-war ones, they were also improved upon in nearly every subsequent year between the wars. Much of the ground was won at Liberal expense; indeed, the Liberals' inability to survive at the local level was underlined by a steady fall in the number of municipal candidates, which continued even when the party was enjoying revivals in parliamentary elections. It was the London Labour Party under Herbert Morrison's leadership which demonstrated the most effective approach to party organization. Here the strategy was characterized by the channelling of funds from the Transport and General Workers Union to the central control point, and by less reliance on major meetings and more on the thorough doorstep canvass in which women members came into their own. Even in some most unpromising seats the LLP established effective organizations, and claimed high membership figures – 2,000 in the case of South Poplar, for instance. Mastery of the canvass, which was particularly appropriate for the huge suburban housing estates around London, was regarded as a key factor in the remarkable Labour gains in such places as North Camberwell in 1922 and Mitcham in 1923. 'The new school of Labour politicians is a scientific school', Morrison claimed, 'It knows that noisy tub-thumping does not make up for careful organization.'[12]

Morrison's hyperbole did highlight another characteristic of Labour's approach to elections during the inter-war years. After 1918 Henderson made great use of regular regional conferences and rallies, and for these, as for parliamentary elections, he relied heavily upon obtaining star speakers. The price was unduly heavy speaking engagements for Henderson himself (who thought nothing of giving a two-hour oration at a by-election) but also for MacDonald. The party's reliance upon the Victorian radical techniques of inspirational rallies and whistle-stop tours, at which MacDonald undoubtedly excelled, is all of a piece with the relative neglect of individual mass membership and efficient local machinery. For although Conservatives also held big rallies this was never such a central part of their approach to the electorate. Their leaders, usually less proficient with the Gladstonian oration, showed, especially in Baldwin's case, considerable facility with the quieter technique of the radio broadcast; and their larger membership, and efficiency with transport, the canvass and the postal vote were far better calculated to mobilize their support from among the enlarged electorate of relatively uncommitted voters than was Labour's traditional radical revivalism. This has sometimes been lost sight of by writers who attribute the Liberal decline to an inherent inability to master the techniques for mobilizing the post-1918 mass electorate, inhibitions from which the more democratic Labour Party should in theory have been free. Yet if there was a basic division in approach it would seem, in practice, to have been between the Conservative Party on the one hand, and, on the other, the Labour and Liberal Parties, whose strengths and weaknesses betrayed a common Victorian origin.

Women in Inter-war Politics

In 1918 women comprised just under 40 per cent of the total electorate; by 1924 their share had risen to 42.8 per cent, and by 1929, following the introduction of equal suffrage, to 52.7 per cent. Only recently has this new majority in the British political system begun to attract the scholarly attention it deserves. This may reflect an assumption that the political impact of women proved to be slight and that the feminist movement entered upon a decline after 1918. No major women's party emerged, as some politicians had feared, and only a handful of women became MPs. After Nancy Astor's breakthrough at a 1919 by-election, two were elected in 1922, eight in 1923, four in 1924, fourteen in 1929, fifteen in 1931 and nine in 1935. Some of the former suffragists and suffragettes eschewed any attempt to enter Parliament because they felt none of the parties were yet willing to treat women equally; Eleanor Rathbone, however, sat as an Independent MP for a university seat from 1929 to 1946. Many activists had been Liberals, but the declining fortunes of their party severely hampered their chances between the wars. A number of very able women chose to pursue a political career within the Labour and Conservative parties, but for most this meant accepting the orthodox priorities of the party rather than promoting feminism.

Nonetheless women made an impact in several ways. Each party felt obliged to overhaul its organization after 1918, to recruit new members, to establish formal representation for women in the party machine, to create a professional hierarchy for women, and to address propaganda to them. The two main parties showed the same recruitment pattern; women's membership rose to a peak in the late 1920s – one million for the Conservatives and 250,000 to 300,000 for Labour – followed by a slight decline in the 1930s as the early enthusiasm wore off.

The concern felt by politicians over the new voters may also be charted in the fluctuating proportion of candidates who made specific appeals to women in their election literature: 46 per cent in 1922, 39 per cent in 1923, 63 per cent in 1924 and 67 per cent in 1929. This reflects the fact that initially Labour were more inclined to bid for female votes, whereas the Conservatives feared that this would be divisive. But the defeat of Baldwin in 1923 was widely attributed to women, especially as the debate over tariffs and free trade had pushed food prices to the top of the agenda. Thereafter Conservatives gave much more attention to women. This was reflected in the pattern of political debate and legislation during the 1920s. The combination of adult male suffrage and the rise of the Labour Party consolidated the Edwardian trend towards giving such questions as standards of living, unemployment and social welfare a high priority on the agenda. Women's entry into the system simply strengthened that trend. Thus the parties competed with one another to offer women essentially the same policies: widows' pensions, equal suffrage and local maternity clinics financed by the state. During the 1920s a large number of measures for women were enacted. But by 1929 the politicians had had sufficient experience of female voters at five general elections to know where they could draw the line. No more feminist reforms were now on their agenda; women's politics could be confined essentially to domestic questions and their interests treated as though they coincided exactly with those of their children and husbands. Thus during the 1930s women's politics appeared to have been contained, though the domestic approach was yet to reach its culmination in the form of the welfare state after 1945.

One of the most important questions, though difficult to answer, is, for whom did the women vote at inter-war elections? Naturally there is a good deal of propagandist and impressionistic evidence here. In 1918 candidates in all parties judged that women had reacted very patriotically and voted for the Coalition government. On the other hand the announcement of equal suffrage in 1927 led the right-wing press to warn that young women were highly susceptible to socialism. Certainly the Tories attributed their setbacks in 1923 and 1929 in part to vacillating females. However, the objective evidence suggests that they were probably wrong to do so. Studies of several elections between 1918 and 1931 have found an *inverse* relationship between the level of the female vote in a constituency and the level of Labour support; in other words, women as a group leaned a little towards the Conservatives.[13] This is consistent with other evidence for the inter-war period. Conservatives clearly mobilized more women within the party than Labour. The experience of working-class women in the field of employment may have played a part in this. Many women were in service occupations, in which trade unions were very weak; even in industry female workers were far less likely to join a union than their male colleagues. Consequently they seldom underwent the same process of political socialization which cemented the loyalty of growing numbers of working men to Labour.

This has been underlined emphatically in a local analysis of politics in Preston, where, after Labour's advance in 1918, the party lost support. This appeared to reflect the character of the local party, which was dominated by male trade unionists who had emerged from the war rather hostile to the employment of women. They opposed municipal and national spending on welfare for women, and discouraged the organization of women within the party. The loss of votes from women forced some modification of these attitudes, but after the policy failure of the second Labour government women proved slow to return to the party even in 1935.[14]

This does not mean that Labour was not gaining support generally among working-class women during the 1920s. The 1924 MacDonald government made the reduction of taxation on food items one of its priorities, and the party placed great emphasis on widows' pensions and improved maternity services. But it was probably more difficult to win over the women's vote than the men's. Consequently by 1929 this was the more vulnerable part of Labour's support, and this manifested itself after 1931 when the party lost votes heavily among women electors.

The General Strike and the
Realignment of the Working Class

In the past it was assumed that the central feature of popular politics between the wars was the emergence of social class as the basic determinant of political allegiance, a development that in itself would account for the replacement of the Liberals by Labour as the party of the working class. As a broad description of what happened this sketch has much to commend it, but as an explanation it does not take us very far. We have already considered the strong empirical grounds for thinking that the shift to a class-based pattern had already occurred before the First World War. Even for the inter-war years an interpretation of the role of class depends very much on the perspective adopted, whether, for example, one studies the Labour vote in terms of its class origin, or whether one examines the total working-class vote in terms of its party loyalty. In the former instance, studies of post-1945 voters suggest that among Labour supporters 87 per cent were working class and 13 per cent middle class; however, of the working-class electorate only slightly over 60 per cent supported the Labour Party in the 1945–51 period.[15] During 1918–39 the proportion must have been considerably lower than this. For what actually happened in this period was that Labour progressively pushed up its share of the total poll so that by 1929 it had reached 37 per cent, falling to 30.5 per cent in 1931, and returning to a similar level (38 per cent) in 1935. It has been rightly pointed out that the pattern was something less than a sudden and complete breakthrough resulting from the incorporation of millions of new voters in 1918;[16] such drastic transformations can occur, as the near eclipse of the Irish Nationalists and the rise of Sinn Fein from none to 73 seats during 1916–18 shows. Yet in Britain the working class, markedly less monolithic than the middle class after 1918, failed to conform at all neatly to a pattern of class allegiance.

An estimate of working-class support for the Labour Party may be obtained from the 1929 figures if one makes an assumption that 76 per cent of the 22,648,000 who actually voted were working class; this leaves 17,212,000 as against a Labour poll of 8,389,000. One cannot be sure what proportion of Labour votes were middle class, but if 13 per cent is taken as a maximum and none at all as the minimum, then Labour's share of the working-class vote would fall within the range 42–8 per cent in 1929. At other inter-war elections, except for 1935, the proportion would of course have been lower. It must be doubtful, in the light of such (admittedly approximate) calculations, whether Labour was any more effective in winning the working-class vote after 1918 than the Liberals had been before 1914. Since the Liberals had been able to draw more strongly on the middle-class electorate they had been more successful, on occasion, in obtaining overall majorities.

Thus we have more than one problem to explain. Why was there a steady and impressive rise in Labour support? And why did it stick at a fairly low ceiling around 37 per cent even after recovering from the check administered in 1931? We have argued earlier that there was so much continuity between pre-war Liberal and post-war Labour support that the explanation for the replacement of one party by the other must be essentially chronological–historical. An alternative approach would involve adopting a structural explanation, namely that while pre-1914 Liberal voters largely continued to support their old party, Labour's new strength was derived from newly enfranchised and, by implication, different, working-class voters. However, these approaches are by no means mutually exclusive. Elements of each are combined in the idea of the political generation as an explanation for the pattern of political change. Clearly the regular arrival of a fresh set of young voters and the removal by death of older ones constitutes a structural transformation of the electorate; but the chronological–historical element is also implicit in that each new generation experiences a different set of political circumstances; young voters have been found to be less set in their loyalty to party than their elders and more impressionable in the face of events. The formation of their political attitudes, therefore, tends to reflect the political conditions that are paramount in the years when they are growing to adulthood and political consciousness.[17] One study of voters alive in 1960 has highlighted the fluctuation between political generations by isolating the allegiance of those who voted for the first time in 1935, of whom 45 per cent supported Labour, those who voted for the first time in 1945, of whom 61 per cent supported Labour, and those who voted for the first time in 1955, of whom 48 per cent supported Labour.[18]

Which were likely to have been the critical formative influences making for political generations between the wars? Those born around 1900 – and consequently voting for the first time in the early 1920s – experienced a traumatic political apprenticeship in the First World War and post-war chaos, which, in view of the sorry conclusion of Lloyd George's Coalition in 1922, may well have disrupted Liberal allegiance more severely than among the older generations. The generation born around 1914–18 grew to political awareness in the late 1920s and early 1930s; it is a matter for speculation whether for them the discrediting of MacDonald's second government weighed more or less heavily than the fact that by this time Labour was plainly the only real alternative government.

In what sense did national events and trends help to mould a generation relatively predisposed to Labour sympathies? We have noted already the groundswell of trade union membership which doubled from 4 to 8 million between 1914 and 1920, and the accelerating industrial militancy during the latter half of the war. In 1917 the number of working days lost in strikes doubled to 5.8 million; but the real explosion came in 1919, with 21 million days lost, in 1920, with 35 million, and in 1921, with 86 million. What stoked up this outburst was the maintenance of full wartime employment by the post-war boom until the summer of 1920, and the abandonment of compulsory arbitration procedures by the government. At this stage, workers sensed that although wages were higher than before the war they had missed the real fruits of victory. Union leaders felt that their patriotic restraint had not been fully reciprocated by the employers who had reaped vast profits, and so they now declined responsibility for holding back their members' demands. These were years of rising expectations which, during 1920–1, suddenly seemed unlikely to be fulfilled. Though few can be said to have been directly influenced by the Russian Revolution, the comparison did serve to highlight a belief that Britain alone was slipping back into the status quo. The hurried Coupon Election soon came to be regarded as a tactic to hamstring the workers' new power; and the impression of the Coalition as a conspiracy of employers to deceive the workers gained credence from the neat defusing of demands for public ownership by timely wage concessions and the Sankey Commission. By the summer of 1921 unemployment had leapt to 2 million, or 18 per cent of the insured workforce, and union membership soon began its inexorable downward slide as long-term unemployment took its toll. This turn of events was significant in several ways; it induced an embattled defensiveness in the labour movement which lasted until the Second World War; and in the short run it generated a sense of betrayal which spilled over into the 1922 general election.

The fusion of Conservative and some Liberal forces in the Coalition after 1918 drove many working men to see Labour as the natural alternative for them; indeed during 1915–22 Lloyd George had established himself in the eyes of their leaders as an enemy more dangerous, because cleverer and more unscrupulous, than the Conservatives, an interpretation vociferously reinforced by the Liberal recruits to Labour. Meanwhile the independent Liberal Party became bereft of those politicians most in tune with labour aspirations, and seemed to have nothing of relevance to say; insofar as it won back the coalitionists it appeared less congenial to labour. Though it developed constructive industrial policies along the lines of the wartime Whitley Councils, no policy was likely to be as effective electorally as an attitude; and in a period of sharply rising unemployment and dashed expectations the Liberal stance of impartiality between the two sides of industry inevitably appeared evasive and insincere. In this way the 1920s were an instrumental phase in severing the Liberal Party from its traditional working-class base; indeed the years from 1918 to 1924 were possibly more important in this respect than 1914–18, which is usually taken as the decisive period. In this process the significance of the Labour government of 1924 cannot be overestimated; for however brief its life, it made the Liberals redundant at a stroke for the working classes.

In some ways the General Strike of 1926 stands out as the key stage in the evolution of politics in the 1920s. There was nothing revolutionary in either the motivation or the methods behind the strike. It was essentially a defensive measure against an imminent threat of general wage cuts in industry. Under the leadership of people like Ernest Bevin and Margaret Bondfield the union movement was wedded to the parliamentary system; they hoped that the threat of a general strike would encourage Baldwin to intervene again in the coal industry, or that he would be driven to hold a general election. Although MacDonald and his colleagues felt apprehensive about the likely effects of the strike on Labour's fortunes, in the event the failure on the industrial front had the effect of strengthening his political position.

In the short run the nine-day strike appeared to be a triumph for Baldwin. But he derived no real advantage from it. This has been obscured by most traditional accounts of the strike written from the perspective of the London leadership. As a result of local and regional studies it is now clear that working-class backing for the strike was remarkably solid; people were keen to join and not at all ready to return to work after nine days. This inevitably had a destabilizing effect on the loyalties of working-class Conservatives. Similarly, Liberal supporters were torn between the views of Sir John Simon and Asquith who considered the strike illegal, and Lloyd George who dissociated himself from his leader. Lloyd George's credentials were by now too besmirched for him to restore his standing with organized labour, however. After 1926 the Liberals continued to lose ground in working-class constituencies even when enjoying a national revival under Lloyd George's leadership.

The General Strike, after all, gave the working class a strong motive for rallying around the unions and the Labour Party. The Baldwin government promoted this by its trade union legislation in 1927 which made general strikes illegal, prohibited certain workers from joining unions, and substituted the practice of contracting in for the political levy for contracting out. In the event it is true that the prohibition on sympathetic strikes was never invoked. And although the new rules had the effect of reducing the Labour Party's income from the levy by about one-third, this was purely temporary. But if the direct consequences were marginal, the 1927 legislation nonetheless served as an important symbolic grievance. It helped to unite the industrial and political wings of the Labour movement around the objective of re-electing Labour to office. After the experience of 1924 unity could not be taken for granted because serious doubts had arisen about the wisdom of taking office without the power to implement a radical economic programme. However, after 1926 MacDonald succeeded in fending off his critics in the ILP. His task was rendered easier by the apparent drift of Baldwin's government on the economic front. After 1926, industry's costs were not significantly reduced, export markets were not fully recovered and unemployment was still 1.1 million in early 1929. The Cabinet attempted to gain the initiative by a set of proposals designed to stimulate industry, including de-rating, safeguarding by means of tariffs, and empire development. However, neither politicians nor voters evinced much enthusiasm and the 'Safety First' strategy fell flat. Labour appeared as the party most likely to tackle unemployment, and its vote went up from 33 per cent to 37 per cent, which produced 287 MPs, only 21 short of an overall majority. The one worrying feature of 1929 for Labour was the Lloyd George Liberal revival which pushed up the party's proportion of the vote to nearly a quarter. However, this was essentially the result of a big increase in the number of candidates financed by Lloyd George. At the grass roots, Liberal organization was still falling back. As the Labour organizers observed, the 'revival' was essentially an ephemeral phenomenon puffed up by the publicity attaching to the arrival of Lloyd George's 'circus' in certain favourable areas rather than a firmly entrenched gain.[19] At the general election in 1929 only 24 of the 43 existing Liberal seats were held; 33 of the 35 gains were at Conservative expense, while 17 of the 19 losses went to Labour. Thus the slide away from the Liberals in working-class areas manifested in municipal activity was repeated in the parliamentary contests notwithstanding the revival.

This working-class realignment was partly a cause and partly a consequence of the collaboration of middle-class Liberals with Conservatives in anti-socialist pacts which took such forms as a Citizens Party in Bristol, a Municipal Association in Hull, and a Progressive Party in Sheffield. While such combinations checked Labour's attainment of majority control in many cities during the 1920s, they left Liberals holding working-class wards which were highly vulnerable to Labour, and merely turned the Liberals into a Conservative force in the long run. For the party could not be sustained by an appeal for cautious, Conservative votes at the municipal level and for radical anti-Conservative votes at the parliamentary level. The confusion was compounded by the growing fluctuations in the number of candidates, which had the inevitable effect of breaking the habit of voting Liberal and obliging erstwhile supporters to make an alternative choice. Radical Liberals were often antagonized by the appearance of ex-coalitionists as Liberal or National Liberal candidates in 1922–3, while the more right-wing and traditionalist supporters withdrew into the Conservative camp in great numbers in 1924. Each subsequent revival began from a lower level and never recouped the losses of 1918. The attrition of the traditional Liberal constituency culminated in 1931–5 when the Liberal MPs – apart from Lloyd George and his family – were absorbed into the National Government, in the case of the Simonites on a permanent basis. After a short interruption Labour then resumed its absorption of the remnants of industrial Liberalism.

The 1920s were also a formative period for other elements within the electorate such as the Irish, hitherto a pillar of the Liberal vote. Though largely working class the Irish had displayed a reluctance to vote Labour.

Yet the war shattered the Liberal–Nationalist alliance, and as early as 1919 the leading Irish politician in Britain, T. P. O'Connor, had begun to urge Irish voters to back Labour; the new alignment was formalized in 1924 when MacDonald made him a privy councillor. On O'Connor's resignation from his Scotland (Liverpool) constituency his successor simply received the Labour nomination. Wherever the Irish were numerous, as in Liverpool or Glasgow, they came to be a bastion of Labour strength – but as Catholics rather than simply as working men. For the transition from one party to another occurred during the early 1920s, when Labour was a staunch Home Rule party free of association with the Easter Rebellion or the 'Black and Tans' policy; Labour thus inherited a role within the traditional sectarian pattern of politics which, in places like Liverpool and Glasgow, still had much life in it.

Similarly, there was no sudden collapse of 'Nonconformity' but rather a political realignment of many Nonconformists to Labour's advantage. Ever since the settlement of certain Nonconformist grievances in the 1860s there had been a gradual drift from radicalism to Conservatism, especially among Wesleyans; and by 1914 groups like Quakers had grown so high in the social scale and so close to the establishment view as to be largely patriotic volunteers, despite their reputation for pacifism. Conversely, those Nonconformists whose sympathies were engaged by the anti-war movement and who had been ardent social reformers often migrated via the ILP to the Labour Party afterwards. By 1924, 86 Labour parliamentary candidates were Nonconformists (as against 120 Liberals) and 45 Labour MPs were Nonconformists (as against only 21 Liberals).[20] However, Liberal support among middle-class Nonconformists did remain relatively firm, so much so that the relationship was still discernible in 1960.[21] The big shift occurred in the working class. One modern study of voters alive in 1960 who had reached voting age before 1914 suggests that whereas working-class Anglicans of their generation were evenly divided between Conservative and non-Conservative allegiance, working-class Nonconformists split 4:1 against the Conservatives.[22] Although this pattern had largely died out among new voters after 1945, for inter-war voters religious traditions remained politically relevant. In County Durham, for example, the smoothness of the transfer of loyalties from Liberal to Labour after the war owed much to the pervading Methodist tradition common to both. A generation before 1914, Durham Methodists had adopted both the secular ideology of radicalism and the institutionalized politics of the miners' lodges. Their mobilization in the post-1918 Labour Party therefore involved little perceptible 'conversion'; for adherence to Labour did not imply adopting socialism except in the general ethical sense in which they were already socialists.

What such shifts did imply was a certain moderation in objectives and methods which characterized the labour movement in general, not just the

Nonconformist element in it. It has been rightly observed that notwithstanding the grievance of unemployment, manual workers during the 1920s and 1930s displayed remarkably little predilection for a drastic soak-the-rich policy, but tended rather to compare their own situation with that of other workers.[23] Their apparently limited aspirations were surely of a piece with their politics; for their characteristic claim – faithfully reflected by the Labour Party – was that the working man was entitled to work, and failing that, maintenance, not that the distribution of wealth in society should be fundamentally altered. Essentially the party appealed to the self-respect of the working class rather than to any militant sense of class-consciousness. This is consistent with Labour's steady accumulation of support up to 1929, which nevertheless fell short of two-fifths of the total vote. Despite its stance as, in essence, the party of the working class at a point in time when the working class came into its own electorally, Labour failed to overturn the existing pattern of approximately class-based loyalties; the persistence of traditional working-class Conservatism ensured that. What Labour did accomplish was the inheritance of one sector within the pattern of political allegiance that had been established before the First World War.

The Election of 1931

The break-up of the second Labour government over the measures designed to deal with the economic crisis led to the formation of a National Government under MacDonald in August 1931. Three months later the new administration called a general election which it won with 67 per cent of the vote and 554 MPs. Labour found itself reduced to a mere 52 MPs; after a decade of progress its share of the poll had dropped to 30.5 per cent.

How are we to understand this dramatic turning point in electoral politics? In the first place, with only 52 MPs returned in 1931 Labour's voters were grossly under-represented. The net loss of 236 is explicable if one remembers that in 1929 the system had worked in the party's favour in giving it more seats than the Conservatives for slightly fewer votes; four out of ten Labour seats had been won on a minority vote and often by very slender margins. In these circumstances a slight shift of votes was bound to be disproportionately damaging. Second, it seems almost certain that even before the extraordinary events in which Labour's leader, along with senior figures like Philip Snowden and J. H. Thomas, joined with their opponents, the party was heading for defeat. The by-elections of 1929–31, in contrast to those of the first MacDonald government, brought substantial falls in the Labour poll, a reflection of its inadequate response to mounting unemployment. However, the scale of the defeat was clearly exacerbated by the peculiar circumstances of the 1931 election. In this connection it is often stressed that the effect of withdrawals by Liberal candidates – down from 513 in 1929 to 173 – was to leave Labour facing far more straight contests than in 1929. Around three-fifths of former Liberal voters seem to have supported National Government candidates and only one-fifth supported Labour. In addition there are grounds for thinking that the Labour leaders, notably Arthur Henderson, made inept attempts at playing what was, admittedly, a weak hand. Before the election Henderson largely gave support to the new government's proposals, thereby exposing the ambivalent position of many former Labour ministers, and creating some confusion in the party. The opposition never managed to put forward a convincing alternative economic policy or shake off the charge of having run away from the crisis.

There is, however, a strong tradition to the effect that, while the National Government achieved its victory by means of special arrangements and stratagems, Labour's own support remained loyal. This does not seem to be borne out by the evidence. In the 49 constituencies which saw a straight Labour–Conservative contest in both 1929 and 1931, Labour's vote fell by almost a quarter. Nationally its poll dropped from 8,389,000 to 6,649,000, despite an increase of a million in the electorate and a turnout of 76 per cent, which was as high as in 1929. However, it is conspicuous that Labour did well in South Wales, where it held almost all its seats in Glamorgan and Monmouthshire. By contrast, in north-east England, a very similar region in many ways, the party fared much worse, losing 14 of the 16 seats it had held in County Durham and Tyneside. Such regional variations have not so far been explained.

Finally, it is of some importance that Labour had expected to blunt the impact of the National Government's attack on their record by playing the free trade card. There were, after all, several precedents to suggest that the electors punished Conservatives whenever protection was made a priority, as it was in 1931. For the first time, however, the voters failed to react, perhaps because after such a serious and prolonged depression free trade seemed an inadequate policy. This is corroborated by the experience of the Samuelite Liberals who, though part of the new government at this stage, vigorously advocated free trade. They suffered as great a loss of votes as Labour candidates. Thus 1931 marked a new post-Victorian era in which protectionism would be taken for granted. Yet for Labour there was a silver lining to this particular cloud. For 1931 represented a worse result for the Liberal Party, which was split exactly in half and whose decline continued in 1935. Labour, on the other hand, remained the alternative party of government, and was quite capable of effecting a recovery from the débâcle, as the 1930s were to show.

CHAPTER TWELVE

From the National Government to the Popular Front 1931–1939

The old pacifists have become warlike. The true blue Tory warmongers now coo like doves. Who knows what the effect of that reversal of parts will be upon the voters at the next General Election?

Daily Mirror, 10 March 1938

The crushing victory won by supporters of the National Government in 1931 was repeated on almost the same scale at the election of 1935, thereby maintaining Neville Chamberlain's premiership until the military disasters of 1940 finally dislodged him from power. But why did a temporary expedient hastily arranged to deal with a crisis develop into a long-term fixture? And how did the political parties react to this decade of coalition? For Labour it proved to be a formative phase in which some of the key issues that had been avoided hitherto were tackled. But for the Conservatives, being in office involved some bitter internal controversies over both domestic and external issues, from which there emerged a younger generation whose ideas were in some ways remarkably close to those of their Labour rivals.

The National Government and Liberal Toryism

Traditionally the National Government has figured so prominently in left-wing demonology that it is easy to overlook the outrage it aroused among right-wing Tories, who regarded it as an effete liberal administration which had been foisted on the country quite unnecessarily. This perspective may seem surprising since the governments were dominated by Conservatives,

THE WRITING ON THE WALLSEND.

MR. BALDWIN (*at the Cookery Exhibition*). 'NOW HERE IS OUR
NEW GRID – THE LATEST NATIONAL LABOUR-SAVER.'
THE LUMP OF COAL (*with smouldering resentment*). 'CALL THAT
A GRID? I CALL IT THE THIN END OF THE WEDGE.
YOU'LL BE NATIONALISING *ME* NEXT.'
['Grid' is the name given to the system of inter-communicating
lines between the Power Stations of the country as proposed by
the Electricity Bill. The Conservative opposition to this excellent
measure is largely based on the apprehension that it is a first
step towards Nationalization.]
Punch, or the London Charivari, 17 November 1926

even though a generous share of posts was conceded to the Labour and Liberal supporters of the National Government. The point is that the governments of the 1930s represented the triumph of a particular school of Conservatism and of several leaders who were determined to drag their reluctant colleagues into the twentieth century.

In accepting the royal invitation to form a coalition in August 1931 Macdonald, Baldwin and Sir Herbert Samuel, the acting Liberal leader, all contemplated co-operating for weeks or months in order to undertake unpopular measures to balance the budget and restore confidence; they would then split and fight the next election separately. However, these expectations collapsed with extraordinary speed. Since the new government enjoyed a perfectly adequate majority and three years of its parliamentary term the decision to hold a fresh election in October 1913 was an unnecessary diversion from its task. The obvious explanation is that it proved too tempting for the Conservatives not to take advantage of Labour's disarray and to use MacDonald as they had used Lloyd George in 1918 to make a national appeal. However, this is far from being an adequate explanation. MacDonald himself actually encouraged Baldwin to go for a dissolution, and he recognised that it would be safer to do so before taking the necessary economic measures rather than after lest 'the feeling of national unity will ebb away'.[1] Having burned his boats with Labour, MacDonald now had no future in politics except in some form of coalition.

It is more surprising that the Conservatives should have gone along with this since many were appalled by the idea of another coalition. Baldwin had assumed that on the fall of the Labour cabinet he would be called upon to form a new government, but the pressure of the king and the willingness of Samuel to join made it difficult for him to refuse. Significantly, once the National Government materialized, Baldwin found compelling reasons to keep it going. Despite his own role in destroying the last coalition in 1922 he actually favoured coalitions, provided that Lloyd George had no part in them; he must have thought it divine intervention that trapped 'The Goat' in hospital with a serious operation during the crisis in 1931. By harnessing MacDonald and the Liberals to the 554-seat election landslide Baldwin executed more than merely a short-term manoeuvre: as the subsequent years were to show, he had imposed his control over the Conservative Party by emasculating his own right wing. For the massive increase in Conservative MPs from the 258 in 1929 to the 471 in 1931 altered the composition of the party. Around 150 of them were unlikely to have been elected on a purely Conservative ticket, and it has been estimated that 100 owed their seats to the withdrawal of Liberal candidates.[2] Their survival at the next election depended on the credibility of the national appeal in the eyes of many erstwhile Labour and Liberal voters. While the Conservatives would have won an election independently in 1931 they could hardly have captured so many working-class constituencies whose new members, Baldwin believed, would give him support for the comparatively liberal brand of Conservatism he favoured. He had long made it clear he wished to follow 'the traditions of Disraeli adapted to the present day', or, in effect, to lead the party from a position to the left of its centre.

Baldwin was in fact well equipped to lead the Conservatives through a period when their chief opponents claimed to represent the working class. Some Labour politicians considered him to be separated from them more by background than by ideology, and his own son, Oliver, had joined Labour in the 1920s. Unlike his leading colleagues, Austen and Neville Chamberlain, Curzon, Birkenhead and Churchill, who refused to conceal their contempt for the Labour politicians, Baldwin treated them as equals; he even reproached his own party for neglecting the workers by drawing its own candidates from a narrow range of men who were able to finance their campaigns from their personal wealth.

However, Baldwin's 1924–9 premiership had demonstrated how difficult it was to maintain his liberal policies and his conciliatory attitude towards the workers. In 1925 he had vetoed a bill prepared by a Tory backbencher to undermine the political levy paid by the unions to the Labour Party, even though his cabinet favoured it. In the same year he had tried to avoid the General Strike by giving a subsidy to maintain miners' wages for nine months. Baldwin's eventual failure checked his influence and led to the punitive legislation of 1927 attacking the unions and the Labour Party's political levy. Despite this Baldwin did succeed in enacting a catalogue of progressive measures, including the Widows', Orphans' and Old Age Pensions Contributory Pensions Act (1925), the Equal Franchise Act (1928), the Unemployment Insurance Act and the Local Government Act (1929), which abolished the poor law unions and introduced block grants for local authorities. Not since Disraeli's ministry had Conservatives adopted such a positive stance in domestic affairs.

The minister responsible for many of these reforms was Neville Chamberlain. Despite the reputation for financial severity he cultivated as Chancellor of the Exchequer under the National Government, Chamberlain proved to be more liberal in practice. In the financial crisis of 1931 the new administration proclaimed orthodoxy and deflation as its aims; but it actually devalued the pound in 1931 and ran modest budgetary deficits from 1932 onwards. By 1934 the expenditure cuts necessitated by the crisis had been rescinded, and the Chancellor deliberately promoted low interest rates to reduce the national debt charges which stimulated the boom in housebuilding.

The policy was more obviously doctrinaire in dealing with declining industries such as shipbuilding, where output dropped dramatically. In iron and steel falling capacity was masked by the construction of new plant, and in coal many inefficient mines were kept in operation by means of a quota system and fixed prices. As a result of the tariffs introduced in 1931 and 1932 three-quarters of all British imports paid duties, a reversal of the historic policy of free trade. But interventionism went beyond this. The government adopted Labour's Agricultural Marketing Act to fix quotas for imports, and it encouraged output by means of subsidies and marketing boards which spent £100 million a year by 1934. A comparatively niggardly £2 million a year was made available for public schemes under the 1934 Depressed Areas Act, and in 1937 Chamberlain introduced remission of rent, rates and taxation for companies moving into such areas.

The National Government also recognized that in certain sectors where private enterprise seemed inappropriate or unwilling to invest, the state should intervene to impose rationalization and control. Back in 1926 the Central Electricity Board (CEB) had been created and a charter had been granted to the British Broadcasting Corporation (BBC). The National Government revived Herbert Morrison's plans for a London Passenger Transport Board in 1933, and it merged the private airlines, which were not viable, into a public body, the British Overseas Airways Corporation (BOAC), in 1939. Such measures of nationalization and economic pump-priming were no doubt empirical responses to immediate problems rather than evidence of an ideological change; but they certainly made the gap between the political parties much narrower than their rhetoric suggested. During these years members of all three political parties participated in organizations committed to rethinking economic strategy, including Political and Economic Planning (formed in 1931) and the Next Five Years Group (formed in 1935). Broadly they propagated a Keynesian strategy for operating the private enterprise system with full employment, high economic growth and social welfare. In the long term this ensured that the economic inheritance of younger Conservatives such as Harold Macmillan and R. A. Butler would be similar to that of their Labour rivals after the Second World War.

Baldwin's success in steering the policy of the National Government towards the centre ground was matched by his skill in reassuring the non-Conservative and uncommitted sections of the electorate, notably women, who comprised 52 per cent of the total electorate after 1928. In many ways he was an ideal leader for a less politically committed mass electorate, radiating as he did a soothing, almost non-political appeal. He paid particular attention to the Liberal voters who were confused by the behaviour of their leaders in this period. In 1931 the entire parliamentary Liberal Party joined the National Government except for a small family group around Lloyd George. But in 1932 the supporters of Samuel resigned in opposition to tariffs, rather too late to be very credible in the country. This left Sir John Simon and around half the Liberal members who fought the

1935 election as National Liberals and thus split the party yet again. Simon's role as Foreign Secretary was part of a strategy designed to convince voters of the government's commitment to disarmament and the League of Nations, which were regarded as symbols of peace. The government was anxious to avoid being blamed for the failure of the disarmament conference at Geneva and to retain the goodwill of the League of Nations Union, which urged voters to support candidates most likely to back the League. Since Liberals were believed to be especially keen about the League, Baldwin took some trouble to reassure them by appointing the popular and seemingly liberal Anthony Eden to the Cabinet as minister with responsibility for League affairs. There was a price to be paid for this, because many Conservative politicians disapproved of Simon's role at the Foreign Office and resented what they saw as a sacrifice of British interests for the sake of the League of Nations, especially when the Soviet Union was allowed to join in 1934. In particular they believed it contrary to national interests to support sanctions against Mussolini following his invasion of Abyssinia in 1935.

It was in fact over foreign and imperial issues that Baldwin's liberal credentials were most severely challenged from within his own party during the 1930s. In retrospect Baldwin emerges as a key figure in leading his party away from its traditional role as defender of the British Empire. His leadership marked a distinct break with that of Bonar Law, for Baldwin simply did not share the same commitment to the Union with Ireland and it was he who dropped the very word 'Unionist' to describe the party. Baldwin expressed his patriotism in a less divisive and more emollient form in terms of a romantic celebration of the English countryside and English traditions.

However, at the time Baldwin was a little lucky in that his right-wing critics found themselves divided between the enthusiasts for the British Raj in India and the proponents of the United Empire Campaign, which renewed the long-standing agitation for protectionism. The government's Indian policy was determined by Baldwin himself, Lord Irwin (the Earl of Halifax) and Samuel Hoare, who broadly shared the liberal belief that westernized Indians could not be excluded indefinitely from the government of their country. Since 1919 Britain had embarked upon a policy of widening Indian participation. This could not be checked, if only because without Indian co-operation it would have become impossible to run the country. The Montagu–Chelmsford reforms were due for revision in 1929, but Baldwin had anticipated this by appointing a commission under Simon in 1928. This was effectively overthrown when Gandhi launched the Civil Disobedience campaign. In order to regain the initiative Irwin, now Viceroy, issued a declaration to the effect that dominion status was the 'natural issue of India's constitutional progress' in October 1929, which led to a series of Round Table Conferences between the two sides. Irwin's concession provoked a storm of protest from the Conservative right wing, especially when he agreed a pact with Gandhi which involved releasing the nationalist agitators from gaol, and struck a demoralising blow to the morale of the British administration. Subsequently Hoare, as Secretary of State, prepared a major reform, the Government of India Act of 1935, which extended virtual self-government to Indians at the provincial level and increased the electorate from five to thirty million. This approach decisively alienated Churchill from the party leadership, and led to his resignation from the shadow cabinet in January 1931 and his exclusion from the National Government. For the next four years Churchill led a bitter attack on Indian policy which attracted far more Conservative support than the 40–50 rebels who voted against the government in the House of Commons. At a meeting of the National Union's Central Council in February 1933 the Cabinet's policy was upheld by only 189 votes to 165; and it was repudiated by both the Conservative women and the Junior Imperial League; at the 1934 party conference the India rebels lost the vote by just 520 to 543.

Baldwin managed to live with this revolt partly because even 50 rebels could not upset the huge majority enjoyed by the National Government in the Commons. Also, the rebels failed to combine with the protectionists under Lords Rothermere and Beaverbrook, who waged a campaign for 'Empire Free Trade' after the party's defeat in 1929. Not content with using their newspapers, the press barons intervened at by-elections to oppose official Conservative candidates. The decisive clash occurred at the St George's (Westminster) by-election in March 1931 in which Baldwin's candidate, Duff Cooper, triumphed over his Empire Free Trade rival. Although Rothermere contributed financially to the India Defence League (a backbench Churchillian group), Churchill was too staunch a free-trader for the two imperialist groups to combine effectively. The greatest danger to Baldwin was Neville Chamberlain, whom the press barons were willing to back as an alternative leader in 1931. A similar motive led Rothermere to adopt Sir Oswald Mosley as a suitable battering ram later in the 1930s.

In the light of these controversies during the 1920s and 1930s Baldwin's distaste for a purely Conservative government is entirely explicable; under the aegis of the National Government he succeeded in resurrecting the liberal or centrist approach to Conservatism that had been threatened by the General Strike and by his defeat in 1929. The imperial controversies are also significant, especially when seen in conjunction with the policy of appeasement with which Conservatives became closely associated later in the 1930s. These issues went a long way to depriving the party of the patriotic high ground which had given it an advantage over its rivals since the late Victorian period. Moreover, although many Conservatives were critical of decolonization after 1945, they never fought it tooth and nail; the decisive battle to save the Empire had been fought and lost in the 1930s.

The Threat from the British Union of Fascists

By deliberately seeking the central ground of politics Baldwin ran the risk of driving his Tory opponents to seek an alternative leadership outside the National Government. For much of the decade the most compelling alternative on the right was that offered by Sir Oswald Mosley and the British Union of Fascists (BUF). Until comparatively recently historians treated the phenomenon of British fascism as quite marginal, regarding it as an inevitable failure. However, this has increasingly been recognized as an inadequate and misleading view. The publication of a serious biography of Mosley by Robert Skidelsky underlined the point that the BUF leader had a coherent programme and a bolder grasp of economic problems than most conventional politicians. Although shortage of evidence for fascist activity has inhibited academic research, the growth of local studies has demonstrated that fascism enjoyed a far wider regional appeal than once realized; it won support at all social levels; and it mobilized women in significant numbers. The traditional assumption that after a rapid rise the movement collapsed in 1934 has also given way to evidence that it revived in 1936 and in 1938–9 in connection with the peace campaign.

During the 1920s several extremist organizations appeared, including the Imperial Fascisti under Rotha Lintorn Orman and the Imperial Fascist League under Arnold Leese. They are best seen as essentially anti-Communist, pro-imperialist groups that feared the rise of labour, and believed in a Jewish conspiracy. They attracted people who felt that Parliament was being ruined by democracy, aristocrats dismayed by the collapse of land prices, and those who admired Mussolini for saving Italy from socialism. As such they were perhaps not strictly fascist. However, adopting strict academic definitions of fascism can easily lead one to underestimate the significance of the phenomenon, for it was precisely because fascists shared so much common ground with people in other organizations that the far right enjoyed so much influence in inter-war Britain. 'If I had been an Italian', said Winston Churchill, 'I am sure I would have been wholeheartedly with [the fascist movement] from start to finish in your triumphant struggle against the bestial appetites and passions of Leninism.'[3] Many influential men such as Lord Salisbury, Henry Page Croft and the Duke of Northumberland, who operated on the fringes of Conservatism, accepted many fascist ideas and welcomed the movement as a check to Bolshevism and as a source of stewards for Tory Party meetings at home. They did not find it necessary to join fascist organizations in the 1920s because the Conservatives were largely able to keep the threat of labour at bay; the defeat of the General Strike in 1926 also seemed to remove the need for a militant fascist organization for a time.

MOSLINI.

THE DUCE (*to Sir Oswald Mosley*). '*FIVE* DICTATORS!
WHY WORRY ABOUT THE OTHER FOUR?'
An early comment on Mosley's dictatorial tendencies.
Punch, or the London Charivari, 17 December 1930

However, the economic crisis of 1931 and the apparent inability of even the National Government to arrest the growth of unemployment during the early 1930s created fresh alarm in British society. It also made it fashionable to decry parliamentary politicians and parties as an effete bunch of failures who were vulnerable to a left-wing takeover, which the fascists alone were ready to prevent. Although Mosley aroused a good deal of suspicion as a man who had betrayed his class and his party by joining Labour, there was always a feeling that he might turn out to be necessary if the crisis returned. Moreover, Mosley's ideas rang bells with many on the right. What he had to say about the protection of British industry and the exploitation of the Empire, even to extent of suppressing the cotton textile industry in India, was highly congenial to rank-and-file Conservatives. There was also a radical edge to his programme in that he distinguished between manufacturers on the one hand and financiers on the other. The latter he attacked on the grounds that they helped Britain's competitors and perpetuated the bankrupt economic policies of nineteenth-century liberalism. Mosley's willingness to use the powers of the state and to stimulate the economy with a mixture of Keynesian and other techniques gave him a bold and coherent strategy which held an appeal on the left, as much as on the right, to those who despaired of the politicians' ability to tackle unemployment. This was why some Labour politicians, including John Strachey, Aneurin Bevan and James Maxton, had supported him briefly in 1930 and another Labour MP, John Becket, followed him even after 1931.

Seen at the grass roots the BUF was an opportunistic movement which varied in character from one region to another and over time. It campaigned effectively in areas of declining industry such as the Lancashire textile belt, where traditional working-class Conservatives sometimes succumbed to its appeal. Mosley also spent a lot of time speaking in market towns where discontented farmers were attracted to his policies. Though accurate figures for membership are not available, the BUF is thought to have had around 500 local branches at its height in 1934–6; something may be discerned from the distribution of parliamentary candidates it planned during 1936– 9: 39 in and around London, 16 in Lancashire, 12 in Yorkshire, 6 in the Midlands, 3 in Wales. The traditional picture of the BUF in the East End of London where it was involved in the notorious 'Battle of Cable Street' in 1936 gives a misleading impression, though anti-Jewish sentiment was certainly a factor in the organization's strength in places such as Leeds and Manchester, where a substantial Jewish community lived.

But by 1938–9 the BUF was attracting large audiences by means of its peace campaign, often in middle-class areas of the country where no violence occurred; in arguing against going into another war with Germany it clearly articulated the fears of an important section of opinion at that time. In these years many influential politicians joined organizations which were sympathetic to fascism without being labelled fascist, such as the Anglo-German Friendship, the Friends of National Spain and the United Christian Front, which is a reminder that fascist sympathies ran far wider than the formal membership of the BUF itself. Our perspective on the strength and character of fascism has also been changed by the evidence of the extensive female participation it aroused. Women comprised a substantial proportion of members and undertook roles in recruiting, selling *The Blackshirt*, and as stewards, speakers and candidates. Some upper-class ladies such as Viscountess Downe and Lady Maud Mosley were simply frustrated by the Conservative Party; others were former suffragettes now disillusioned with liberal democracy, who found in the military style of the BUF the excitement of militant campaigns before 1914.[4]

Despite this, the BUF ultimately failed to reach the level of support achieved by continental fascist movements. This has conventionally been ascribed to reactions aroused by the violence used by Blackshirt stewards at the notorious rally at Olympia in June 1934, which provoked a debate in Parliament and the loss of the favourable publicity previously given by Rothermere's *Daily Mail*. However, things were far more complicated. Violent events such as Olympia and the Battle of Cable Street in 1936 actually attracted fresh recruits as well as alienating others. Moreover, supporters of the National Government often reacted favourably because they regarded the BUF as justified in using violence against Communist disruption. In the debate in 1934 members made a point of praising 'the thousands of young men who have joined the Blackshirt Movement. They are among the best elements in this country.' One Tory summed it up: 'The Blackshirts have what the Conservatives need.'[5] Alarmed at the evidence that thousands were joining Mosley, these politicians appreciated that their own vote would be split by BUF candidates at the next election, thereby giving Labour the chance to return to power. This electoral calculation, as well as reluctance to interfere with freedom of speech, made the National Government very cautious about curtailing BUF violence. Not until 1936 did they pass the Public Order Act, which outlawed political uniforms and empowered the police to ban marches. By that time they thought it safe to legislate because the movement was past its peak.

However, the underlying explanation for the BUF's decline lay less in reactions to violence or to government intervention than in the modest economic revival from 1934 onwards. Fascism was only likely to succeed if it enjoyed the opportunity to step in to save a collapsing and discredited capitalist economy from chaos. By 1935 this seemed unlikely to materialize, which is why Mosley wisely kept out of the general election in that year. His best chance had been a very brief one between 1931 and 1934 when the National Government had appeared likely to fail, but his movement was too new to be ready to take full advantage. More generally, the relatively light impact of the depression in Britain, which spared the middle classes from inflation, restricted the scope for a Fascist movement. After 1935 much of Mosley's natural constituency felt safe enough with the National

Government. Moreover, although the British were not immune to a Fascist appeal, they differed from many continental people in having emerged victorious from the war with their system of government, their monarchy and their Empire intact and popular. Many found Mosley's thesis that Britain should concentrate on a self-contained Empire, leaving Nazi Germany to do the same in east and central Europe, very attractive; however, by the late 1930s, while some still saw this as a way to maintain peace, others had begun to regard him as a potential agent of Hitler.

Labour, Socialism and Keynesianism

Under Baldwin's leadership the National Government skilfully presented itself as Britain's bulwark against the dictatorships of both the Right and the Left. This meant depicting the Labour Party, which in the 1920s had enjoyed a growing reputation as moderate and respectable, as extremist and subversive. Although some socialists found inspiration in the five-year economic plans of the Soviet Union, the Labour movement remained fundamentally parliamentarian and continued to devote much energy to dissociating itself from Marxism and purging Communists from its ranks. The discussion about 'planning', which became fashionable in the 1930s, masked the fact that Labour's thinking was steadily evolving as a blend of Keynesianism and Fabianism rather than as Soviet-style central control.

Inevitably, in the aftermath of the collapse of MacDonald's government some left-wingers asked whether it would ever be possible to achieve a socialist programme under the British parliamentary system. But most socialists recognized that it was not the bankers or the House of Lords that had really prevented this in 1929–31 but rather the absence of a majority and a lack of clear policies on Labour's part. Socialist intellectuals recognized that Britain's strong central system of government, the tradition of secrecy and the tendency of the electoral system to deliver large majorities was actually advantageous for the enactment of a socialist programme; and they had no desire to change it in more than marginal ways.

A more pertinent question for the post-1931 Labour movement was not whether but *how* socialism might be achieved in Britain. Inevitably, there was a reaction against the whole style of leadership offered by MacDonald, which had been uplifting but ultimately shallow. None of his successors, Henderson, Lansbury and Attlee, were to enjoy the kind of personal standing that MacDonald had achieved at his peak. Labour retained MacDonaldism insofar as it continued to want to work within a gradualist, parliamentary framework, but after 1931 it focused much more on a precise and practicable economic policy. Although the ILP decided to sever its links with the party in 1932, in the process condemning itself to a fatal loss of members and influence, its ideas about managing the economy by stimulating demand did become more central to the party's thinking. One of the most important effects of 1931 was to encourage the trade union leaders to shift the party towards Keynesianism as the most feasible means of managing or 'planning' the economy and avoiding the horrors of mass unemployment. Even before the cabinet broke up, the TUC's General Council, led by Ernest Bevin, had concluded that retrenchment, deflation and attempts to defend the exchange rate were futile, and they refused to accept the need to wait for capitalism either to collapse or to recover its health before any move could be made towards socialism. Instead, they looked for ways of boosting employment and demand in the short and medium term.

By 1933 this train of thought led the TUC to recommend the New Deal programmes being implemented in America by President Roosevelt as worthy of emulation in Britain.[6] It identified its priorities as a programme of public works financed out of national credit, a 40-hour maximum working week, raising the school-leaving age to 16 and the prohibition of labour by those under 16. Some on the left seized on this as proof that the union leaders, lacking a socialist ideology, had been seduced by reformist capitalism. It was tempting to believe that the emergence of fascist regimes and the deterioration of the free enterprise system heralded the final collapse of capitalism, and on that assumption strategies such as the New Deal could be seen as doomed attempts to avert fundamental change, or even as a variation on fascism. However, the pragmatic instincts of the Labour movement led it to appreciate the significance of Rooseveltian policy in greatly extending the capacity of the state to manage the economy in the interests of the working class.

Consequently, during the later 1930s, Labour developed a strategy that combined Keynesian techniques with planning in the form of public ownership of certain sectors of the economy. In *For Socialism and Peace* (1934) the party proposed to nationalize coal, gas, electricity, water, transport, agriculture, iron and steel, shipping, shipbuilding, engineering, textiles, chemicals, insurance and banking. Subsequently this ambitious list was curtailed to incorporate a more limited selection of public utilities and ailing industries where the opposition to public ownership from vested interests was likely to be slight. Even this programme of nationalization left four-fifths of the economy in private hands. Equally as important as the extent of these proposals, however, was the evolution of a definite procedure for taking these industries into the state sector and running them. The chief architect of this was Herbert Morrison, the one minister in the last Labour government, apart from Addison, to have shown a real grasp of the practicalities. His London Transport Bill established the principle of paying compensation to the dispossessed owners, and the operation of publicly owned industries by small boards of experts and businessmen selected by ministers and responsible to the Cabinet rather than to Parliament or to the employees. Although the exclusion of workers' participation and trade union representation drew severe criticism from Bevin, and can be seen in retrospect as a political error, Morrison's scheme largely survived as the nearest thing to a blueprint for the nationalization programme after 1945. It translated the hitherto vague idea of state control into something concrete for the first time, and it left the party advocating a mixed economy rather than a Soviet-style system of planning. Even this remained vulnerable to attack in the late 1930s, but wartime experience rapidly removed much of the controversy and novelty from state control.

The Left, Rearmament and Public Opinion

The most surprising aspect of 1931 is that it did not lead to a takeover of the Labour Party by the Left. It did, however, generate protracted internal debates and struggles within the movement, and as a result historians have often depicted the 1930s as a period of divisiveness, poor leadership and missed opportunities for Labour. This, as we shall see, is unduly negative. There was, however, a vacuum in terms of leadership. The electoral holocaust of 1931 reduced the parliamentary party to a mere 52 members, most of whom had been loyal to MacDonald and felt lost without him. Labour's founding fathers had largely disappeared, and only three members had any ministerial experience; as a result George Lansbury became leader, with Clement Attlee as deputy. On the other hand, defeat accelerated the rise of three talented politicians who were to leave their mark on the party's domestic and external policy for the next 20 years – Herbert Morrison, Ernest Bevin and Hugh Dalton. But in the short term the small size and mediocrity of the parliamentary party robbed it of its previous dominance; whereas during 1918–31, 16 of the NEC's 23 members had, on average, been MPs, only three were MPs in 1931–5. Inevitably this left a gulf separating the cautious trade unionist MPs and the rebellious socialists among the rank and file.

Despite this the Left struggled to gain significant influence. Union membership had fallen since 1920 and did not begin to recover until 1934. But neither the ILP, the Socialist League nor the Communist Party managed to recruit more than a fraction of the lost members. The most successful were the Communists, whose membership increased from 2,500 in 1930 to 6,000 in 1931 and eventually reached 18,000 by 1938. More worrying to the trade unions was the National Unemployed Workers' Movement (NUWM), led by Wal Hannington, which at its peak in 1931–3 mobilised 50,000 men. Yet despite the apprehension of the orthodox labour leaders the NUWM was by no means a revolutionary movement. Its methods were hunger marches and petitions, and its demands centred on the restoration of the cuts in unemployment benefit and the abolition of the means test. What violence accompanied its meetings was half-hearted and unintended, and by 1933 the movement was already dwindling. Significantly, the Labour Party felt it could afford to shun the NUWM without danger to itself; the loss of working-class support to the National Government remained a more serious concern.

The leaders bore even more lightly the disaffiliation of the ILP in 1932. Its departure led to the formation of a new body, the Socialist League (SL), a small but vigorous group of intellectuals including G. D. H. Cole, Stafford Cripps, Harold Laski, Sir Charles Trevelyan, R. H. Tawney, D. N. Pritt, Ellen Wilkinson and Aneurin Bevan. Though intended as a research and propaganda group within the party, the SL rapidly ran into the difficulties of offering a rival programme to the party as the ILP had done. The Left did derive some advantage from the only effective challenge to the leadership – the Constituency Parties Movement (CPM) – though this developed quite independently. The CPM emerged as a spontaneous expression of rank-and-file feeling that the constituencies had been largely excluded from influence in the party despite their right to fill 5 of the 23 places on the NEC. At a time of general decline individual membership was expanding to reach 419,000 in 1935. Speaking for loyal party workers, the CPM could not be brushed aside as easily as the socialist societies, and in 1937 the conference raised constituency representation to seven and allowed for separate election. This had the effect of strengthening the Left since Cripps, Laski and Pritt were elected to fill these seats on the NEC.

Despite its internal divisions the Left played a crucial role in the debates over defence and foreign policy during the 1930s. In the 1920s the party had largely accepted its interpretation of the Treaty of Versailles as a punitive settlement designed to satisfy the French, its condemnation of the pre-war arms race and its belief in disarmament. From a party point of view the only flaw in this was that Conservative governments followed much the same policy by revising reparations, assisting Germany with her currency difficulties, admitting her to the League, accepting an early evacuation of the Rhineland and generally seeking to appease Germany's legitimate grievances. By 1922 expenditure on the armed forces had been reduced to £110 million, from £600 million in 1920, and it remained around that level until 1935. However, many Labour politicians felt that this did not go far enough, for in backing the League the government was simply upholding the territorial status quo which benefited the victorious powers. The party contained many socialist and Christian pacifists who advocated unilateral disarmament as a sure way to peace, and in 1922 and

1926 the conference voted against participation in any future wars. Though few MPs fully shared these pacifist views, they regularly voted against the defence estimates and argued that it would be dangerous to support rearmament under the National Government.

In retrospect, the apologists for the appeasers often argued that the government's timidity in dealing with the dictators was dictated largely by the pacifism of the British public between the wars. However, if opinion had been as clear-cut as this, the Labour Party would have garnered much more support than it did. Many of the famous manifestations of public opinion require careful interpretation. For example, the success of several 'anti-war' books, including Robert Graves's *Goodbye To All That* (1929) and Vera Brittain's *Testament of Youth* (1933), point to the pessimism at this time owing to the failures of the League and the Disarmament Conference at Geneva; but they reflect a repudiation of the appeals used to justify war in 1914 rather than opposition to war in all circumstances. Nor can the findings of the famous and misleadingly titled 'Peace Ballot' in 1934 be interpreted as proof of popular pacifism. Against the background of Germany's withdrawal from the Disarmament Conference in 1933, the ballot was intended to demonstrate to the government the extent of public support for the League and collective security. In a poll of 11.5 million people some 6.7 million votes were cast in favour of applying sanctions, including *military* sanctions, against aggressor states who flouted arbitration by the League, and only 2.3 million against. Clearly support for the League was not to be equated with pacifism, and the ballot showed that by 1935 the public had concluded that the dictators must be resisted; in effect it was the National Government that lagged behind public opinion, not the other way round.

On the other hand historians sometimes cite electoral evidence to show how the government was constrained, notably by a famous by-election held at East Fulham in October 1934 when a Conservative majority of 14,000 was turned into a Labour one of nearly 5,000. The assumption was that the result reflected support for the Labour candidate's disarmament policy and a reaction against the warmongering by the Conservative candidate. However, this interpretation has been discredited. Although the 1931 result made East Fulham appear a strong Tory seat, it was actually marginal, returning Conservatives by 1,700 votes in 1929 and by 1,000 in 1935; consequently its loss at a mid-term by-election was not remarkable. Also, the by-election was fought on domestic issues, not primarily over defence, and the Liberal supporters voted Labour in the absence of a candidate of their own. Finally, this one result has to be set in the context of other by-elections in which Conservative candidates won comfortable victories by frankly advocating rearmament, such as Basingstoke and Twickenham in 1934 and South Aberdeen in 1935.

It also remains unproven whether the National Government, which after all enjoyed a huge majority, was sufficiently fearful of public opinion to allow it to influence its defence policy. In fact the chief restraint on re-armament was the financial policy of Neville Chamberlain as Chancellor. Following the Treasury view, he refused to allow his budgets to be unbalanced by major increases in defence spending, and insisted that the expansion of one sector would force the government into massive borrowing and weaken other parts of the economy. In 1934 the Defence Requirements Committee reported that Germany should now be regarded as Britain's most likely enemy and that the air force and the army should be expanded with this in mind. However, under Chamberlain's influence the cabinet opted to spend only an extra £52 million rather than the £97 million recommended and to expand the Royal Air Force (RAF) but to avoid any new expeditionary force.

While the government hesitated over a major rearmament programme, Labour embarked upon a major change of policy in the mid-1930s. Under the influence of Dalton, Bevin and Attlee, who argued in favour of collective security through the League of Nations, the party became committed to imposing sanctions against aggressor states. This reflected the fears aroused by Japanese aggression in Manchuria and Hitler's seizure of power in Germany. In 1934 the annual conference voted by 1.5 million to 0.67 million for Henderson's resolution backing collective security, a step which precipitated the resignation of Stafford Cripps and Arthur Ponsonby, the leader in the Lords; the following year Lansbury himself quit as Labour leader. Though the party was reluctant as yet to say so, this shift of policy implied the necessity for major rearmament, but the need to maintain party unity dictated caution until the deteriorating international situation prompted a further step away from pacifism.

The General Election of 1935

For the first few years of its life it seemed uncertain whether the National Government would survive, especially as it failed to avoid a devaluation of the pound, unemployment continued to rise, the BUF gained strength, and the Labour Party enjoyed a marked recovery. In the 1932 municipal elections Labour gained 458 seats and exceeded its previous peak in 1929; progress continued in 1933, culminating in Labour's capture of the London County Council in 1934. Individual membership increased by 100,000 in 1933, though by 1935 it had levelled out at 419,000. By-elections also produced two gains in 1932, two in 1933 and four in 1934. However, this was less impressive when put in the context of 40 by-elections in which the government retained most of the gains made in 1931; East Fulham did not indicate a general trend.

Indeed, when the depression reached its nadir in 1932–3, Labour failed to derive the full benefit because its own credentials were still tarnished by the events of August 1931; and once unemployment began to fall the sense in the country that the corner had been turned took the pressure off the government. Between 1931 and 1935, when the election was held, a million houses had been built, the cuts in salaries and unemployment benefits had been reversed, and Chamberlain's budget brought additional tax reliefs. Only in 1934 did the government run into serious conflict with the unemployed when it decided to remove unemployment assistance from the Public Assistance Committees and administer it on a uniform basis through the Unemployment Assistance Board. The realization that the new uniform scales would reduce the income of many families provoked a rare display of outrage throughout the country early in 1935. Thereupon the scales were promptly dropped and Baldwin took care to get the election out of the way before new ones were introduced in 1936. Thus the autumn of 1935, when the country was happily celebrating the Silver Jubilee of King George V, seemed a safe time for an early election. Still saddled with the charge of having run away from the financial crisis in 1931, the Labour leaders found it impossible to erase the impression that if they returned to office the crisis would return with them.

Despite the importance of economic issues, the defenders of Baldwin and his ministers have sometimes claimed that the 1935 election was fought on defence and foreign policy, the point being that not until 1935 did he obtain a mandate for rearmament. This, however, is far from clear. Rearmament could not become an election issue, however intrinsically important, unless the two main parties adopted and articulated distinct views on the subject. But although by this time Labour was gradually retreating from its earlier position, it remained cautious. Meanwhile Baldwin played down the issue by promising 'there will be no great armaments' and insisted that the Cabinet intended only to 'repair gaps in our defences'. It was thus not easy to tell the difference between the parties. If any clear message emerged from the election it was that both parties attached great importance to the League of Nations and, by implication, would support it in restraining Mussolini's recent aggression in Ethiopia. Since neither party had been especially supportive of the League in the past, this carried little credibility.

Labour entered the election in some disarray, having to devote attention to repudiating the Communist Party and disclaiming any sympathies with totalitarianism. Unfortunately the resignations of Cripps, Lansbury and Ponsonby so close to the election drew attention to internal divisions. Henderson's death in 1935 robbed the party of a familiar and reassuring figure and Attlee lacked the oratorical ability to make any impact in the short time that he had been party leader. Labour also continued to be handicapped by a largely hostile press. Only the *Daily Herald* and the *Daily Chronicle* opposed the National Government at this stage; it was not until the later 1930s when the *Daily Mirror* swung to Labour that the balance shifted significantly. Even more important were the cinema newsreels, which catered to a huge working-class audience. But they were invariably calculated to foster an optimistic, patriotic view of current events in which ministers received the bulk of attention for their efforts; the soporific character of the newsreels militated against the emergence of any issues which might have undermined the government of the day. Similarly, the programmes and news reports by the BBC reflected a distinct bias towards ministerial achievement and neglected the Opposition's case.[7] By this time Baldwin himself had become a master of the quiet, reassuring radio broadcast, which contrasted with the more formal style of traditionalists such as Attlee.

In these circumstances the comfortable victory won by the National Government, including its Simonite Liberal and National Labour allies, is explicable. Labour recorded a net gain of 94 seats, bringing its total to 158, but this should be contrasted with the 288 won in 1929. Despite an average swing to Labour of 9.4 per cent since 1931 the government retained 435 seats, of which 388 were Conservative. In the West Riding, Durham, Northumberland and Scotland, barely touched by economic recovery, the swing exceeded this; but in the buoyant west Midlands it reached only half the average. In Birmingham, where Labour had won six of the twelve seats in 1929, it won none in 1935. Many industrial working-class constituencies returned National Government supporters, including all three in Salford and all four in Newcastle. Even Jarrow was only narrowly recovered by Ellen Wilkinson. A measure of Baldwin's success is contained in the 40 constituencies that enjoyed a straight Conservative-Labour contest in 1929, 1931 and 1935; there the swing away from Labour was 15.1 per cent from 1929-31 and only 9.9 per cent back to Labour from 1931-5. In effect Baldwin had managed to retain much of the middle ground. Although Labour's share of the poll (38 per cent) narrowly exceeded that of 1929 (37 per cent), it yielded 130 *fewer* seats because of the concentration of non-Labour votes on a single candidate where they had previously been divided between Conservative and Liberal. Having received a boost from the electoral system in 1929, Labour was now seriously under-represented by it.

Labour and the Popular Front 1936–1939

Mussolini's invasion of Ethiopia in the spring of 1935 destroyed all remaining confidence in the League of Nations, and, by driving the Italians into alliance with Hitler, accelerated Europe's descent into war. This growing sense of crisis profoundly affected the political parties and created conditions which were greatly to Labour's advantage. The outbreak of civil war between Republicans and Nationalists in Spain in the summer of

1936 also had a powerful effect in uniting the left and right wings of the Labour Party and creating an acceptance of the inevitability and justice of a war to defend democracy and to rid Europe of fascism. This view was widely held in all political parties, though some right-wing Tories argued that the Nationalists were fighting for Christian civilization. The determination of Neville Chamberlain to retain the friendship of Mussolini and to remain neutral over Spain gradually discredited the government, and meanwhile it provoked fresh initiatives on the left in the shape of the United Front and the Popular Front.

The theory behind this strategy was that all opponents of fascism, regardless of their party allegiance, should co-operate against the National Government and put an end to the policy of appeasement. The electoral success of the Popular Front in France led leading Labour intellectuals, including G. D. H. Cole and Hugh Dalton, to consider seriously whether it could be repeated in Britain. On the assumption that Labour could not win the next election, or even the one after that, Cole considered a Popular Front worth trying. Dalton, though attracted, felt that it would be difficult to implement under the British electoral system and that none of Labour's potential allies would be able to deliver the vote.[8]

In any case, the Labour Party showed a marked reluctance to accept the strategy. When the TUC met in 1936 the Right backed a policy of non-intervention in Spain, partly because to sell arms to the Republicans threatened to bring a general war much closer and partly because the Popular Front Government in France took the same view. Later that year the party conference also adopted non-intervention, despite pressure from the Left. 'I say you are beggared of policy at this moment', declared Charles Trevelyan, one of the leading opponents of war who had now switched to a Popular Front policy. He and Stafford Cripps exacerbated the division in the party by formally launching the Popular Front in January 1937, for which they were eventually expelled. The underlying fear of the Labour leadership was that Popular Front activities were simply expedients for allowing the Communists to infiltrate local Labour parties and evade the ban on Communist membership of the party. Though understandable, this was an error since it allowed Communists to gain credibility by taking the lead in opposition to fascism, and in any case the Labour leaders' writ did not run at the grass roots. When the 1936 conference rejected another Communist application for affiliation some 400,000 votes were cast against the official line – a clear indication of the growing sympathy for a Popular Front.

This is a reminder that the negative view traditionally taken by historians towards the Popular Front stands in need of some revision; it suffers from taking a national perspective rather than a local one, and it overlooks the long-term significance that the campaign had on Labour's appeal in the country. During these years party members co-operated with Communists,

ILP-ers, Liberals and Conservatives in a multitude of 'Aid Spain' Committees. They assisted Republican refugees, raised funds for food ships, demanded that Britain sell arms to the Republicans and organized celebrations to mark the return of volunteers who had fought in the International Brigade.[9] By 1937 the Labour Party had recognized that non-intervention in Spain was ineffective, and the MPs began to vote for the defence estimates after opposing them for many years. Prominent Labour politicians, including Ellen Wilkinson, openly supported 'Aid Spain' activities, and even Attlee visited Spain where he inspected the British contingent of the International Brigade.

Thus, although the Popular Front did not succeed in a formal sense by 1939, its effects on the National Government were significant. For one thing it left the Conservatives open to Labour accusations of weakness and even of failure to stand up for British interests.[10] In this way Labour began to recover the language of patriotism which it had not used since the First World War. Conservative disquiet with Chamberlain's policy was more extensive than it appeared to be partly because politicians felt reluctant to lend support to Churchill, whom they regarded as disloyal and overambitious. In any case, since several of the Tory anti-appeasers, including Churchill and Duff Cooper, continued to seek better relations with Mussolini, their position was somewhat compromised. Few were prepared to go as far as the Duchess of Atholl, who resigned the Tory whip and fought a by-election at Perth in December 1938 against an official Conservative. She narrowly lost partly because she failed to appeal to the non-Conservative vote. But Popular Front candidates also challenged the Conservatives unsuccessfully at Oxford in October 1938, and scored a notable victory at Bridgwater, Somerset in November that year. By the spring of 1939, when the Munich settlement collapsed following the entry of German troops into Czechoslovakia, Chamberlain rapidly lost credibility in the country. One of the most striking symptoms of the momentum gathering behind the Popular Front was the withdrawal of support from the National Government by the *Daily Mirror* between 1936 and 1939. As a former pro-Conservative paper it was in a good position to undermine the electoral support of the government, and conversely, its new pro-Labour stance helped the Opposition to project a national, patriotic appeal which yielded dividends in 1945. In spite of this one should not exaggerate the extent to which domestic politics had changed by 1939. The National Government would probably have won a peacetime general election. On the other hand, conventional accounts have underestimated the extent to which Labour had recovered and repositioned itself, largely through its stance on national defence and the Popular Front during the last years of peace. The outbreak of the Second World War simply accelerated a process that was already under way.

CHAPTER THIRTEEN

The Politics of
the 'People's War'
1939–1945

Socialism as practised in the war, did no one any harm, and quite a lot of
people good.

Sarah Churchill to Winston Churchill, 5 June 1945

The Second World War represented a major watershed in British politics.
It brought an end to a prolonged period of Conservative dominance and
turned Labour into a majority party with real power for the first time. It
moved the agenda to the left and ushered in a phase of 'consensus' which
lasted until the 1970s. Finally, the subsequent polarization of votes between
the two main parties during the 1950s led many political scientists to conclude that a class-based pattern of politics was a natural or even inevitable
result of mass democracy in an industrial society such as Britain.

The Churchill Coalition

Although Neville Chamberlain's administration entered the war backed by
a parliamentary majority of 200, after nine months of what contemporaries
called the 'Phoney War' the hegemony of the National Government had
been effectively destroyed. The rot set in during the early days of September
1939 when the prime minister disappointed the House of Commons by
his failure to make a prompt announcement of Britain's entry into the war.
Many members expected him to contrive another 'Munich'. Chamberlain's
statement on 2 September was received in ominous silence by the Conservatives, one of whom, L. S. Amery, in a remark that crystallized the
political significance of the war, called across to the Labour front-bench
spokesman: 'Speak for England!'

THE CABINET BUILDER.
'Quite effective in its way! I hope the one I've just made
will do as well.'
The Pick of 'Punch', February 1941

For a time Chamberlain went some way to shoring up his position by
offering Churchill a post as First Lord of the Admiralty, possibly calculat-
ing that his chief rival and critic would discredit himself by sponsoring
some reckless scheme as he had in the previous war. But the refusal of the
Labour Party to join the government forced Chamberlain to bear the
responsibility for the early military setbacks; they felt no confidence in him
as a war leader and believed they would have little influence in a coalition
under him.[1] During the next few months, while German troops swept
across Europe, Britain seemed to have little fighting to do; consequently
the public missed any strong sense of patriotism and unity and soon
concluded that the country was not receiving proper leadership. This

feeling was relentlessly exploited by newspapers such as the *Daily Mirror*, whose attacks on Chamberlain reached a peak after the fiasco of the Norwegian Campaign in May 1940: 'the Prime Minister is an expert at this art of explaining away failure. He gets so much practice in it! He has had little else to do since Munich.'[2] Meanwhile the opponents of appeasement, including the Liberal, Clement Davies, the Conservatives, Duff Cooper, L. S. Amery and Robert Boothby, along with Attlee and Arthur Greenwood on the Labour front bench, created a parliamentary popular front by co-ordinating their attacks on the government. This culminated in a two-day debate provoked by the Norwegian Campaign on 7–8 May 1940, which the government survived by 281 votes to 200. Forty Conservatives had voted against Chamberlain and another eighty had abstained. This, combined with the continued refusal of Labour to serve under him, forced the prime minister to resign.

In this crisis most Conservatives preferred Lord Halifax as Chamberlain's successor; but Churchill was the only alternative who looked like a war leader and could command the support of the Opposition and much of the press. Even so, Churchill's position remained at least as precarious as that of Lloyd George in 1916, for he, too, was a prime minister who did not lead a political party. Embarrassingly, his early speeches as premier were cheered by Labour members but heard in sullen silence by the Conservatives, who realized that the formation of a coalition including Labour and Liberal ministers had suddenly marginalized them. Churchill attempted to soothe their feelings by retaining Chamberlain, Simon, Halifax and Hoare in the Cabinet. Things improved, especially after Chamberlain's resignation from the Cabinet in September and his death later that year. Reluctantly the Conservatives then accepted Churchill as party leader, though many found it impossible to see him as a genuine Conservative. Moreover, the military setbacks of 1941 and 1942 convinced many politicians that the Coalition would not survive the war.

Conversely, the Coalition transformed the standing of the Labour Party. Not only were Attlee and Greenwood members of the War Cabinet, but later Attlee became deputy prime minister; moreover, its leaders enjoyed much greater prominence than the Conservatives because of their role on the home front, notably Herbert Morrison as Minister for Supply and Home Security, Ernest Bevin as Minister for Labour, and Hugh Dalton as Minister for Economic Warfare. Even more remarkably, the largely unknown Stafford Cripps returned from his ambassadorship in Moscow in 1942 at a time when Russia had become Britain's much-needed ally against Hitler, and delivered a broadcast which, according to Mass Observation, won the approval of 93 per cent of the public. Twelve days later Cripps had joined the War Cabinet, become leader of the House, and emerged as a popular choice to succeed Churchill as premier. Interestingly, Cripps soon began to pressurize Churchill, rather as Lloyd George had done with Asquith in 1916, by demanding a small War Cabinet free from departmental ministers, on the grounds that the war was not being run effectively.[3] Although this criticism was widely accepted, Churchill was rescued from further danger by General Montgomery's success at the Battle of El Alamein.

It also appeared that the war was going to restore the fortunes of the Liberals. The party's leader, Sir Archibald Sinclair, was a popular Air Minister in the Coalition and Gwilym Lloyd George served as Minister for Fuel and Power, but Lloyd George himself hovered in the wings, apparently ready to join the government when Churchill failed. More importantly, Sir William Beveridge, who became something of a national hero after the publication of his famous report on social security in 1942, was also a Liberal and entered the Commons as member for Berwick in 1944. These developments convinced many contemporaries that the next election would see a Liberal revival. However, these expectations failed to materialize.

On the other hand, the Labour Party's stance was complicated by its uncomfortable dual role as a key element in the government and as the chief opposition to it. While the Labour leaders sat on the government front bench, their followers remained opposite them and, in effect, were led by discontented members such as Emmanuel Shinwell and Aneurin Bevan. They forced a confidence motion on the government in May 1941 after the failure of the Allied campaign in Greece, and led a revolt over the level of old-age pensions in July 1942. By that stage the government's approval rating in the polls had fallen to 41 per cent. The most severe challenge came during the three-day debate on the Beveridge Report in February 1943 when Labour moved a hostile amendment, despite appeals from Bevin and Morrison, because it felt the government's response was too negative. Though the government won by 325 to 119, only two Labour backbenchers, in addition to the ministers, had supported them. 'This division,' commented James Griffiths, 'makes the return of a Labour Government to power at the next election a certainty'.[4] This, however, was not reciprocated by the party's leaders, who simply felt angry about the revolts. Conversely, the rank and file believed that their leaders had failed to make the most of their influence to force the Coalition towards more egalitarian policies on the home front. Consequently, as the fortunes of the Allies improved, the members looked increasingly to the time when they could return to normal party politics. Attlee bowed to this pressure in October 1944 when he accepted the decision of the NEC that Labour should quit the Coalition once Germany had been defeated, a decision that helped determine the timing of the general election.

In retrospect, the Conservatives complained that Labour had taken an unfair advantage by maintaining its organization during wartime. There was some basis for this in that Labour held annual conferences, whereas the Conservatives' were suspended. Churchill himself gave no real leadership to his party and neglected its organization; in any case his only close Conservative colleagues were marginal and maverick figures such as Brendan Bracken and Lord Beaverbrook. In this situation the party inevitably became moribund and rudderless. On the other hand, both parties' organizations suffered considerable disruption, especially as local agents left to undertake war work. Labour's real advantage lay in its greater sense of purpose and its underlying optimism that things were moving decisively its way at last.

Public Opinion and the Swing to the Left

By comparison with the First World War, historians have a better range of evidence about changes in popular attitudes between 1939 and 1945 in the form of the Mass Observation reports, opinion polls which some newspapers had been printing since the late 1930s, and the Ministry of Information's surveys. Not surprisingly, the disappointments of the early stages of the war generated a sharp reaction against the leading proponents of appeasement, most of whom, including Chamberlain, Halifax, Simon and Hoare, remained in office and could thus be blamed for military setbacks. The mood was nicely caught by the authors of *Guilty Men*, a slim volume which went through ten impressions during July 1940 alone. They concluded: 'Let the guilty men retire, then, of their own volition, and so make an essential contribution to victory upon which we are implacably resolved.'[5] This public hostility towards Chamberlain and the 'Old Gang' was confirmed by the Ministry of Information. However, the party-political significance of this feeling was not immediately apparent, partly because the three main parties agreed on a truce covering by-election vacancies during the war. Despite this, 75 of the 141 seats which fell vacant actually saw a contest – a sign that many people felt the need to fill the vacuum left by the suspension of normal political conflict and the agreement to postpone the general election which had been due in 1940. Initially the running was made by Independents who gained seats from the Conservatives at Grantham, Rugby, Wallasey, West Derbyshire and Maldon. The first Scottish Nationalist MP was also elected at Motherwell in 1945. In 1942 a new party was formed by Sir Richard Acland. Common Wealth was a left-wing, middle-class movement which won safe Tory seats at by-elections in Eddisbury, Skipton and Chelmsford. Many of these contests, notably that of Tom Driberg at Maldon, took the character of Popular Front campaigns, and almost all the Independent and Common Wealth candidates stood on Labour-cum-Liberal programmes.[6] In effect, then, the wartime by-elections were a foretaste of the post-war general election and an indication not just of a negative anti-appeaser reaction but of a positive shift of opinion to the left.

However, the traditional view of the war goes further than this, suggesting the spread of egalitarian views and a weakening of class prejudices. One can certainly see manifestations of such attitudes in the belief that the suffering and sacrifices of wartime ought to be shared equally, especially as this had not been the case in the previous war. A symptom of this was the popularity of J. B. Priestley's radio broadcasts in 1940 in which he suggested that a better future would be denied 'if the privileges of a few are seen to be regarded as more important than the happiness of the many'.[7] This was intensified by the experience of the Blitz. The king and queen showed an awareness of the force of public opinion by remaining in London throughout the war. 'Now we can look the East End in the face', the queen is believed to have remarked after Buckingham Palace had sustained damage from enemy bombing.

On the other hand, it has rightly been argued that there was a great deal of exaggeration in claims about wartime egalitarianism. Wealthy people scrambled for advantage by sending their children to safety in Canada, and the class system emerged largely unscathed from the conflict. And although measures such as food rationing were generally popular, there were limits to public tolerance. Male manual workers, for example, wanted more meat than they were officially allowed; and once the war was over patience with the system began to dwindle. Yet in spite of such qualifications, it would be wrong to dismiss the wartime mood. This is best understood by comparing reactions with those of the First World War. In the previous conflict popular patriotism had been much more deferential and responsive to the king-and-Empire appeal; by contrast, during 1939–45 people were more critical and irreverent and readier to assert that the purpose of the war was to benefit the general population. This is underlined by the industrial militancy that characterized the Second World War. This time there was no patriotic interlude; strikes increased in 1939 and continued to do so right up to 1945, as workers showed their determination not to lose the benefits of a booming economy. Critical attitudes towards those in authority were revealed by the regular Mass Observation surveys, which showed how the public had lost confidence in most of the newspapers for misleading them over appeasement before the war. It also became clear from these investigations that women were much less caught up by wartime patriotism than men; their vulnerability to the privations of war in the shape of food queues, the blackout, evacuation, and deteriorating housing undermined women's morale and their acceptance of authority. More generally the public displayed a surprising disrespect for official propaganda which was directed at them daily and monitored unofficially by Mass Observation. Much of the advice about not discussing the war in public and about food economy was regarded as absurd and irrelevant. The reaction against one government poster – 'Your Courage, Your Cheerfulness, Your Resolution Will Bring Us Victory' – actually forced the authorities to withdraw it from circulation.

However, in recent years some historians have argued that the wartime mood should not be seen as increasingly radical or left-wing and thus as having implications for the general election, but rather as detached, cynical, ignorant and non-party. Yet this involves a considerable misunderstanding to which well-informed and politically aware academics are often susceptible when analysing the political attitudes of ordinary people. For much of the war people were not offered a normal party-political choice due to the truce and the loyalty of the Labour leaders to the Coalition; nor were the usual forms of local party activity available to them. To that extent people had become disengaged from politics. However, their interest clearly reasserted itself before 1945. For despite a very outdated electoral register and the difficulties in casting a vote a, *higher* proportion of people voted in 1945 (73 per cent) than at the previous peacetime election in 1935 (71 per cent). A longer perspective suggests that the country had suffered from apathy during the 1930s in the face of a depression that seemed to defy solution. But during the war the possibility of improvement had begun to raise expectations and foster a more assertive attitude. The key stage in the politicization of this mood came early in 1943 with the debate over the Beveridge Report, which won the overwhelming endorsement of the public. The failure of Churchill and his Conservative colleagues to be sufficiently supportive of Beveridge crystallized the negative feelings of the early war years into something more positive and party political. From 1943 onwards people were determined that there should be no return to the mass unemployment and hardship which they associated with the inter-war period.

Consensus Politics

Analysis of wartime politics has given rise to a fresh interpretation of the significance of the period for British party politics. In *The Road to 1945* (1975) Paul Addison drew attention to the way in which the need to mobilize national resources and achieve national unity set the pattern for reconstruction. But this was not simply an ephemeral response to a crisis. It involved a range of men and women who comprised an enlightened elite of politicians, intellectuals and experts in a new consensus about the aims of public policy. The impact of their thinking was to last through several decades and even changes of government. Apart from the obvious Labour and Liberal figures, consensus included prominent Conservatives such as R. A. Butler and younger MPs who joined the Tory Reform Group in 1943 with a view to supporting the Beveridge Report. In domestic affairs consensus manifested itself in a number of policies common to all the main parties, of which the most important was full employment; this aim was enshrined in the famous white paper of 1944 which committed the government to maintaining a high and stable level of employment. Other elements of the consensus were the welfare state, the mixed economy, and collaboration between government and trade unions to resolve disputes.

Since the 1970s this thesis has attracted a good deal of criticism. There is, for example, a legitimate question about timing. During the war the politicians agreed chiefly about the need to defeat Hitler but were less able to co-operate on domestic issues. Nationalization of industry was postponed although the Minister for Fuel and Power suggested nationalizing coal as a wartime measure to improve efficiency and output. And it has been argued that reconstruction was only at the planning stage by 1945. This is valid only to a limited extent, for the Coalition government had an impressive record in social reform in the shape of the 1944 Education Act and the Family Allowances Act, for example. On the other hand, by the end of the war friction between the two main parties was growing and the Conservatives had not fully embraced the new agenda. There is thus some ground for the view that consensus was a product of the 1945 election as much as of wartime experience. Since the Conservatives evidently expected to win the election, their heavy defeat naturally put them under pressure to rethink their programme and appeal.

However, many of the criticisms of the consensus thesis involve misrepresenting it by exaggerating the claims behind it. It does not, for example, suggest that *all* Conservatives and *all* Socialists subscribed. Naturally the leadership of both parties was subject to pressure to be true to their parties' principles, though significantly, they managed to resist it with some ease. Some historians have examined wartime policy-making in detail and found, not surprisingly, differences between Labour and Conservatives. For example, the Conservative, Henry Willink, was involved in plans for a National Health Service which did not go as far as Aneurin Bevan's post-1948 scheme; yet as Bevan himself fell short of the ideas of the Socialist Medical Association this tends to confirm the idea of a consensus as much as to undermine it. It has also been claimed that R. A. Butler's Education Act fell short of Labour views on multilateral or comprehensive schooling; yet this overlooks the fact that comprehensive education was only a minority interest in the Labour Party at this stage, and the Act was happily implemented by Ellen Wilkinson under the post-war Attlee government. In short, criticisms over details do not pose a fundamental challenge to the idea of consensus.

As so often in historical debates, much depends on how narrow or how wide a perspective one adopts. For example, the manifestations of enthusiasm over social reconstruction during the Second World War may seem similar to those of 1914–18. Yet there is no suggestion of a consensus in connection with the previous war, for after an initial flurry of social reforms around 1919 the political impetus for innovation and interventionism was blown away; thus the aftermath of the two wars was quite different. It is of course true that by 1945 both parties had become keen to abandon the *Coalition*; but that did not in itself indicate hostility towards the principles of consensus. The extent to which *both* parties moved is especially apparent if one takes account of foreign, defence and imperial issues after 1945. Under Ernest Bevin, who was greatly admired by the Conservatives, the Labour government strove to maintain Britain as a Great Power, to develop atomic weapons, to retain the Empire and to support a huge peacetime army – all of which would have been a shock to the post-1918 Labour Party.

Inevitably most doubt centres around the extent to which the Conservatives can be seen in terms of consensus. Again, perspective is important here. As we have seen, during the 1930s younger Tories had become impatient with their party's negative position in economic and social affairs, and the war helped to accelerate their influence in changing priorities and policies. Of course, Churchill devoted many a speech after 1945 to the demand to 'set the people free', implying a reversal of wartime interventionism. Yet historians must beware of taking party rhetoric at face value. As Opposition Leader Churchill had a duty to arouse the party faithful and try to distinguish himself from Labour to some extent. But his own record as a minister in the Edwardian period made him a social reformer – indeed, he was in some ways a product of the same turn-of-the-century thinking as Beveridge himself. Critics have pointed to his reluctance to commit his government to the implementation of the Beveridge Report as wartime prime minister, but that really reflected his fear of pledging more than could be afforded by a government strapped for cash and of encouraging the public to relax its self-discipline by the contemplation of improvements to come. No doubt Churchill's heavy defeat in 1945 added an element of opportunism to Conservative tactics; the party accepted that it could not afford to be seen to threaten the National Health Service or full employment. But after recovering power in 1951 Churchill made only marginal changes to Labour's programme and generally upheld the central principles of the consensus. To that extent the war had left an enduring mark on British politics.

The Labour Landslide of 1945

The much-delayed general election that took place in July 1945 was unquestionably a turning point in modern history. The unprecedented 12 per cent swing from Conservative to Labour left Attlee with 393 seats and thus a big overall majority for the first time. Perhaps surprisingly this event has not been intensively researched and has failed to generate much controversy among historians, no doubt because the main explanations for the discrediting of the Conservatives and the popularity of Labour have seemed to be obvious. The remarkable feature of the election was how unexpected the outcome was amongst most contemporaries. Churchill evidently expected a majority somewhere between 30 and 80, especially since the Opposition had rejected his offer to maintain the Coalition until the defeat of Japan and thus forced an early contest while his popularity was at its height. On the Labour side Hugh Dalton believed it lunacy to fight Churchill, and, like his colleagues, would have settled for a Coupon-style arrangement in 1945 had not the party been so keen to abandon the coalition. All parties clearly assumed that the victory won by Lloyd George in 1918 offered a reliable precedent.

In this assumption contemporaries discounted the evidence of the war-time by-elections which had exposed the Conservatives' unpopularity. In view of the absence of official Labour opposition they considered that the by-elections had no party significance, even though the defeated Tory candidates had enjoyed very strong endorsement from Churchill, who had become very depressed by the defeats he suffered. In addition, the opinion polls published by the *News Chronicle* had consistently indicated a Labour lead of anything between 7 per cent and 18 per cent since 1943 and the appearance of the Beveridge Report. These polls were, however, still a novelty and not regarded as reliable. They encouraged Labour to expect an improved result, but not an outright victory.

In analysing the election it is helpful to distinguish between long-term structural changes, medium-term factors that emerged during the war, and the short-term impact of the election campaign itself. Of these relatively little consideration has been extended to long-term factors. This is under-standable since in 1945 there were no sweeping reforms of the electoral system of the kind that had affected the 1918 election. Despite this, the composition of the electorate had changed greatly since 1935. The unusu-ally long gap since the last general election meant that no fewer than one-fifth of all electors in 1945 were voting for the first time. In effect they

TABLE 13.1   *General Election Results 1935–1950*

	1935 seats	Vote %	1945 seats	Vote %	1950 seats	Vote %
Con.	432	53.7	213	39.8	298	43.5
Lab.	154	37.9	393	47.8	315	46.1
Lib.	20	6.4	12	9.0	9	9.1

represented a fresh political generation whose formative political period had been the 1930s, mass unemployment and appeasement, and the phase of rising expectations engendered by the war; they now looked towards peacetime fearful that their gains would be swept away by an economic depression. Later surveys revealed that no fewer than 61 per cent of the first-time voters of 1945 had supported the Labour Party, making them a uniquely pro-Labour generation. Their influence would have enabled the party to perform much better at a normal peacetime election in 1939, though probably not sufficiently well to win. Many of the new voters were, of course, servicemen. At the time officers in the army and the RAF told politicians that their men were going to swing sharply to Labour. This seems credible partly because they were relatively young and conscious of the need to obtain employment once the war had ended. It was also claimed that the activities of the Army Bureau of Current Affairs in encouraging the men to take an interest in politics had stimulated a left-wing outlook, though this is probably an exaggeration. More influential may have been the *Daily Mirror*, which was read by a high proportion of soldiers and which articulated their grievances and promoted support for Labour.

Most of the discussion about the election has focused on the impact of wartime in shaping opinion in various ways. The immediate effect was to discredit the Conservatives who were seen as having been too committed to appeasement, slow to rearm and sympathetic towards the fascist regimes. 'It was not Churchill who lost the 1945 election', wrote Harold Macmillan, 'it was the ghost of Neville Chamberlain.'[8] By contrast, Labour, in spite of its own record between the wars, was free of responsibility for failure to prepare adequately for the war. By 1945 Labour politicians were as vociferous as anyone else in demanding that the leading Nazis be brought to trial for their crimes. Consequently they were not vulnerable to aspersions on their patriotism as they had been at the end of the First World War; and although the role of Churchill in 1945 appeared similar to that of Lloyd George as the head of a victorious administration, his position was not in fact as strong because of his association with men who were thought to have let the nation down. The two elections bear further comparison since on the face of it they seem to have produced opposite results in similar circumstances. Much of the explanation lies in the timing. In 1918 few had expected victory so soon. The Coupon Election was hurriedly called within a month of the armistice and therefore caught the emotions of war at their height; voters refused to listen to promises about building homes for heroes in their desire for revenge on Germany. But in the Second World War people had begun to take victory for granted since 1942 when the combined might of the United States and Russia was brought to bear. As a result the public had had several years in which to refocus its thoughts on post-war domestic conditions, thereby pushing war issues down the agenda even though the country was still at war with Japan after the defeat of Germany. According to surveys of opinion the major issues in the minds of the voters in 1945 were housing, health and unemployment. Moreover, on these questions they felt more inclined to trust the Labour Party to reflect their views than the Conservatives. Opposition tactics were designed to exploit this by inviting electors to 'Ask Your Father' – thereby reminding them that their interests had been betrayed after the last war.

By 1945 the leading Labour figures had become familiar, reassuring faces; their close association with the war effort had largely erased the reputation for incompetence which had dogged them throughout the 1930s. The party's willingness to implement the Beveridge proposals clearly coincided with the mood of the moment. But Labour also entered the election with an extensive programme of nationalization which in the past had appeared vulnerable to attack by its opponents. However, this had to a large extent ceased to be controversial partly because nationalization appeared to be a continuation of the wartime controls which had worked well enough for several years. Previous associations between economic planning and the Soviet Union now seemed more of a recommendation than a drawback, in view of the popular impression that Russia had stood up remarkably well to the onslaught of the Germans which had carried everything else before it. In any case, the argument for nationalization was expressed in terms of the need to save key industries which had been starved of investment by private enterprise. These perceptions enabled the left to capture the patriotic high ground for socialism.

The Labour Party also derived the maximum benefit from these shifts in public attitudes and perceptions because its case was put across to a larger proportion of the country than had been usual. Since 1935 the *Daily Mirror*, whose circulation increased from 1.7 million in 1939 to 3 million by 1946, had abandoned its pro-Conservative loyalties and swung towards Labour. This proved to be crucial in enabling the party to reach the patriotic, Tory working-class communities which had been slowest to respond to its appeal in the past. In addition the paper enjoyed a wide female readership – another weak point for Labour – and, as we have seen, it had earned credibility by ventilating the grievances of the troops during the war.[9] The *Mirror* adopted a shrewd tactic by launching the 'Vote for Him' campaign in June 1945. This was calculated to exploit the 2.8 million service voters and the 1.8 million proxy voters who were often their female relations. The assumption behind the campaign was that the proxy voters would wish to ensure that the opinions of the men at the front made their mark by voting the Opposition into power.[10] More generally, the *Daily Mirror* helped to propagate the impression of the Labour Party as moderate and its proposals as non-revolutionary ones that had been proved to be viable by experience. It did not describe the party as socialist but as pragmatic and collectivist: 'Labour's Declaration offers a typically British solution for British problems.'[11] In combination with the reputation of Attlee, Morrison and Bevin this propaganda clearly made Labour far more difficult to attack than in the 1930s.

Turning to the election campaign itself we encounter one aspect which has caused some uncertainty or inconsistency among historians' accounts: the role of Churchill. The traditional view tends to blame him for adopting an unduly negative approach to post-war reconstruction and for undermining his reputation as a national leader by reverting to the role of a party politician. There is clearly something in this. Churchill had offered Labour the chance to continue in the Coalition until Japan had been defeated, and on its refusal he had formed a purely Conservative caretaker government until the election took place. But his mind was inevitably on the war and the international situation, and he had insufficient time to reorientate himself to peacetime politics. Insofar as he did so he resorted to the partisan tactics used by Conservatives during the 1930s. In a notorious speech on 4 June he claimed that as socialism could not be established without a political police, a Labour government would introduce a 'Gestapo' into Britain. This was generally thought a blunder because it reminded people of his earlier role as an extremist and allowed Attlee to appear more dignified.

On the other hand, Churchill's triumphal tours around the country suggest that he retained a great deal of popularity. Whereas in May the gap between the two parties stood at 16 per cent, it narrowed sharply to 8 per cent in the poll itself, an improvement which can only be attributed to his influence. The point is that Churchill's personal standing was not sufficient to overcome the unpopularity of his party. This may have reflected some real confusion amongst voters because of his detachment from the Conservatives. For five years they had grown accustomed to seeing him working alongside Attlee and the other Labour leaders, and as a result some voters believed that voting for Labour did not necessarily imply rejecting Churchill. His recent role as Tory Leader may not have erased his long-term role as the leading critic of the Conservative leadership under Baldwin and Chamberlain before the war. Consequently, though he remained an asset in 1945, Churchill did not carry enough weight to rescue his party from its unpopularity.

Conclusions

Though Labour had done very well in 1945, the outcome in terms of seats exaggerated the party's strength in the poll. One existing weakness – the gender gap – remained prominent; whereas Labour's lead over the Conservatives stood at almost 20 per cent among men, it shrank to 2 per cent among female voters. This apart, 1945 marked the party's evolution from being essentially a sectional party to a national, majority one. The move of middle-class voters into Labour's camp was reflected in victories in suburban constituencies in the South-East, including no fewer than 42 of the 62 seats in London. Moreover, Labour's traditional claim to be the party of the working class was now justified by its success in extending its support into areas conspicuous for their working-class Conservatism, which had maintained a nineteenth-century pattern of loyalties up to this point. This was dramatically underlined by Labour's success in 12 out of the 13 constituencies in Birmingham and in 8 of the 11 Liverpool seats. In these districts Labour had achieved a distinct advance in 1929 but the collapse of 1931 had delayed the real breakthrough until 1945. Another way of looking at this is to compare the electoral maps of Edwardian Britain with those of the post-1945 era. They are similar in that the areas of Liberal strength before 1914 had largely become Labour strongholds. But there are two differences. Labour never did as well in south-west England, East Anglia and the highlands and borders of Scotland as the Liberals. But it more than compensated by gaining urban areas, especially in the west Midlands and Lancashire, in which the Liberals had returned few members since the late 1880s. Although Labour was to lose power in 1951, the new pattern can be regarded as a lasting one in that its support exceeded 48 per cent even in that year and remained over 40 per cent through the 1950s and 1960s.

In this way the process of change that had begun with the widening of the electorate during the 1860s can be seen to have reached a conclusion. By stages and through several different organizations the working class had been absorbed into the political system. Women, too, had gained a footing as voters, though their role in Parliament was as yet marginal. This had involved changes in the scope and agenda of British politics as well as the personnel, but it had not led to anything like an overthrow of the existing system. To some extent this reflected Britain's success in the two world wars which left her institutions intact and spared her the destabilizing effects which carried away other regimes all over Europe. But it was also the result of the peculiar loyalty of the Labour movement towards the traditional system and its reluctance to advocate radical changes even to the hereditary elements in it. Even socialists concluded that Britain's strong, centralized government, her tradition of secrecy, and her electoral system which usually endowed governments with larger majorities than their vote merited, was well calculated to enable a party to carry through its legislative programme. Constitutional reform was thus widely regarded as an irrelevance. As a result of the demise of the Liberals the great debates over political innovations which had loomed so large during the Victorian and Edwardian periods had largely disappeared from British politics by 1945. For several decades to come the two main parties found themselves in broad agreement about the viability of the British system of government.

Notes

CHAPTER 1: **Party and Participation 1867–1900**

1   Brian Harrison, *Separate Spheres: The Opposition to Women's Suffrage in Britain* (1978), pp. 59–64, 71.
2   J. R. Vincent, 'The Electoral Sociology of Rochdale', *Economic History Review*, 16 (1963–4), pp. 79–81.
3   Neal Blewett, 'The Franchise in the United Kingdom 1885–1918', *Past and Present*, 32 (1965), pp. 33–4.
4   Ibid., pp. 46–7.
5   R. J. Olney, *Lincolnshire Politics 1832–85* (1973), pp. 158–81.
6   G. E. Mingay, *The Gentry* (1976), pp. 79, 172, 177; F. M. L. Thompson, *English Landed Society in the Nineteenth Century* (1963), p. 342.
7   T. J. Nossiter, *Influence, Opinion and Political Idioms in Reformed England* (1975), pp. 48–9.
8   Ibid., p. 53.
9   J. Howarth, 'The Liberal Revival in Northamptonshire 1885–95', *Historical Journal*, 12 (1969), pp. 90–1.
10 Countess of Warwick, *Joseph Arch: The Story of His Life Told by Himself* (1898), p. 329.
11 P. F. Clarke, *Lancashire and the New Liberalism* (1971), p. 251.
12 Charles Roberts, *The Radical Countess: The History of the Life of Rosalind, Countess of Carlisle* (1962), p. 85.
13 Before decimalization in 1971, three monetary units were in use: the pound (symbol £), the shilling or *s* (one-twentieth of a pound) and the penny or *d* (one-twelfth of a shilling).
14 Patrick Joyce, 'The Factory Politics of Lancashire in the Later Nineteenth Century', *Historical Journal*, 18 (1975), pp. 533–41.
15 Ibid., pp. 541–3.
16 Nossiter, *Influence*, pp. 125–8.

17 Surviving two-member boroughs were Bath, Blackburn, Bolton, Brighton, Derby, Devonport, Halifax, Ipswich, Leicester, Newcastle, Northampton, Norwich, Oldham, Plymouth, Portsmouth, Preston, Southampton, Stockport, Sunderland, York, Merthyr Tydfil and Dundee.

18 Derek Fraser, *Urban Politics in Victorian England* (1976), pp. 115–24.

19 L. Kitchen, 'The 1892 Election in the Tyneside Area' (Newcastle M.Litt. thesis, 1979), pp. 268, 284.

20 Leeds Liberal Federation Executive Committee Minutes 1894–1924; Keighley Conservative Association Minutes 1885–1904.

21 J. A. Garrard, 'Parties, Members and Voters after 1867: A Local Study', *Historical Journal*, 20, (1977), p. 151.

22 NUCCA Conference Minutes, 1897.

23 Quoted in the *Campaign Guide* (1892), published by the Conservative Party.

24 W. L. Guttsman, *The British Political Elite* (1965), p. 104.

25 R. Pumphrey, 'The Introduction of Industrialists into the British Peerage', *American Historical Review*, 65 (1959–60), p. 7.

26 H. H. Asquith, *Memories and Reflections* (1928), vol. II, p. 105.

CHAPTER 2: **The Evolution of the Gladstonian Liberal Party 1867–1895**

1 In full: The Society for the Liberation of Religion from State Patronage and Control.

2 Henry Pelling, *America and the British Left* (1956), pp. 16–27.

3 C. Harvie, *The Lights of Liberalism: University Liberals and the Challenge of Democracy* (1976), pp. 112–14.

4 Robert Spence Watson, *The National Liberal Federation 1877–1906* (1907), pp. 3–4.

5 D. A. Hamer, ed., *Joseph Chamberlain and the Radical Programme* (1971 edn), pp. xxii–xxv.

6 T. W. Heyck, 'Home Rule, Radicalism and the Liberal Party 1886–95', *Journal of British Studies*, 13 (1974), p. 69.

7 Michael Barker, *Gladstone and Radicalism 1885–94* (1975), p. 24.

8 P. C. Griffiths, 'The Caucus and the Liberal Party in 1886', *History*, 61 (1976), p. 192.

9 Barker, *Gladstone*, p. 75.

10 Quoted in D. A. Hamer, *John Morley* (1968), p. 236.

CHAPTER 3: **The Conservative Revival 1874–1900**

1 *The Times*, 6 June 1865.

2 Balfour to Salisbury, 27 August 1891, J. P. Cornford, 'Parliamentary Foundations of the Hotel Cecil', R. Robson, ed., *Ideas and Institutions of Victorian Britain* (1967), p. 296.

3 NUCCA, *Annual Conference Report, 1867*, fol. 3–4.
4 NUCCA Conference Minutes, 23 July 1880.
5 Ibid., 14 November 1882.
6 R. E. Quinault, 'Lord Randolph Churchill and Tory Democracy 1880–85', *Historical Journal*, 22 (1979), pp. 144–5.
7 NUCCA, pamphlet No. 24 (1873), p. 4.
8 Quinault, 'Randolph Churchill', pp. 158–9.
9 Peter Marsh, *The Discipline of Popular Government* (1978), p. 152.
10 R. B. McDowell, *British Conservatism 1832–1914* (1959); Samuel Beer, *Modern British Politics* (1965).
11 Olney, *Lincolnshire*, pp. 188, 217.
12 NUCCA, *Campaign Guide* (1892).
13 Marsh, *Popular Government*, p. 160.
14 J. P. Dunbabin, 'The Politics of the Establishment of County Councils', *Historical Journal*, 6 (1963), pp. 228–36.
15 G. Stedman Jones, *Outcast London* (1971), pp. 227–30.
16 Quoted in Dunbabin, 'County Councils', pp. 239–40.

CHAPTER 4: The Social Roots of Political Change in Late Victorian Britain

1 Nossiter, *Influence*, pp. 177–92.
2 Henry Pelling, *The Social Geography of British Elections 1885–1910* (1967), p. 415.
3 Quoted in Olney, *Lincolnshire*, p. 229.
4 See Raphael Samuel, *Village Life and Labour* (1975), on Headington Quarry in Oxfordshire.
5 Marsh, *Popular Government*, p. 207.
6 Olney, *Lincolnshire*, p. 214.
7 Karl Marx, 'The Chartists', *New York Daily Tribune*, 25 August 1852.
8 Pelling, *Social Geography*, p. 419.
9 Frank Gray, *Confessions of a Candidate* (1925), pp. 9–10.
10 Warwick, *Joseph Arch*, p. 55.
11 Ramsay MacDonald, *The Socialist Movement* (1911), p. 93.
12 NUCCA, *Annual Conference Minutes*, 13–14 November 1892.
13 C. Green, 'Birmingham's Politics 1873–91: The Local Basis of Change', *Midland History*, 2 (1973), p. 92.
14 Quoted in A. McKenzie and A. Silver, *Angels in Marble* (1968), p. 60.
15 R. Price, *An Imperial War and the British Working Class* (1972), pp. 200–28.
16 NUCCA, pamphlet No. 3, 'Promise Versus Performance' (1892).
17 'Labour Problems', *Campaign Guide* (1892), by the Conservative Party.
18 Warwick, *Joseph Arch*, p. 255.
19 *Campaign Notes* (1901), by the Conservative Party, p. 516.
20 Green, 'Birmingham's Politics', p. 91.
21 Ibid.
22 Nossiter, *Influence*, pp. 147–8, 163–7.

CHAPTER 5: **The Edwardian Crises 1895–1914**

1   H. A. Tulloch, 'Changing British Attitudes towards America in the 1880's', *Historical Journal*, 20 (1977).

2   H. C. G. Matthew, R. I. McKibbin and J. A. Kay, 'The Franchise Factor in the Rise of the Labour Party', *English Historical Review*, 91 (1976), pp. 742–3.

3   Minutes of the Society of Certificated and Associated Liberal Agents, 1895–1945.

4   See A. J. Lee, *The Origins of the Popular Press 1855–1914* (1976), and S. E. Koss, *Fleet Street Radical: A. G. Gardiner and the Daily News* (1973), p. 40.

5   S. E. Koss, 'Wesleyanism and Empire', *Historical Journal*, 18 (1975).

6   See C. P. Trevelyan Papers, vol. 4; Martin Pugh, 'Yorkshire and the New Liberalism?', *Journal of Modern History*, 50 (1978), p. 1142; Kitchen, 'The 1892 Election', pp. 70–1.

7   Barker, *Gladstone*, pp. 50, 89–96, 197–8.

8   C. P. Trevelyan to Herbert Samuel, 2 October 1898, Trevelyan Papers, 4.

9   T. Boyle, 'The Liberal Imperialists, 1892–1906', *Bulletin of the Institute of Historical Research*, 52 (1979), pp. 51–5.

10 R. B. Haldane to Lord Rosebery, 24 April 1895, Rosebery Papers, 24.

11 Peter Cain, 'Political Economy in Edwardian England: the Tariff Reform Controversy', in Alan O'Day ed., *The Edwardian Age* (1979), p. 37.

12 Contemporary estimates after the 1906 suggested 11–16 free-traders, 32 Balfourites and 109 tariff reformers, though historians have thought this an overestimate of protectionist strength.

13 Richard Rempel, *Unionists Divided* (1972), pp. 94–5.

14 G. R. Searle, 'Critics of Edwardian Society': The Case of the Radical Right', in O'Day ed., *The Edwardian Age*.

15 He had been parliamentary secretary at the Board of Trade 1902–5, worked for a firm of merchant bankers, and became a partner in a Glasgow iron merchant's company.

16 H. H. Asquith, *Memories and Reflections* (1928), vol. I, p. 202.

17 H. H. Asquith to W. S. Churchill, 12 September 1913, Randolph S. Churchill, *Winston S. Churchill*, vol. II, companion part 3 (1969), p. 1399.

18 Clarke, *Lancashire*, p. 387.

19 J. Liddington and J. Norris, *One Hand Tied Behind Us: The Rise of the Women's Suffrage Movement* (1979), pp. 193, 205, 219.

20 Paul Thompson, *The Edwardians: The Re-making of British Society* (1975), pp. 240–64.

21 D. Lloyd George, *Better Times: Speeches on the Social Question* (1910).

CHAPTER 6: **Edwardian Progressivism**

1   See, Vincent, 'Rochdale', p. 85.

2   Published as Charles Booth, *Life and Labour of the People of London*, 17 vols (1902–4); B. S. Rowntree, *Poverty: A Study of Town Life* (1901).

3 J. M. Robertson, *The Meaning of Liberalism* (1912), p. 64.

4 Clarke, *Lancashire*, p. 223.

5 Memorandum, 6 September 1903, Herbert Gladstone Papers 46106.

6 C. P. Trevelyan to W. S. Churchill (draft), undated 1903, Trevelyan Papers 13.

7 Bruce K. Murray, *The People's Budget 1909–10* (1980), pp. 112–21.

8 Notably the British Medical Association, Friendly Societies and insurance companies with their armies of collectors. Part 1 of the Act provided health insurance and part 2 unemployment insurance for three groups of workers.

9 A. E. Pease to Herbert Samuel, 19 August 1908, Samuel Papers A/155(III).

10 W. Runciman to H. H. Asquith (copy), 27 February 1908, and W. Crawshaw to W. Runciman, 2 April 1912, Runciman papers 21 and 63.

11 See Lloyd George papers C/21/1/17.

12 W. D. Rubinstein, 'Wealth, Elites and the Class Structure of Modern Britain', *Past and Present*, 76 (1977); and 'The Victorian Middle Classes: Wealth, Occupation and Geography', *Economic History Review*, 30 (1977).

13 See Runciman papers 66 and 74.

14 H. V. Emy, *Liberals, Radicals and Social Politics 1892–1914* (1973), p. 219.

15 Leslie Scott to D. Lloyd George, 29 September 1913, Lloyd George Papers C/8/2/1.

16 P. Poirer, *The Advent of the Labour Party* (1958), p. 110.

17 Memorandum, Ramsay MacDonald Papers PRO 30/69/5/81.

CHAPTER 7: **The Electoral Struggle 1906–1914**

1 Roy Gregory, *The Miners and British Politics 1906–14* (1968), p. 189.

2 Blewett, 'Franchise', pp. 30–42.

3 Duncan Tanner, *Political Change and the Labour Party 1900–1918* (1990), pp. 111–23.

4 *The Labour Leader*, 18 July 1912.

5 16 November 1911, PRO CAB 37/108/148.

6 Gregory, *Miners*, p. 9.

7 See Labour Party Archives LP/EL/08.

8 See Master of Elibank to Lord Knollys (copy), 7 November 1906 and 'Memorandum on the Socialist and Labour Movements in Scotland', Elibank Papers 8801.

9 See undated memorandum, J. A. Pease Papers 88, and memorandum by Scottish Liberals, Asquith Papers 23, fol. 298.

10 Tanner, *Political Change*, pp. 325–37.

11 Austen Chamberlain, 9 March 1910, Chamberlain Papers AC/8/8/15.

12 George Young to C. P. Trevelyan, 26 June 1906, Trevelyan Papers 6.

13 J. Cochrane Shanks to D. Lloyd George, 9 February 1914, and Mrs L. Bulley to Mrs M. Lloyd George, undated, Lloyd George papers C/10/3/19 and C/10/1/68.

CHAPTER 8: **The Impact of the Great War on British Politics**

1 Which is why Ponsonby, fearing to embarrass the government, failed to call the Liberal Foreign Affairs Group in the week before the declaration of war: A. Ponsonby to W. S. Churchill, 31 July 1914.

2 E. I. David ed., *Inside Asquith's Cabinet: From the Diaries of Sir Charles Hobhouse* (1977), pp. 179–80.

3 A. Bonar Law to H. H. Asquith, 2 August 1914, Robert Blake, *The Unknown Prime Minister* (1955), p. 222.

4 See Bonar Law papers 36/1/12, 14, 18 for correspondence on this point.

5 Bonar Law to Curzon (copy), 29 January 1915, and memoranda by Curzon and Long in the Balfour Papers 49693.

6 Richard Denman to C. P. Trevelyan, 28 May 1915, in M. Swartz, *The Union of Democratic Control in British Politics during the First World War* (1971), p. 66.

7 C. P. Scott's diary, 3 September 1915.

8 Notes on the Report of the Speaker's Conference, 3 February 1917, Steel-Maitland Papers 202.

9 F. E. Guest to D. Lloyd George, 20 July 1918, Lloyd George Papers F/21/2/28.

10 I. G. Hunter, 'Working-Class Representation on Elective Local Authorities on Tyneside 1883–1921' (Newcastle University M.Litt. thesis, 1979), pp. 115–38.

11 Labour Party Archives ORG/14/1 and 2.

12 Ramsay MacDonald Papers PRO 30/69/7/51; G. Morgan to A. Ponsonby, 20 December 1917, Ponsonby Papers 666.

13 A. Rowntree to A. Ponsonby 3 January 1919, Ponsonby Papers 667; K. O. Morgan, *Consensus and Disunity* (1979), pp. 152–3; D. Marquand, *Ramsay MacDonald* (1977), p. 235.

14 John Turner, 'The Labour Vote and the Franchise after 1918', in P. R. Denley and R. Hopkins eds., *History and Computing* (1987), pp. 139–40; J. Rasmussen, 'Women in Labour: the Flapper Vote and Party System Transformation', *British Electoral Studies*, 3, 1, (1984).

15 Report by S. Higgenbottam, 17 January 1919, MacDonald papers PRO 30/69/7/51; A. Rowntree to A. Ponsonby, 3 January 1919, Ponsonby Papers 667.

CHAPTER 9: **Patriotism, Ideology and the State in the Great War**

1 PRO CAB 42/1/21.

2 David French, *British Economic and Strategic Planning 1905–1915* (1982), pp. 101–3.

3 C. P. Scott's diary, 11–12 December 1917.

4 C. P. Trevelyan, *From Liberalism to Labour* (1921).

5 Christopher Addison to Arthur Henderson (copy), 19 November 1923, Addison Papers 82.

6 K. O. and Jane Morgan, *Portrait of a Progressive* (1980), pp. 182–7.
7 William Wedgwood Benn to A. Munro (copy), 25 January 1927, Stansgate Papers 85/1.
8 J. H. Thomas, *My Story* (1937), p. 154.
9 Martin Pugh, 'Class Traitors: Conservative Recruits to Labour 1900–30', *English Historical Review*, CXIII (1998), pp. 42–3.
10. John Turner, 'The British Commonwealth Union and the General Election of 1918', *English Historical Review*, 93 (1978), pp. 530–9.
11 Rodney Lowe, 'The Erosion of State Intervention in Britain 1917–24', *Economic History Review*, 31 (1978), p. 278.
12 J. M. McEwen, 'The Coupon Election of 1918 and the Unionist Members of Parliament', *Journal of Modern History*, 34 (1962), pp. 298–302.

CHAPTER 10: **The Elevation of Labour and the Restoration of Party Politics 1918–1931**

1 M. Kinnear, *The Fall of Lloyd George* (1973), pp. 79–85.
2 John Ramsden, *The Age of Balfour and Baldwin* (1978), pp. 134–5.
3 M. Cowling, *The Impact of Labour* (1971), pp. 72–5.
4 Kinnear, *Fall*, pp. 89–90.
5 K. Middlemas and J. Barnes, *Baldwin* (1969), p. 216.
6 Arthur Henderson, speech at Nottingham, 2 November 1918.
7 *Daily Graphic*, 10 March 1923.
8 MacDonald's diary, 26 September 1924.
9 R. MacDonald to Vernon Hartshorn (copy), 20 December 1930, MacDonald papers PRO 30/69/5/174.
10 See correspondence of MacDonald, Loyd George, Snowden and Hartshorn 1930–1 in MacDonald Papers PRO 30/69/5/174, 175.
11 Memoranda and correspondence on electoral reform in MacDonald Papers PRO 30/69/5/166.

CHAPTER 11: **Origins of the Conservative Electoral Hegemony 1918–1931**

1 For 1922 the total poll can be recalculated by estimating the likely vote in the 42 Conservative seats uncontested and in the 14 Liberal and Labour ones on the basis of subsequent performances; this would raise the Conservative share by around 3 per cent, from 38 to 41 per cent.
2 MacDonald Papers PRO 30/69/5/166.
3 M. Kinnear, *The British Voter: An Atlas and Survey 1885–1964* (1969), pp. 70–1.
4 They were: Cambridge 2; Oxford 2; London 1; Combined English Universities 1; Wales 1; Combined Scottish Universities 3; Dublin 2; National University 1; Belfast 1.

5   Memorandum dated October 1916, Steel-Maitland Papers 202.
6   Colonel R. A. Sanders's diary, 15 June 1917.
7   Memorandum on seats by Walter Long, 19 January 1918, Long Papers.
8   J. P. D. Dunbabin, 'British Elections in the Nineteenth and Twentieth Century: A Regional Approach', *English Historical Review*, 95 (1980), pp. 244–5.
9   Kinnear, *British Voter*, pp. 122–4.
10 Ramsden, *Balfour and Baldwin*, p. 239.
11 Ibid., p. 249.
12 R. I. McKibbin, *The Evolution of the Labour Party 1910–1924* (1974), p. 145.
13 J. Rasmussen, 'Women in Labour: the Flapper Vote and Party System Transformation in Britain', *Electoral Studies*, 3, 1 (1984), pp. 55–8.
14 Michael Savage, *The Dynamics of Working-Class Politics* (1987), pp. 162–73.
15 Mark Abrams, 'Social Class and British Politics', in Lewis A. Coser ed., *Political Sociology* (1966), pp. 206–71.
16 Dunbabin, 'British Elections', p. 243.
17 D. Butler and D. Stokes, *Political Change in Britain* (1971 edn), pp. 65–89.
18 Ibid., p. 77.
19 MacDonald Papers PRO 30/69/5/160.
20 S. E. Koss, *Nonconformity in Modern British Politics* (1975), p. 234.
21 Butler and Stokes, *Political Change*, p. 163.
22 Ibid., pp. 166–7.
23 W. G. Runciman, *Relative Deprivation and Social Justice* (1972 edn), p. 82.

CHAPTER 12: **From the National Government to the Popular Front 1931–1939**

1   R. MacDonald to Stanley Baldwin (copy), 5 September 1931, MacDonald Papers PRO 30/69/5/180; R. MacDonald to the King (copy), 14 September 1931, MacDonald papers PRO 30/69/5/180.
2   C. T. Stannage, 'The General Election of 1935' (Cambridge University Ph. D. thesis, 1973), pp. 30–1.
3   *The Times*, 20 January 1927.
4   Julie Gottlieb, *Feminine Fascism: Women in Britain's Fascist Movement 1923–1945* (2000), pp. 74, 147–60.
5   House of Commons Debates, 14 June 1934, c.2018; Sir Thomas More, *Daily Mail*, 25 April 1934.
6   B. C. Malament, 'British Labour and Roosevelt's New Deal: The Response of the Left and the Unions', *Journal of British Studies*, Spring (1978), pp. 158–9.
7   Stannage, 'Election of 1935', pp. 287–99.
8   Hugh Dalton, 'The Popular Front', and G. D. H. Cole, 'A People's Front', *Political Quarterly*, 7 (1936).
9   *Annual Report*, Birmingham Trades Council and Borough Labour Party, 1937–8, p. 62.
10 Ibid., 1938–9, p. 6.

CHAPTER 13: **The Politics of the 'People's War' 1939–1945**

1 Ben Pimlott, ed., *The Political Diaries of Hugh Dalton 1918–1940* (1986), p. 297.
2 *Daily Mirror*, 4 May 1940.
3 Stafford Cripps to W. S. Churchill, 21 September 1942, in C. Cooke, *The Life of Richard Stafford Cripps* (1957), pp. 298–9.
4 James Griffiths, *Pages From Memory* (1969), pp. 71–2.
5 'Cato', *Guilty Men* (1940), pp. 124–5.
6 Paul Addison, 'By-Elections of the Second World War', in C. Cook and J. Ramsden eds., *By-Elections in British Politics* (1997), pp. 138–9.
7 J. B. Priestley, *Postscripts* (1940), pp. 96–100.
8 Harold Macmillan, *Tides of Fortune 1945–55* (1979), pp. 31–2.
9 Mass Observation, file report 1173, March 1942.
10 *Daily Mirror*, 27, 29, 30 June 1945.
11 *Daily Mirror*, 21 April 1945.

Guide to Further Reading

CHAPTER 1: **Party and Participation 1867–1900**

For general surveys of attitudes towards the political system see: Brian Harrison, *The Transformation of British Politics* (1996); Ian Machin, *The Rise of Democracy in Britain 1830–1918* (2001); Walter Bagehot, *The English Constitution* (1867, repr. 1963); Brian Harrison, *Separate Spheres: The Opposition to Women's Suffrage in Britain* (1978); and Martin Pugh, *The Evolution of the British Electoral System 1832–1987* (Historical Association pamphlet 1988).

More specifically on the franchise and reforms see: F. B. Smith, *The Making of the Second Reform Act* (1967); Andrew Jones, *The Politics of Reform 1884* (1972); C. Seymour, *Electoral Reform in England and Wales 1832–85* (1915, repr. 1970); M. Cowling, *Disraeli, Gladstone and Revolution: The Passing of Second Reform Act* (1967); Neal Blewett, 'The Franchise in the United Kingdom 1885–1914', *Past and Present*, 32 (1965); Duncan Tanner, 'The Parliamentary Electoral System, the "Fourth" Reform Act and the Rise of Labour in England and Wales', *Bulletin of the Institute of Historical Research*, 56 (1983); C. C. O'Leary, *The Elimination of Corrupt Practices in British Elections* (1962); and W. B. Gwyn, *Democracy and the Cost of Politics in Britain* (1962).

Aspects of the operation of the system in the country are discussed in: H. J. Hanham, *Elections and Party Management: Politics in the Time of Gladstone and Disraeli* (1959); T. J. Nossiter, *Influence, Opinion and Political Idioms in Reformed England* (1975); J. A. Garrard, 'Parties, Members and Voters after 1867', *Historical Journal*, 20 (1977); D. Richter, 'The Role of the Mob in Victorian Elections', *Victorian Studies*, 15 (1971); Patrick Joyce, 'The Factory Politics of Lancashire in the Later Nineteenth Century', *Historical Journal*, 18 (1975); Trevor Lloyd, 'Uncontested Seats in British General Elections 1852–1910', *Historical Journal*, 8 (1965); and R. J. Olney, *Lincolshire Politics 1832–1885* (1973).

Changes in the parliamentary sphere are analysed in: T. A. Jenkins, *Parliament, Party and Politics in Victorian Britain* (1996); W. L. Guttsman, *The British Political Elite* (1965); G. R. Searle, *Corruption in British Politics 1895–1930* (1987); H. J. Hanham,

'The Sale of Honours in Late Victorian England', *Victorian Studies*, 3 (1960); R. Pumphrey, 'The Introduction of Industrialists into the British Peerage', *American Historical Review*, 65 (1959–60); E. A. Smith, *The House of Lords in British Politics and Society 1815–1911* (1992); David Cannadine, *The Decline and Fall of the British Aristocracy* (1990); Hugh Berrington, 'Partisanship and Dissidence in the Nineteenth Century House of Commons', *Parliamentary Affairs*, 21 (1967–8); P. Fraser, 'The Growth of Ministerial Control in the Nineteenth Century House of Commons', *English Historical Review*, 75 (1960); and Trevor Lloyd, 'The Whip as Paymaster: Herbert Gladstone and Party Organisation', *English Historical Review*, 89 (1974).

CHAPTER 2: **The Evolution of the Gladstonian Liberal Party 1867–1895**

There is a range of interesting volumes dealing with the development of the Liberal Party and its ideas: J. R. Vincent, *The Formation of the British Liberal Party 1857–68* (1966); T. A. Jenkins, *The Liberal Ascendancy 1830–1886* (1994); C. Harvie, *The Lights of Liberalism: University Liberals and the Challenge of Democracy* (1976); H. S. Jones, *Victorian Political Thought* (2000); Ian Bradley, *The Optimists: Themes and Personalities in Victorian Liberalism* (1980); Henry Pelling, *America and the British Left* (1956); and Asa Briggs, *Victorian People* (1954).
The causes and issues that made up the fabric of Liberal politics are analysed in: D. A. Hamer, *The Politics of Electoral Pressure* (1977); Ian Machin, *Politics and the Churches in Great Britain 1869–1921* (1987); D. W. Bebbington, *The Nonconformist Conscience* (1982); J. P. Parry, *Democracy and Religion: Gladstone and the Liberal Party 1867–1875* (1986); Eugenio Biagini, 'Popular Liberals, Gladstonian Finance and the Debate on Taxation 1869–74', in E. F. Biagini and A. S. Reid eds, *Currents of Radicalism* (1990); D. A. Hamer ed., *Joseph Chamberlain: the Radical Programme* (1971); K. O. Morgan, *Wales in British Politics* (1970); T. W. Heyck, 'Home Rule, Radicalism and the Liberal Party 1886–95', *Journal of British Studies*, 13 (1974); and P. C. Griffiths, 'The Caucus and the Liberal Party in 1886', *History*, 61 (1976).
On the relationship between the parliamentary leadership and the wider party and its supporters see: Eugenio Biagini, *Liberty, Retrenchment and Reform: Popular Liberalism in the Age of Gladstone 1860–1880* (1992); and T. A. Jenkins, *Gladstone, Whiggery and the Liberal Party 1874–1886* (1988). For detailed analyses of the machinations of the parliamentary elite see: D. A. Hamer, *Liberal Politics in the Age of Gladstone and Rosebery* (1972); A. B. Cooke and J. R. Vincent, *The Governing Passion* (1974); and W. C. Lubenow, 'Irish Home Rule and the Social Basis of the Great Separation in the Liberal Party in 1886', *Historical Journal*, 28 (1985).
For biographical studies see: Eugenio Biagini, *Gladstone* (2000); Roy Jenkins, *Gladstone* (1995); H. C. G. Matthew, *Gladstone 1809–1874* (1986), and *Gladstone 1875–1989* (1996); E. J. Feuchtwanger, *Gladstone* (1975); Peter Marsh, *Joseph Chamberlain: Entrepreneur in Politics* (1994); Richard Jay, *Joseph Chamberlain* (1981); and D. A. Hamer, *John Morley: Intellectual in Politics* (1968).

CHAPTER 3: **The Conservative Revival 1874–1900**

General surveys of the Conservative Party include: Bruce Coleman, *Conservatism and the Conservative Party in Nineteenth Century Britain* (1988); Robert Blake, *The Conservative Party from Peel to Churchill* (1970); Noel O'Sullivan, *Conservatism* (1976); Frank O'Gorman ed., *British Conservatism: Conservative Thought from Burke to Thatcher* (1986); R. B. McDowell, *British Conservatism 1832–1914* (1959); D. Southgate ed., *The Conservative Leadership 1832–1932* (1974); and Lord Butler ed., *The Conservatives* (1977).

On Disraeli see: Robert Blake, *Disraeli* (1966); Paul Smith, *Disraelian Conservatism and Social Reform* (1967); G. I. T. Machine, *Disraeli* (1995); Stanley Weintraub, *Disraeli: A Biography* (1993); Paul Smith, *Disraeli: A Brief Life* (1996); Sarah Bradford, *Disraeli* (1983); Peter Ghosh, 'Disraelian Conservatism: A Financial Approach', *English Historical Review*, 99 (1984); and Paul Smith, 'Disraeli's Politics', *Transactions of the Royal Historical Society*, 37 (1987).

After a long period of neglect Lord Salisbury has attracted scholarly attention, notably in the important revisionist study by David Steele: *Lord Salisbury: A Political Biography* (2000). The other original treatment is Peter Marsh, *The Discipline of Popular Government: Lord Salisbury's Domestic Statecraft 1881–1902* (1978); both Marsh and Steele tend to emphasize the adaptive rather than the inflexible aspects of Salisbury. Other works include: Andrew Roberts, *Salisbury* (2000); Paul Smith, *Lord Salisbury on Politics* (1972); M. Pinto-Duschinsky, *The Political Thought of Lord Salisbury* (1967); R. E. Quinault, 'Lord Randolph Churchill and Tory Democracy', *Historical Journal*, 22 (1979); A. B. Cooke and J. R. Vincent, *The Governing Passion* (1974); J. P. D. Dunbabin, 'The Politics of the Establishment of County Councils', *Historical Journal*, 6 (1963); Peter Davis, 'The Liberal Unionist Party and the Irish Policy of Lord Salisbury's Government 1886–92', *Historical Journal*, 18 (1975); and J. E. B. Munson, 'The Unionist Coalition and Education 1895–1902', *Historical Journal*, 20 (1977).

On party organization see: Richard Shannon, *The Age of Disraeli 1868–1881* (1992); E. J. Feuchtwanger, *Disraeli, Democracy and the Tory Party* (1968); R. T. McKenzie, *British Political Parties* (1955); and Viscount Chilston, *Chief Whip* (1961).

The methods adopted by late Victorian Conservatives for mobilising their support in the country have attracted a number of studies: Martin Pugh, *The Tories and the People 1880–1935* (1985); Jon Lawrence, *Speaking for the People: Party, Language and Popular Politics in England 1867–1914* (1998); Jon Lawrence, 'Class and Gender in the Making of Urban Toryism 1880–1914', *English Historical Review*, 108 (1993); J. P. Cornford, 'The Transformation of Conservatism in the Late Nineteenth Century', *Victorian Studies*, 7 (1963); J. P. Cornford, 'Parliamentary Foundations of the Hotel Cecil', in R. Robson ed., *Ideas and Institutions of Victorian Britain* (1967); H. J. Hanham, *Elections and Party Management: Politics in the Time of Gladstone and Disraeli* (1959); and J. P. D. Dunbabin, 'Parliamentary Elections in Great Britain 1868–1900: A Psephological Note', *English Historical Review*, 81 (1966). See also the reading on working-class Conservatism in chapter 4.

CHAPTER 4: **The Social Roots of Political Change in Late Victorian Britain**

For analyses of elections and trends see: Henry Pelling, *Social Geography of British Elections 1885–1910* (1967); J. R. Vincent, *Pollbooks: How Victorians Voted* (1967); Trevor Lloyd, *The General Election of 1880* (1968); Paul A. Readman, 'The 1895 General Election and Political Change in Late Victorian Britain', *Historical Journal*, 42 (1999); J. P. D. Dunbabin, 'British Elections in the Nineteenth and Twentieth Century: A Regional Analysis', *English Historical Review*, 95 (1980); S. E. Koss, 'Wesleyanism and Empire', *Historical Journal*, 18 (1975); and Alan Simon, 'Church Disestablishment as a Factor in the General Election of 1885', *Historical Journal*, 18 (1975).

On the politics of rural areas see: Raphael Samuel ed., *Village Life and Labour* (1975); Alan Howkins, *Reshaping Rural England* (1991); R. J. Olney, *Lincolnshire Politics 1832–1885* (1973); P. Horn, 'Agricultural Trade Unionism and Emigration 1872–81', *Historical Journal*, 15 (1972); F. M. L. Thompson, 'Land and Politics in England in the Nineteenth Century', *Transactions of the Royal Historical Society*, 15 (1965); J. P. D. Dunbabin, *Rural Discontent in Nineteenth Century Britain* (1974), and 'The Revolt of the Field: The Agricultural Labourers' Movement in the 1870's', *Past and Present*, 26 (1963); and Countess of Warwick, *Joseph Arch* (1898).

On working-class attitudes towards politics see: Robert Roberts, *The Classic Slum* (1971); Robert Tressel, *The Ragged Trousered Philanthropists* (1955); Stephen Renbolds, *Seems So! A Working Class View of Politics* (1911); Henry Pelling, 'The Working Class and the Origins of the Welfare State', in Pelling, *Popular Politics and Society* (1968); R. I. McKibbin, 'Why was there no Marxism in Great Britain?', *English Historical Review*, 99 (1984); Paul Thompson, *The Edwardians: The Re-making of English Society* (1975); G. Stedman Jones, *Outcast London* (1971); and Standish Meacham, *A Life Apart* (1977).

On the origins of and influences on the early Labour Party see: Paul Ward, *Red Flag and Union Jack: Englishness, Patriotism and the British Left 1881–1924* (1998); John Callaghan, *Socialism in Britain since 1884* (1990); David Howell, *British Workers and the Independent Labour Party 1888–1906* (1983); R. G. Gray, *The Aristocracy of Labour in Nineteenth Century Britain* (1985); Brian Harrison, 'Traditions of Respectability in British Labour History', in Harrison, *Peaceable Kingdom* (1982); Noel Thompson, *Political Economy and the Labour Party* (1996); K. O. Morgan, *Keir Hardie: Radical and Socialist* (1975); Caroline Benn, *Keir Hardie* (1997); David Powell, *British Politics and the Labour Question 1868–1990* (1992); Andrew Thorpe, *A History of the British Labour Party* (1996); Royden Harrison, *Before the Socialists: Studies in Labour and Politics 1861–81* (1965); James Hinton, *Labour and Socialism* (1983); and James D. Young, *Socialism and the English Working Class* (1989).

On the role and attitudes of women in politics see: Olive Banks, *Becoming a Feminist: Social Origins of First Wave Feminism* (1986); Barbara Caine, *English Feminism 1780–1980* (1997); Martha Vicinus, *Independent Women* (1985); Patricia Hollis, *Ladies Elect: Women in English Local Government 1865–1914* (1987); Martin

Pugh, *The March of the Women: A Revisionist Analysis of the Campaign for Women's Suffrage 1866–1914* (2000); David Rubinstein, *Before the Suffragettes* (1986); and Susan Kingsley Kent, *Sex and Suffrage in Britain 1860–1914* (1987). For working-class Conservatism see: Frank Parkin, 'Working Class Conservatives', *British Journal of Sociology*, 18 (1967); A. J. Lee, 'Conservatism, Traditionalism and the British Working Class', in D. E. Martin and D. Rubinstein eds, *Ideology and the Labour Movement* (1979); R. L. Greenall, 'Popular Conservatism in Salford 1868–1886', *Northern History*, 9 (1974); C. Green, 'Birmingham's Politics 1873–91', *Midland History*, 2 (1973); and R. T. McKenzie and A. Silver, *Angels in Marble* (1968). See also chapter 3 on the Conservatives. On working-class imperialism see: John MacKenzie, *Propaganda and Empire* (1984); Henry Pelling, 'British Labour and British Imperialism', in Pelling, *Popular Politics and Society* (1968); and Richard Price, *An Imperial War and the British Working Class* (1972). The lower middle class is discussed in works cited above by Nossiter, Vincent, Price and Paul Thompson in addition to: G. Crossick ed., *The Lower Middle Class in Britain 1870–1914* (1977); G. L. Anderson, *Victorian Clerks* (1976); Avner Offer, *Property and Politics 1870–1914* (1981); and Arno Mayer, 'The Lower Middle Class as a Historical Problem', *Journal of Modern History*, 47 (1975).

CHAPTER 5: **The Edwardian Crises 1895–1914**

For Liberal perspectives on the crisis see: H. C. G. Matthew, *The Liberal Imperialists* (1973); T. Boyle, 'The Liberal Imperialists 1892–1906', *Bulletin of the Institute of Historical Research*, 52 (1979); K. O. Morgan, *The Age of Lloyd George* (1971); Robert Rhodes James, *Rosebery* (1963). The themes of national decadence and national efficiency are covered in: G. R. Searle, *The Quest for National Efficiency* (1971), and *Country Before Party: Coalition and the Idea of 'National Government' in Modern Britain 1885–1987* (1995); F. Clarke, *Voices Prophesying War 1763–1884* (1966); Michael Balfour, *Britain and Joseph Chamberlain* (1985); R. Scally, *The Origins of the Lloyd George Coalition: The Politics of Social Imperialism 1900–1918* (1975); A. Gollin, *Proconsul in Politics* (1966); and B. Semmel, *Imperialism and Social Reform* (1960). There are several general surveys of the Edwardian crisis: David Powell, *The Edwardian Crisis: Britain 1901–1914* (1996); David Brooks, *The Age of Upheaval: Edwardian Politics 1899–1914* (1995); Mary Langan and Bill Schwartz eds, *Crises in the British State 1880–1930* (1985); Paul Thompson, *The Edwardians* (1975); Alan O'Day ed., *The Edwardian Age* (1979); S. Hynes, *The Edwardian Turn of Mind* (1968); and George Dangerfield, *The Strange Death of Liberal England* (1935). Scholarly recognition that the political crisis of this period was a crisis for the Conservatives rather than the Liberals is reflected in the volume of work on the dilemmas faced by the Conservatives: Alan Sykes, *Tariff Reform in British Politics 1903–13* (1979); E. H. H. Green, *The Crisis of Conservatism: The Politics, Economics and Ideology of the British Conservative Party 1880–1914* (1995); G. R. Searle, 'Critics of Edwardian Society: the Case of the Radical Right', and Peter Cain, 'Political Economy in Edwardian England: the Tariff Reform Controversy', both in Alan O'Day, *The Edwardian Age* (1979); Frans Coetzee, *For Party or Country: Nationalism and the Dilemmas of Popular Conservatism in Edwardian England* (1990); Matthew Fforde, *Conservatism and Collectivism 1886–1914* (1990); Martin Pugh, '1886–1906', in Anthony Seldon, *How Tory Governments Fall* (1996); Robert Blake, *The Unknown Prime Minister: The Life and Times of Andrew Bonar Law* (1955); R. J. Q. Adams, *Bonar Law* (1999); and Richard Rempel, *Unionists Divided: Arthur Balfour, Joseph Chamberlain and the Unionist Free Traders* (1972).

On the House of Lords controversy see: E. A. Smith, *The House of Lords in British Politics and Society 1815–1911* (1992); Andrew Adonis, *Making Aristocracy Work: The Peerage and the Political System in Britain 1884–1914* (1993); Roy Jenkins, *Mr Balfour's Poodle* (1954); David Cannadine, *The Decline and Fall of the British Aristocracy* (1990); and Gregory D. Phillips, *The Diehards* (1979).

On the suffragette campaign see: Andrew Rosen, *Rise Up Women!* (1974); Martin Pugh, *The March of the Women: A Revisionist Analysis of the Campaign for Women's Suffrage 1866–1914* (2000), and Historical Association pamphlet, *Votes for Women in Britain 1867–1928* (1994); David Morgan, *Liberals and Suffragists* (1975); Sylvia Pankhurst, *The Suffragette Movement* (1931, repr. 1984); and Jane Marcus ed., *Suffrage and the Pankhursts* (1987).

On industrial militancy see: H. Clegg, A. Fox and A. F. Thompson, *A History of British Trade Unions since 1889, vol. I 1889–1910* (1964); H. A. Clegg, *A History of British Trade Unions vol. II 1911–1939* (1985); Bob Holton, *British Syndicalism 1900–1914* (1976); Keith Burgess, *The Challenge of Labour* (1980); Henry Pelling, 'The Labour Unrest 1911–1914', in Pelling, *Popular Politics and Society* (1968); Chris Wrigley, *David Lloyd George and the British Labour Movement* (1976); and Jane Morgan, *Conflict and Order: Police and Labour Disputes in England and Wales 1900–1939* (1985).

CHAPTER 6: **Edwardian Progressivism**

The New Liberalism is discussed in: M. Freeden, *The New Liberalism* (1978); M. Richter, *The Politics of Conscience* (1964); P. F. Clarke, 'The Progressive Movement in England', *Transactions of the Royal Historical Society*, 24 (1974), and *Liberals and Social Democrats* (1978); and Rodney Barker, *Political Ideas in Modern Britain* (1978). For some contemporary restatements of Liberalism: Herbert Samuel, *Liberalism* (1902); J. A. Hobson, The Crisis of Liberalism (1909); C. F. G. Masterman, *The Condition of England* (1912); L. T. Hobhouse, *Democracy and Reaction* (1904) and *The Labour Movement* (1912); D. Lloyd George, *Better Times; Speeches on the Social Question* (1910); and J. M. Robertson, *The Meaning of Liberalism* (1912).

On some of the policies of New Liberalism see: H. V. Emy, *Liberals, Radicals and Social Politics 1892–914* (1973), and 'The Impact of Financial Policy on English Party Politics Before 1914', *Historical Journal*, 15 (1972); Bruce Murray, *The People's Budget 1909–10* (1980); R. J. Hay, *The Origins of the Liberal Welfare Reforms 1906–1914* (1975); Avner Offer, *Property and Politics 1870–1914* (1981); Ian Packer, 'The Land Issue and the Future of Scottish Liberalism in 1914',

Scottish Historical Review, 11, 1992; H. V. Emy, 'Lloyd George as a Social Reformer: the Land Campaign', in A. J. P. Taylor ed., *Lloyd George: Twelve Essays* (1971); and Roy Douglas, 'God Gave the Land to the People', in A. J. Morris ed., *Edwardian Radicalism 1900–1914* (1974).

Useful biographical studies are: E. I. David, 'The New Liberalism of Charles Masterman'; K. D. Brown ed., *Essays in Anti-Labour History* (1974); John Grigg, *Lloyd George: The People's Champion 1902–11* (1978); Martin Pugh, *Lloyd George* (1988); Ian Packer, *Lloyd George* (1998); Paul Addison, *Churchill on the Home Front* (1992); B. Wasserstein, *Herbert Samuel* (1992); Roy Jenkins, *Asquith* (1964); and S. E. Koss, *Asquith* (1976).

For Labour's approach to co-operation with the Liberals see: Rodney Barker, 'Socialism and Progressivism in the Political Thought of Ramsay MacDonald', in K. D. Brown ed., *Edwardian Radicalism* (1974); David Marquand, *Ramsay MacDonald* (1977); Frank Bealey and Henry Pelling, *Labour and Politics 1900–1906* (1958); Frank Bealey, 'The Electoral Arrangement between the Labour Representation Committee and the Liberal Party', *Journal of Modern History*, December 1965; and for a hostile treatment, Ralph Miliband, *Parliamentary Socialism* (1961).

The programme and ideology of the Labour movement is analysed in: Duncan Tanner, Pat Thane and Jim Tomlinson eds, *Labour's First Century* (2000), which includes essays by Jose Harris, 'Labour's Political and Social Thought', Jim Tomlinson, 'Labour and the Economy', and Pat Thane, 'Labour and Welfare'; Noel Thompson, *Political Economy and the Labour Party* (1990); John Callaghan, *Socialism in British Society since 1884* (1996); G. Foote, *The Labour Party's Political Thought: A History* (1986); K. D. Brown, *Labour and Unemployment 1900–1914* (1971); K. O. Morgan, *Keir Hardie: Radical and Socialist* (1975); and Fred Reid, *Keir Hardie* (1978).

Recently there have been some interesting discussions of working-class attitudes towards social reform: Pat Thane, *Old Age in English History* (2000), and 'The Working Class and State Welfare in Britain 1880–1914', *Historical Journal*, 27 (1984); Sheila Blackburn, 'Working Class Attitudes to Social Reform: Black Country Chain Makers and Anti-Sweating Legislation 1880–1930', *International Review of Social History*, 33 (1988); and Henry Pelling, 'The Working Class and the Origins of the Welfare State', in Pelling, *Popular Politics and Society* (1967).

CHAPTER 7: **The Electoral Struggle 1906–1914**

An important starting point for the revisionist view of Edwardian electoral politics is P. F. Clarke, *Lancashire and the New Liberalism* (1971). See also Neal Blewett, *The Peers, the Parties and the People* (1910); A. K. Russell, *Liberal Landslide* (1973); G. R. Searle, *The Liberal Party: Triumph and Disintegration 1886–1929* (1992); and P. F. Clarke, 'The Electoral Position of the Liberal and Labour Parties 1910–1914', *English Historical Review*, 90 (1975).

For recent studies which throw some doubt on the traditional emphasis on class see: Duncan Tanner, *Political Change and the Labour Party 1900–1918* (1990); Jon Lawrence and Miles Taylor eds, *Party, State and Society: Electoral Behaviour in Britain since 1820* (1997); Jon Lawrence, *Speaking for the People: Party, Language and Popular Politics in England 1867–1914* (1998); Duncan Tanner, 'Elections, Statistics and the Rise of the Labour Party 1906–1931', *Historical Journal*, 34 (1991); and Neville Kirk, ' "Traditional" Working-Class Culture and the "Rise of Labour": Some Preliminary Questions and Observations', *Social History*, 16 (1991).

A classic statement of the traditional view that Labour was bound to replace the Liberals as the working-class party is: Henry Pelling, 'Labour and the Downfall of Liberalism', in Pelling, *Popular Politics and Society* (1968). The best modern version of this approach is R. I. McKibbin, *The Evolution of the Labour Party 1910–1924* (1974), though the author bases the case on class, not on ideological grounds. The significance or otherwise of the electorate is discussed in H. C. G. Matthew, R. I. McKibbin and J. A. Kay, 'The Franchise Factor in the Rise of the Labour Party', *English Historical Review*, 91 (1976); K. Laybourn, 'The Rise of Labour and the Decline of the Liberals: the State of the Debate', *History*, 80 (1995); and C. Chamberlain, 'The Growth of Support for the Labour Party in Great Britain', *British Journal of Sociology*, 24 (1973). The franchise thesis is effectively challenged in Duncan Tanner, 'The Parliamentary Electoral System, the "Fourth" Reform Act and the Rise of Labour in England and Wales', *Bulletin of the Institute of Historical Research*, 56 (1983); and J. Davis, 'Slums and the Vote 1867–1890', *Historical Research*, 64 (1991). On the municipal evidence see: M. G. Shephard and J. L. Halstead, 'Labour's Municipal Election Performance in Provincial England and Wales 1901–1913', *Bulletin of the Society for the Study of Labour History*, 39 (1979); and C. Cook, 'Labour and the Downfall of Liberalism', in A. Sked and C. Cook eds, *Crisis and Controversy: Essays in Honour of A. J. P. Taylor* (1976).

The complications involved in the electoral pact are discussed in: Roy Gregory, *The Miners and British Politics 1906–14* (1968); M. Petter, 'The Progressive Alliance', *History*, 58 (1973); Roy Douglas, 'Labour in Decline', in K. D. Brown and R. I. McKibbin eds, 'James Ramsay MacDonald and the Problem of the Independence of the Labour Party 1910–1914', *Journal of Modern History*, 42 (1970); and Martin Pugh, *Electoral Reform in War and Peace 1906–1918* (1978). George L. Bernstein tends to argue that the pact could not work at local level in his *Liberalism and Liberal Politics in Edwardian England* (1986).

For studies of particular regions see: P. J. Waller, *Democracy and Sectarianism: A Political and Social History of Liverpool 1868–1939* (1980); K. O. Morgan, 'The New Liberalism and the Challenge of Labour: the Welsh Experience 1885–1929', *Welsh History Review*, 6 (1973); M. Savage, *The Dynamics of Working Class Politics: The Labour Movement in Preston 1880–1940* (1987); A. W. Purdue, 'Arthur Henderson and Liberal, Liberal–Labour and Labour Politics in North East England 1892–1903', *Northern History*, 11 (1975); Sam Davies and Bob Morley, 'The Politics of Place: A Comparative Analysis of Electoral Politics in Blackburn, Bolton, Burnley and Bury', *Manchester Region History Review*, XIV (2000); Tony Adams, 'Labour Vanguard, Tory Bastion or the Triumph of New Liberalism? Manchester Politics 1900–1914', *Manchester Region History Review*, XIV (2000); and K. Laybourn and J. Reynolds, who make very selective use of evidence to argue that Liberalism was in decline in West Yorkshire in *Liberalism and the Rise of Labour 1890–1918* (1984).

CHAPTER 8: **The Impact of the Great War on British Politics**

The high politics of the war is analysed in John Turner, *British Politics and the Great War* (1992); G. R. Searle, *Country Before Party: Coalition and the Idea of 'National Government' in Modern Britain, 1885–1987* (1995); Cameron Hazlehurst, *Politicians at War* (1971); John Bourne, *Britain and the Great War 1914–1918* (1989); Lord Hankey, *The Supreme Command 1914–1918* (1961); and E. I. David ed., *Inside Asquith's Cabinet: From the Diaries of Sir Charles Hobhouse* (1977). The strains and divisions on the Liberals have been examined in a multitude of works. Trevor Wilson places the chief blame for Liberal problems on Lloyd George in his classic account: *The Downfall of the Liberal Party 1914–35* (1966). See also: M. Swartz, 'A Study in Futility: the British Radicals at the Outbreak of the First World War', in A. J. A. Morris ed., *Edwardian Radicalism* (1974); G. L. Bernstein, 'Yorkshire Liberalism during the First World War', *Historical Journal*, 32 (1989); Trevor Wilson ed., *The Political Diaries of C. P. Scott 1911– 1928* (1970); Martin Pugh, 'Asquith, Bonar Law and the First Coalition, *Historical Journal*, 17 (1974); E. I. David, 'The Liberal Party Divided 1916–1918', *Historical Journal*, 13 (1970); Michael Hart, 'The Liberals, the War and the Franchise', *English Historical Review*, 97 (1982); and J. M. McEwen, 'The Liberal Party and the Irish Question during the First World War', *Journal of British Studies*, 12 (1972).

As a corrective to Wilson's hostile account, see more sympathetic treatment of Lloyd George in: John Grigg, *Lloyd George: from Peace to War 1912–1916* (1985); Peter Lowe, 'The Rise to the Premiership', in A. J. P. Taylor ed., *Lloyd George Twelve Essays* (1971); and Martin Pugh, *Lloyd George* (1988). Lloyd George's system of government is analysed in K. O. Morgan, 'Lloyd George's Premiership', *Historical Journal*, 13 (1970); John Turner, *Lloyd George's Secretariat* (1980); and J. Ehrman, 'Lloyd George and Churchill as War Leaders', *Transactions of the Royal Historical Society*, 11 (1961).

The Conservatives have received less attention, but their reaction to the war is examined in: J. O. Stubbs, 'The Impact of the Great War on the Conservative Party', in G. Peele and C. Cook eds, *The Politics of Reappraisal* (1975); Robert Blake, *The Unknown Prime Minister* (1955); R. J. Q. Adams, *Bonar Law* (1999); Martin Pugh, *Electoral Reform in War and Peace 1906–1918* (1978); N. R. McCrillis, 'Taming Democracy?: The Conservative Party and House of Lords Reform 1916–1929', *Parliamentary History*, 13 (1993); D. Close, 'The Collapse of Resistance to Democracy: the Conservatives, Adult Suffrage and Second Chamber Reform 1911–28', *Historical Journal*, 20 (1977); and D. Rubinstein, 'Henry Page-Croft and the National Party 1917–22', *Journal of Contemporary History*, 9 (1974).

The means by which Labour coped with the war are analysed in: R. I. McKibbin, *The Evolution of the Labour Party 1910–1924* (1974); David Marquand, *Ramsay*

MacDonald (1977); Chris Wrigley, *Lloyd George and the British Labour Movement* (1976); Chris Wrigley, *Arthur Henderson* (1990); C. Howard, 'MacDonald, Henderson and the Labour Party in 1914', *Historical Journal*, 20 (1977); J. M. Winter, 'Arthur Henderson, the Russian Revolution and the Reconstruction of the Labour Party', *Historical Journal*, 15 (1972); and R. I. McKibbin, 'Arthur Henderson as Labour Leader', *International Review of Social History*, 23 (1978). For developments affecting rank-and-file members see: Julia Bush, *Behind the Lines: East London Labour 1914–19* (1984); A. Clinton, 'Trades Councils during the First World War', *International Review of Social History*, 15 (1970); Royden Harrison, 'The War Emergency Workers' National Committee', in A. Briggs and J. Saville eds, *Essays in Labour History 1886–1924* (1971); James Hinton, *The First Shop Stewards Movement* (1973); S. R. White, 'The Leeds Soviet', *International Review of Social History*, 19 (1974); and Ian McLean, 'Red Clydeside 1915–19', in J. Stevenson and R. Quinault eds, *Popular Protest and Public Order* (1974).

On the circumstance in which the 1918 election took place see: R. Douglas, 'The Background to the Coupon Election Arrangements', *English Historical Review*, 86 (1971); Trevor Wilson, *The Downfall of the Liberal Party 1914–1935* (1966); John Turner, 'The British Commonwealth Union and the General Election of 1918', *English Historical Review*, 93 (1978); D. Englander and J. Osborne, 'Jack, Tommy and Henry Dubb: the Armed Forces and the Working Class', *Historical Journal*, 21 (1978); B. McGill, 'Lloyd George's Timing of the 1918 Election', *Journal of British Studies*, 14 (1974); and Martin Pugh, *Electoral Reform in War and Peace 1906–1918* (1978). For analysis of the outcome of the election see: Duncan Tanner, *Political Change and the Labour Party 1900–1918* (1990); John Turner, *British Politics and the Great War* (1992); R. I. McKibbin, *The Evolution of the Labour Party 1910–1924* (1974); Michael Hart, 'The Liberals, the War and the Franchise', *English Historical Review*, 97 (1982); John Turner, 'The Labour Vote and the Franchise After 1918', in P. Denley and D. Hopkin eds, *History and Computing* (1987); and J. M. McEwen, 'The Coupon Election of 1918 and the Unionist Members of Parliament', *Journal of Modern History*, 34 (1962).

CHAPTER 9: **Patriotism, Ideology and the State in the Great War**

On state interventionism and the retreat from it under the Coalition see: James Cronin, *The Politics of State Expansion: War, State and Society in the Twentieth Century* (1991); David French, *British Economic and Strategic Planning 1905–1915* (1982); Keith Grieves, *Sir Eric Geddes* (1989); K. Burke ed., *War and the State: the Transformation of British Government 1914–1919* (1982); P. K. Cline, 'Eric Geddes and the Experiment with Businessmen in Government 1915–1922', in K. D. Brown ed., *Essays in Anti-Labour History* (1974); Rodney Lowe, 'The Erosion of State Intervention in Britain 1917–1924', *Economic History Review*, 31 (1978); and K. O. Morgan, *Consensus and Disunity: the Lloyd George Coalition 1918–1922* (1979).

The impact of the war on Labour's ideas is examined in: J. M. Winter, *Socialism and the Challenge of War* (1974); Noel Thompson, *Political Economy and the Labour Party* (1996); and John Callaghan, *Socialism in Britain since 1884* (1990). The significance or otherwise of the adoption of Clause IV is considered in: Rodney Barker, 'Political Myth: Ramsay MacDonald and the Labour Party', *History*, 61 (1976); and R. I. McKibbin, *The Evolution of the Labour Party 1910–1924* (1974). Working-class patriotism is a neglected subject, but see: Paul Ward, *Red Flag and Union Jack: Englishness, Patriotism and the British Left 1889–1924* (1998); Andrew Thorpe, 'J. H. Thomas and the Rise of Labour in Derby 1880–1945', *Midland History*, 15 (1990); and David Howell, '"I loved my Union and my Country": Jimmy Thomas and the Politics of Railway Trade Unionism', *Twentieth Century British History*, 6 (1995). The process by which Labour attracted men and women from the other parties is another crucial but neglected aspect, but is examined in: Martin Pugh, 'Class Traitors: Conservative Recruits to Labour 1900–1930', *English Historical Review*, 113 (1998); C. A. Cline, *Recruits to Labour* (1963); A. J. A. Morris, *Charles Trevelyan* (1977); and Jane and Kenneth Morgan, *Portrait of a Progressive: the Political Career of Viscount Addison* (1980).

Histories of the Conservatives tend to neglect the impact of ideas, though something can be gleaned from the biographies of leading figures. Aspects are examined in: J. O. Stubbs, 'The Impact of the Great War on the Conservative Party', in G. Peele and C. Cook eds, *The Politics of Reappraisal* (1975); R. Scally, *Origins of the Lloyd George Coalition: The Politics of Social Imperialism* (1975); John Ramsden, *The Age of Balfour and Baldwin 1902–1940* (1978); John Turner, 'The British Commonwealth Union and the General Election of 1918', *English Historical Review*, 93 (1978); and D. Rubinstein, 'Henry Page-Croft and the National Party 1917–22, *Journal of Contemporary History*, 9 (1974).

CHAPTER 10: **The Elevation of Labour and the Restoration of Party Politics 1918–1931**

The collapse of the Coalition and Lloyd George's subsequent career are discussed in: K. O. Morgan, *Consensus and Disunity: The Lloyd George Coalition Government 1918–1922* (1979); John Campbell, *Lloyd George: The Goat in the Wilderness* (1977); M. Kinnear, *The Fall of Lloyd George* (1973); G. R. Searle, *Corruption in British Politics 1895–1930* (1987); and K. O. Morgan, 'Lloyd George's Stage Army: the Coalition Liberals', in A. J. P. Taylor ed., *Lloyd George: Twelve Essays* (1970).

The Conservatives' inter-war strategy and their attitude towards coalition has been analysed in detail in many volumes including: John Ramsden, *The Age of Balfour and Baldwin 1902–1940* (1978); Stuart Ball, *Baldwin and the Conservative Party: The Crisis of 1929–1931* (1988); G. R. Searle, *Country Before Party: Coalition and the Idea of National Government in Modern Britain 1885–1987* (1995); Phillip Williamson, *National Crisis and National Government: British Politics, the Economy and the Empire 1926–1932* (1992); Maurice Cowling, *The Impact of Labour*

1920–1924 (1971); Stuart Ball, '1916–1929', in Anthony Seldon ed., *How Tory Governments Fall* (1996); John Ramsden, 'The Newport By-Election and the Fall of the Coalition', in C. Cook and J. Ramsden eds, *By-elections in British Politics* (1997); Robert Self, *Tories and Tariffs: The Conservative Party and the Politics of Tariff Reform 1922–1932* (1986); Paul Addison, *Churchill on the Home Front* (1992); P. F. Clarke, 'The Politics of Keynesian Economics', in M. Bentley and J. Stevenson eds, *High and Low Politics in Modern Britain* (1983); Robert Self, 'Conservative Reunion and the General Election of 1923: A Reassessment', *Twentieth Century British History*, 3 (1992); and Phillips Williamson, '"Safety First": Baldwin, the Conservative Party and the 1929 General Election', *Historical Journal*, 25 (1982).

For Labour during this period see: Andrew Thorpe, *A History of the British Labour Party* (1997); Neil Riddell, *Labour in Crisis: The Second Labour Government 1929–1931* (1999); Robert Skidelsky, *Politicians and the Slump* (1967); David Marquand, *Ramsay MacDonald* (1977); R. I. McKibbin, 'The Economic Policy of the Second Labour Government', *Past and Present*, 36 (1975); Adrian Oldfield, 'The Independent Labour Party and Planning 1920–1926', *International Review of Social History*, 21 (1976); Chris Wrigley, *Arthur Henderson* (1990); C. Cook, 'By-elections of the first Labour Government', in C. Cook and J. Ramsden eds, *By-elections in British Politics* (1997); R. Lynam, *The First Labour Government* (1957); and R. Miliband, *Parliamentary Socialism* (1961).

CHAPTER 11: **Origins of the Conservative Electoral Hegemony 1918–1931**

The significance of the electoral system in influencing party fortunes is examined in: David Butler, *The Electoral System in Britain 1918–1951* (1953); M. Kinnear, *The British Voter: An Atlas and Survey since 1885* (1969); Michael Dawson, 'Money and the Real Impact of the Fourth Reform Act', *Historical Journal*, 35 (1992); Martin Pugh, *Electoral Reform in War and Peace 1906–1918* (1978); Enid Lakeman, *Voting in Democracies* (1955); and S. E. Finer ed., *Adversary Politics and Electoral Reform* (1975).

On election results and trends see: C. Cook, *The Age of Alignment* (1975), and 'Liberals, Labour and Local Elections', in C. Cook and G. Peele, *The Politics of Reappraisal* (1975); Andrew Thorpe, *The British General Election of 1931* (1991); D. H. Close, 'The Realignment of the British Electorate in 1931', *History*, 67 (1982); C. Cook and J. Ramsden eds, *By-elections in British Politics* (1973); and David Butler and Donald Stokes, *Political Change in Britain* (1969).

Aspects of Conservative electoral strategy are examined in: David Jarvis, 'British Conservatism and Class Politics in the 1920s', *English Historical Review*, 111 (1997), '"Mrs Maggs and Betty": the Conservative Appeal to Women Voters in the 1920s', *Twentieth Century British History*, 5 (1994), and 'The Shaping of the Conservative Electoral Hegemony 1918–1939', in Jon Lawrence and Miles Taylor eds, *Party, State and Society* (1997); R. I. McKibbin, 'Class and Conventional Wisdom: The Conservative Party and the "Public" in Inter-War Britain', in McKibbin, *The Ideologies of Class: Social Relations in Britain 1880–1950* (1991);

R. I. McKibbin, *Classes and Cultures in England 1918–1951* (1998); and John Ramsden, *The Age of Balfour and Baldwin 1902–1940* (1978).

On Liberal fortunes see: Barry M. Doyle, 'A Conflict of Interests? The Local and National Dimensions of Middle Class Liberalism 1900–1935', *Parliamentary History*, 17 (1998), and 'Urban Liberalism and the "Lost Generation": Politics and Middle Class Culture in Norwich 1900–1935', *Historical Journal*, 38 (1995); and Trevor Wilson, *The Downfall of the Liberal Party 1914–1935* (1966).

On Labour support and organization between the wars see: M. Savage, *The Dynamics of Working-Class Politics* (1987); J. Rasmussen, 'Women in Labour: The Flapper Vote and Party System Transformation in Britain', *Electoral Studies*, 3 (1984); C. Howard, 'Expectations Born to Death: Local Labour Party Expansion in the 1920s', in J. M. Winter ed., *The Working Class in Modern British History* (1983); Duncan Tanner, 'Labour and Its Membership', in D. Tanner, P. Thane and N. Tiratsoo eds, *Labour's First Century* (2000); Neil Riddell, 'The Catholic Church and the Labour Party 1918–1931', *Twentieth Century British History*, 8 (1997); Sam Davies, *Liverpool Labour* (1996); Duncan Tanner, 'The Labour Party and Electoral Politics in the Coalfields 1910–1945', in A. Campbell, D. Howell and N. Fishman eds, *Miners, Unions and Politics 1910–1947* (1996), 'Class Voting and Radical Politics: the Liberal and Labour Parties 19190–1931', in J. Lawrence and M. Taylor eds, *Party, State and Society* (1997), and 'Elections, Statistics and the Rise of the Labour Party 1906–1931', *Historical Journal*, 34 (1991); Andrew Thorpe, 'The Membership of the Communist Party of Great Britain 1920–1945', *Historical Journal*, 43 (2000); Peter Catterall, 'Morality and Politics: The Free Churches and the Labour Party Between the Wars', *Historical Journal*, 36 (1993); and Ian McLean, 'Party Organisation', in C. Cook and I. Taylor eds, *The Labour Party* (1980).

Recently women's role in the political system has attracted much more attention: Pamela Graves, *Labour Women: Women in British Working-class Politics 1918–1939* (1994); Martin Pugh, *Women and the Women's Movement in Britain 1914–1959* (1992); G. E. Maguire, *Conservative Women* (1998); Brian Harrison, *Prudent Revolutionaries: Portraits of British Feminists between the Wars* (1987); Brian Harrison, 'Women in a Men's House: The Women M.P.'s 1919–1945', *Historical Journal*, 29 (1986); and Harold L. Smith ed., *British Feminism in the Twentieth Century* (1990).

CHAPTER 12: **From the National Government to the Popular Front 1931–1939**

On the adaptation of the Conservatives under the National Government the following are helpful: C. T. Stannage, *Baldwin Thwarts the Opposition: The General Election of 1935* (1980); Nicholas Pronay, 'British Newsreels in the 1930s', *History*, 56 (1971) and 57 (1972); T. J. Hollins, 'The Conservative Party and Film Propaganda between the Wars', *English Historical Review*, 96 (1981); Philip Williamson, *Stanley Baldwin, Conservative Leadership and National Values* (1999); Siân Nicholas, 'The Construction of a National Identity: Stanley Baldwin, Englishness and the Mass Media in Inter-War Britain', and Martin Francis, 'The

Conservatives and the State 1920–1960', both in M. Francis and I. Zweiniger-Bargielowska eds, *The Conservatives in British Society 1880–1990* (1996); Lord Butler ed., *The Conservatives* (1977); David Butler ed., *Coalitions in British Politics* (1978); G. R. Searle, *Country Before Party: Coalition and the Idea of National Government in Modern Britain 1885–1987* (1995); Arthur Marwick, 'Middle Opinion in the Thirties: Planning, Progress and Political Agreement', *English Historical Review*, 79 (1965); J. A. Cross, *Sir Samuel Hoare* (1977); and Robert Rhodes James, *Anthony Eden* (1994).

On aspects of the growth of fascism see: Richard Thurlow, *Fascism in Britain: A History 1918–1985* (1987); Robert Skidelsky, *Oswald Mosley* (1975); Julie Gottlieb, *Feminine Fascism: Women in Britain's Fascist Movement 1923–1945* (2000); Martin Durham, *Women and Fascism* (1998); Gerry Weber, 'Patterns of Membership and Support for the British Union of Fascists', *Journal of Contemporary History*, 19 (1984); Martin Pugh, 'The British Union of Fascists and the Olympia Debate', *Historical Journal*, 41 (1998); Andrew Thorpe ed., *The Failure of Political Extremism in Inter-War Britain* (1989); K. Lunn and R. Thurlow eds, *British Fascism* (1980); Tony Kushner and Kenneth Lunn eds, *The Politics of Marginality* (1990); Tony Kushner and Nadia Valman eds, *Remembering Cable Street: Fascism and Anti-Fascism in British Society* (2000); Nigel Griffiths, *Fellow Travellers of the Right* (1983); and R. Benewick, *The Fascist Movement in Britain* (1972).

On Labour's dilemmas with the economy see: Noel Thompson, *Political Economy and the Labour Party* (1996); David Howell, *British Social Democracy* (1976); Robert Skidelsky, *Politicians and the Slump* (1967); R. I. McKibbin, 'The Economic Policy of the Second Labour Government', *Past and Present*, 36 (1975); Adrian Oldfield, 'The Labour Party and Planning – 1934 or 1918?', *Bulletin of the Society for the Study of Labour History*, 25 (1972); Barbara Malament, 'British Labour and Roosevelt's New Deal: The Response of the Left and the Unions', *Journal of British Studies*, Spring (1978); David Marquand, *Ramsay MacDonald* (1977); Ben Pimlott, *Hugh Dalton* (1985); Michael Newman, *John Strachey* (1989); and Alan Bullock, *The Life and Times of Ernest Bevin vol. I* (1960).

Studies of the strategy of the Left in the 1930s have been fairly critical, notably Ben Pimlott, *Labour and the Left in the 1930s* (1977). See also: James Jupp, *The British Radical Left 1931–1941* (1978); John Naylor, *Labour's International Policy* (1969); Martin Ceadel, *Pacifism in Britain 1914–1945* (1980), and 'The First British Referendum: the Peace Ballot 1934–35', *English Historical Review*, 95 (1980); C. T. Stannage, 'The East Fulham By-Election', *Historical Journal*, 14 (1971); Jonathan Schneer, *George Lansbury* (1989); P. Kingsford, *The Hunger Marchers in Britain 1920–1939* (1982); H. Harmer, 'The Failure of the Communists: The National Unemployed Workers' Movement 1921–1939, A Disappointing Success', in A. Thorpe ed., *The Failure of Political Extremism in Inter-War Britain* (1989); N. Branson, *History of the Communist Party of Great Britain 1927–1941* (1985); and Andrew Thorpe, 'The Membership of the Communist Party of Great Britain 1920–1945', *Historical Journal*, 43 (2000).

On the Popular Front and opposition to appeasement see: Tom Buchanan, *The Spanish Civil War and the British Labour Movement* (1991), and 'Britain's Popular Front? Aid Spain and the British Labour Movement', *History Workshop Journal*,

31 (1991); Nigel Copsey, *Anti-Fascism in Britain* (2000); R. Eatwell, 'Munich, Public Opinion and the Popular Front', *Journal of Contemporary History*, 6 (1971); Ian McLean, 'Oxford and Bridgwater', in C. Cook and J. Ramsden eds, *By-elections in British Politics* (1975); Martin Pugh, 'The *Daily Mirror* and the Revival of Labour 1935–1945', *Twentieth Century British History*, 41 (1998); N. J. Crowson, *Facing Fascism: The Conservative Party and the European Dictators 1935–1934* (1997); Stuart Ball, 'The Politics of Appeasement: The Fall of the Duchess of Atholl and the Kinross and West Perth By-Election, December 1938', *Scottish Historical Review*, 69 (1990); N. Thompson, *The Anti-Appeasers: Conservative Opposition to Appeasement in the 1930s* (1971); and Richard Cockett, *Twilight of Truth: Chamberlain, Appeasement and the Manipulation of the Press* (1989).

CHAPTER 13: The Politics of the 'People's War' 1939–1945

On the high politics of the war see: Stephen Brooke, *Labour's War: The Labour Party during the Second World War* (1992); Kevin Jeffreys, *The Churchill Coalition and Wartime Politics 1940–1945* (1991); Paul Addison, *Churchill on the Home Front* (1992); Trevor Burridge, *Clement Attlee* (1985), and *British Labour and Hitler's War* (1976); Robert Pearce, *Attlee* (1995); Ian S. Wood, *Churchill* (2000); Ben Pimlott, *The Second World War Diary of Hugh Dalton* (1986); Kevin Jeffreys, *Labour and the Wartime Coalition: From the Diaries of James Chuter Ede 1941–45* (1987), and 'May 1940: The Downfall of Neville Chamberlain', *Parliamentary History*, 10 (1991); D. M. Roberts, 'Clement Davies and the Fall of Neville Chamberlain 1939–1940', *Welsh History Review*, 8 (1976); Henry Pelling, *Britain and the Second World War* (1970); Alan Bullock, *The Life and Times of Ernest Bevin, vol. II* (1967); and B. Donoghue and G. W. Jones, *Herbert Morrison* (1973).

Changes in popular attitudes and expectations as a result of wartime experience are discussed in a wide range of books including: Angus Calder, *The People's War 1939–1945* (1971); 'Cato', *Guilty Men* (1940); Ina Zweiniger-Bargielowska, *Austerity in Britain: Rationing, Controls and Consumption 1939–1955* (2000); Tom Harrison, *Living Through the Blitz* (1976); Tony Mason and Peter Thompson, 'Reflections on a Revolution: The Political Mood in Wartime Britain', in N. Tiratsoo ed., *The Attlee Years* (1991); Paul Addison, 'By-elections of the Second World War', in C. Cook and J. Ramsden eds, *By-Elections in British Politics* (1973); S. Fielding, P. Thompson and N. Tiratsoo eds, *England Arise: The Labour Party and Popular Politics in the 1940s* (1995); and Harold L. Smith ed., *War and Social Change: British Society in the Second World War* (1986).

For the origins and character of wartime consensus see: Paul Addison, *The Road to 1945* (1975), and 'The Road from 1945', in Anthony Seldon ed., *Ruling Performance* (1987); Dennis Kavanagh and Peter Morris, *Consensus Politics from Attlee to Thatcher* (1989); Rodney Lowe, 'The Second World War, Consensus and the Foundation of the Welfare State', *Twentieth Century British History*, 1 (1990); Kevin Jeffreys, 'British Politics and British Social Policy During the Second World War', *Historical Journal*, 30 (1987); Ben Pimlott, 'The Myth of

Consensus', in L. M. Smith ed., *The Making of Britain* (1988); Brian Harrison, 'The Rise, Fall and Rise of Political Consensus in Britain since 1940', *History*, 84 (1999); Jose Harris, *William Beveridge* (1977); James Cronin, *The Politics of State Expansion* (1991); Martin Francis, '"Set the People Free"? Conservatives and the State 1920–1960', in Martin Francis and Ina Zweiniger-Bargielowska eds, *The Conservatives in British Society 1880–1990* (1996); M. Holmes and N. Horsewood, 'The Post War Consensus', *Contemporary Record*, 2 (1988); Corelli Barnett, *The Audit of War* (1986); and Harold L. Smith ed., *War and Social Change: British Society in the Second World War* (1986).

The 1945 general election has not attracted much attention until fairly recently: R. McCallum and Alison Readman, *The British General Election of 1945* (1947); David Butler, *British General Elections since 1945* (1989); Richard Sibley, 'The Swing to Labour during the Second World War: When and Why?', *Labour History Review*, 55 (1990); Martin Pugh, 'The *Daily Mirror* and the Revival of Labour 1935–1945', *Twentieth Century British History*, 9 (1998); J. A. Crang, 'Politics on Parade: Army Education and the 1945 General Election', *History*, 81 (1996); Stephen Brooke, 'The Labour Party and the 1945 General Election', *Contemporary Record'*, 9 (1995); S. Fielding, 'What did the People Want? The Meaning of the 1945 General Election', *Historical Journal*, 35 (1992); and Henry Pelling, 'The 1945 General Election Reconsidered', *Historical Journal*, 23 (1980).

Index